By the same author

The Arabs

Peter Mansfield

A History of the
Middle East

VIKING

To Luis Cañizares

VIKING

Published by the Penguin Group
Viking Penguin, a division of Penguin Books USA Inc.,
375 Hudson Street, New York, New York 10014, USA
Penguin Books Ltd, 27 Wrights Lane, London W8 5TZ, England
Penguin Books Australia Ltd, Ringwood, Victoria, Australia
Penguin Books Canada Ltd, 2801 John Street, Markham, Ontario, Canada L3R 1B4
Penguin Books (NZ) Ltd, 182–190 Wairau Road, Auckland 10, New Zealand

Penguin Books Ltd, Registered Offices: Harmondsworth, Middlesex, England

First American edition published 1991
10 9 8 7 6 5 4 3 2 1

Set in 10½/12½ pt Lasercomp Ehrhardt

CIP data available

ISBN 0–670–81515–2

Contents

Maps

THE MIDDLE EAST TODAY

International Boundary

0   1000 Km
0   600 Miles

CASPIAN SEA

briz

● Tehran

I R A N

dad

Isfahan ●

Abadan

asra ●

● Shiraz

● Kuwait   ● Bushire

WAIT

Jubail ●

Damman ●

Dhahran ●

Sharja

Dubai

QATAR

BAHRAIN   Abu Dhabi ●

● Riyadh

UNITED ARAB EMIRATES

RABIA

GULF OF OMAN

● Muscat

O M A N

A R A B I A N
S E A

PUBLIC OF YEMEN

● Salala

● Mukalla

Socotra Island

en

LF OF ADEN   SOMALIA

I N D I A N   O C E A N

P E R S I A N   G U L F

rce: Peter Mansfield (ed.), *The Middle East: A Political and Economic Survey*, Oxford University Press, 1980

1. Introduction: from Ancient to Modern

'The Middle East' is a modern English term for the most ancient region of human civilization. Before and during the First World War, 'the Near East', which comprised Turkey and the Balkans, the Levant and Egypt, was the term in more common use. 'The Middle East', if employed at all, referred to Arabia, the Gulf, Persia (Iran)/ Mesopotamia (Iraq) and Afghanistan. After the First World War Allies had destroyed the Ottoman Turkish Empire and established their hegemony over its former Arab provinces, 'the Middle East' gradually came to encompass both areas. This trend was reinforced during the Second World War, when the entire region was seen as a strategic unit in the struggle against the Axis powers. Egypt was the site of the Allies' Middle East Supply Centre. At the end of the war, Cairo also became the headquarters of the Arab League, which linked Egypt with the independent Asian Arab states. The Turkish Republic, which had joined NATO and saw its destiny as part of Europe, scarcely belonged to the Middle East any more.

The term 'the Middle East' is Eurocentric. The people of the Indian subcontinent understandably find it irritating. For them after all, the region is 'the Middle West'. 'Why not "West Asia"?' they might ask. But this has the disadvantage of excluding Egypt. Similarly, 'the Arab world', now in common usage, excludes Israel and Iran which, to say the least, are both at the centre of the region's concerns, although 'the Arab world' does have the advantage of including the North African Maghreb states, which are increasingly partners in the affairs of the region in spite of the practical failure to achieve political union of the two halves of the Arab world. 'The Middle East' seems likely to continue in use for some time. It is not even confined to European languages: in Arabic – *Asharq al-Awsat* – it is the title of the Saudi Arabian newspaper with the largest international circulation of all Arab newspapers.

Common usage, however, should not allow us to lose sight of the drawbacks of the term, of which the most important is that it assumes a Western domination of the world. That distinguished scholar the late General John Bagot Glubb enjoyed reminding his readers that, in terms of civilization and culture, the Middle East region was in advance of western Europe for all but the last five hundred of the five thousand or so years for which human history can be traced back. Archaeologists will continue to dispute whether the Nile Valley and Delta, narrow but richly fertile, or Mesopotamia, the land of the twin rivers, the Tigris and the Euphrates, can claim precedence as the cradle of human civilization, but it is their joint role in the development of mankind which matters.

Hammurabi, King of Babylon in the eighteenth century BC, formulated the first comprehensive code of law which has survived. Akhenaten, Pharaoh of Egypt in the fourteenth century BC, had the first conception of a single all-powerful deity. Some fifty years later Rameses II – 'the Great' – created an empire which covered most of the Middle East region.

In the huge arc of territory which stretches from the Euphrates around the northern edge of the Syrian Desert along the eastern Mediterranean to the Nile Valley, much of human history was made. It was the Fertile Crescent, because either river irrigation or winter rainfall nurtured productive farmland and settled populations. The central portion of this arc is the isthmus of land which connects Egypt with Anatolia (central Turkey). Bounded on the west by the Mediterranean and on the east by the Syrian Desert, it is some 500 miles long and 75 miles wide. Later called the Levant, it today comprises Lebanon, Israel and the western parts of Syria and Jordan. All the great powers of the ancient world fought over and occupied this stretch of land; it contains the oldest continuously inhabited towns on the earth, such as Jericho and Byblos (Jubail). It was the birthplace of Judaism and Christianity. The name of its most famous city, Jerusalem, still arouses more passionate responses than any other.

The glorious if violent history of this territory was shaped by its geography. Its features run north and south. First the narrow coastal plain, then the upland chain from the Alawite or Nusairiyah mountains of Syria to the north, through Mount Lebanon, Galilee, Samaria and Judaea to Beersheba. To the east of this a deep rift is formed by the valley of the Orontes, the Bekaa Plain, the Jordan Valley leading to the Dead Sea, the Gulf of Aqaba and the Red Sea, and then another mountain chain – the Anti-Lebanon, Mount

Hermon, Kerak and the mountains of Moab. Because the winter rains are blown in from the west, the land is most fertile on the coast and the western slopes of the mountains. Eastwards the farmlands become pasture, until they merge into the limestone steppe of the Syrian Desert stretching to Mesopotamia. The city of Damascus stands like a port on the western edge of this wilderness, which was always a more formidable barrier than the Mediterranean Sea.

This short causeway along the eastern Mediterranean between Egypt and present-day Turkey was the scene of an astonishing and productive mixture of peoples and cultures. They came from all directions. The non-Semitic and highly civilized Sumerians from Mesopotamia dominated Syria for about a thousand years, from 3500 BC. They were defeated by the Semitic Amorites, nomads from central Arabia, but the Sumerians taught their conquerors how to write and how to farm the land. Babylonians in the middle of the third millennium were followed by Egyptians, who first conquered the coastal plain of Syria at about the same time. The Egyptians were frequently driven out by the new invaders such as the warlike Hittites from Asia Minor, who took all of Syria in 1450 BC, but just as often they returned and recovered control.

The settled inhabitants of Syria and Palestine were known as Canaanites from about 1600 BC. Almost certainly they did not constitute a single race but were formed through a mingling of peoples, some of whom came from the sea and some from the desert. They never created a powerful imperial state of their own; they submitted to the successive waves of conquerors, paid them tribute and traded with them. They were skilful workers in metal.

One people who came to settle on the Levant coast in about 1400 BC was the extraordinary seafaring Phoenicians, who established trading colonies on most of the Mediterranean shore and even on the Atlantic coasts of Europe and Africa. Carthage, Tyre and Sidon are the most famous of these. The name 'Phoenician' derives from the Greek word for purple – the Tyrian purple dye was renowned throughout the ancient world. Many Lebanese of today like to think of the Phoenicians as their ancestors.

Another wave of invaders came from central Arabia – the Aramaeans. By about 1200 BC they had gained control over Damascus. They took their culture from the more civilized, settled inhabitants of Syria, but it was their Semitic language – Aramaic – which became the *lingua franca* of the region and was spoken by Jesus Christ a thousand years later.

About a century after the Phoenicians the Hebrews, having escaped from Egypt, invaded the land of Canaan from the east, seized Jericho and gradually subdued its settled population in the hills. But they had to contend with a new wave of invaders from across the Mediterranean – the Philistines – who settled on the coastal plain, giving their name to the region: Palestine (*falastin* in Arabic). The struggle ebbed and flowed until David, King of Israel, united the Hebrew tribes, captured the Jebusite town of Jerusalem and made it his capital. There his son Solomon built the first Jewish temple. The Kingdom of Israel lasted some two centuries before it split into two – the Kingdoms of Israel and Judah. In about 720 BC the newest great power from northern Iraq – the Assyrians – overran the two little Jewish states and caused them to disappear. From then on there was never an independent Jewish state until the present century, although the Jews had a degree of autonomy in the Maccabean kingdom (166–163 BC) and its successor, the House of Herod. When the Jews rebelled against the Roman Empire in AD 70, the Emperor Titus destroyed Jerusalem. Their final revolt was put down by Hadrian in AD 135 and the Jews were scattered; only a few thousand remained in Galilee.

The Jews stood apart from the other peoples who invaded and settled in Syria and Palestine in two important respects. One was that in general they did not intermarry and assimilate with the other peoples of the region. The other was their religious genius, which produced the first of three great monotheistic faiths. The Ten Commandments and the Judaic legal code which derives from them were by far the highest system of morality to be developed by mankind before the coming of Christ. But because the Jews regarded themselves as a distinctive people, specially chosen by God, Judaism was never a proselytizing religion. There was no question of huge masses of humanity converting to the Jewish faith, as was the case with its two successors – Christianity and Islam.

From about the end of the ninth century BC, the character of the invasions of Syria/Palestine began to change. It was now less a matter of migrating peoples seeking a better place in which to settle – 'a land of milk and honey' – than of great powers aiming to conquer and impose their rule over the existing inhabitants. The Assyrians, who had their capital at Nineveh near Mosul in modern Iraq, first appeared in Syria in about 1100 BC, but it was their King Shalamaneser III (859–824 BC) who founded the Assyrian Empire, which lasted for more than two centuries and finally conquered Egypt. The former great empire of the Pharaohs had been in sad decline since the time of Rameses III of the Twentieth Dynasty (twelfth century BC), who was the last to display military genius in the field of battle. Irrigation works fell into disuse and trade decayed. Egypt was governed by local despots in the cities of the Nile Delta, which were constantly attacked and finally defeated by the Assyrians.

The Assyrians were in turn defeated and overthrown by the Chaldean dynasty of Babylon. In 597 BC their King Nebuchadnezzar took Jerusalem. But the Chaldean Empire was short-lived. Further east, in present-day Iran, a new and dynamic state was formed by the uniting of Medes and Persians. Their King Cyrus II – 'the Great' – reigned from 559 to 530 BC and founded an empire which covered the whole of western Asia in the modern Middle East and more, from the Indus River to the Aegean Sea and the borders of Egypt.

In 525 BC the successors of Cyrus conquered Egypt with little difficulty, and it could be said that for the Egyptians two thousand years of foreign rule had begun.

The Persians were then masters of the whole civilized world of the time, apart from China. In the western province of Syria and Palestine, Aramaic was the official language. Administration was efficient, roads were built and taxes were collected regularly. The region enjoyed two hundred years of peace and prosperity.

As we have seen, the local indigenous population was a melting-pot of races, both non-Semites who had come mainly from the west and north and Semites who had come mainly from the east – the Arabian peninsula. The word 'Semite' derives from Shem, the eldest son of Noah, from whom all the Semitic peoples are supposed to be descended. However it is not a racial but a linguistic term, invented in the late eighteenth century by the German historian Schlözer to denote the languages which were spoken in Mesopotamia, Syria and the Arabian peninsula and which from the first millennium BC spread into North Africa. All the Semitic languages have striking similarities in their syntax and basic vocabularies, just as there are affinities between the social institutions, religious beliefs and even the psychological traits of the peoples who speak them. Almost certainly there was once a single 'proto-Semitic' language spoken by the people of Arabia which had dialectical variants.

The northwards migration of Semitic peoples from the Arabian peninsula was continuous, tending to reach a peak about every thousand years. The Arabs are first mentioned in Assyrian inscriptions of about 850 BC as a nomadic people of the north Arabian desert who paid their tribute to their Assyrian overlords in the form of camels – which had first been domesticated in the Arabian peninsula some five hundred years earlier.

The racial origins of the Arabs are highly obscure. The Arabs of today have inherited a tradition that they come from two stocks – the Qahtanis and Adnanis. The former originated in the rain-fed highlands of south-western Arabia and are descended from the patriarch Qahtan. The latter came from the north and centre of the peninsula and are descended from the patriarch Adnan. Almost every Arab tribe claimed descent from one or the other. Of the two, it is the southerners or Yemenis who now form half the population of Arabia and are called the 'true Arabs', the sons of Adnan being called *Mustarib* or arabized peoples. Although today there is no obvious racial difference between those who call themselves Qahtanis and those who call themselves Adnanis, there are two recognizable racial types among the general population of Arabia. The tall people with clean-cut, hawk-like features come mainly from the north; while those in the south tend to be shorter with softer and more rounded features – in origin they are probably related to the Ethiopians. It is therefore ironic that it is the southerners who are considered the 'true Arabs', for it is the northerners who provide the popular image of the Arab and it was in central and northern Arabia that the classical Arabic tongue – the vehicle of Arab/Islamic civilization – developed.

It was many centuries before the whole Middle Eastern and North African region (apart from Persia and Turkey) became arabized. In 336 BC Philip, King of Macedon, united the warring Greek city-states, and it was his son Alexander who launched the astonishing series of conquests which overthrew the magnificent but decadent Persian Empire. Greek thought and culture had already started to penetrate Syria/Palestine and Egypt before Alexander the Great's arrival. A thousand years of Graeco-Roman civilization on the eastern and southern shores of the Mediterranean had begun.

The Persian/Arabian Gulf was included in Alexander's empire.

When he reached the limits of his eastern conquests, in India in 326 BC, he set out to return to Persia by land. But he had in mind a great sea-traffic between Babylon, the capital of his eastern empire, and India. So he ordered his admiral, Nearchos, to return to the Euphrates via the Gulf at the head of his huge fleet. Nearchos reported on the existence of two strategic islands at the head of the gulf. The larger had wild goats and antelope, which were sacred to the Goddess Artemis, and Alexander ordered that it should be named Ikaros after the island in the Aegean Sea which it resembled. A fortress outpost was established which lasted about two hundred years. Today Ikaros is called Failaka and is part of Kuwait.

Alexander's dream of a vast united Hellenistic empire did not survive his early death, as his conquests were disputed between his generals. But Hellenistic civilization remained dominant in the successor empires which stretched from Persia to Egypt, and the cities which Alexander founded continued to flourish. Egypt prospered under the wise rule of the early Ptolemys. Alexandria, with its library and museum, became a splendid city and the intellectual centre of the world. Palestine for a time came once again under Egyptian rule. The rest of Syria and Asia Minor (Turkey of the present day) fell into the hands of Seleucus, the Persian ruler of Alexander's former eastern empire. He founded Antioch, which he named after his father, and this became the capital of Syria for the next nine centuries.

Hellenism first began to retreat in Persia, but even here it was a slow process. Two hundred years after Alexander's death, the Seleucids in Persia were overthrown by the Parthians, a predatory nomadic tribe from the region of the Caspian Sea. The Parthians assimilated Greek government practice and continued to make use of the Greek language in addition to their own. Some Greek cities of Seleucid foundation continued to flourish. Hellenistic influence began to weaken only in the first century AD.

In Syria/Palestine Hellenism was more lasting, but its degree of influence varied greatly. As might be expected, it was greatest to the north and west on the Mediterranean coast, where Laodicea (modern Latakia) and Berytus (Beirut) were typical Greek cities. East of Mount Lebanon, towards the Syrian Desert, Hellenistic influence declined. In fact the whole region was a blend of Hellenism and Semitic Aramaic culture in varying proportions. In both the Ptolemaic and Seleucid Empires the senior civil servants, and the leading businessmen, scholars and intellectuals were Greek. Both empires encouraged immigration from Greece, but the Greeks remained a minority. In their armies the Greeks formed the core or phalanx bearing pikes, but the archers and slingers were Arabs, Kurds and Persians.

Little more than a century after Alexander's death saw the beginning of the rise to power of the Roman Republic. After the final defeat of Carthage in 211 BC, Rome gained mastery over the western Mediterranean. It then turned its attention to the east and invaded Greece. There followed more than 150 years of chaos and war in the eastern Mediterranean region. The rival Seleucid and Ptolemaic Empires fought each other beneath the looming shadow of Rome, and went into a long decline. As always, local powers in Syria took the opportunity to assert themselves.

In Palestine, the small Jewish community enjoyed some freedom to manage its own affairs in the Judaean hills around Jerusalem. The Jewish people were divided between a Hellenized educated upper class which broadly accepted Seleucid rule and a peasantry which clung to their Judaic faith. When, in 168 BC, the Seleucid King Antiochus Epiphanes ordered the altar of Zeus, 'the abomination of desolation', to be set up in the Holy Temple in Jerusalem, Judas Maccabaeus, the son of a priest, led the fervent Jews in a revolt. Although Judas was killed, his family founded a dynasty of priest-princes – the Hasmonaeans – who gradually extended their rule to cover most of Palestine as the Seleucid Empire disintegrated. They were succeeded under the Romans by the related House of Herod.

Further to the east another independent state was established by the Nabataeans, with their headquarters in Petra (south Jordan) and Madain Saleh (Saudi Arabia). In the second century BC their powerful commercial kingdom stretched deep into the Arabian peninsula and flourished by controlling the caravan trade which brought Chinese and Indian spices, perfumes and other luxuries from southern Arabia to Syria and Egypt. The Nabataeans spoke Arabic, but their writing was Aramaic. Their culture was superficially Hellenic. The people of present-day Jordan regard them as their ancestors.

The consolidation of Roman power in the eastern Mediterranean was delayed by the civil war and anarchy in Rome. However, in 71 BC the triumvirate of generals Pompey, Caesar and Crassus took power, and Pompey set about establishing Roman power in Asia Minor and the eastern Mediterranean. He invaded Syria and took Jerusalem. But Roman rule was not yet firmly established. The Parthians inflicted a savage defeat on the Roman legions and for a time occupied Syria. It was not until after both Pompey and Caesar had been assassinated that Caesar's successor Octavian – the Emperor Augustus, who reigned from 29 BC to AD 14 – incorporated the entire Middle East region from Egypt to Asia Minor into the Roman Empire. Only Persia and present-day Iraq remained under Parthian control. Augustus ignored the demands of some of his generals that the defeat of the Roman legions be avenged, preferring to have peace in order to organize Rome's new eastern provinces.

The eastern Mediterranean region – Asia Minor, Syria and Egypt – settled down to several centuries of the Pax Romana, which in general meant efficiency, good order and justice in accordance with Roman law. The road and tax systems were greatly improved. Egypt became an important supplier of food to the imperial capital and a military base for the Roman armies. The Romans cleared the Red Sea of pirates and revived the trade through it to India. Egypt was a Roman colony in the fullest sense, living under iron military government and paying exorbitant taxes. The Greek ruling class co-operated with the colonial power and retained its privileged position.

Egypt, with its population densely concentrated in the Nile Valley and Delta, lends itself to authoritarian centralized government. Roman rule in Syria was rather more relaxed. In the eastern or 'Semitic' half of the region, the Romans allowed the local rulers to retain their autonomy – provided they did not become over-ambitious and threaten the settled populations to the west. It was indirect rule of the kind employed by the British in their empire in Asia and Africa some eighteen centuries later. Thus the Nabataeans continued to control east Jordan and Damascus until in AD 106 the Emperor Trajan, exasperated by their spirit of independence, brought them under the subjection of Rome. A century later, Palmyra in the central Syrian Desert emulated the Nabataeans in achieving power and prosperity through control of the caravan trade-routes to the east until its queen, Zenobia, defied Roman authority, only to be defeated and to have the region's autonomy repressed.

The western or Mediterranean region of Syria, with its great and flourishing Greek cities founded under the Seleucids, was more directly incorporated into the Roman Empire. The educated urban population, a fruitful synthesis of Mediterranean and Semitic races, was part of the empire's professional and intellectual élite. These people mixed easily with the Roman officials, and many acquired Roman citizenship. Many Syrian lawyers, doctors, historians and administrators – not to mention poets and actors – achieved distinction and fame. Hellenized Egyptians played a similar role. Antioch and Alexandria were, after Rome, the two largest and most magnificent cities of the empire. While Latin was the official language of government, Greek was the *lingua franca*. Several of the later Roman emperors were either wholly or partly Syrian, although it has to be said that two of these – Caracalla and Elagabalus, from Homs – were among the least admirable. However, Caracalla can claim credit for the decision to grant Roman citizenship to the whole empire in AD 212. Philip 'the Arab', an able ruler, did something to redeem Syria's reputation during his brief reign.

Despite the easy racial mixture of the cities, a gulf – and especially a linguistic gulf – remained between the cities and the peasants and tribesmen of the countryside. In Syria these spoke Aramaic; the nomads and semi-nomads on the fringes of Arabia spoke Arabic. In Egypt the majority of the population spoke the ancient Egyptian language. But it was in Palestine that the clash of cultures was most violent, and yet perhaps most productive.

In 40 BC the Romans appointed Herod from Idumaea (Edom) in southern Palestine as king of Judaea, with Jerusalem as his capital. In his long reign he extended his effective rule over most of Palestine, earning the title of 'Herod the Great'. An Arab by race, he was a Jew by practice and he saw himself as the protector of the Jews. He rebuilt the Temple of Jerusalem, but as a Hellenizer and a Roman protégé he was detested by the pious Jews. His reign ended in bitterness and violent dispute over his succession in which he ordered the notorious massacre of the innocent infants of Bethlehem. Thus he also became the ogre of Christian tradition, as it was in the little Herodian kingdom that the Jewish founder of the Christian religion was born, lived and was executed – the founder of the religion which in time triumphantly converted the entire Graeco-Roman world.

Jesus and his Apostles were Jews, and Christianity was originally a movement within Judaism. But the Christian message made little headway among the Jewish people and so it was soon directed towards the gentile world instead. It was the task of the early

Christian apologists to define the Christian gospel as both the correction and the fulfilment of Greek and Roman philosophy, and their intellectual achievements in the first three centuries after Christ were considerable. However, the simple message of the Sermon on the Mount made its first appeal to the poor and underprivileged masses of the Graeco-Roman world. Despite official persecution, it thrived and spread – the martyrdom of Jesus providing a model for suffering and endurance. Christianity is thought to have arrived in Egypt with St Mark, before the end of the first century AD, and it spread rapidly among the mass of the Egyptian people, although the Greeks and the Hellenized upper class generally remained pagan.

The persecution of Christianity in the empire occurred in waves which were interspersed by periods of toleration, but for three centuries Christianity gained converts. Although still a minority – the majority clinging to the old state religions, of which the cult of the emperor was the most popular – Christians formed a substantial proportion among all classes, including members of the imperial family and the Roman aristocracy, by the time the last wave of persecution was instituted by Diocletian, at the beginning of the fourth century AD. They were dynamic and well-organized, and within a few years of Diocletian's abdication his successor, Constantine the Great, declared Christianity to be the official religion of the Roman Empire. Whether Constantine's conversion was genuine or whether he had recognized Christianity as the conquering faith is immaterial.

The rise of Christianity was favoured by the decline of the empire. Throughout the third century AD it had been beset by internal divisions – indeed, for periods it was ruled by rival emperors – and assaulted from outside its borders by Goths and Persians. At times the empire had seemed on the verge of collapse, until it was rescued once more by an able emperor or army commander. In the east, the Parthian Empire was replaced in AD 224 by that of the Sassanids from west Persia, who claimed descent from the great dynasty of Cyrus and Darius. The Sassanian Empire lasted for four centuries in which it was almost constantly at war with the rival great power in the west. Shapar I, the second Sassanid ruler, took the title of 'King of Kings of Iran and non-Iran', thus emphasizing his claim to dominion of the world.

In AD 330, on the ancient site of Byzantium on the Bosporus

where Europe meets Asia, Constantine founded the city that bore his name. Constantinople became the capital of the eastern half of the Roman Empire – still formally united – and, as the centre of power and wealth shifted eastwards, Constantinople overtook Rome in magnificence. Half a century later, on the death of the Emperor Theodosius, the empire was divided between his two sons. The Christian, Hellenic–oriental Byzantine Empire was born. While the western half of the empire collapsed under the weight of barbarian invasions, Byzantium continued to rule the Balkans, Asia Minor, Syria, Palestine and Egypt.

The eastern Roman Empire was able to maintain control over the Middle East region for three centuries. The greatest threat it faced was not from Goths and Germans in Europe but from the aggressive and expansionist Sassanian Persians to the east. However, for at least two hundred years the Byzantines were able to secure peace with the Persians through diplomacy. It was only when Justinian the Great (527–65) decided to devote his energies to the reconquest of the western Roman provinces and the reuniting of the empire – efforts which were partially and temporarily successful – that the Persian danger increased. Between 534 and 628 the Persians repeatedly invaded and occupied Syria and had to be thrown back. In 616 they conquered both Egypt and Asia Minor and laid siege to Constantinople. By the time the Emperor Heraclius defeated the Persians and restored the empire's frontiers, Byzantium and Persia, although still the two superpowers of the ancient world, were overstretched and weakened. Meanwhile, in AD 570 or 571, in obscure and impoverished Arabia an extraordinary man had been born who would plant the seeds of a new and much greater power that would come to overwhelm them. The Prophet Muhammad, who was born in Mecca, one of the largest settled and trading communities in western Arabia, was a man of genius and inspiration who helped to transform the history of mankind – a fact which is acknowledged not only by the one-fifth of the human race who subscribe to the faith that he founded.

There are two aspects of the Islamic religion which are of special importance to the subsequent history of the Middle East. The first of these is that while Muslims do not believe Muhammad to be divine – for Islam is the most fiercely monotheistic of faiths, adhering to the belief that 'there is no God but God' – they do regard him as the last of God's messengers, or the seal of the prophets, who include Moses and Jesus. They therefore hold that Islam is the ultimate faith, which completes and perfects the two other heavenly religions – Judaism and Christianity. If mankind as a whole has not yet accepted the truth, it is due to the failings of the community of Muslim believers.

The other important fact is that, while Muslims believe in paradise and the soul's immortality, their faith is far from other-worldly. The Prophet, unlike Jesus, was a political leader and organizer of genius, and in Islam there is no separation between religion and politics and no concept of a secular state. The Holy Koran, which for Muslims is the literal word of God, is the continuing inspiration for all Muslim thought and actions, but it is not a comprehensive code of law. Muslims have therefore looked also to the example of the Prophet and his companions. Their words and deeds, known as their *sunnah* or habitual modes of thought and action, were collected in the *hadith*, or traditions of the prophet, which were handed down through a line of reliable witnesses. Together the Koran and the *sunnah* form the sources of the Islamic *sharia*. This is normally translated as 'Islamic law', but it is much more than this. It is neither canonical law (Islam has no priesthood) nor secular law, because no such concept exists in Islam: it is rather a whole system of social morality, prescribing the ways in which man should live if he is to act according to God's will. If he contravenes the *sharia*, his offence is against God and not the state.

This is the ideal. Since the earliest times, Arab and Muslim rulers have assumed secular powers to some degree – and none more so than those of today – but the ideal continues to have a powerful influence on the hearts and minds of all Muslims. It accounts for the potent force of utopianism among Arabs – the belief that if they were to return to the ways of the Prophet and his companions the triumph of Islam in this world would be assured. In the West this is usually described as fundamentalism, but in a real sense all Muslim believers are fundamentalist, because they know that the Holy Koran was God's final message to mankind. The triumph of the West in the last two or three centuries is seen by Muslims as an aberration of history.

It is not surprising that the Arabs of today are still inspired to the point of obsession by the story of the first achievements of Islam. When, at the age of forty, Muhammad underwent the religious experience which turned him into a prophet and leader, the Arabian peninsula was a conglomeration of petty autonomous states grouped around tribal confederations. The largely nomadic people were mainly animists by religion, worshipping a variety of spirits who were often based in a particular rock or shrine. They had no written codes of laws; crimes were restrained by the lasting fears of vengeance. No such restraints applied to communal acts of violence, however, and the frequent inter-tribal disputes could be settled only by reference to an arbiter, a wise authority on tribal customs. This was not a high culture which could remotely be compared with that of Byzantium or Persia, but it had a matchless asset in the Arabic language, with its limitless power and flexibility and the supreme artistic achievement of its poetry.

Although proud and independent, the people of Arabia were not immune to outside influences. Through their contacts with the Christian Byzantines and Abyssinians, and Zoroastrian Persians, they had begun to acquire some monotheistic ideas when Muhammad began his mission. By the time he died, in his early sixties, the new faith had been accepted throughout most of Arabia. In one generation he had succeeded in welding the scattered and idolatrous tribes of the peninsula into one nation worshipping a single, all-powerful god.

If the achievements of the Islamic faith in the lifetime of Muhammad were remarkable, those during the brief rule of his three successors, or caliphs – the Rashidoun or Rightly Guided Ones – were even more astonishing. The small forces of the faithful went on to challenge the two great empires of Byzantium and Persia. Within ten years they had defeated the Sassanid Persians, captured their capital Ctesiphon on the Tigris and driven them out of Mesopotamia. They then turned their attention to the Byzantine provinces of Syria and Egypt. The Arab army swept on through North Africa, and within another fifty years, in AD 711, had crossed into Spain.

After the conquest of Syria and Egypt, the Arabs spent another ten years destroying what remained of the Sassanid Empire. The Byzantine Empire, however, was to last another eight hundred years. Although the Arabs took Cyprus, Rhodes and Cos and twice besieged Constantinople, they never conquered and held Anatolia, which continued for several more centuries to be shared between the Byzantines and the Christian kingdom of Armenia.

Within thirty years of the Prophet's death, decisive events were to shape the future of Islam and of the Prophet's Arabian homeland. In

AD 656 the Caliph Omar's successor, Othman, was assassinated. His natural successor seemed to be Ali, first cousin of the Prophet and husband of his daughter Fatima. But Ali was opposed by the ambitious and able Arab general Muawiya, whom Omar had appointed governor of Syria and who, like Othman, belonged to the powerful Umayyad family of Mecca. The defeat of Ali and his son Hussein by the Umayyads led to the first and only great division in Islam: between the Sunnis, or 'people of the sunnah', who are the great majority, and the Shia or 'partisans' of Ali, who continue to regard Muawiya and his Umayyad successors as secular usurpers.

Today about 10 per cent of the world's Muslim population are Shiite, and most of these are in Iran and the Indian subcontinent. There are scarcely any Shiites in Africa. In the Levant they are important in Lebanon, where they form 30 per cent of the population and probably outnumber the Sunnis.

In the Arabian peninsula the great majority of the people have remained Sunni, although there are important Shiite minorities on the eastern fringes. The Zaydis, who inhabit the mountains of Yemen, also belong to a branch of Shiism. But Sunnism and Shiism continued in dispute over Persia (Iran) until, in the sixteenth century, Sunnism was adopted as the ruling faith. In Mesopotamia (Iraq), the majority of the population have remained Shiite, and the Shia holy cities of Nejaf and Kerbala are on Iraqi territory, but Sunnis are still politically dominant. This has a significant bearing on the modern history of the region.

The triumph of the Umayyads not only caused a split in Islam: it made Damascus the capital of the new Arab/Islamic empire. After a century, in AD 750, the defeat of the Umayyads by the Abbasids, a rival revolutionary movement based in east Persia, shifted the centre of power to Baghdad, inaugurating the Golden Age of Islam – one of the highest peaks of human civilization.

In the vast territories in which Islam was triumphant, two processes – allied but not identical – began to operate: 'arabization' and 'islamization'. In Iraq, Greater Syria, Egypt and the North African countries of the Maghreb, the Arabic languages began gradually to overwhelm the existing tongues. (Kurdish in northern Iraq and Berber in Algeria and Morocco, neither of which is a written language, have survived.) In Syria/Palestine and Egypt, Greek continued to be used in administration for a time until Arabic was made the official tongue. In the

Fertile Crescent, the Arabic which was already spoken in the east and in the Arabian peninsula steadily replaced Aramaic, which now barely survives in one or two villages north of Damascus and in northern Iraq. Similarly, the Coptic language of the ancient Egyptians was progressively extinguished as the Arab occupation changed into full-scale colonization and assimilation, although it survived at least until the seventeenth century.

Islamization was less complete than arabization because substantial communities of Christians and Jews, respected and tolerated by Islam as 'People of the Book', clung to their faith and survived. But the spread of Islam was more extensive than that of the Arabic language. It moved swiftly to Samarkand and the borders of India, and in subsequent centuries huge populations in the Indian subcontinent, in China and in south-east Asia converted. But here Arabic was confined to religious observance. The language and culture of the Persians survived both their conquest by the Arabs and their acceptance of the Islamic faith, although the Persian Farsi language adopted the Arabic script and an extensive Arabic vocabulary. Today only about one-fifth of the Muslims in the world are Arabic-speaking.

The Turks were not conquered by the Arabs, but they were largely converted to Islam in the tenth century, and their language was invaded by a stream of Arabic words from the vocabulary of religion, science and culture. Turkish was also written in the Arabic script. The twelfth century, when Persian became the literary language of western Asia, saw a second linguistic invasion. Turkish writers adopted Persian and Arabic grammatical constructions as well as words, to create the synthesis of Ottoman Turkish.

Three languages – Arabic, Persian and Turkish – therefore came to be spoken or written by the vast majority of the inhabitants of the Middle East region. According to modern nationalist terminology, the people who spoke these languages were Arabs, Persians and Turks.

Only two important minorities resisted assimilation and retained their national identity – Armenians and Kurds. The Armenians had a continuing national existence from the sixth century BC, in what is now eastern Turkey and part of Soviet Transcaucasia, and they can claim to be the oldest Christian nation, with their own Armenian Apostolic Church. They had an independent kingdom for several centuries before their conquest and absorption into an Islamic Empire in the fourteenth century, and, although later dispersed throughout the Middle East and beyond, they remain loyal to their language, religion and culture.

The Kurds are a mountain people whose ancient history has often overlapped with that of the Armenians. They speak an Indo-European group of dialects, related to Persian. Unlike the Armenians, they have never had their own independent state, but they have been less dispersed and today they inhabit an arc of territory from north-western Iran through north-eastern Iraq and Syria to eastern Turkey.

The Arabs were aided in their conquest by the debilitating struggles between the Byzantine and Persian Empires, and also by the unpopularity of the imperial rulers among their subject peoples. To create their own lasting empire the Arabs had to succeed better in the art of government than their predecessors. The achievement of these former barbarian nomads was astonishing, and undoubtedly the nature of the Islamic faith – austere, simple, comprehensible and just – provides the reason. There is no cause for surprise that Arabs of today should believe that a return to the principles and practice of those days should restore their greatness.

Initially the tribal warriors of pure Arab descent formed a military aristocracy who numbered no more than a few hundred thousand. Non-Arabs who embraced Islam – Persians, Egyptians, Levantines of mixed race or North African Berbers – were called *mawalis* or clients. But this aristocracy of the Arabs did not last.

Although Islam's relationship with Arabia and the Arabic language is indestructible, racial distinction among the faithful is contrary to both the letter and the spirit of the Holy Koran. As marriage with *mawali* women was frequent, assimilation proceeded swiftly, and in the process the term 'Arab' began its gradual change from the name for a beduin nomad of the Arabian peninsula to its present meaning of anyone whose culture and language are Arabic.

Under the Abbasid caliphate, a great movement of ethnic as well as cultural assimilation took place within the Islamic Empire. While Arabic came to be accepted first as the dominant language and then as the *lingua franca*, the 'pure' Arabs also gradually abandoned their claims to aristocracy. The principle of ethnic equality came to be accepted. Thus the language and religion of the Arabs acted as the cement which held this great edifice together. Its strength and prosperity lay in the fact that the splendid Persian and Hellenic civilizations which had been overwhelmed were not destroyed: for a time the new Arab rulers left the existing systems of government and administration largely intact, until they had assimilated them and developed their own synthesis.

The transfer of the empire's capital from Damascus to Baghdad shifted its centre of gravity eastwards. Interest in the Mediterranean declined, and oriental influences, such as the Persian taste for absolute monarchy, increased. The removal of frontier barriers made Baghdad the centre of a vast and increasingly prosperous free-trade area in which most sections of the population had the opportunity to engage in vigorous commercial activity. Arab ships sailed to China, Sumatra, India and southwards along the east coast of Africa as far as Madagascar. Learning and culture also flourished in this Islamic Golden Age. At first it was mainly a question of translation into Arabic of the great scientific and philosophical works of the ancient civilizations, but soon the Islamic Empire brought forth its own towering achievements in science, literature and the arts.

As in all other human empires, the seeds of decline were already sprouting when this empire was apparently at its zenith. Despite the remarkable system of communications radiating from Baghdad, effective power could not be exerted over the more distant provinces for long. In Egypt and in eastern Persia, authority was delegated to local commanders who made themselves autonomous. The Arabs who had earlier supplied the vanguard of the imperial forces felt alienated from their new arabized rulers and no longer enlisted, so the caliph took to importing Turkish slave-boys known as Mamlukes from what is now Soviet Turkestan to be trained as soldiers who would maintain the security of the empire. Although speaking Turkish, the Mamlukes were not all ethnic Turks but included Kurds, Mongols and other central Asian peoples. These mercenaries made effective soldiers, but they soon realized their ability to seize control for themselves. In 861 they assassinated the caliph in Baghdad and set up a military dictatorship. In 867 a Turk named Ibn Tulun seized power in Egypt. He easily occupied Syria and once again brought it into an association with Egypt. This was to last, with intermissions, until the whole region came under the domination of the Ottoman Turkish Empire in the sixteenth century.

The great Arab/Islamic Empire which had lasted more than two centuries and covered the whole of the contemporary known world except for northern Europe and China was breaking up. In the early part of the eighth century the Arabs had held Spain and half of France. They soon withdrew from France, but later occupied Sicily and much of southern Italy. However, the move of the capital from Damascus to Baghdad weakened the empire's control in the Mediterranean and now, at the end of the ninth century, this was broken entirely. The Arabs retained their cultural dominance for at least another two centuries, and Baghdad continued to be a great centre of culture and learning, but effective power was exercised by the uncultivated Turkish military caste.

This Turkish hegemony was broken for a time, however. In AD 969, Egypt, after a century of unstable rule by Turkish military dynasties, was invaded from the west by a new Arab power. This was the Fatimid dynasty, which took its name from the Prophet's daughter Fatima, the wife of the caliph Ali. Before moving to North Africa the Fatimids had originated in Syria as leaders of the Shiite Ismaili movement, which was dedicated to the overthrow of the Abbasid caliphate. Thus they were regarded as heretical enemies by Baghdad.

Just north of the old Arab/Muslim capital of Fustat, the Fatimids founded Cairo as their new capital and established a rival caliphate to that of Baghdad, with its own empire of great splendour. For a time this stretched westwards across the Maghreb to the Atlantic and into Sicily. Although Fatimid power did not extend eastwards, the instability in Baghdad meant that much of the oriental trade which was the source of Abbasid wealth was diverted from the Persian/Arabian Gulf to the Red Sea. Cairo prospered at Baghdad's expense.

Syria/Palestine resumed its historical role as the battlefield for the struggle between the rival rulers of the Tigris–Euphrates and Nile Valleys. But a new element added to Syria's misery: the Byzantines, who had suffered three centuries of Arab/Muslim invasions, took their opportunity for revenge. Between 962 and 1000, Syria was invaded thirty-eight times by successive Byzantine emperors.

In 1018 the Fatimid Caliph Hakim became insane and declared himself to be God. After his death, a new religion emerged with the belief that Hakim had not died but had only disappeared, and would return in triumph to inaugurate a golden age. Taking their name from one of their leaders who fled to Mount Lebanon, Ismail al-Darazi, the Druze are important because, although never numerous (some 250,000 now live in Lebanon, Syria and Israel), they are one of the few of the many sub-Shiite sects which appeared at that time to have survived to the present day and have played a crucial role in the history of the region. (Another sub-Shiite sect is the Alawite or Nusairi, that first flourished around Aleppo in the tenth century. This sect has also survived and today forms about 10 per cent of the population of Syria. The fact that President Assad and other key members of his regime belong to this sect has had a significant bearing on the modern history of Syria.)

In spite of their repeated invasions of Syria/Palestine, the Byzantines were not able to hold this region. In fact the Byzantine, Abbasid and Fatimid Empires were all in a state of decline in the first half of the eleventh century, when a new force burst on the scene. Oghuz Turkish nomads from central Asia, who became known as Seljuks, after one of their chiefs, invaded Persia and in 1050 captured Baghdad, reducing the Abbasid caliph to the status of a vassal. In 1071, they took Syria and Palestine and drove the Fatimids back to Egypt. By the end of the century the Seljuk Empire included Persia, Mesopotamia, Syria and Palestine. But the Turkoman warriors of the Seljuk army were looking to the rich lands of the Byzantine Empire to the west. In 1071 the Seljuk sultan Arp Arslan routed a huge Byzantine army and captured the Byzantine emperor. The Muslim Turks were then able to settle in Asia Minor.

For four centuries, Byzantium had protected western Christendom from Islamic invasion and expansion from the east. With the Byzantine Empire now in danger of collapse, the Emperor Alexius Commenus (1081–1118) appealed to Pope Urban II for men to help fight the infidel invaders. On 27 November 1095 the Pope called for recruits to march to the relief of their fellow-Christians in the east and to restore the security of the western pilgrim-routes to the Holy Land.

The consequent invasion of the Middle East by the Christians of western Europe – the First Crusade – was initially successful. Jerusalem was captured in 1099 and its Muslim and Jewish populations were massacred. A Latin kingdom of Jerusalem and three other crusader principalities were established. The Abbasid caliphs of Baghdad and the Seljuk sultans were largely indifferent to Syria and Palestine, which lay on the periphery of their interests. After one abortive attempt, the Fatimids of Egypt abandoned any effort to recover Jerusalem for Islam. In Syria itself the local Turkish regimes, normally in a state of mutual hostility, frequently allied themselves with the crusaders against each other.

The petty Christian states, which were manifestly inferior in culture and civilization (the Muslims were astonished by the crusaders' primitive medical knowledge, for example), were not regarded as a serious threat to the world of Islam. But the crusader states were not content with mere tolerated survival. They became embroiled with their neighbours, and eventually caused the divided Muslim states to unite in a *jihad* or holy war against them. In 1187 the Kurdish leader Saladin recovered Jerusalem (and, in contrast to the crusaders eighty-eight years previously, spared the lives of those who surrendered). Further crusades were launched in the following century which enabled the diminished Christian states on the coast of Syria and Palestine to survive for a time, but after little more than two centuries they had disappeared.

Apart from a few magnificent castles and some of their blood through intermarriage, the crusaders left little which endured. Their greatest achievement was drastically to weaken the superior civilization they encountered and to undermine its moral standards. However, in one vitally important respect the crusaders showed that they had an advantage over their Muslim enemies: this was their ability to create sound and workable political institutions. These were feudal rather than democratic, but they enshrined the notion of the rights and obligations of the different sections of society – princes, knights, merchants and peasants. The power of the ruler was not unlimited, and the succession was usually achieved by consent rather than force. In the Muslim lands, on the other hand, although both the principles and procedures of law governing human relationships were more sophisticated and rational, the practice of government was normally arbitrary and unlimited. The tribal democracy of the early caliphs, whose power was limited by a *Majlis al-Shura* or consultative council, had generally given way to despotism.

It has been wisely observed that the most disastrous effect of the crusades on the Islamic heartland was Islam's retreat into isolation:

Although the epoch of the Crusades ignited a genuine economic and cultural revolution in Western Europe, in the Orient these holy wars led to long centuries of decadence and obscurantism. Assaulted from all quarters, the Muslim world turned in on itself. It became over-sensitive, defensive, intolerant, sterile – attitudes that grew steadily worse as world-wide evolution, a process from which the Muslim world felt excluded, continued.

This was the long-term consequence. At the time, the triumphant elimination of the Christian invaders was seen as proof of the superiority of the Islamic faith, which, as always has to be remembered, Muslims believe to be designated by God to succeed and perfect the other monotheisms. A few contemporary Muslim chroniclers were prepared to acknowledge the virtues of the system of government in the crusader states, but such comparisons were considered irrelevant once these states had been eliminated.

With the final defeat and expulsion of the crusaders, Islam was triumphant throughout the Middle East region. In Egypt, the splendid but short-lived Ayyubid dynasty founded by Saladin was replaced by the Mamlukes, who at the end of the thirteenth century extended their empire to Syria. The Seljuks gradually pushed forward their domains in Anatolia at the expense of Byzantium, whose decline had been accelerated by the crusaders who in their Fourth Crusade, at the beginning of the thirteenth century, caused a struggle in Constantinople between western Latin and eastern Greek Christians. The Seljuk dynasty in Asia Minor was known as 'the Sultanate of Rum' (Arabic for Rome), a Muslim inheritor of the eastern flank of the Roman Empire.

In the beginning of the thirteenth century, the Muslim world had to face a new and terrifying threat: the Mongols. Like the nomadic Turkish tribes before them, the Mongols burst out of central Asia into the rich lands of the Fertile Crescent. In 1220 Genghis Khan seized Persia; in 1243 his successors routed the entire Seljuk army and went on to occupy the sultanate of Rum. In 1258 Gengis Khan's grandson Hulagu captured Baghdad and eliminated the last ghostly relic of the Abbasid caliphate, as his armies completed the destruction of the great irrigation works of Mesopotamia.

It seemed as if nothing could prevent the Mongols from overruning Syria and Egypt. But the Egyptian Mamlukes rallied to inflict a crushing defeat on the Mongols at Ain Jalout in Palestine in 1260. In that it saved the heartlands of the Muslim world from being overwhelmed, this was one of the decisive battles in the history of the world. The Mongol threat was far greater than that of the Christian crusaders, but it was also short-lived. Eastern and western Christians both nursed hopes that the Mongols could be converted to Christianity. Instead, in 1295, the Mongol khan announced that he had become a Muslim. The struggle for the Middle East continued to be within the world of Islam.

The three centuries of Mamluke rule in Egypt and Syria showed many of the aspects of an advanced civilization. With the demise of Baghdad and the reduction of Muslim Spain, the great centres of Islamic learning and literary and artistic achievement were now Cairo, Damascus and Aleppo. Exquisite architecture and artefacts have survived from the period. These cities were wealthy and prosperous, as trade poured through both to and from the East. But these centuries were disastrous in the way that power was exercised and in the development of political institutions. If Muslim society was relatively stable, its rulers were not. The Mamlukes' code prevented the founding of a hereditary dynasty, and in matters of government they fell back on their ferocious and unyielding military tradition. Mamluke sultans of Egypt rarely lasted more than a few years before they were ousted by a stronger rival. Similarly, Mamluke generals fought each other for the governorship of Syria. As the Mongol Empire declined, there was no longer an external threat to enforce the unity that had been achieved at Ain Jalout.

The Mamlukes were not aware that their fate was being sealed by events that were taking place in Asia Minor. At the end of the thirteenth century this was the territory of some dozen Turkish warrior-princes, or ghazis, who had overwhelmed most of the provinces of the Byzantine Empire. Nominally tributaries of the Mongol Khans, they had become increasingly independent. One of these, named Osman, was the founder of a dynasty and empire which grew to control most of the world of Islam for four centuries.

The first Osmanlis – or Ottomans, as they became known in the west – were distinguished among their fellow-ghazis by their wisdom and statecraft. In many ways they resembled the first caliphs of Islam – the Rashidoun or Rightly Guided Ones – in that they combined a passionate and simple faith with a chivalrous and tolerant attitude towards the mainly Christian inhabitants of the lands they conquered. Some of these Christians converted to Islam, but even those who did not frequently welcomed the firm justice of Ottoman rule in contrast to the anarchic misgovernment of the decadent Byzantine Empire.

In the second half of the fourteenth century, Osman's grandson

Murad I, the first great Ottoman sultan, crossed the Hellespont to extend the young empire into the Christian Balkan states. He applied the principle of toleration to allow non-Muslims to become full citizens and rise to the highest offices of state, so at this very early stage establishing the character of the vast multilingual and multi-ethnic Ottoman Empire, which had much in common with the Roman Empire.

Murad conquered the Balkans; his son Bayezid I devoted himself to the acquisition of the whole of Asia and the final reduction of Constantinople. He failed at the final hour because of a sudden new threat from the east – the Tartars, who appeared like a reincarnation of their Mongol cousins two centuries earlier. Tamerlane, the terrifying Tartar leader, came close to destroying the Ottoman Empire in its infancy and restoring the ghazi principalities to Byzantium, but he died on his way to new conquests in China. The Ottomans recovered and a generation later produced another outstanding leader in Mohammed II – 'the Conqueror' – who in 1453 finally captured Constantinople and overwhelmed the last relics of the Byzantine Empire.

Western schoolchildren have been taught that, by scattering the legacy of Greece and Rome, the Muslim conquest of Constantinople launched western Christendom into the Renaissance. In fact, although this momentous event had a profound and lasting effect on the imagination of mankind, it marked only the final stage of the withdrawal of non-Muslim power from the Middle East: for many generations the Byzantine Empire had been no more than a shadow of its former dominating presence.

Europe was already well aware of the Ottoman threat. The Venetians, Hungarians and others had tried to stem the tide by forming temporary alliances with the Ottomans' rivals in Asia Minor. After the fall of Constantinople, the infidel Turk was for two centuries a towering menace which threatened to burst out from the Balkans and overrun central Europe. Twice – in 1529 and 1683 – the Ottoman forces were on the point of occupying Vienna and overwhelming the Habsburg Empire. In weapons and military strategy – especially the early use of firearms – they were superior, and they had rapidly turned themselves into a formidable naval power which could match anything the Europeans could put to sea. Edward Gibbon's famous speculation about the consequences for Europe if the Arab/Muslim armies had continued their advance northwards into France in the eighth century (students of Oxford and Cambridge studying the Holy Koran instead of the Bible) could equally have been applied to the Turkish invasions eight centuries later. The Arabs were turned back as much by the unappealing climate of northern Europe as by the army of Charles Martel, leader of the Christian Franks; the Turks from Asia Minor were more accustomed to the frost and snow. The Renaissance monarchs of Europe constantly attempted to combine their forces for new crusades against the world of Islam but, in contrast to their predecessors in the earlier crusades, they were acting not on behalf of Christian pilgrims to the Holy Land or Christian minorities in the Middle East but to protect themselves.

In its first two centuries, the greater part of the Ottoman Empire's remarkable energies was directed towards Christian Europe. However, after Mohammed the Conqueror had consolidated the Ottoman hold on Asia Minor, his grandson Selim I, known as 'the Grim', turned his attention towards Asia. In Persia the Safavid dynasty had been established when Ismail, known as 'the Great Sufi', proclaimed himself shah in 1502. Shortly afterwards he declared Shiite Islam, which was already the faith of most of his subjects, to be the official religion of the empire. In 1508 he occupied Iraq. Selim the Grim – also known as 'the Just' for his severe Sunni orthodoxy – defeated Ismail in a great battle in the Valley of Chalderan, near Tabriz. In 1514 he went on to annex the high plateau of eastern Anatolia, which provided the Ottoman Empire with a vital strategic defence against invasion from the west.

More than two centuries of struggle and intermittent warfare between the Sunni and Shiite Empires ensued. Militarily the Ottomans usually had the upper hand, but Persian cultural influence remained a powerful force in the Turkish Empire, and even when the Ottomans established their definitive control over Mesopotamia in the seventeenth century the majority of its Arabic-speaking people remained Shiite. Shah Ismail may be regarded as the founder of modern Persia (Iran). Unlike the Ottomans, the Safavids had no ambitions to invade and conquer Christian lands. Apart from disputed Mesopotamia, the territories of the Persian Empire remained roughly the same until modern times. But within these borders a great national and religious revival took place. Shah Abbas I, who reigned from 1587 to 1629, was an outstanding military leader, administrator and patron of the arts. Although a zealous Shiite Muslim, he was tolerant towards Christians, allowing the Carmelites and other orders to set up missions and build churches at Isfahan and elsewhere. The Safavid dynasty declined under his less able successors, but Persia remained established as a dominant power in the region. Although encroached upon by its neighbours, it never suffered the dismemberment which was the fate of the Ottoman Empire.

After his defeat of Persia, Selim turned upon the Mamlukes. Although courageous fighters, in their weakened and semi-anarchic condition these were no match for the superior training and discipline of the Ottoman army. After a battle near Aleppo in 1516, in which the aged Mamluke sultan Qansuh al-Ghawri died of a stroke and his army was annihilated, Selim easily occupied Syria and Palestine. The following year he invaded Egypt and inflicted a final defeat on the Mamlukes outside the walls of Cairo. While he was in Egypt, Selim received a delegation from the Arab sharif, or ruler, of Mecca, who offered him the keys of the Holy City of Islam and the title of 'Protector of the Holy Places'. The standard and cloak of the Prophet were transferred to Istanbul.

The North African or Barbary states as far as Morocco soon accepted Ottoman suzerainty. Yemen in south-western Arabia became an Ottoman pashalik, or governorate, in 1537. Of the Arabic-speaking world, only Morocco in the far west, Oman in south-eastern Arabia and the central Arabian peninsula, sparsely inhabited by beduin, remained outside Ottoman control. Although it was not until the eighteenth century that the Ottoman sultans officially adopted for themselves the title of 'Caliph of Islam', their claim to leadership of Sunni Islam was henceforth disputed only by rebels with local followings in outlying provinces.

It is hardly surprising that the Arabs of today tend to see their four Ottoman centuries in the darkest terms. Their ancestors had allowed first military leadership and then political leadership in the Islamic world to pass into Turkish hands. Except in the outer extremities of the Arab world, where the Arabs retained some political independence, the Turks were indisputably the governing race. In contrast, the Persians in their own vast homeland were rivals rather than subjects of the Ottoman Turks. Just as wounding to Arab pride was the fact that the Arabic language, the glory of Arab civilization, had yielded its cultural leadership in Islam. Arabic remained the language of religion, as it was bound to be, but Turkish and Persian, after absorbing profound Arabic influence, developed more vital independent cultural worlds of their own.

Nevertheless, the Ottoman Empire was a splendid Islamic civilization. It reached its zenith under the son of Selim the Grim – Sulaiman the Magnificent, or Lawgiver, who reigned from 1520 to 1566 and was therefore an exact contemporary of the great Renaissance monarchs of Europe – the Habsburg Emperor Charles V, Francis I of France and the Tudor Henry VIII of England. Sulaiman added Hungary, Rhodes and North Africa to his empire, although he failed to take Vienna. But he was much more than a great military campaigner: he was a fine administrator and a stern but humane dispenser of justice. A considerable poet in his own right, he encouraged all the arts at his court. Like all great civilizations, the Ottoman absorbed and transformed various external cultural influences. The first sultans took from the Byzantines. Selim and Sulaiman brought in craftsmen from Tabriz in western Persia to beautify Istanbul. Under Sulaiman, with the help of Sinan – the son of a Christian from Anatolia and one of the finest architects of all time – the work that had begun with Mohammed the Conqueror was completed, and Istanbul became a city of true magnificence at the point of confluence of eastern and western civilization.

All great multiracial empires decline and dissolve. The Ottoman Empire was far more extensive and enduring than the powerful states that had been established by other warrior nomads from central Asia – the Seljuks, Mongols and Tartars – but decline began rather less than halfway through the five centuries of the empire's life, and from then on the decadence was virtually unremitting. Attempts to reform and revive the empire actually contributed to its break-up and decline.

It is not possible to ascribe the decline to any single cause; it is certain only that the seeds of the empire's decadence had been sown when it was apparently at its zenith under Sulaiman the Magnificent. For some further hundred and fifty years it remained a great power that was still capable of instilling in successive Popes and the Christian states of western Europe a lively dread that they would be overwhelmed by the Turkish infidel. It was the second Ottoman defeat at the gates of Vienna – in 1683, at the hands of the forces of the king of Poland – which finally removed the Turkish threat. The balance of power had turned unremittingly against Istanbul. But in 1683 no one in Europe could be confident of turning back the Muslim advance. It took time for fears to recede.

While no simple diagnosis can be made of the cause of the transformation of the empire into the 'Sick Man of Europe', there are certain characteristics which suggest themselves. Often they were originally reasons for the empire's strength and success, but they became weaknesses as they were unadaptable to changing circumstances. In the first place the empire was a huge military organization in which military values and ideals were supreme. It was also highly centralized, in the sense that virtually all land within the empire belonged to the Ottoman state. It was feudal in so far as much of the best land was allocated as fiefs to the Ottoman military aristocracy; but only in rare cases could this land be inherited, and thus the empire never developed a European kind of feudal nobility to balance the power of the monarch. If this European type of feudalism is an essential stage towards the ultimate development of capitalism, this suggests a reason why the empire gradually fell behind the European states in terms of material and industrial power. On the other hand, the lack of a landed aristocracy meant that the early empire was socially egalitarian to an exceptional degree. Not only Muslims but also Christians and Jews – ex-slaves and men of the humblest birth – could rise to the highest offices of state, provided they converted to Islam. Sulaiman the Magnificent's outstanding grand vizier Ibrahim was born a Christian Greek. Beyond doubt the empire benefited from the use of these unusual sources of talent and ability.

Converted Christians were the source of one of the strangest and most distinctive institutions of the Ottoman empire – the Janissaries (that is *yeni-cheris*, or new troops). In the fourteenth century, Murad I began the practice of recruiting Christian boys, handpicked for their good physique and ready intelligence, to form a highly disciplined and superbly trained militia which became the core of the Ottoman army. Forbidden to marry, they lived monastic lives which were devoted to the sultan. As the empire expanded, they were used to put down ruthlessly any signs of disorder or insurrection among its huge population.

The empire did not have a hereditary aristocracy, but it did have a ruling class. This consisted of the army officers, the senior civil servants and the men of religion – the muftis and leading *ulama*

(Muslim scholars). They represented the sultan's authority which it was their function to preserve. Beneath them were the *rayas* (*rai'yah* in Arabic – the 'flock' or 'shepherded people'), who consisted of the mass of peasant farmers and some of the craftsmen of the towns. Originally the term '*raya*' applied to all subjects of a Muslim ruler, but it was later limited to those non-Muslims who, unlike the Muslims, paid the poll tax. Since they formed the great majority of the population in the empire's European provinces, they provided the bulk of its revenues. They were organized into *millets* or self-governing communities headed by their patriarch or bishop, who was responsible for their good behaviour. They lacked any political power within the structure of the empire, and they were not allowed to join the army or the civil service, but in time they gained increasing commercial and economic influence.

The Muslim Arabs who formed the great majority in the empire's Middle Eastern and North African provinces were not treated as second-class citizens in this institutionalized manner, but in Syria/Palestine and Iraq an Ottoman ruling class of governors and administrators was imposed upon them. A large military garrison and a staff of civil officials was established in the principal cities. The members of this ruling class not only remained Turkish-speaking but also, in contrast to their Mamluke predecessors, failed to put down roots where they were living. There was no Turkish colonization of the land. Officials were frequently moved to other provinces of the empire, which might not be Arabic-speaking, and they normally expected to retire to the Turkish heartland. At the same time, there was no attempt to turkify the non-Turkish Muslims who were Ottoman subjects. Only a very small minority adopted Turkish as their first language and entered the Ottoman ruling class; the vast majority carried on their lives much as before. Only a few Turkish words entered their language, mostly related to the army or cuisine. Mount Lebanon, inhabited by Maronites (a small Christian sect in union with Rome) and Druze, remained especially untouched. Here the Ottomans recognized the Lebanese amirs in their hereditary fiefs and allowed them the same autonomous privileges as they had enjoyed under the Mamlukes. Hence Lebanon was the only part of the empire in which something similar to European feudalism flourished. Charles Issawi, the noted economic historian, has suggested that this is why the Lebanese alone among the Arabs have made a marked success of capitalism.

There was some difference in the administration of Egypt as an Ottoman province. Selim the Grim had been prepared to leave the last Mamluke sultan as governor provided he accepted the status of vassal. But the sultan rebelled and was executed, and Selim appointed an Ottoman governor, or pasha. However, he left Mamluke amirs in charge of the twelve *sanjaks* or provinces of Egypt and they enjoyed a high degree of autonomy, which enabled them to treat their territories as personal fiefs, collecting taxes and commandeering supplies for their troops. There was a constant struggle for power between the pashas and the Mamluke aristocracy of amirs and beys, in which the Mamlukes frequently gained the upper hand before Istanbul again imposed its authority. During the three centuries of direct Ottoman rule in Egypt more than a hundred pashas came successively as the sultan's viceroy.

The conditions for the ordinary Egyptians were even worse than in the last years of anarchic Mamluke rule before the Turkish occupation. They could expect neither security nor justice. Ottoman administrators and Mamluke beys competed to squeeze them for taxes by use of the *kurbaj* (whip). No public works were carried out, the irrigation canals silted up and famine and disease were rampant. The population drastically declined. It is no surprise that Egyptians look on this period as a dark age. But Egypt suffered more than other Ottoman provinces. Because of its unique dependence on the Nile and the population's confinement within the narrow space of the Valley and Delta, Egypt's prosperity since the time of the Pharaohs had derived from a strong and wise central government controlling the waterway and providing security.

Syria, with its naturally autonomous mountain and desert regions, fared rather better. Mesopotamia was a remote and stagnant backwater of the empire with little to recall its former glory. A pasha with his court ruled in Baghdad, and there was little attempt to incorporate the tribes who occupied most of the land into the state. But at least the Janissaries secured the province from external dangers until the revival of the Persian threat in the eighteenth century.

The achievement of the Ottoman Turks, recent descendants of uneducated nomadic warriors from the Asian steppes, in building and administering their vast empire should not be underestimated. The trouble was that the institutions they created, while initially more effective and enduring than those employed by the empires which had preceded them in the region, could not be developed and transformed to meet changing needs and circumstances. An obvious example is that of the Janissaries. The idea of selecting young Christian slaves to be compulsorily converted to Islam and trained to form the core of the Ottoman army was original and certainly had no equivalent in any western Christian army. The Janissaries were not only a superb fighting force in the campaigns against the sultan's enemies: they also maintained the internal security of the entire empire. It was probably inevitable that they should in time become not only an autonomous power but also one that was fiercely opposed to any change in the system. As the clear Ottoman superiority in military skills over the empire's enemies declined, the Janissaries rejected all attempts to reform the army along the new lines that had been developed in the West. Whenever they felt that their privileges were being curtailed or that they were being superseded by their principal rivals, the *sipahis* or cavalrymen, they rose in rebellion leading to acts of atrocious violence and barbarity on both sides. Eventually they were suppressed, but by then it was too late for Ottoman military power to catch up with that of the West.

Another rigid institution was the sultanate itself – a despotism which never contemplated any sharing of power. It had a fierce sense of self-preservation. When Bayezid I succeeded his father Murad in 1389, his first act as sultan was to order the strangulation of his younger brother, a potential rival. He thus instituted a tradition of imperial fratricide. There was some basis for his action in the Islamic principle that anything is preferable to sedition, and Mohammed the Conqueror a century later gave the practice the force of law. Selim the Grim had not only his two brothers strangled but his five orphaned nephews as well.

The elimination of rivals in the imperial family avoided the disastrous civil wars of the Mamlukes and can be said to have preserved the Ottoman dynasty for five hundred years. But it was at a terrible price. The sultan's palace became a cauldron of mistrust and fear which increased as he aged and the mothers of his sons intrigued, in most cases in vain, to preserve the sons' lives. Sometimes it was the least able son who succeeded, as when Sulaiman the Magnificent was succeeded by Selim the Sot. In moral terms the practice of executing royal princes for potential rather than actual sedition aroused horror in western Christendom and seemed to justify the denunciations of

Turkish inhumanity. When an heir apparent had been clearly designated, he was kept under virtual house arrest in the seraglio in a small room known as the 'cage', to preserve him from possible rivals, with the result that on his succession he lacked any experience in government. He was also often in poor health or even physically deformed from his long confinement. The Safavid shahs of Persia had a similar system of immuring the heir apparent in the palace compound, and the dynasty suffered accordingly.

The fear of sedition extended outside the royal family throughout the imperial system. Grand viziers and governors were regularly disgraced or executed if they appeared to be gaining too much power. Under Selim the Grim this happened so regularly that it became astonishing that anyone was still prepared to accept the highest offices. Even the humane Sulaiman, under the influence of his ambitious wife Roxelana, had his outstanding grand vizier Ibrahim executed. With a system based on mistrust, sultans increasingly came to rely on a vast web of espionage centred on Istanbul to watch over their subjects. It was not a situation that helped to foster talent and initiative.

The well-being of the empire depended overwhelmingly on the character and ability of the sultan. When he was inadequate, the state suffered disastrously, unless the sultan was prepared to delegate the powers of government to a grand vizier of outstanding capacity. This occurred in the second half of the seventeenth century, when a series of grand viziers of the Koprulu family temporarily arrested the empire's long decline. On the other hand, after a period in which the central government had been weakened by incompetence or neglect, an incoming sultan found it necessary to restore his authority through measures of ruthless severity. These were accepted as necessary for the empire's preservation.

From the empire's foundation, its vital spirit was one of holy war for the furtherance of Islam. For at least two centuries it was militarily superior to its opponents, and the Ottoman devotion to military ideals could be justified. But, in contrast to the Abbasids in the Golden Age of Islam, Ottoman militarism was combined with a contempt for industry and commerce. The consequence was that when the empire was still in its heyday it was already being overtaken in material strength by the more innovative and industrializing economies of the Christian European states. Soon this was reflected in the military balance of power.

One factor in the empire's economic decline could not be avoided. In 1497 the Portuguese rounded the Cape of Good Hope and opened a new route to India and the Far East which outflanked the traditional link between Europe and Asia through Egypt and the Red Sea. Soon the Portuguese, followed by the French and the British, were competing for control of the parallel route through the Gulf. The influence of this factor should not be exaggerated. Its most disastrous effect was on Egypt. Syrian merchants concentrated on the land route from Alexandretta (the modern Iskenderun) through Aleppo to Baghdad and Basra, and a flourishing transit trade to and from the east survived. However, much of this trade came to be dominated by non-Muslim foreigners who were granted special legal and financial privileges for their protection when the empire was strong which they were able to exploit as it weakened.

More important than the diversion of trade was that the economy of the Muslim Middle East as a whole was transformed from the commercial and monetary economy that it had been in the Middle Ages and which could quite easily have continued to match that of Europe to one of military feudalism based on subsistence agriculture. This did not, however, immunize the empire from the economic scourge which affected the whole Mediterranean region in the sixteenth century. This was the huge influx of bullion from the Spanish Americas, which caused the depreciation of the Ottoman silver currency, leading to high inflation and increased taxation. The government was already beset with problems in financing its vast military expenditure. The lack of flourishing industrial and financial sectors in the Ottoman economy in contrast to those of western Europe greatly contributed to the shift in the balance of power over the years.

It is far from correct that the Ottomans were always hostile to learning and the arts, as their later reputation suggested. Sulaiman the Magnificent was a man of the Renaissance, and the exhibition illustrating his life and times held in 1988 in Washington and London was enough to correct any impression of philistinism. Certainly the Arabs regard their Ottoman centuries as years of cultural stagnation, but this is largely because of the downgrading of Arabic combined with the loss of political self-confidence. What is undeniable is that, as the empire weakened and declined, its leaders – sultans, pashas, generals and men of religion – turned in upon themselves to become increasingly hostile and outwardly contemptuous towards innovation, originality and external influences of all kinds. Muslim national pride demanded that attempts should be made to match the European powers by adopting some of their ideas and techniques, but these could succeed only if the rigid and reactionary Ottoman system was reformed from within. Efforts to achieve these reforms, although sincere and far-reaching, ultimately came to nothing.

The second Ottoman failure to take Vienna, in 1683, marked a decisive stage in the long decline of Ottoman power in Europe and the enforced shift in the empire's centre of gravity in the east. At the end of the seventeenth century, a new rival and enemy emerged in the form of aggressive and expansionist imperial Russia. Tsar Peter the Great was bent on making Russia a great European and Asian power, and the Ottoman Empire was his principal obstacle. Two centuries of intermittent Russo-Turkish wars, separated by periods of hostile peace, had begun.

Although the Ottoman Empire was more often than not on the defensive, its withdrawal from Europe was slow and irregular. The Ottoman armies were still brave and formidable, and they benefited from rivalries between the Christian powers of Europe. In the first half of the eighteenth century some lost ground – the Grecian Morea, Belgrade – was recovered. At the end of the century, Empress Catherine the Great failed in her declared aim of dismembering the Ottoman Empire and making Constantinople the capital of a New Byzantium. Nevertheless, under the Treaty of Küchük Kainarja, Sultan Mustafa III lost not only his control over some of his Christian subjects but also his suzerainty over the Muslim Tartars of the Crimea. As he claimed to be the caliph of Islam, this was a greater blow than his conceding to Catherine a virtual protectorate over his Orthodox Christian subjects.

2. Islam on the Defensive, 1880–

At the end of the eighteenth century, the balance of power between the European Christian states and the Islamic world represented by the Ottoman Empire had swung decisively against Istanbul. The progressive retreat from Europe meant that the focus of the empire moved eastwards. In the first three centuries of its existence, the weight of Ottoman interest was directed towards the conquest and control of Christian lands – the spread of the world of Islam towards the West. It was from this that the empire's power and glory derived. Possession of the vast territories inhabited mainly by Muslim Arabs – including the Islamic holy place in Arabia and the great Muslim cities with a prestigious past such as Cairo, Damascus and Baghdad – was important but might be said to have been taken for granted. The Arabic-speaking provinces, economically stagnant or declining, enjoyed a large measure of autonomy under local dynasties such as the Mamlukes in Egypt and Mesopotamia or the Druze amirs in Mount Lebanon.

In the nineteenth century the Ottoman Empire had become the Sick Man of Europe in Western eyes. In reaction, successive Ottoman sultans placed greater emphasis on their leadership of Islam: the Sick Man of Europe could still be the Strong Man of Asia. The title of 'Caliph of Islam' – disused for five centuries – was revived and, through a false analogy between the caliphate and the papacy, the sultan's representatives began to claim spiritual authority over all Muslims, even when they were under non-Muslim rule.

The expansionist and colonizing empire of the first centuries was becoming an Islamic fortress under siege. The world of Islam did not face a frontal assault of the kind it had confronted seven hundred years earlier, in the First Crusade: it was being penetrated in a more subtle and insidious manner. The foreign non-Muslim trading communities had originally been granted their privileges and immunities, which came to be known as the Capitulations, in order to benefit the empire's economy. The first were given to the Genoese in the Galata suburb of Constantinople immediately after the capture of the city in

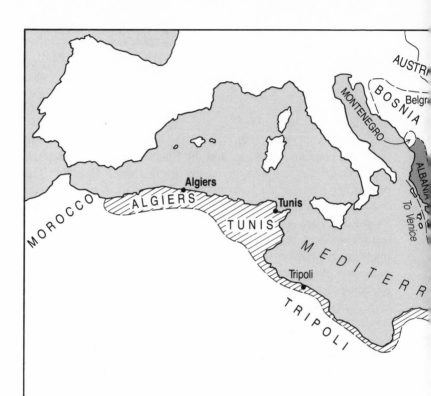

AUSTR[

BOSNIA

MONTENEGRO

Belgr[

ALBANIA

To Venice

MOROCCO

ALGIERS

Algiers

TUNIS

Tunis

M E D I T E R R

Tripoli

TRIPOLI

THE OTTOMAN EMPIRE IN 1792

Approximate limits of the Empire

North African States under Ottoman suzerainty

Areas under autonomous and tribal rulers

Lands lost, 1774 - 1792

| 0 | | | | 1200 km |
| 0 | | | | 800 Miles |

RUSSIA

1775

MOLDAVIA
Jassy
1792
1774
1774

PIRE

WALLACHIA
Silistre
CRIMEA

IN
Ruschuk

MELIA

BLACK SEA

CASPIAN
SEA

Edirne

Istanbul

Trabzon

GEORGIA

Bursa

Ankara

Erzurum

KURDISTAN

Izmir

NOMAD
TRIBES

D E R E B E Y S

Kayseri

rete

DEREBEYS

Konya

Adana

PERSIA

Mosul

CYPRUS

Aleppo

BAGHDAD

E A N S E A

Beirut

SYRIA

Damascus

Baghdad

Akka

Alexandria

Jerusalem

Cairo

EGYPT

HIJAZ

WAHHABIS

Aswan

Medina

RED

Mecca

Jedda

SEA

Suakin

Massawa

Source: Bernard Lewis, *The Emergence of Modern Turkey,* Oxford University Press, 1961

1453. The most famous were probably those granted to Francis I of France by Sulaiman the Magnificent in 1535 as a reward for French co-operation with the sultan against the Christian Habsburgs. The Capitulations were not only commercial: they granted full religious liberty to the French in the Ottoman Empire and, more significantly, the right to guard the Christian holy places. What amounted to a French protectorate was established over all the Latin Catholics in the Levant. In the mid eighteenth century these privileges were confirmed and extended as a reward for French diplomatic support in negotiations with Austria. The extraterritorial privileges created by the Capitulations were remarkable. Special consular courts had complete jurisdiction over the nationals of the countries concerned. Non-Muslim foreign nationals living in Turkey were not subject to Ottoman law, however grave the crime they might have committed.

France was ahead of its European rivals, but not by far. Russia claimed similar protective rights over Orthodox Christians in the empire. England's special ties were only with the smaller religious minorities such as Jews and the Druze, but these were supported by England's growing maritime and commercial dominance in the world.

By the end of the eighteenth century, British sea-power and trading ambitions formed another threat to Ottoman sovereignty in the world of Islam, on the eastern fringes of the empire. The English were not the first Europeans to arrive in force in the Persian/Arabian Gulf: the Portuguese came some thirty years before the Ottomans and, to further their aim of building a great empire in India and the East, attempted to dominate the Red Sea and the Gulf. They attacked and pillaged the eastern Arabian coast from Muscat to Bahrain, leaving forts and garrisons to dominate the indigenous Arab trading and pearling communities. Throughout the sixteenth century the Portuguese controlled the waters of the Gulf and the Straits of Hormuz. Occasionally the Turks, with the help of local tribes, were able to challenge their supremacy and drive the Portuguese out of Bahrain and Muscat, but it was Portuguese naval supremacy which counted.

The Portuguese presence was also a deep affront to the Persians on the northern side of the Gulf. Shah Ismail I, founder of the Safavid dynasty which ruled from 1501 to 1736, protested vigorously but, owing to his life-and-death struggle with the Ottoman Turks, he could do little more. In fact, throughout the sixteenth century it was the presence of Persia as a hostile neighbour on the Ottoman Empire's eastern border which reduced the power of the Turks to expand into Europe. In 1599 the English even attempted – unsuccessfully – to persuade the Persians to ally themselves with the Christian powers against the Turks.

The real challenge to the Portuguese came from two rival powers: England and Holland. By the end of the sixteenth century, English and Dutch adventurers (or pirates) were competing with the Portuguese for the spice trade. Shah Abbas I of Persia (1571–1629), a great military leader and administrator, encouraged the English and Dutch East India companies to establish special branches in Persia, giving the fledgeling companies special privileges. In 1602 he was able to oust the Portuguese from their foothold on the Persian mainland north of the island of Hormuz, and twenty years later, with the aid of the fleet of the English East India Company, he ousted the Portuguese from Hormuz itself. In gratitude he gave the Company special privileges in the port which bears his name, Bandar Abbas. Although a powerful ruler and a passionate defender of the Shiite branch of Islam, Shah Abbas, like the Ottoman sultan Mohammed the Conqueror, set a precedent for the granting of concessions to non-Muslims which was to provide the opportunity for foreigners to gain control over a large share of the economic life of Islam.

However, this Western penetration of the material world had little effect on the minds and beliefs of Muslims in the empire. Secure in the knowledge of the superiority of Islam, they showed no interest in the ways of non-Muslim people. The contrast with the Golden Age of the first Islamic Empire, which had not hesitated to benefit from the wisdom and knowledge of other civilizations, was striking. Only a few individuals pondered on the reasons for the advances in Christian power. As might be expected, the most serious efforts to adopt Western innovations were in the military and naval fields, and these brought with them some revival of interest in mathematics, navigational sciences and cartography. In the early eighteenth century the mild and pleasure-loving sultan Ahmed III introduced some French manners and architecture into the capital, but the effect was entirely superficial. Almost incredibly, there was a total ban on printing in Turkish or Arabic. Printing was known because Jews, Armenians and Greeks began to introduce it from Europe from the late fifteenth century and to set up their own presses, but the religious authorities maintained the ban for Muslims. In 1727 reluctant permission was given for the first Turkish press to print books on subjects other than religion. By the time it was closed in 1742 it had printed seventeen books on language, history and geography. It was not allowed to reopen until 1784.

The practice of employing non-Turkish converts as high officials had changed since the early days of the empire, and officials were now mainly Turkish. But they were usually illiterate and both unable and unwilling to learn foreign languages, having little interest in the rest of the world. The empire thus depended on Christians and Jews as interpreters. The Greek chief dragoman, or interpreter, was an individual of power and responsibility.

Thus it was that the great movements of ideas in western Europe from the Renaissance through the Reformation and Counter-Reformation left the Ottoman world almost untouched. *A fortiori* the same applied to Safavid Persia.

In the Arab-speaking provinces of the Middle East and North Africa, where Muslims were the great majority, Turkish leadership of the Muslim *umma* or nation was accepted. Where local dynasties achieved considerable autonomy as in Egypt, Tunisia and Mesopotamia in the eighteenth century, they nevertheless stopped short of challenging Ottoman sovereignty or attempting to establish an independent nation on a territorial basis – a term which had no meaning at that time. Similarly the Christian minorities, organized in their self-governing *millets*, accepted the overall structure of the empire. Their loyalties were religious rather than political, but they were resigned to their subordinate status.

The most notable exception to Muslim acceptance of Turkish leadership of Islam came from Arabia. In the middle of the eighteenth century in Nejd in the centre of the peninsula, a remarkable religious reformer named Muhammad Ibn Abd al-Wahhab appeared spreading the essential doctrine of *Tawhid* or the uniqueness of God, denouncing the prevalent backsliding and idolatry, and calling for a return to the purity of early Islam. Abd al-Wahhab formed a formidable alliance with an outstanding local tribal dynasty, the House of Saud (and thus planted the seed which nearly two centuries later grew into the kingdom of Saudi Arabia). In the second half of the eighteenth century the Wahhabi warriors spread northwards to the Gulf and into Mesopotamia, where they sacked the Shiite holy places of Kerbala and Nejaf. They then turned westwards and in 1806 took the Hejaz with the Islamic holy places of Mecca and Medina. They destroyed many of the saints' tombs and stripped the Kaaba – Islam's holiest shrine, in the Mecca Great Mosque – of its ornaments, which outraged their fierce puritanism. The Amir Muhammad al-Saud had the public prayers read in his name instead of that of the Ottoman caliph/sultan – he did not regard the Ottoman Turks as worthy guardians of the holy places.

However, all this still lay in the future; as the eighteenth century drew to its close, the caliph's authority over Sunni Islam was still largely intact. In 1789 two events occurred which helped to crack the Ottoman insulation – the outbreak of the French Revolution and the accession as sultan of the reforming Selim III. The French Revolution introduced the novel concepts of political liberty and equality. It also created the basis of nationalism as it has been known in the last two centuries – derived from dedication and loyalty to a nation-state. The most important element was that the movement was secular; it was not only non-Christian but, at least initially, anti-Christian. As such it did not provoke the immediate Muslim hostility which would have been aroused by anything in the nature of a crusade.

More than any of his predecessors Selim III was interested in fresh external ideas and the possibilities of restoring the strength of the empire through reform. He had been conducting a secret correspondence with King Louis XVI before the Revolution, and he greatly admired French culture. He was not deterred by the regicide of the revolutionaries. Indeed the triumphant success of French arms against the Revolution's adversaries encouraged him to import French instructors into his new military and naval schools, where French was made a compulsory subject. A whole new class of young Turkish officers began to emerge – familiar with Western ways and prepared to learn from Western technical superiority. As part of the opening to the West, Sultan Selim for the first time allowed the establishment of embassies in five leading European capitals on a reciprocal basis.

It was even more significant that Selim III tried to apply his reforms to the internal administration of the empire. When he heard of his army's defeat by Catherine the Great of Russia, he called a council which enumerated the causes of defeat and disaster and proposed reform as the only remedy. He also insisted that the people should elect their own mayors and councillors without the interference of his governors, and he attempted to end illegal extortion and tax-farming (the practice of allowing local governors or tax-collectors to take a cut of the tax revenues).

Sultan Selim's reforms, however, did not extend to the Arab provinces of the empire, where power was largely in the hands of local rulers. Damascus for most of the eighteenth century was ruled by governors of the Azm family, who remained loyal to the sultan but independently managed the province's affairs. Sidon district, on the Syrian coast, was governed on similar lines by a ruthless Bosnian, Ahmad al-Jazzar, and his band of Mamlukes. They controlled the Janissaries and kept the predatory beduin at bay. But while the cities prospered, the countryside was insecure and derelict. Squeezed for taxes, the peasant farmers flocked into the cities. Agriculture flourished only in the mountainous areas controlled by local Maronite and Druze amirs.

The situation in Mesopotamia was similar. Here there was constant strife between a series of contenders for power, but the contrast was even greater than in Syria between the rich courts of the pashas of Baghdad and Basra and the backwardness and poverty of the ruined countryside. The great food-producing region of medieval times was on the brink of starvation.

In the vital province of Egypt the situation was rather different. The productivity of the Nile Valley and Delta – perhaps the richest agricultural land on earth – could not be destroyed. With a minimum of secure and effective government, Egypt could export coffee, wheat and rice to the empire. The artisans of the towns produced fine textiles. For a few years (1768–72) an outstanding Mamluke, Ali Bey, provided the strong central government the country needed, but on his death the long-standing struggle between Ottoman officials and Mamluke beys was resumed. They competed to wrest more money from the unfortunate *fellahin* or peasants. The population had sunk to less than two million, compared with an estimated seven or eight million in Roman times, but the land of Egypt was still a glittering prize.

Apart from its natural fertility, Egypt enjoyed a remarkable geo-strategic position at the hinge of the Asian and African continents, guarding the principal route to India and the East. In 1798 the 29-year-old Napoleon Bonaparte, the aspiring dictator of France who had defeated Austria in a series of brilliant campaigns, saw the occupation of Egypt as a means of striking at the source of wealth of France's remaining arch-enemy, Britain, and of controlling the route to India. And his ambitions went further. Talleyrand represented his views to the Directory who then ruled France: 'Our war with this Power [England] represents the most favourable opportunity for the invasion of Egypt. Threatened by an imminent landing on her shores she will not desert her coasts to prevent our enterprise. This further offers us a possible chance of driving the English out of India by sending thither 15,000 troops from Cairo via Suez.' Such an achievement would have destroyed Britain's nascent world empire.

After landing near Alexandria in July 1798, Bonaparte marched up the Nile and defeated the Mamluke army at the battle of the Pyramids. The two Ottoman-appointed Mamluke beys fled to upper Egypt, leaving Bonaparte to set up his own military government of occupation. This momentous event marked the first non-Muslim invasion of the heartlands of Islam since the time of the crusades. Bonaparte went out of his way to show his respect for Islam. He even told the shaikhs of the great Islamic university mosque of al-Azhar that he was a disciple of Muhammad and that he and his army were under the Prophet's special protection. The shaikhs were not impressed and wondered why he and his soldiers did not become Muslims. Bonaparte also tried to convince the Egyptians that his quarrel was not with the Ottoman sultan but with the Mamlukes, from whose tyranny he had come to deliver them. He treated the Egyptian shaikhs and notables as political leaders, appointing them to *diwans* or councils to administer the large cities, with a French commissary as chairman and adviser. It was an enlightened form of indirect colonial rule. But he notably failed to win the hearts and minds of the Egyptians. Al-Jabarti, the shaikh of Al-Azhar and a historian who left an account of the French occupation, described it as the beginning of the reversal of the natural order. Like his fellow-Muslims, he was alarmed by the promotion of Christian Copts and Greeks as officials and tax-collectors, and at the training of Christians for the army. The French were still regarded as intruders, and their claim to be upholding the authority of the sultan was not believed.

Despite his tendency towards Caesarism, Bonaparte was a product of the eighteenth-century Enlightenment, and he brought with him to Egypt a party of 165 scientists, artists and men of letters. This mission of savants set up Arabic and French printing-presses in

Cairo and founded the Institut d'Égypte in imitation of the Institut National in Paris. Its members studied the antiquities and languages of ancient Egypt and laid the foundations of Egyptology. They also examined the economy and society of contemporary Egypt and made a survey for a future Suez Canal. The magnificent twenty-volume *Description de l'Égypte* which was the result of their work aroused Europe's interest in both Pharaonic Egypt and the contemporary world of Islam, which was mysterious and unknown. Orientalism in the West received a wholly new impulse.

Learned Egyptians, such as Shaikh al-Jabarti, visited the Institut and the printing-press and watched chemical and scientific experiments. Al-Jabarti saw a balloon launched at Cairo's Ezbekiyah Square. But while the Egyptians were politely curious about these displays of Western technology, their fundamental beliefs were unshaken.

With regard to its strategic objectives, Bonaparte's expedition to Egypt was a failure. Sultan Selim formed an alliance against him with France's enemies England and Russia. The destruction of Bonaparte's fleet in Abukir Bay by Nelson on 1 August 1798 placed his only line of communication with France at their mercy. When he advanced into Syria to forestall a Turkish invasion, he was turned back at Acre and forced into a disastrous retreat. In August 1799 he abandoned Egypt and with a handful of followers slipped back to Paris, where a crucial struggle for power was taking place. His successors in Egypt held on for another two years, facing sporadic insurrections in Cairo and attacks by Anglo-Turkish troops to enforce their withdrawal. Although they successfully repulsed these more than once, their weakening situation finally forced them to capitulate and evacuate Egypt.

Bonaparte's invasion was a brief episode in the long history of Egypt, but it had lasting significance. It not only aroused in the West a wave of interest in the Arab/Islamic regions of the Ottoman Empire; it also marked the opening of a prolonged struggle between the powers of Europe for influence and control over these territories. The struggle lasted a century and a half. It primarily involved England and France, but Russia was also concerned with the Middle East region on its southern borders, and in the latter part of the nineteenth century the newly united states of Germany and Italy also began to intervene.

Britain responded to Bonaparte's threat to its vital interests by helping the Ottoman sultan to expel the French from Egypt. Anglo-French rivalry also extended to the Gulf and the Indian Ocean. After the outbreak of war between France and England in 1793, France sent various missions to Istanbul and Tehran to try to secure a friendly alliance between Turkey and Persia against Russia, and to revive French influence in Persia. French agents also appeared in the Gulf, studying the movements of British shipping between the Arabian waters and India. French intervention received a wholly new impulse with Bonaparte's invasion of Egypt. Attacks on British merchant shipping were stepped up by French war vessels and privateers based in Mauritius. A 'Napoleonic era' in the region lasted until the French were expelled from Mauritius in 1810.

The first British reaction to Bonaparte's arrival in Egypt was the East India Company's signature of a treaty with the sultan of Muscat. In the 1820s, similar treaties were signed with other local rulers along the Gulf coast. These treaties developed into annually negotiated truces through which Britain endeavoured to establish a Pax Britannica over the waters of the Gulf. At this stage British ambitions in the region were maritime/commercial rather than imperial. There was still no question of challenging the authority either of the Ottoman and Persian empires or of the independent Arab rulers who were outside Ottoman control. Provided these rulers did not make concessions to Britain's rivals, Britain's concern was only that they should help to suppress piracy.

3. Muhammad Ali's Egypt: Ottoman Rival

The Napoleonic episode had minimal direct effect on Egypt; but, through the defeat of the Mamluke beys and the weakening of their hold on the country, it had important indirect influence. When the French departed, the beys came out of hiding and attempted to reimpose their authority. At the same time, Sultan Selim III tried to oust them and restore direct control from Istanbul. But he failed, as the British who still occupied Alexandria took the side of the beys. When the British departed in 1803, they left a situation in which neither the Turkish governor nor the beys were strong enough to prevail, and two years of chaos and civil war ensued. The situation worsened when the Albanian Ottoman troops rebelled against the governor, and power shuttled between the sultan's representatives, the uncontrollable soldiery and the beys (who were split into two factions).

In the midst of this anarchy Muhammad Ali, the commander of one of the Albanian contingents which had landed with the Anglo-Ottoman expeditionary force in 1801, came to prominence as an ally of some of the Mamluke leaders against the nominal Ottoman governors. On 13 May 1805 the *ulama* (Muslim scholars), leading merchants and other notables who were regarded by the people of Cairo as their spokesmen and representatives, asked Muhammad Ali to be their ruler.

Understandably, Sultan Selim was suspicious of Muhammad Ali's intentions. There is little doubt that he helped to intensify the anarchy which led the Egyptians to appeal to him as their saviour. In an attempt to remove him from Egypt, the sultan had appointed him *wali* (governor-general) of Jeddah in Arabia. The Cairo notables, with the backing of the people, united to declare that they wanted Muhammad Ali to replace Khurshid Pasha, the existing Ottoman governor. After a few more months of chaos, Sultan Selim bowed to reality and confirmed Muhammad Ali as *wali* of Egypt.

In this way one of the remarkable figures of the nineteenth century came to control Egypt. His dynasty was to rule, either in reality or nominally, for a century and a half, until his great-great-grandson Farouk was ousted from the throne in 1952.

Born on the Aegean coast of Macedonia, Muhammad Ali was the rare combination of a soldier and a political leader of genius. Although almost illiterate, he was no narrow-minded bigot. Having worked as a tobacco merchant in his youth, he was accustomed to dealing with non-Muslims and Europeans. His sharp intelligence was quick in absorbing new facts and analysing their importance. Ruthless, fiercely ambitious and capable of harsh cruelty, he could also charm, and foreign visitors, however exalted, would quail at his piercing gaze before remaining to admire.

Muhammad Ali did not regard himself as an Egyptian or an Arab and he never spoke Arabic. But in 1805 he had already decided to make Egypt the basis of his power, and to do this he had to turn the Ottoman province into the nation-state which in a sense it had been in the time of the Pharaohs. Having done this, he came close to overthrowing the Ottoman Empire itself.

His appointment as *wali* did not give him control of Egypt; the Mamluke beys still dominated the countryside outside Cairo, and Britain continued to intervene on their behalf. With a mixture of cunning and ruthlessness he set about the destruction of the Mamlukes; but first he had to deal with the British threat. In this he was helped by the fact that, while Britain and Russia were competing to force Selim into an alliance against France, the sultan had reconciled himself with Bonaparte. Selim still admired the heirs of the French Revolution, and French officers continued to train his artillery. No doubt he was also impressed by Bonaparte's new victories over Austria. He recognized him as emperor of the French. Outraged, Britain and Russia stepped up their bullying pressure. In 1807 a British fleet under Admiral Duckworth sailed into the Sea of Marmara to demand the surrender of the Ottoman fleet, failing which, he said, he would burn the fleet and bombard Istanbul. With the help of Sebastiani, a French soldier/ambassador, the sultan organized his capital's defences and drove the British fleet away. Duckworth then sailed to Alexandria and landed an expeditionary force to forestall an expected new French offensive in the Mediterranean.

However, the British were rebuffed. Al-Jabarti records that Muhammad Ali's officials told them that they had no interest in letting them land to protect Egypt from the French, for this was the sultan's territory. The Mamlukes refused the British offer of support because they would not join Christians to fight Muslims. Popular resistance was aroused and inflicted a sharp defeat on the British at Rosetta. Muhammad Ali astutely avoided a full confrontation with the British at Alexandria and agreed on lenient terms for the withdrawal of their naval and military forces. He retained a permanent suspicion of British intentions towards Egypt, and ultimately Britain would be his nemesis – but that was many years in the future.

Muhammad Ali still had to face the Mamluke challenge to his rule, and his campaign against the beys lasted several years. It was no simple matter as, despite their unpopularity, they were entrenched in Egyptian society and his own Ottoman troops were unruly and demanding. He persuaded some Mamluke beys to settle on the outskirts of Cairo, where he could supervise them. Some remained in Upper Egypt, which they tried to make their stronghold. Muhammad Ali then defeated them in a series of small engagements. There remained a rump of beys in Cairo of whose loyalty he was justifiably uncertain. On 11 March 1811 he invited them to a reception at the Citadel, where he had them massacred. Tradition has it that only one escaped – by leaping with his horse from the Citadel.

The way was now open for Muhammad Ali to realize his dream of turning Egypt into a powerful centralized state which, while nominally an Ottoman province, would in reality be independent. Several factors were favourable to his aims. Although the Egyptian people had become accustomed to instability after more than two centuries during which the Mamlukes had struggled for power both among themselves and with a series of Ottoman governors, they longed for the security on which the country's prosperity depended. Although the *ulama* and other notables had played an important role in bringing Muhammad Ali to power, few of them had any relish for official responsibility. Moreover, Egypt – 'the gift of the Nile', as Herodotus observed – lends itself to centralized rule: anyone who could control the river and its delta would dominate the country. All the aspiring despot needed was to dispose of his rivals.

Muhammad Ali made liberal use of the sword and the gallows to stamp out the lawlessness which had plagued the country for many decades. The natural commercial and agricultural wealth of the country was then at once displayed. He set up a highly centralized administrative bureaucracy with the aim of raising revenues and combating the corruption and tax-fraud which had become endemic. At the same time he tried both to modernize and to expand the economy. The growing of high-quality long-staple cotton and sugar was introduced during his reign. He was prepared to seek advice and technical expertise from any quarter, including Christian merchants in Eygpt and Europeans. As an admirer of France he invited French engineers to Egypt and with their help built dams and canals and introduced in the Delta a system of perennial irrigation to replace the ancient basin irrigation using the Nile flood. One million new acres of land were brought under cultivation. Hitherto, Egyptian industry had been confined to the manufacture of textiles; he now established a range of factories, protected with heavy tariffs against imports. The factories were crude and primitive, but they were the first of their kind in Egypt.

Muhammad Ali learned to read only at the age of forty-seven, but he understood the importance of education. He sent several hundred young Egyptians to Paris (and a few to London) to study industry, engineering, medicine and agriculture. In Egypt, where teaching until then had been confined to the Koranic schools, his French advisers helped to establish a system of state education which at least on paper was highly impressive. French doctors helped to found hospitals and a rudimentary system of public health.

His ambitions went far beyond turning Egypt into the most advanced province of the Ottoman Empire in European terms. For Egypt to act beyond its borders required the creation of an independent army and navy, and the major part of his energies were devoted to this end. His concentrated drive to increase revenues served this purpose. One of his first actions had been to order a much needed cadastral survey of all land in Egypt, and within a few years he had settled about two million acres or one-third of the cultivated area on a small class of big land-owners drawn from members of his family (he had thirty children), senior army officers, village shaikhs and beduin chiefs. But the greater part of the increased revenues accrued to the central government, so it has been said that he converted most of Egypt into a huge farm under the direct administration of the government.

The new industries that he created were also directed mainly to providing the land and naval forces with weapons and equipment, although they also turned out non-military goods such as machine tools, pumps, clothing, paper and glass.

The Egyptian *fellahin* or peasants had never been thought of as promising military material, but properly trained and led they proved that they could fight with discipline and courage. They were at their best in defensive positions; they lacked the panache in attack of the Sudanese. On the other hand, unlike the Sudanese, their health stood up remarkably well to campaigns in colder climates. Virtually all the officers and non-commissioned officers were non-Egyptian. Some of the Mamluke officers came over to Muhammad Ali's side but, when the Ottoman sultan banned all further export of Mamluke recruits to Egypt, other officers were recruited from among local Turks and Albanians. After 1820 Muhammad Ali reorganized the armed forces entirely with a *nizam al-jadid* or 'New Order'. His eldest son, Ibrahim (1789–1848), proved to be an outstanding general and leader of men. At its height in the 1830s, the Egyptian army amounted to a quarter of a million men and was the most formidable force in the Middle East.

In consolidating his personal power and the independence of Egypt, Muhammad Ali was helped by a weakening in authority at the centre of the empire. In 1807 the Janissaries, in rebellion against the reforms and European innovations introduced by the New Order of Selim III, deposed the sultan and replaced him with his cousin Mustafa, who promptly abolished all the reforms. Fourteen months later Mustafa was assassinated, and his brother – the last surviving male of the House of Osman – succeeded as Mahmud II. He was a reformer like Selim, and ultimately he went much further than Selim in his long reign of thirty-one years, but in the first decade he had to proceed cautiously in order to consolidate his own power. It was not until 1826 that he was able to confront the problem of the Janissaries and destroy them in a massacre.

During this period Muhammad Ali was able not only to resist interference from Istanbul but also to make the new sultan dependent on him for holding the empire together. In 1807 he was asked to send an expeditionary force to the Hejaz to recover the holy places of Islam from the Saudi/Wahhabi invaders. He succeeded in procrastinating for four years while he was consolidating his hold on Egypt, but in 1811 he dispatched his second son, Tussun, with an army. Tussun was an indifferent general; he recovered Mecca and Medina but suffered heavy casualties and more than one defeat at the hands of the Wahhabi warriors. The indisciplined behaviour of the Albanian officers no doubt helped Muhammad Ali to decide on the subsequent remodelling of his armed forces. He went personally to the Hejaz to share the command with Tussun, and on his return to Cairo to deal with pressing domestic problems he replaced Tussun with the much more able Ibrahim as commander-in-chief.

Making full use of his cavalry and artillery, Ibrahim carried the campaign against the Saudis into their Nejd homeland. In May 1818 the Saudi capital Daraiyya (twelve miles from Riyadh) fell after a six-month siege in which the Turco-Egyptian army suffered heavy losses. Abdullah Ibn Saud, the Saudi ruler, was sent to Egypt where he was treated with honour and then to Istanbul where he was summarily executed. The first Saudi state had come to an end. However, the Egyptian garrisons remained only a few years in Nejd. In 1824 the Saudis established their second state with their new capital in Riyadh and successfully resisted further attempts to conquer them. However, Muhammad Ali and Ibrahim had their prize in the Hejaz. This enabled them not only to reopen the sea-routes from Egypt to the Indian Ocean but also to monopolize the entire Red Sea trade. The *wali* even exacted an annual tribute from the imam of Yemen. He brushed aside a British proposal for Anglo-Egyptian co-operation in pacifying southern Arabia to protect the sea-routes to India against attacks by local tribesmen; instead he sent his own ships to occupy all the western Arabian seaports as far as Aden. Britain was obliged to concentrate on the Gulf region, where in 1820 it succeeded in concluding a General Treaty of Maritime Peace in perpetuity with the small shaikhdoms of the Trucial Coast (the United Arab Emirates of today). The British did not occupy Aden and found a colony there until 1839.

Sultan Mahmud was duly grateful to Ibrahim for the recovery of the Islamic Holy Land and promoted him to the rank of pasha with three tails as well as governor. This in theory made him superior in rank to his father, and it is probable that the sultan – by now alarmed at Muhammad Ali's ambitions – hoped to estrange him from his son. But Ibrahim remained loyal and continued to defer to his father throughout his life.

Sultan Mahmud sharply rebuffed Muhammad Ali's suggestion that he should be given the permanent governorship of Syria, but the *wali* of Egypt was not yet ready for a direct challenge to Istanbul.

The vast lands lying to the south of Egypt, known to medieval

Arab writers as Bilad as-Sudan or the 'country of the blacks', provided a different opportunity. Islam and the Arabic language had advanced more slowly than in the Middle East and North Africa, but by AD 1500 the great majority of the inhabitants of the north and centre of today's republic of Sudan were Muslim and Arabic-speaking. For the past three centuries these lands had been dominated by the kingdom of the Fur – a people of uncertain origins – but there had been frequent incursions by Mamlukes from Egypt in search of slaves and gold. A group of them in flight from Muhammad Ali's repression had set up their own state in Dongola, on the west bank of the Nile, and were interfering with the river trade.

Muhammad Ali therefore had both political and commercial motives in attempting to conquer the Sudan. An additional motive was the provision of suitable employment for his unruly Albanian troops. In 1821 he sent an army commanded by his third son, Ismail, followed in the next year by two more under Ibrahim, victor of the Hejaz, and his son-in-law Muhammad. Between them they conquered an area half the size of Europe, nominally on behalf of the Ottoman sultan but in greater reality to add to his Egyptian viceroy's domains. In some ways the conquest was a disappointment. Muhammad Ali's dream of creating his own army of black slaves failed because they were too few in number and their health deteriorated when they were brought to Egypt. The gold mines were poorer than anticipated, and there was no breakthrough to the fabled wealth of tropical Africa. When Ismail was ambushed and killed by a resentful local chieftain, Muhammad Ali ordered a massacre which left its memory in Sudanese minds.

However, Muhammad Ali's conquest laid the foundations of the modern Sudan. The addition by his successors of the three Negro and tropical provinces in the south created the giant of Africa – part Arab and Muslim and part Christian and pagan and black. Even when, after sixty years, Turco-Egyptian rule came to an end, Egypt and Sudan remained inextricably linked.

The acquisition of Sudan had not been completed before the opportunity arose for expansion northwards, into the eastern Mediterranean. Sultan Mahmud invited Muhammad Ali to help put down the uprising in 1821 of his Greek subjects, who were demanding independence. The weakened and demoralized Ottoman troops were proving incapable of dealing with the rebels. Muhammad Ali's troops landed first in Crete and then in Cyprus to quell the uprising. But the heart of the rebellion was in the Morea on the mainland. The sultan hesitated to order him there because he rightly feared that Muhammad Ali's well-organized and disciplined forces might threaten his own authority. However, he finally had no alternative. In 1825 Ibrahim moved with his fleet to the Morea, landed troops and two years later captured Athens.

When the Greek rebellion broke out, the powers of Europe paid little more than lip-service to the principle of Greek Christians breaking away from the Ottoman Empire to form an independent nation. They were deeply suspicious of each other's intentions. Russia did not favour the birth of a new Christian state in the Levant unless it would be under tsarist control. The other powers, led by Britain, were equally determined to prevent such Russian domination; however, they would probably not have been spurred into action if the Greek nationalists, who engaged in piracy when they were not fighting the Turks, had not begun to interfere with the Levant trade. An equally alarming development was the appearance of Muhammad Ali's forces to defeat the Greeks. With his control of the Morea, he would be able to dominate the region – raising the unwelcome possibility of the establishment of a new Muslim power in the eastern Mediterranean.

France had sympathetic ties with Muhammad Ali but was eventually induced to join Britain and Russia in the Treaty of London of 6 July 1827. Through this, the three powers aimed to mediate between the Ottoman government and the Greek patriots in order to bring about an armistice which would lead to the establishment of Greek autonomy under the suzerainty of the sultan. An additional purpose was to make Ibrahim's presence unnecessary and bring about his withdrawal.

When the sultan prevaricated, the Russian and French fleets joined the British fleet at Navarino and on 20 October blew the combined Turkish and Egyptian fleets out of the water.

The sultan broke off relations with the three powers and summoned his Muslim subjects for a *jihad* or holy war. But there was little he could do. In the previous year he had destroyed the Janissaries, and the reconstruction of the Ottoman army had hardly begun. His best protection was that Britain and France wanted neither the dismemberment of his empire nor the aggrandizement of Russia. Five years later, on 7 May 1832, in accordance with a new Treaty of London, Greece became an independent kingdom under the Bavarian prince Otho. All the powers of Europe could claim a share in this settlement, and it had not led, as the sultan had feared, to the disintegration of the empire.

Muhammad Ali's forces had suffered severe losses, and the financial strain on Egypt was heavy. But the disaster of Navarino had not dampened the ambitions of the *wali* or his son. Muhammad Ali believed he had been promised the pashalik of Syria as a reward for his help against the Greeks, but Sultan Mahmud said that he would have to be content with the pashalik of Crete. Muhammad Ali therefore decided to seize Syria for himself. While rebuilding his fleet, he dispatched Ibrahim at the head of an army which routed the Ottoman forces near Homs and again near Aleppo. Ibrahim then passed through the Taurus range into Anatolia and defeated the sultan's army at Konya. When he reached Bursa, he was poised to take Istanbul and overthrow the Ottoman Empire.

A desperate Sultan Mahmud appealed to Britain to send the Royal Navy to the Dardanelles and Alexandria. Palmerston, the British prime minister, was in favour, but the majority in his cabinet refused. The sultan was therefore obliged to turn to Russia. (Palmerston later wrote that 'No British cabinet at any period of the history of England ever made so great a mistake in foreign affairs.') The Russians sent ships and landed troops; Ibrahim prudently agreed to negotiate. By now alerted to the danger of Russian ascendancy in the eastern Mediterranean, Britain and France intervened to insist on a Russian withdrawal in return for the sultan's agreement to make concessions to Muhammad Ali – the sultan granted him the pashalik of the whole of Syria. The Russians did withdraw, but the Sultan was obliged to accept an agreement known as the Treaty of Hunkiar Iskelessi, which bound him to an alliance with Russia. This included a secret clause which allowed Russian warships to pass freely through the Dardanelles if Russia should be at war but made a similar concession to other powers conditional on Russian consent. Palmerston's regrets are easy to understand.

Muhammad Ali's ambition to build a predominantly Arabic-speaking empire on the ruins of Ottoman power no longer seemed fanciful. He controlled the Nile Valley, the Red Sea and the eastern Mediterranean. He even thought of making a bid for the caliphate.

However, his dream was a chimera. The pan-Arab idea did not exist in the consciousness of the people, and the Albanian Muhammad Ali could not be its inspiration. Ibrahim could conceivably have provided such an inspiration. Unlike his father, he spoke Arabic, regarded himself as Egyptian and was prouder of his Egyptian private soldiers than of their Ottoman officers. But he never challenged his father's authority and, although he was more cultivated and civilized, he was not equal to Muhammad Ali's formidable political abilities.

Ibrahim was placed in charge of Egypt's new Syrian possessions. But, although he had a powerful army under his command, his task of imposing a strongly centralized and modernizing administration was not easy. The various sects of Syria – Sunni and Shia Muslims, Druze and Maronites – had become accustomed to a high degree of autonomy, whether under local dynasties, such as the Azms in Damascus or the Shihabs in Lebanon, or Ottoman *walis* who remained only for periods too brief to establish their authority. Ibrahim was confronted by a variety of vested interests who had no desire to be incorporated into a centralized economy based on the type of government monopolies Muhammad Ali had instituted in Egypt. The Ottomans had had their monopolies, but the system was inefficient and could easily be subverted. In Syria and Lebanon there were flourishing cotton and silk textile industries, although they faced increasing competition from European imports, and the Levantine merchants prospered on the transit trade to the East. They resented Egyptian interference, as did the Druze landowners growing cereals on the Hauran plains of southern Syria.

Ibrahim was faced with various acts of rebellion, which he suppressed with his customary ruthlessness. Nevertheless his achievements during the decade of his governorship (1831–40) were considerable. He streamlined the administration, reformed the tax system and began the process of expanding and improving education. His aims accorded with those of his father in Egypt, who guided and directed his actions: to lay the foundations of a strong state with a self-sustaining economy. Eventually he hoped that Syria's manufacturing industries would compete with those of Europe.

His plans would have been over-ambitious even if he had had more time to realize them. The Syrian merchants and landowners could be dynamic and enterprising, but they were not ready to be moulded into an alien system. Ibrahim did succeed in expanding and improving trade with Europe and in increasing the area under cultivation, but this was through more efficient government rather than the encouragement of local initiative. For all Ibrahim's attempts to identify with his subjects, he remained a foreign occupier. (Many of the same problems beset the next Egyptian attempt to rule Syria, 120 years later.)

As part of Ibrahim's policy of modernization, Christian missionaries were for the first time allowed to open schools. These missionaries were principally American Protestants and they founded several schools, including one for girls. They also established the first Arabic printing-press in Syria. Ibrahim went further to attempt to establish the principle of equality between Muslims and Christians. Within the Ottoman Empire this meant favouring Christians at Muslim expense. In Egypt Muhammad Ali had always made use of talent and expertise wherever he found it, and he did not hesitate to employ Europeans or to promote local non-Muslims when he deemed it necessary. In Syria this policy meant favouring the Christian merchants, who had the best contacts with Europe (and frequently held *berats* or patents granted by European consulates). Ibrahim imposed a special poll tax on the Muslims of the cities, which equated them with the non-Muslims who had always paid such a tax.

Not unnaturally, the Muslims were not in favour of this innovation. Their resentment greatly increased when Muhammad Ali insisted that Ibrahim begin conscripting Syrians into the Egyptian army. Ibrahim, who was much closer to identifying himself with his Arab subjects than his father, protested that this was unwise; but Muhammad Ali insisted.

However, Muhammad Ali and Ibrahim might have been able to subdue opposition and hold on to their east-Mediterranean/Arabian empire if they had not incurred the implacable opposition of the European powers, led by Britain. Muhammad Ali could defy his nominal master the Ottoman sultan Mahmud – and indeed could contemplate his overthrow – but Britain preferred that a weakened Ottoman Empire should survive rather than be dismembered and swallowed by one of its rivals. Britain was still less enthusiastic that the empire should be replaced by a dynamic and expansionist Muslim power, but it was precisely this possibility which alarmed the powers of Europe.

This was the period in which the Palmerstonian doctrine of imperialism was developed. It was directed not towards the acquisition of colonies – that was to come later in the century – but to the instant protection of British interests wherever they were threatened. As the world's leading industrial and commercial power, Britain saw these interests as largely economic. British manufactured goods were flooding eastwards to Asian markets by the Gulf and Red Sea routes. The era of the steamship had arrived, and Muhammad Ali had greatly eased the passage to India by developing the overland route between Alexandria and Suez. But although British trade was expanding throughout the eastern Mediterranean, it was severely obstructed by the system of monopolies in the Ottoman Empire. Palmerston directed all his powerful diplomacy with the Ottoman Empire towards having these removed. In 1838 he succeeded when an Anglo-Turkish treaty was signed giving Britain and the other European powers the right to trade throughout the Ottoman Empire in return for a tariff of only 3 per cent.

At one stroke Palmerston's treaty had opened the way to foreign commercial domination of the Ottoman Empire. It had also removed a principal source of the sultan's revenue from the state monopolies. Muhammad Ali rightly regarded the terms of the treaty as disastrous for his ambitions, and he refused to apply them to Egypt. He had done everything in his power to protect and facilitate British trade across Egypt, but he could not allow Britain to destroy the sources of his independence. A few weeks before the signature of the treaty, he had announced his decision to declare Egypt and Syria an independent, hereditary kingdom and had offered to pay the sultan the high sum of 3 million pounds as the price for his acceptance of this. Palmerston immediately registered his strong disapproval and made it clear that, if war should ensue between Muhammad Ali and the Ottoman Empire, Britain would be on the side of the sultan.

Britain was determined to foil Muhammad Ali's ambitions. It had become seriously alarmed by the spread of his power along the whole eastern coast of the Red Sea from Bab al-Mandab to Mecca. He had even seized the Tihama coast of Yemen, bought the city of Taez from its corrupt governor (an uncle of the imam of Yemen) and gained control over its valuable coffee trade. The vital route to India seemed to be threatened at a time when the importance of the Arabian coast had been increased by the arrival of steamships and the need for secure coaling-stations. 'I think that it will be absolutely necessary to have a possession of our own on or near the Red Sea,' wrote the Governor of Bombay, Sir Robert Grant, in 1837.

The opportunity to acquire such a possession soon arose. The sultan of Lahej, in whose territory on the south-eastern corner of Arabia lay the tiny port of Aden, was accused of permitting the molestation of British shipping. In January 1839 Commander Haines of the Bombay Marine landed with a small force and seized the town, inaugurating 130 years of British rule in Aden and increasing influence in the tribal hinterland. The Aden settlement was attached to the Bombay presidency, emphasizing its importance to India, and so remained until it became a Crown Colony.

A *de facto* alliance against Muhammad Ali was now in existence between Palmerston and Sultan Mahmud. In the summer of 1839, the sultan declared war on his ambitious viceroy and sent an army across the Euphrates into northern Syria. In spite of the new training of the Ottoman forces by the German military mission headed by Moltke, at the battle of Nazib they were once again soundly defeated by Ibrahim. (He successfully bribed some of the Ottoman troops to desert.) At the same time the admiral of the Ottoman navy, which had been ordered into action, decided to sail the entire fleet to Alexandria and surrender to Muhammad Ali.

Sultan Mahmud died suddenly, before the news of the Nazib disaster could reach him, and he was succeeded by his 16-year-old son Abdul Mejid. The boy sultan and his government were at Muhammad Ali's mercy.

Ibrahim wanted to consolidate his victory by advancing into the Anatolian heartland. There was nothing to prevent him, but his father commanded restraint. He understood that the destruction of the Ottoman Empire would provoke the powers of Europe. He still hoped that they would accept his more limited ambition of holding on to his possessions in the Levant, North Africa and Arabia. However, this was no longer possible. Palmerston had come to regard him as a dangerous menace. 'I hate Mehemet Ali,' he wrote to the British ambassador in Paris, 'whom I consider as nothing better than an ignorant barbarian who by cunning and boldness and mother wit has been successful in rebellion . . . I look upon his boasted civilization of Egypt as the arrantest humbug, and I believe that he is as great a tyrant and oppressor as ever made a people wretched.'

Palmerston had his own share of humbug. He knew that the

Ottoman sultan was no less tyrannical than Muhammad Ali or Ibrahim and had a rather worse record for his treatment of minorities. The difference was that the Egyptian dictatorship was relatively effective while a weak sultan could be manipulated. Palmerston set about organizing the five powers of Europe (Britain, France, Prussia, Austria and Russia) behind a move to expel Muhammad Ali from the Levant. France was his greatest problem, because it still regarded Muhammad Ali as a valuable ally whose naval power – particularly in combination with that of France – would act as a counterpoise to Britain in the eastern Mediterranean. Palmerston used a masterly combination of diplomacy and bullying to overcome French resistance. Although half his own cabinet was afraid that he might be provoking a European war, Palmerston played on the fact that King Louis-Philippe of France was even more cautious because of his fears of an attempted *coup d'état*.

At the Conference of London in July 1840 the five powers, including a reluctant France, agreed to the 'Pacification of the Levant' under which Muhammad Ali would be obliged to withdraw all his troops from Syria and to restore the Turkish fleet to the sultan. His family would be recognized as hereditary viceroys of Egypt, but would not inherit his viceroyship of Syria.

When Muhammad Ali indignantly refused these terms, a British fleet under Admiral Napier appeared off the Syrian coast and sent out emissaries calling upon the population to revolt. All the resentment against conscription, high taxation and Ibrahim's flouting of local traditions found expression in rebellions which broke out all over the country. After failing to bribe Ibrahim's governor of Beirut to defect, the British fleet bombarded the city and an Anglo-Turkish force landed. When Napier sailed on to Alexandria, Muhammad Ali realized he was beaten. His French allies had deserted him and he could not fight the European powers alone.

Through the terms of the Treaty of London of 1841, the powers of Europe cut back Muhammad Ali's ambitions and restored his vassal status within the Ottoman Empire. He was stripped of all his possessions except the Sudan, which meant that Crete, Syria and the Hejaz were restored to direct Ottoman rule. At the same time he was obliged to reduce his armed forces, which at one time had approached a quarter of a million men, to 18,000. The instrument of his expansionism was removed, and he no longer could threaten to seize Constantinople.

His consolation was that his position as hereditary pasha of Egypt was confirmed. Although this had been the limit of his original ambitions, his horizons had subsequently expanded. But now he could no longer hope to dominate the trade routes to Asia or challenge the growing hegemony of the European powers in the eastern Mediterranean.

A semi-independent Egypt was still a country of some political and economic importance. Although tired and elderly (he was seventy-two at the time of the Treaty of London) Muhammad Ali was not entirely broken in spirit. Maintaining his enormous army had imposed an impossible burden of taxation on the Egyptian people. (As Palmerston typically observed, 'Like all countries Egypt has rich and poor. The rich is Muhammad Ali and the poor is everyone else.') He had already been seeking ways of retrenchment before the Treaty of London, and the enforced reduction in military spending could have brought relief. The trouble was that the focus of his entire economic policy – the *raison d'être* of his industrialization programme – was the servicing of the needs of his military power. Without demand for their products, the military factories would collapse.

It could be argued that Muhammad Ali's attempt to industrialize Egypt was already a failure. Unlike the European countries, led by Britain, which were achieving a rapid industrial revolution in the first half of the nineteenth century, Egypt had no natural resources of coal or timber to produce steam power and no steel industry. The 40,000 industrial workers, helped by camels and donkeys, produced nearly all their own power. The imported machinery was badly serviced and continually broke down. It was even more of a disadvantage that no class of independent entrepreneurs or trained managers was developing under Muhammad Ali's authoritarian regime. Although he sent some young Egyptians for training in Europe, it was mainly members of the Turco-Circassian officer class that he placed in charge of the factories. Crucial hydraulic and other engineering works were in the hands of foreign technicians, and commerce was increasingly controlled by European merchants.

It is possible, as some Egyptian economic historians have argued, that without European interference the mistakes could have been rectified and Egypt might have achieved a genuine industrial revolution in the wake of Europe. But the auguries were poor, and it would have required a successor to the aged Muhammad Ali of equal forcefulness and ability but greater enlightenment. Ibrahim might conceivably have filled the role and, with his health and reason failing, Muhammad Ali delegated his powers to his son in 1847. But in little more than a year Ibrahim succumbed to a fever, and Muhammad Ali followed him within a few months, on 2 August 1849, without realizing that his son was dead.

In accordance with the terms of the Treaty of London, Muhammad Ali was succeeded by his eldest male descendant – his grandson Abbas, the son of Tussun. Abbas was a gloomy reactionary who repudiated the European influences introduced by his grandfather and uncle. He dismissed the foreign advisers and closed the secular schools. However, he was far from being an Egyptian patriot and had no love for the Egyptians. Because he detested the French, he showed some favour towards the British and allowed them to build the Cairo–Alexandria railway – the first in Africa or Asia – which greatly enhanced Britain's imperial route to India. But Abbas was essentially a xenophobic Ottoman, loyal to the sultan. He had no imperial ambitions of his own. Moreover, a provision of the Treaty of London was that appointment of senior officers in his much diminished army must be approved by Istanbul. This ensured that the high command was in the hands of the Turco-Circassian ruling class rather than native-born Egyptians.

Abbas ruled only five years before he was murdered by two of his Albanian slaves. His uncle Said, who succeeded, was nine years younger than Abbas, corpulent, amiable and Francophile. His contrasting character did not, however, mean that he regarded himself as an Egyptian or cared for the interests of the Egyptians. His liberal attitude towards trade and enterprise resulted in the rapid growth in the size and importance of the foreign communities, and his friendship with the French engineer Ferdinand de Lesseps led to the building of the Suez Canal which, under foreign ownership, was to be a prime cause and justification of Egypt's subjection to European control.

In his classic work *The Arab Awakening* (first published in 1938) the Palestinian writer George Antonius describes the development of the concept of an Arab nation in modern times. His chapter on Muhammad Ali and Ibrahim is entitled 'The False Start'. He quotes one of their contemporaries as observing that Muhammad Ali's genius 'was of a kind to create empires, while Ibrahim had the wisdom that retains them'. The suggestion is that, if Ibrahim had survived his father and the Western powers led by Britain had not combined against him, a revived Arab empire controlling the Nile Valley, the Red Sea and the Levant could have replaced the Ottomans as the world's leading Islamic power.

Such a development is hard to conceive. Muhammad Ali had no vision of Arab national regeneration. When he considered claiming the caliphate from the sultan it was not to restore it to Arab hands. He remained an Albanian/Turk who never learned to speak Arabic. Ibrahim, it is true, chose to regard himself as an Egyptian – much to his father's disgust. He spoke Arabic and could identify with his Arab soldiers. He dreamed of a revived Arab empire and sometimes rallied his troops with references to Arab historical glory. But none of this amounted to much. Centuries of Turkish political and military dominance in the Muslim world could not be erased. Neither Muhammad Ali nor Ibrahim had time to create new institutions which would last. Their dynasty survived, but their descendants were much lesser men.

4. The Struggle for Reform, 1840–1900

When 16-year-old Sultan Abdul Mejid I (1839–61) succeeded, his empire was in mortal danger. The reforms of his father, Mahmud II, had disrupted the old order while their benefits were still to be realized. The Janissaries, the core of the armed forces, had been repressed, but the training and weaponry provided by Moltkes's military mission had yet to prove effective, as the ignominious defeats by Ibrahim's *fellahin* army had proved. The reforms in education – the new medical, engineering, naval and military schools staffed by foreign instructors; the student missions to European universities; and the creation of the first basis for compulsory primary education – were only beginning to produce a new generation of young Ottomans who could understand and cope with the great technical and scientific advances of the nineteenth century.

The young sultan lacked his father's force of character, although for a time he was backed by his formidable mother, but he decided to continue and extend the reforms. Mustafa Reshid Pasha, the outstandingly able foreign minister who was on a mission to London when Mahmud II's death was announced, was brought back to the capital to take charge of the reform programme and on 3 November 1839 the historic Noble Rescript of the Rose Chamber was promulgated – the first of a series of edicts which are known collectively as the *Tanzimat* or Reorganization. More than once, Mustafa Reshid fell from power, only to be restored again. Others carried on his work after his death in 1858. Conservative opposition was powerful, because the reforms were revolutionary in purpose and content. Although their achievements fell well short of their intentions, they initiated notable changes in the way the empire was governed and administered.

Two of the changes were truly revolutionary, in that they broke with the Islamic principles by which the empire had always been governed. The mere declaration of these changes, which were closely related, was shocking to traditional opinion. One was that all Ottoman citizens were to be perfectly equal before the law, regardless of race or creed. The other was the introduction of a new legal code which was distinct from that of the Islamic *sharia* administered by the *qadis* or Islamic judges.

Equality of all citizens before the law was a secular non-Islamic principle derived from the European Enlightenment and the nationalist ideals of the French Revolution. Islamic tradition and law prescribed tolerance and protection for non-Muslim subjects of the state, and it was according to these principles that non-Muslims were allowed a substantial degree of autonomy under the *millet* system. But this did not mean that the members of these minorities were equal to the Muslim majority.

The new concept of equality inevitably affected the supremacy of the Islamic *sharia*. Once again it was a principle which was at stake. Muslim rulers since the earliest days had in practice encouraged or allowed the creation of tribunals in which their own administrative decisions or customary law was applied. But these were on the fringes; the *sharia* courts were dominant, and nowhere more so than in the Ottoman Empire. Now the first steps were being taken towards the demotion of the *sharia* by creating a new body with powers of drafting legislation. The change was not immediate. The religious authorities fought against it and they were able for a time to prevent the introduction of a new commercial code outside the *sharia*. Nevertheless the process of secularization of the world's leading Islamic power had begun.

Because the sultan and his reformist advisers always claimed that the changes were in accordance with Islam, the mass of the population was not aware of their importance. They were none the less revolutionary. Turks and Arabs of today, depending on their point of view, would regard them as either milestones on the road to catastrophe or as steps towards the modernization of the Islamic world which were essential if it were to resist the encroaching power of Christian Europe.

The other reforms of the *Tanzimat* were aimed at this central purpose of regenerating the empire's strength. Sultan Mahmud's policy of opening new military schools with foreign instructors was greatly extended. Of greater importance was the new recruiting law, reducing military service from its hitherto indefinite period to a fixed term of five years followed by seven in the reserves. A body of civil police, or gendarmerie, was also instituted.

Modernizing the armed forces, although requiring time and energy, was simple compared with the task of raising educational standards. Mustafa Reshid understood that this was a prerequisite for the success of all the other reforms. The only existing educational institutions were the Koranic schools maintained by the *ulama* with private donations. A vast programme was launched for the creation of a state university and a centralized network of primary and secondary schools. A Ministry of Education was established. Although religion was proclaimed as having primacy in the new curriculum, in effect a system of secular education was being created. Many fewer schools were founded than had been hoped, but it was the principle that mattered.

Because these reforms were expensive, they were related to the single greatest weakness of the empire and the primary reason for its failure to match the power of Europe – finance. In the first great Ottoman centuries, the empire's vast resources had fed its conquering armies, although even then successive sultans had found that shortage of funds placed limits on their ambitions. By the mid nineteenth century the balance of economic strength had shifted wholly in favour of western Europe – and especially Britain and France, as they passed into the second stage of the industrial revolution which Turkey had barely begun. The European powers were able to use their political and economic power to force the empire to allow its economy to be incorporated into the nineteenth-century liberal capitalist system. British, French and Austrian textiles and other manufactures began to pour into the Middle East from the early years of the century. Facing the onslaught of Muhammad Ali's armies, the sultan was in no position to resist Europe's demands. As we have seen, the Anglo–Turkish treaty of 1838 removed all restrictions on European imports.

Free trade was by no means entirely harmful to the empire. As European manufactures flooded in, the traditional handicrafts and textile industries suffered, but there was a huge growth in demand for raw materials such as Syrian silk, Egyptian cotton and Anatolian wool. Production of cereals and fruit also expanded to meet the needs of the growing cities. The merchant class prospered and with it the capitalist institutions of banks, insurance and limited commercial companies began to develop for the first time in the empire. However, there were two drawbacks for the rulers of the empire. One was that so much of the newly created wealth accrued to foreigners, who benefited from the Capitulations, rather than to Ottoman subjects.

The other was that the ending of the traditional system of government monopolies eliminated the principal source of state revenues.

Mustafa Reshid and his colleagues were aware of the dangers of the traditional policy of debasing the currency to meet the empire's chronic deficits. They took steps to avoid this by withdrawing the old coinage and issuing a new currency on European lines, consisting of a gold pound divided into 100 piastres. This ensured monetary stability for a period. However, at the same time they took the unavoidable but potentially disastrous course of issuing treasury bonds as a means of raising revenue. Before long these bonds were circulating as a form of currency, causing alarming inflationary pressure. The temptation to resort to Europe for state loans in order to withdraw the treasury bonds became overwhelming. The banking institutions now existed through which the savings of the willing European middle classes could be channelled into foreign investment. In 1851 Mustafa Reshid signed an agreement with a British and a French bank for a state loan of 55 million francs. This was the first step on the road which led to the bankruptcy of the empire two decades later.

Because the Ottoman armaments factories were inefficient and outmoded, new equipment had to be imported from Europe. Even in time of peace the effort to restore the military balance with the West placed a heavy strain on the empire's finances. At this point it became involved in war with its traditional European enemy – Russia. The Crimean War was not of its own choosing; it was more the consequence of rivalry between the powers of Europe.

Russia was mildly concerned at the prospect of a reformed and revived Turkey; however, the autocratic and ambitious Tsar Nicholas I believed that the collapse of the empire was a more likely outcome of the reform programme. In 1844 he proposed to the British government a plan for the empire's partition: Britain would have Crete and Egypt, Istanbul would be a 'free city', and the Balkan states would be autonomous under Russian protection. The Tsar denied that he entertained Catherine the Great's dreams of restoring the Byzantine Empire – he said that Russia was in the fortunate position of requiring no more territory – nevertheless, Britain remained extremely suspicious of his intentions. It was still the policy of Britain – as well as of France and Austria – to keep the Sick Man of Europe alive as long as possible, to prevent any of his vital organs from falling into Russian hands. The British response to the Tsar was guarded.

The empire might have been left in peace had it not been for a dispute between France and Russia over the control of the holy places in Palestine. In 1740 Sultan Mahmud I, through the Capitulations agreement signed with France, had granted privileges to the Roman Catholic monks in the holy places and had placed the French pilgrims as well as those of other Latin Catholic nations under the protection of the French flag. However, under the secular influence of the French Revolution, French interest in the holy places declined, and Russia took the opportunity to enlarge the privileges of the Orthodox Church in the Holy Land at Latin Roman Catholic expense. In 1850 Louis Napoleon, needing the support of the French Catholic Church in his struggle for power, decided to reassert Catholic rights in Palestine and made a formal demand in this respect to the sultan. When the tsar refused to relinquish any of the rights that Russia had acquired, the Ottoman government proposed a compromise through which both sides would retain their privileges but the sultan would undertake the protection of the holy places and the Christian pilgrims. Both France and Russia rejected this.

Britain was naturally concerned. Unlike Russia and France it was not spoiling for war but, disliking Russian ambitions towards the Ottoman Empire more than those of France, it was inclined to side with France and Turkey. The British government endeavoured to keep the peace, but it became clear that Russia was aiming to secure a protectorate over not only the Orthodox monks but also the twelve million Orthodox Christian subjects of the empire. This was something the sultan was bound to refuse. When the Russians occupied the Danubian principalities of Moldavia and Wallachia, Turkey declared war. Ottoman troops crossed the Danube and secured four initial victories. Although vast, the Russian armed forces were as much in need of modernization as the Turkish, and it seemed at first as if the Ottoman reforms were achieving results. The British and French fleets entered the Dardanelles strait. Britain hoped that this would be enough to cause the Russians to withdraw, but Tsar Nicholas was not deterred. The Russian fleet bombarded the Black Sea ports and destroyed a Turkish squadron. On 27 March 1854 Britain and France declared war on Russia, with strong support from public opinion at home.

The war lasted less than two years and ended when Austria threatened to intervene against Russia. If the hostilities revealed serious defects in both the British and the French armies – in some respects they were still fighting the Napoleonic wars – the Russians were in even worse condition. Although the war was fought over the internal affairs of the Ottoman Empire, Turkish troops played an insignificant role. After their initial successes on the Danube, only one Turkish division was involved.

The terms for the ending of the war were negotiated in the Treaty of Paris of March 1856. Russia abandoned its claims to the protection of the Ottoman Christians, and the exclusive Russian protectorate over the Danubian principalities was replaced by a joint protectorate of the powers of Europe. Free navigation on the River Danube was entrusted to the supervision of an international commission and the Black Sea was neutralized.

Under the treaty, the Christian powers undertook to respect the independence and territorial integrity of the Ottoman Empire and to maintain it, if necessary, by armed intervention. This could be regarded as the admission of Turkey into the so-called Concert of Europe, but the manner in which it was done was highly patronizing. In effect the Christian powers were claiming the right to interfere in the internal affairs of the empire if they felt that their interests were threatened by one of their rivals. At the same time, the powers were expressing their approval of Turkey's essentially westernizing re-forms. A new charter or Imperial Rescript was announced as a prelude to the Treaty of Paris, reaffirming the *Tanzimat* and carrying the reforms a stage further. This had been drafted in collaboration with the representatives of the powers, notably the energetic British ambassador Stratford Canning. On the insistence of the powers, the terms of the charter were incorporated into the Treaty of Paris.

The Imperial Rescript reiterated in stronger and more specific terms than ever before the full equality of all Ottoman subjects 'without prejudice of class or creed' in all matters relating to taxation, ownership of property, education and justice. If applied in full, this concept would have amounted to the dismantling of the Islamic order which was the basis of the empire. This was only very partially achieved, but the charter did have some important consequences: new commercial, maritime and penal codes, which were largely based on French law, were introduced, and the holy *sharia* ceased to be dominant in many areas of life.

However, the measure which had the most immediate and far-reaching effect on Ottoman society was the new land law, based on Western practices which it was hoped would enable the empire to catch up with Christian Europe. The traditional system, in which the land was the property of the state but the cultivators had a variety of established rights in return for the payment of a regular tax (the *miri*), was replaced by one which was based on individual freehold land ownership with full rights of disposal and succession.

Such a revolutionary reform could not be fully applied. It was often circumvented, and many traditional practices survived. The results were highly discouraging. The old system was harsh and inequitable in many respects – the practice of tax-farming had been monstrously abused, and it was a long-standing aim of the Ottoman reformers to abolish it – but the practical result of the new land code was to turn many of the more influential tax-farmers into freeholders and the bulk of the cultivators into sharecroppers or hired labourers. A powerful new landlord class was thus created. Very few of the new class of large land-owners were enlightened or progressive farmers. A prosperous peasantry on the Western model – investing in and developing its own property – was not created. Well-intentioned efforts by the reformers to increase agricultural output by the distribution of free seed and to create a network of rural co-operative banks to provide the farmers with cheap and easy credit were failures – the necessary administrative system and technical expertise were lacking. The only minor success was in the settlement of some hundreds of thousands of refugees from Russia on hitherto uncultivated lands in Anatolia.

Similar problems beset all the efforts of the Ottoman reformers to increase the productive capacity of the empire's economy as an essential means of raising revenues, as Western ambassadors in Istanbul were urging. In fact it was the liberal free-trade principles that had been imposed by Europe which prevented the reformers from providing the Ottoman infant industries with the protection they needed in order to survive.

The truth was that there was no prospect of a 'great leap forward' in the Ottoman economy which would have enabled it to compete with those of the industrialized powers of western Europe. The main features of advanced nineteenth-century capitalism and the expertise to manage them were lacking, and it would take much more than a generation to develop them. Moreover, the system of Capitulations meant that much of the more progressively managed parts of the economy were in foreign hands and therefore outside Ottoman control. In 1867 an amendment to the land code for the first time allowed foreigners to own land in the empire.

The reformers did attempt to develop the backward infrastructure of the Ottoman economy – roads, railways and ports. But every effort in this direction only increased the burden of government debt. Despite some improvement in the collection of taxes, expenditure always outran revenues. Soon the Ottoman government was forced to take the fatal step of using receipts from foreign loans to meet the growing deficits. Finally, in October 1875, the government issued a public declaration that only half the amount needed to service the foreign debt could be paid in cash; the remainder would be covered with a new issue of government bonds. This was equivalent to a declaration of bankruptcy. Although twentieth-century experience has shown how debtor nations can skilfully exploit their position with their creditors, this was an appalling position in which the proud Ottomans found themselves.

Sultan Abdul Mejid had died in 1861, at the age of thirty-eight. If he had been a more forceful character and had given more support to Reshid Pasha and his successors, Ali and Fuad Pashas, it is possible that the reforms would have produced more concrete results. But this is extremely doubtful. There was a narrow limit to what decisions taken at the centre could achieve in trying to transform society in such a vast empire. Through the new schools and academies, the most lasting accomplishment was to further the process, begun much earlier in the century, of developing an Ottoman élite which for the first time in centuries was open to the outside world, could speak foreign languages and could absorb fresh ideas. By its very nature this process could only be gradual, but it was also difficult for reactionaries to reverse. Towards the end of the century the results were apparent in the emergence of a substantial class of educated young Turks with a real understanding of their country's needs. The reformers were no longer a tiny band of lonely men.

The changes at the heart of the empire had their negative aspect, however. Partly as a means of initiating reforms, Sultan Mahmud had greatly increased his autocratic powers. He had suppressed the Janissaries and reduced the power of the feudal dynasties and local magistrates in the provinces. The process was reinforced by the reduction of the authority of the *ulama* over matters of religion, education and law. Sultan Abdul Aziz, who succeeded his brother Abdul Mejid in 1861, emphasized his title as caliph, which hitherto had been purely nominal; he claimed to be the spiritual as well as the political head of the empire. One by one the various countervailing forces with which even the greatest of the earlier sultans had to contend had been removed. But it was inevitable that eventually the Western concepts of constitutional government and the separation of legislative, executive and judicial powers which had penetrated the new Ottoman élite should be turned against the sultan's despotism.

Abdul Aziz had a more muscular personality than his brother but was of more limited mental capacity. Although initially declaring himself a reformist, he soon showed his sympathies with the reactionaries. However, he was incapable of reversing the process of reform. He was under constant pressure from the powers of Europe, led by France, and given the empire's weak financial condition he was in no position to resist. Grudgingly, he allowed Ali and Fuad Pashas to pursue the legal and educational reforms.

By 1871 Ali and Fuad Pashas were both dead. France, the inspiration of liberal reformist ideas, had been defeated by Prussia. External pressures were reduced and there were no men of standing to pursue the reforms. However, it was at this time that internal pressures began to emerge from a lower level.

Until the nineteenth century, hardly any Ottoman Turks were even aware of the immense technical and material advances achieved by Christian Europe. They neither spoke foreign languages nor travelled abroad, and their education and upbringing helped to convince them of the inevitable superiority of the world of Islam. By the middle of the nineteenth century this situation had changed, however. It was not so much that Western concepts of freedom and equality derived from the Enlightenment and French Revolution had penetrated the empire through the reformed educational system and the new printing-presses; indeed, these concepts were enshrined in the imperial charters which were the basis of the *Tanzimat*. It was much more that the young Ottomans who were now familiar with these concepts were travelling abroad in increasing numbers and were able to see for themselves what had happened in the countries where such ideas flourished. They reacted with shame and anger that Ottoman society had become so backward and impoverished in comparison with the West. Some of them concluded that the first necessity was to introduce Western concepts of constitutional government, although they always maintained that these were compatible with the Islamic faith. For others the solution was to revive and restore the true principles of Islam, which had been allowed to decay. These opposing trends exist throughout the Muslim world in the present day. But in the 1860s the supporters of both approaches agreed on the urgent need to reduce the despotic powers of the sultan.

In 1865 a secret revolutionary society was formed which became known as the Young Ottomans. In effect this was the first political party in the Ottoman Empire. Its intellectual inspiration was provided by a new literary movement which was strongly influenced by French writing and ideas but also intensely patriotic. Namik Kemal and Ziya Pasha were poets and dramatists of high quality. When exiled for their political agitation, they continued to publish opposition journals and pamphlets in European capitals and smuggled them into Turkey.

The empire had suffered a series of new humiliations at the hands of the European powers. In 1861, following civil war in Lebanon between Maronite Christians and Druze, Napoleon III, as the protector of the Christians, landed troops in Beirut. The sultan had to accept autonomy for Lebanon under a Christian governor to be chosen by the European powers with the consent of the sultan. When the Serbs revolted in the 1860s, Western pressure forced Turkey to withdraw its troops from the area. Then the Cretans rebelled and declared their union with Greece. Although the Ottoman forces were able to quell the revolt, the Western powers convened a conference in Paris at which Turkey accepted Crete's autonomy under Christian governors.

Personally extravagant and capricious, Sultan Abdul Aziz helped the empire to sink further into debt. The situation was worsened by a world-wide economic depression. In 1876 a revolt by Bulgarian peasants was suppressed with outstanding ferocity. The atrocities committed by the Turks helped to turn public opinion in the West even further against the Ottomans.

The sultan appointed and, after a few months, dismissed a series of grand viziers. One of these was to prove his undoing. Midhat Pasha, the greatest Turkish statesman of the late nineteenth century, was a closet constitutionalist who shared the opinions of the Young Ottomans. In 1873 he had told the British ambassador that the only way to avoid the imminent destruction of the empire lay in making the sultan's ministers responsible, especially in matters of finances, to a national popular assembly which would have to be truly national by avoiding all distinctions of class and religion. The empire would also have to be decentralized by the establishment of local provincial control over the governors.

As the political and economic crisis deepened, with Russia threatening war over the Balkans, a mass demonstration of theological students before the seat of government in Istanbul forced the sultan to recall the dismissed Midhat to office. He succeeded in persuading his fellow-ministers of the necessity for constitutional change, and they persuaded the chief mufti to issue a *fetwa* announcing the sultan's deposition on the ground of his 'mental derangement and ignorance of public affairs'. In the face of a show of force by troops and naval vessels, Abdul Aziz offered no resistance. But it was student power which had initiated the *coup d'état* – setting an ominous precedent.

High hopes were placed in the new sultan, Abdul Aziz's nephew Murad, who had a reputation for liberal constitutionalist sympathies. But Murad proved already to be suffering a nervous breakdown. He had to be instantly replaced by his younger brother, Abdul Hamid.

Abdul Hamid II, whose thirty-three-year reign (1876–1909) led to the final stages of the Ottoman Empire, was the last sultan of consequence. In many respects his complex character was strikingly different from that of most of his predecessors. Austere and pious in his personal life, he was ferociously hard-working. Before his accession, which he had not expected, he managed a farm and learned something of finance by investing in the Istanbul stock exchange. He could be ruthless, but he was not gratuitously cruel or vindictive. His considerable energies were dedicated to the survival of the empire, and his method was to pursue those modernizing reforms which might strengthen its defences and restore its power while maintaining an archaic personal despotism.

Inclination and necessity made him supremely devious in his dealings both with his own people and with overbearing foreign powers. He began his reign by deceiving both. The Balkans were in a state of acute crisis as a warlike Russia continued to support Serbian and Montenegran rebels against the sultan and to claim the right to protect Ottoman Christian subjects. In an effort to avert war, the British government led by Disraeli, as anxious as its predecessors to prevent the destruction of the Ottoman Empire, called a conference in Istanbul to discuss the outstanding problems. As the conference made slow but real progress during December 1876, the young sultan promulgated a new constitution. Devised by Midhat Pasha and based on the Belgian constitution of 1831, this provided for an elected parliament and embodied the principle that men of all creeds should be treated as equals. It was the first of its kind in any Muslim state. As was intended, it deflated the Istanbul conference because it seemed to provide for the kind of reforms for which the European powers had been calling. The parliament assembled in March 1877 and promptly passed a resolution declaring that there was no need for Russian protection of Ottoman Christians. Frustrated and exasperated, Russia declared war on the Ottoman Empire, having arranged Austria's neutrality by means of a secret agreement which divided the Balkans into their respective spheres of influence.

Initially the Ottoman forces gave a good account of themselves, winning several victories against vastly superior numbers. But over-confident tactics led to disaster. An army surrounded in Plerna was forced to surrender. Slav troops rose in rebellion in all parts of the Balkans. One Russian arm occupied the Armenian areas of eastern Anatolia, and another advanced on Istanbul. Abdul Hamid was obliged to sign the humiliating Treaty of San Stefano which specified the virtual dismemberment of his empire in Europe through the creation of two enlarged and independent Slav states of Bulgaria and Montenegro.

Disraeli was appalled. As he saw it, the sultan had been 'reduced to a state of absolute subjugation to Russia'. He contended that all the powers had rights and interests in the Balkans under the terms of earlier treaties. However, Disraeli had to act carefully. He had the support of the Russophobe Queen Victoria (who regarded the Russians as 'the retarders of all liberty and civilization that exists'), but half his cabinet was opposed to any war on Turkey's behalf. British public opinion, which had been aroused by the oratorical denunciations of Turkish atrocities by the Liberal opposition leader William Gladstone, was also generally anti-Turkish. But, the British public was fickle. As the Russians continued to advance on Istanbul despite the armistice, Disraeli succeeded in rallying his cabinet and the nation behind a threat to intervene.

The Congress of Berlin, which in 1878 brought the powers together under the chairmanship of the German chancellor Bismarck, effectively annulled the Treaty of San Stefano and repartitioned the Balkans to take account of the interests of the powers of Europe other than Russia. The independence of Romania, Serbia and Montenegro were recognized, but the large Bulgarian state which Russia had provided for in the Treaty of San Stefano was reduced and divided into two provinces, one of which became a Turkish self-governing province called Eastern Rumelia. Bismarck commented, 'There is once again a Turkey in Europe.'

It was the persistence of Disraeli (now ennobled by Queen Victoria as Lord Beaconsfield) which enforced this Russian retreat. He also enabled the sultan to regain large Armenian territories in eastern Anatolia which had been occupied by the Russians, in return for clear undertakings made to the Congress of Berlin of reforms in the interests of the Armenian population and guarantees of their security from attack by Muslim Circassians and Kurds. The *quid pro quo* for Britain's assistance in protecting substantial parts of the Ottoman Empire from Russia was a secret Anglo-Turkish agreement two months earlier by which Britain was allowed to occupy and administer the island of Cyprus – 'the key to western Asia' in Disraeli's imperial conception. To allay France's fears that this gave Britain too much hegemony in the eastern Mediterranean, France was allowed to understand that it could have a free hand in Tunisia, where Britain had hitherto entertained strong ambitions. Three years later France took Britain at its word by invading Tunisia and declaring it a French Protectorate, but this made it more difficult for France to protest when Britain invaded and occupied Egypt in the following year.

Abdul Hamid pursued with some skill his diplomatic policy of playing off the mutually suspicious European powers against each other, and he prevaricated over the implementation of the terms of the Treaty of Berlin as much as he could. But there was a limit to what he could do. In 1885 the Bulgars of Eastern Rumelia rose in rebellion. The two Bulgarian provinces were united, and the sultan appointed Prince Alexander of Battenburg, the prince of Bulgaria, as governor of Eastern Rumelia as a diplomatic way of accepting the annexation. Abdul Hamid was more successful with Greece. He resisted ceding to Greece the area of Epirus inhabited by Muslims, and he succeeded in holding on to Crete. Nevertheless, the Ottoman Empire in Europe had virtually ceased to exist.

In the empire's Anatolian heartland the situation was different. In

Armenia there was agitation for the reforms promised in the Treaty of Berlin to be carried out. But, inspired by the series of independent non-Muslim governments which had been founded in succession to the empire in Europe, Armenian nationalists went much further and demanded national independence.

Abdul Hamid had no intention of allowing the Christian powers to dictate the way in which he ruled what was left of his empire. As soon as the 1876 Constantinople Conference had ended he had dismissed Midhat Pasha – the prime force behind the liberal constitution which he had accepted – and had sent him into exile. (In 1878 he was appointed governor of Syria, but in 1881 he was again banished. Allowed back into Turkey after British pressure, he was put on trial on a charge of plotting against the sultan. He was sentenced to life banishment and was later quietly murdered in prison in Arabia.)

As we have seen, Abdul Hamid allowed the Ottoman parliament to meet in March 1877. Despite the limits to its powers, the parliament showed worrying signs of independence – to the extent of demanding that some of the sultan's ministers should appear before it to answer charges. Abdul Hamid responded by dissolving the assembly after a session of three months. Six months later he recalled it, hoping that in the continuing international crisis created by the Russian menace it would be more docile. But, once the Treaty of Berlin was concluded in January 1878, parliament renewed both its accusations against certain ministers and its demands that they should answer them. This time Abdul Hamid felt strong enough to dissolve parliament and suspend the constitution indefinitely. The suspension was to last for thirty years. The reform movement of the Young Ottomans was crushed and destroyed.

The young sultan built up his own remarkable system of autocracy. Gradually he reduced the powers that had been delegated to the grand vizier and reinforced his personal bureaucracy, which reported directly to him. His deeply mistrustful nature caused him to rely on an elaborate system of espionage with Istanbul as the heart of the spider's web of imperial intrigue. He had no friends and trusted no one. His fears of abduction or assassination became paranoid to the extent that he always extracted his own teeth and prepared his own medicines. His emissaries not only reported on individuals or groups in the provinces who showed signs of becoming too powerful or ambitious but also acted on the sultan's orders to promote local rivalries and antagonisms. He preferred the use of the silken cord to the sword.

While Abdul Hamid had no sympathy for constitutionalism or democracy, he was not a hidebound reactionary. In contemporary terms he was a modernizer rather than a westernizer. Like certain of his predecessors, he accepted the need to learn from Europe in order to stand up to its power. In the early years of his reign he was prepared to fulfil the *Tanzimat* reforms and went some way towards carrying them through.

His first grand vizier, Mehmed Said Pasha – known as 'Ingiliz Said' because of his Anglophile tendencies – declared in a lengthy memorandum on the subject of reform that 'the advancement of a state can only be secured through knowledge and uprightness.' The people must be better educated; the state must be more just and less corrupt.

Public education was the field in which reform was most successful – especially at the higher level. The Mulkiye, or civil-service training-college, and the Harbiye, or war college, were greatly expanded and improved and some eighteen new higher and professional schools were established. The long-delayed project for the University of Istanbul – described as 'the first truly indigenous modern university in the Muslim world' – was carried through, although it was not until 1900 that it opened its doors.

Elementary and secondary education were also expanded. New schools were needed to supply the training-colleges with pupils. They still served only a small minority of the population, and a truly public education system was still a distant goal; nevertheless, the new Turkish élite, trained in modern languages and disciplines, had become much more numerous by the end of the century. The spread of literacy, the growth of higher education and the expansion of printing transformed the intellectual and cultural life of the cities. However, under Abdul Hamid the censorship which already existed was tightened to an absurd degree. Although newspapers multiplied, they were emasculated by the censor. Because the sultan was terrified of assassination, no report of the violent death of a head of state could be published. When the king and queen of Serbia were murdered in 1903, Turkish newspaper-readers were informed that they had died of indigestion.

The ban on political activity and discussion limited the new generation of Turkish intellectuals to literary or academic writing.

But there was no way in which they could be insulated against revolutionary or secular ideas. Political feelings were merely driven underground.

Discontent was fed by the constant, humiliating erosion of Ottoman power at the hands of Europe, despite all the efforts of the sultan and his grand vizier. Since the Capitulations were one of the most obvious manifestations of Ottoman weakness, the Ottoman government endeavoured to bring them under control. The privileges of the Capitulations had been granted to non-Muslims within the empire in the sixteenth century, when Ottoman power was at its height. In order to stimulate trade and industry, they exempted non-Muslims from taxes and gave them the right to be tried in their own consular courts. As Ottoman power declined, these privileges were reinforced and became flagrantly abused. The foreign communities were not only privileged and protected: they were virtually above the law. The European powers argued that, in spite of the reforms introduced in 1869, the Ottoman legal system was in no way suitable to be applied to their nationals in the empire.

In the first few years of Abdul Hamid's reign an effort was made to meet these objections. A newly established Ministry of Justice was given control first over the commercial courts and then over all non-religious courts. A new law attempted to regulate the mixed courts which had been created earlier in the nineteenth century to try cases between Muslim and non-Muslim Ottoman subjects. All these efforts were a failure. The European powers brusquely refused to recognize the new regulations. The extraterritorial privileges were unassailed and continued to flourish. The impetus behind all legal reform was removed, and in 1888 the sultan disbanded the official drafting committee which had been set up by his predecessor to prepare the new laws.

The fact that the extraterritorial privileges of the powers of Europe remained unscathed was bad enough; it was far worse that the empire itself was bankrupt and forced to submit to a measure of outside financial control.

Bankruptcy had in effect been declared in 1875, in the last year of the reign of Sultan Abdul Aziz, when his government announced that, in view of the size of the budget deficit, it would service only half of the external debt in cash and would make up the rest by a new issue of treasury bonds. The deficit was caused partly by a series of disastrous harvests in Anatolia but much more by the heavy military spending involved in the suppression of Balkan rebels and the war with Russia. The rival European powers had difficulty in co-ordinating their policies towards Istanbul but they moved inexorably towards imposing their financial conditions on the empire. The Congress of Berlin made the situation much worse by forcing the sultan to give up his richest Balkan provinces. A committee representing European holders of Ottoman bonds attended the Congress to press their claims, and they secured warm support from their governments.

In his desperate need to satisfy his European creditors, Abdul Hamid in 1881 issued the Decree of Muharrem, setting up a Council of the Public Debt in agreement with the bond-holders to ensure that the Ottoman debt would continue to be serviced. The Council was to include both bond-holders and Ottoman representatives. Although it was not a full international commission with official foreign-government representatives, as the powers had proposed at the Congress of Berlin, and the sultan could deny that it infringed Ottoman sovereignty, it was difficult to disguise the fact that the empire had submitted to a large measure of foreign financial control, and this became increasingly apparent over the years. Several of the more economically backward European states – not to mention the Latin American countries – had defaulted on their debts and the powers had given their bond-holders varying degrees of support to resolve the situation. But it was a wholly different matter for the caliph/sultan – the leader of the only Muslim great power – to accept such humiliation.

European manufactured goods had already begun to flow into Turkey in the first half of the nineteenth century as the Ottoman efforts at protection collapsed. European financial control assisted the flood of imports. Three major foreign-controlled banks – the National Bank of Turkey, the Imperial Ottoman and the Deutsche Bank – as well as the foreign embassies were always ready to provide support for the policies of the Council of the Public Debt. However, the European powers were not attempting to stifle local Turkish industry – on the contrary, they encouraged the Ottoman reformers' efforts to increase production as the best means of raising the taxable capacity of the population and hence the ability of the Ottoman government to pay its debts. Both Abdul Aziz and Abdul Hamid were aware of the dangers of increasing economic dependence on Europe, and the *Tanzimat* reforms attempted to address the problem. But the measures were half-hearted and incompetently administered. New infant industries not only lacked protection but also, amazingly, still suffered from Ottoman internal taxes on the movement of goods which were only gradually and grudgingly removed. Existing local industries were unable to compete with the imports of increasingly sophisticated products from Europe – armaments factories, for example, found themselves confined to producing small arms, ammunition and military clothing.

Attempts to increase agricultural output and exports were rather more successful. Much of this success was not due to the government. The rising prosperity of industrializing western Europe had already increased the demand for exports of Turkish crops. British imports in particular received a powerful boost from the repeal of the Corn Laws in 1841. The American Civil War created a boom for Turkish cotton which did not entirely disappear when the war ended. The richer agricultural areas of the coastal plains and the Anatolian river valleys prospered.

The trouble was that the twin objectives of the nineteenth-century Ottoman reformers were contradictory: the creation of a prosperous class of peasant freeholders was incompatible with the desire for a powerful centralizing government which would re-establish the rights of the state wherever they had been eroded. Inevitably the progress of reform was extremely slow and, equally inevitably, wherever freehold rights were established they went to the richest and most powerful or to those with the best connections.

A new factor in the situation was the right granted to foreigners to own land and property, under the reform law of 1867. The Ottomans had hoped and expected that, in return, the Europeans who acquired estates in the empire would forgo their privileges under the Capitulations. They were disappointed: the Europeans insisted on retaining their rights to immunity from police interference or the payment of Ottoman taxes.

Ottoman reformers and their European advisers were under no doubt that the biggest single obstacle to the improvement of the Turkish economy was the poor communication systems. When Abdul Hamid came to the throne there were only a few hundred miles of railway; the road system was rudimentary and the ports were primitive. The costs of moving farm produce across the country for export were prohibitive.

Road-building schemes were largely a failure because those roads that were built were not maintained and soon fell into disrepair. Railway building, largely by foreign concession-holders, achieved more results, and from the 1880s a boom in railway construction linked the regions of Anatolia with Europe and extended from Turkey to the Arab provinces of the empire. The length of track in this vast region was still modest by European standards, but the railway was of huge symbolic importance. In August 1888 the first Istanbul Express left Vienna.

It can be seen that much of the nineteenth-century development of the Ottoman Empire's heartland was due to the privileged foreigners. Railways were built by Europeans; banking and finance were largely in foreign hands; and foreign entrepreneurs were even responsible for the investment and installation of machinery that turned cotton into Turkey's most successful export industry. However, there was one aspect of nineteenth-century technical progress which Abdul Hamid and his ministers were determined to keep in Turkish hands; this was the telegraph. When Abdul Hamid came to the throne, in 1876, a French concessionnaire had already linked the entire empire to Istanbul with a telegraph network. Initially the system was operated by foreigners using the French language, but from the 1860s onwards the Ottomans made a special effort to turkize the system and place it under the control of a new Ministry of Posts & Telegraphs. Abdul Hamid immediately recognized the importance of the telegraph as a means of maintaining his despotic and centralized control over the empire. He could issue immediate orders to his officials in the most distant provinces, who found that they could no longer act as if they were semi-autonomous. Foreign ambassadors of despotic rulers were soon to make the same discovery.

Turkish indebtedness and relative military weakness forced Abdul Hamid to use intrigue and diplomacy to keep the powers of Europe divided in their Eastern policies. He had enjoyed some success in this following the Congress of Berlin in 1878. Although the powers were shocked to varying degrees by the sultan's reneging on his promises concerning the treatment of his Armenian subjects, joint action was prevented because Bismarck, chairman of the Congress, said he would co-operate on any matter except the imposition of Armenian reform on the sultan.

The Armenian situation drastically worsened during the following two decades. As Abdul Hamid made use of the Kurds, who coveted much of the same territory, to suppress the Armenian rebellion, the Armenians intensified their organized political activities. They raised their demands to seek a fully independent homeland in eastern Turkey and internationalized their movement by forming branches in western European capitals. Its most extreme form was the Hunchak (or 'Bell'), established in Geneva in 1881, which was the first revolutionary socialist movement in the Ottoman Empire. In 1890 the Armenian Revolutionary Federation was founded at Tiflis (the modern Tbilisi) in Russian Georgia, and armed bands began to make raids into Ottoman territory. The sultan responded by encouraging increased anti-Armenian activities among the Kurdish tribesmen, whom he trained and formed into cavalry regiments. There was no attempt to conceal the fact that their role was to suppress the Armenians.

The response of the inflamed Armenians was an exceedingly unwise attempt to stir up a revolt among the sultan's Muslim subjects in Anatolia. This gave Abdul Hamid the excuse to incite a series of horrific massacres which took place throughout 1895 and 1896. Both regular Turkish troops and Kurdish irregulars took part. In some places the ordinary Muslim population was incited by rumours that the Armenians were about to murder them while they were at prayers in their mosques. Sometimes the Armenians sought refuge in their churches and asked for protection, but this was of no avail. The sound of a bugle was a signal for the massacres to begin. Most of eastern Turkey was affected, and perhaps a hundred thousand Armenians were murdered or died from subsequent disease and starvation.

It was possible to keep the scale of these massacres hidden from the outside world. News only trickled out and was often dismissed as exaggerated rumours. But in August 1896 a group of Armenian revolutionaries with characteristic foolhardiness took their struggle into the heart of Istanbul, where they raided and occupied the Ottoman Bank with the declared purpose of drawing the attention of the European embassies to the plight of their people. In the inevitable reprisal, the Istanbul mob led by religious fanatics was allowed to murder and pillage through the Armenian quarter. Now the powers of Europe could not ignore what was happening. In a series of joint notes they denounced the massacres and made clear their view that these were not spontaneous communal disturbances but had been deliberately provoked by the sultan and his agents. They made veiled threats of intervention by suggesting that the survival of the sultan and his dynasty were at stake.

Abdul Hamid's replies were evasive and unsatisfactory. The rumour spread through the capital that the British fleet would force the Dardanelles and land troops. But once again the sultan was saved by the jealous rivalry of the powers. In England the aged William Gladstone might rage against the 'unspeakable Turk' as a 'disgrace to civilization' and demand that Britain should if necessary act alone, but he was in opposition and the prudent prime minister Lord Salisbury, who like his monarch Queen Victoria always detested and feared the Russians more than the Turks, had no intention of doing such a thing. Public opinion might be aroused against the empire throughout Europe, but the governments of the powers still had no desire to see it dismembered. Russia did not want to see a powerful independent Armenia on its borders. France did not wish to risk its huge investments in the Ottoman Empire, which were now much larger than those of Britain. Germany had its own ambitions for political and commercial expansion to the east which could succeed only through an alliance with the sultan and his government. An international conference on the Armenian question in 1897 ended in failure, and the collapse of the Empire was again forestalled. The Armenians, whose aims had never been realistic, were left to their fate.

Since his accession Abdul Hamid had regarded Germany, recently united under Bismarck, with the greatest favour among the powers of Europe. It not only lacked Britain, France and Russia's imperial ambitions towards the Muslim world but also acted to restrain them. Backed by its rising industrial strength, which was soon to outstrip that of Britain, and allied with Austro-Hungary, imperial Germany created a new focus of power in central Europe. But there were strict limits to Bismarck's ambitions: his own view was that the concept of eastwards expansion was a futile dream. One of his most notable observations was that the whole Eastern Question was 'not worth the bones of a single Pomeranian grenadier'.

However, Germany's foreign policy dramatically changed when, in 1888, the young Kaiser Wilhelm II acceded to the throne on the early death of his father. Intelligent but unstable, autocratic and ambitious, Wilhelm – although half-English through his mother, the daughter of Queen Victoria – was a passionate German nationalist. Against Bismarck's advice he was easily persuaded by Marshal von der Goltz, who headed the German military mission in Istanbul, that Asiatic Turkey was ripe for the growth of German influence. The policy of 'Drang nach Osten' (or 'drive to the east') was born. Abdul Hamid, always suspicious of liberal influences emanating from London and Paris and seeing nothing equivalent in Berlin, welcomed the new German interest. In 1889 he gave a lavish reception to the young kaiser and kaiserin when they made their first visit to Istanbul.

German engineers and scientists now joined the military experts in the difficult task of modernizing the Ottoman Empire. The principal German contribution was the building of the railway across Anatolia to Baghdad, with the prospect of extending it through Basra to Kuwait on the Persian Gulf. In 1898 the kaiser, who by now 'dropped the pilot' and dispensed with Bismarck's services, made a second visit to Istanbul of much greater significance. This time he went on from Turkey to the Arab provinces of the empire. With doubtful symbolism he entered Jerusalem dressed as a crusader knight, after praying on his knees outside the walls of the Holy City. But he went on to Damascus where, in a memorable speech at the tomb of Saladin, he swore Germany's disinterested protection for the 300 million subjects of the sultan caliph.

The foundations had been laid of an Ottoman–German alliance which two decades later was to result in the destruction and dismemberment of the empire. But it was wholly understandable that Abdul Hamid should have clutched at Germany as an ally to help preserve from British and French imperial ambitions his Arab Asian dominions which were virtually all that remained of his empire. Morocco had never been Ottoman, Algeria was lost to France in the 1830s and Tunisia in 1881. Turkish governors still ruled the desert provinces of Libya, but, partly through accident and bungling, Egypt had come under lasting British control.

5. Britain in Egypt, 1882–1914

In 1841, combined European and Ottoman pressure had forced Muhammad Ali of Egypt to abandon all his dreams of empire except for possession of Sudan. However, he nevertheless left his successors a cohesive semi-independent state whose strategic position gave it considerable importance in the eastern Mediterranean. They also inherited gigantic problems which they were ultimately incapable of managing.

Some of these problems closely mirrored those of the Ottoman sultan. The abolition of Muhammad Ali's system of monopolies and the opening up of Egypt to European trade and enterprise (equivalent to the *infitah* or open-door policy of President Sadat more than a century later) not only removed the basis of the state's revenues but also made it impossible for the rulers of Egypt to maintain control over the country's economic development. There was no question of Egypt becoming an industrial power.

There were also important differences from Turkey, however. The enforced reduction of the armed forces to 18,000 men, under the 1841 Treaty of London, removed the need for high military spending which had bled the country. But this also meant that Egypt was no longer a military power of any consequence, even though the Ottoman sultan was neither willing nor able to offer protection against occupation by a European power.

Egypt's open-door policy promoted a more intensive and comprehensive economic development than was taking place in Turkey. In area Egypt is the size of France and Spain, but only 3 per cent of this was inhabited, its population being less than one-tenth of what it is today. Good communications and a modern infrastructure were relatively easy to install, and by the 1870s the inextensive but intensely fertile lands of the Nile Valley and Delta were producing valuable crops for export, of which cotton was the most important.

Unfortunately this did little to improve the lot of the mass of Egyptians, for two reasons. One was that the foreign entrepreneurs who were responsible for so much of the new development made little contribution to Egypt's revenues; under the protection of the Capitulations, they paid virtually no taxes. Secondly, while the trend towards the granting of freehold property rights was more advanced than in Ottoman Turkey, the principal result was that more and more land was concentrated into vast estates owned by the Turco-Circassian ruling class, and especially the numerous members of the family of Muhammad Ali. At the same time, many of the small farmers – the *fellahin* – actually lost control over lands that their families had farmed for generations. The *kurbaj* (whip) might no longer be used to force them into the ranks of Ibrahim Pasha's armies, but it was employed to conscript labour among the landless peasants.

Abbas, Muhammad Ali's immediate successor (1844–54), was an embittered reactionary who dismissed his grandfather's French advisers and willingly closed schools and halted public works. But though generally xenophobic he was curiously Anglophile, and he allowed James Stephenson to build the Cairo–Alexandria railway in 1850–1, the first railway in Africa or Asia. Despite his meanness, Egypt's lack of revenues forced him into borrowing. On his murder by two household slaves (possibly as an act of revenge by his aunt, Princess Zohra, whom he had banished for amorous activities), he was succeeded by a man of very different temperament, his genial and Francophile uncle Said (1854–63). Said launched a vastly expensive new programme of public works – digging new canals, repairing dams and expanding both the railways and steamer transport on the Nile. He set a precedent by negotiating a loan from Fruhling and Goschen of London at 8 per cent. As European entrepreneurs, supported by their consuls and protected by the Capitulations, extracted expensive and one-sided concessions from the Egyptian government, Egypt's debts mounted dangerously.

The consequences of this extravagance were overshadowed by one decision which was to be fateful for Egypt. As a youth, one of Said's closest European friends had been Ferdinand de Lesseps, a young engineer who was son of the French political agent. De Lesseps was interested in a scheme to cut a canal from the Mediterranean to the Red Sea across the isthmus of Suez. This was not a new idea. Napoleon had wanted to do it in order to gain control of the Red Sea for France, but his engineers had told him it was impossible because of the different levels of the Mediterranean and Red Seas. This was contradicted by a British engineer in the 1830s, and Muhammad Ali and his French advisers favoured the project. Palmerston, however, was strongly opposed – especially if the canal was to be built by French engineers. British interests would make control of the canal imperative, and this would mean the occupation of Egypt. As he famously remarked,

We do not want Egypt or wish it for ourselves, any more than any rational man with an estate in the north of England and a residence in the south would have wished to possess the inns on the road. All he could want would have been that the inns should be well-kept, always accessible, and furnishing him, when he came, with mutton-chops and post-horses.

Britain preferred the trans-Egyptian route to the East to be opened by extending the Cairo–Alexandria railway to Suez.

One of Said's first actions on his accession was to sign a canal concession agreement with de Lesseps. The terms were hugely unfavourable to Egypt: it had to provide a corvée of 20,000 unpaid labourers a year, pay for all the extensive ancillary works and abandon its rights to the land on both banks of the canal. In addition, when nearly half the shares in the Suez Canal Company were left unsold by public subscription, de Lesseps persuaded Said that he must purchase them.

Britain still opposed the scheme, and endeavoured to use its influence with the Ottoman sultan. But Said was sufficiently independent, and de Lesseps had the enthusiastic support of Napoleon III. In April 1859 the work began. The Canal was half completed when Said died and was succeeded as viceroy by Ismail, son of Ibrahim Pasha. Ismail was a man of ambition, intelligence and enterprise, but his failings were to destroy Egypt's hopes of independence. Work on the Canal was pushed ahead and was completed by 1869, when Ismail played the lavish host to the Empress Eugénie and other European royalty for the official opening. The cost to Egypt was gigantic. The sultan, encouraged by Britain, had maintained his right to veto the concession. Although de Lesseps persuaded him to refer the dispute to Napoleon III for arbitration, the French emperor's award, which was intended finally to determine the status of the Suez Canal Company, placed an unbearable burden on Egypt. Ismail had to pay the Company the extortionate sum of 130 million francs to relinquish its rights to land, navigation and free labour under the original concession. The sultan issued his firman of approval, but Egypt was rapidly approaching bankruptcy.

The Suez Canal was the most important single expense for Egypt, but there was much more. During Ismail's reign, 8,400 miles of canal were dug and the railway system was extended from 275 to 1,185 miles. Telegraphs, bridges, docks and lighthouses gave Egypt the infrastructure of a modernizing nineteenth-century state. In a remark which is still remembered in Egypt, Ismail claimed that 'My country no longer belongs to Africa; it is part of Europe.' Even *The Times*'s correspondent concurred when he wrote in 1876 that 'Egypt is a marvellous instance of progress. She has advanced as much in seventy years as many other countries have done in five hundred.' The cultivated area was extended by some 15 per cent, and between 1862 and 1879 the value of exports and imports nearly tripled.

There were two disastrous weaknesses in this apparent prosperity. One was that it depended so heavily on the export of a single primary product – cotton. Manufactured goods were mostly imported. Like Turkey, Egypt benefited from the effects of the American civil war on cotton output from the southern states. The boom encouraged Ismail to further extravagance but swiftly faded. The other weakness was the mountain of debt on which the apparent prosperity was based. Within five years of Ismail's Canal concession he had borrowed over £25 million at rates of interest nominally varying between 7 and 12 per cent but in reality amounting to between 12 and 26 per cent. One of his troubles was that as viceroy appointed by the sultan, rather than an independent sovereign, he had no legal power to pledge the revenue of the state, so the terms on which he could borrow were proportionately more expensive. In 1867 he managed to secure from the sultan the style and title of khedive together with the right to change the law of succession in favour of his direct descendants instead of succession passing, as previously, to the eldest surviving member of the house of Muhammad Ali. In 1873 he obtained an Imperial Rescript which made him virtually an independent sovereign with the right to raise loans and secure concessions without reference to the sultan. All this was achieved only with heavy bribes, but it meant that what had previously been the personal liability of the viceroy now became that of the Egyptian state and ultimately of the long-suffering *fellahin*.

By 1875 Ismail's debts were so great that he was obliged to sell his 44 per cent of the Suez Canal Company's shares to the British government for the modest sum of £4 million. The prime minister,

Disraeli, who had once supported Palmerston in his opposition to the building of the canal, arranged for a loan to make the purchase through the London House of Rothschild. Gladstone, leader of the Liberal opposition, saw it as 'an act of folly fraught with danger' to involve Britain so intimately in Egyptian affairs. The French, of course, were furious.

The sale of Canal shares was not enough to save Ismail or Egypt from bankruptcy. Moreover the financial collapse of the Ottoman Empire was imminent and, despite Egypt's relative independence, this had a disastrous effect on Egypt's international credit. In fact Egypt's formal declaration of bankruptcy, in April 1876, followed that of Turkey by only seven months.

The consequences for Egypt were similar to those for Turkey but more profound. Whereas with Turkey and other defaulting countries the British government confined itself to moral support for the bond-holders and refused to become directly involved, Egypt was different because it lay across the route to India. As Palmerston had foreseen, the way in which was governed had become of vital interest to the British Empire.

When Ismail asked Britain for help, the British government sent out a high-level mission headed by a cabinet minister. The hope of the bond-holders and the British public was that Britain would now impose a form of financial control over Egypt. But the French were quite unprepared to allow the British to monopolize the external intervention in Egypt's affairs, and they sent out their own financial mission. Britain and France each proposed solutions which were favourable to their respective bond-holders and, after some diplomatic wrangling, a compromise was reached under which a Caisse of Public Debt (or *Caisse de la Dette*) would be established through which Egypt's total debts would be consolidated with repayments fixed at 7 per cent, absorbing some two-thirds of the state's revenues. The British and French governments were each represented by an independent executive controller-general. Anglo-French dual control of Egypt had begun. The English commissioner in the Caisse was a former secretary of the Viceroy of India, Captain Evelyn Baring, who was to set the tone for Britain's special relationship with Egypt during the next generation.

The controllers-general set about proving their worth and, through a variety of additional taxes, Egypt began to pay its debts at the rate that had been imposed. But the British and French officials in Egypt soon realized that the strain on the population was becoming intolerable. A low Nile flood and cotton pest added to the sufferings of the *fellahin*. Even liberal use of the *kurbaj* could not squeeze any more taxes from them. The controllers-general concluded that an international commission of inquiry was needed to examine the khedive's financial management. Reluctantly, the khedive accepted. As expected, the commission concluded that the source of Egypt's problems lay in the khedive's unlimited authority and that he must delegate some of his powers to 'responsible ministers'. Ismail agreed, in the spirit of his contention that Egypt was now part of Europe. He appointed a cabinet with the wily Armenian Nubar Pasha as prime minister, a British minister of finance and a French minister of public works.

But Ismail had no real intention of becoming a constitutional monarch. When his 'European' government took unpopular measures, as it was bound to do in view of Egypt's financial condition, he refused to share responsibility. He showed his authority by sharply suppressing a mutiny of officers who had not been paid for eighteen months and then dismissing Nubar as incapable of maintaining public order. Britain and France were still unprepared for direct military intervention, partly because the general public in their countries was not very sympathetic towards the bond-holders; they still vainly hoped to persuade Ismail to retain constitutional government. Partly at Ismail's own instigation, a coalition of army officers, pashas and *ulama* had formed something resembling an Egyptian National Party, determined to prove that Egypt could govern itself. Conceivably a balance between the khedive and some form of representative institutions could be achieved. Ismail shrewdly chose Sherif Pasha, a leading constitutionalist, as his new prime minister.

Intervention came from an unexpected quarter. Germany and Austria were indignant at the measures Sherif's government proposed to reduce the burden of the floating debt to the bond-holders, most of whom were of German or Austrian nationality. They persuaded the by now exasperated British and French that Ismail must go, and together they put pressure on Sultan Abdul Hamid to use his residual powers to force Ismail to abdicate in favour of his son Tewfik. Ismail sailed into exile. He left few defenders. His real achievements were forgotten because of the disasters his reign had brought: after consolidating Egypt's independence, he had destroyed it through his extravagance.

The new young khedive lacked Ismail's courage and determination, but he had no wish to accept any form of liberal constitution. However the political situation in Egypt was no longer simple to control. Although the rising national movement consisted of several disparate and incompatible elements, it was now formidable as they were temporarily united against the dangers of foreign domination and arbitrary government.

The ideological strand in the movement consisted of the politico-religious reformers who were disciples of Jamal al-Din al-Afghani, a formidable Iranian of obscure origin who was one of the most powerful intellectual influences in nineteenth-century Islam. Al-Afghani preached the need for the restoration of true Islamic principles, but he also declared the need for national and Islamic unity as a defence against Christian European intervention. However, he had no faith in the Ottoman caliphate and opposed its power. He favoured constitutional government. Exiled, not surprisingly, from Turkey in 1871, he came to Egypt where he was tolerated by Ismail. Tewfik expelled him shortly after his accession – almost certainly with the encouragement of the Anglo-French dual control – but his influence survived. Later he lived in Paris, where he founded a secret society and published a journal dedicated to Islamic reform.

The second strand in the national movement consisted of the pashas, *ulama* and other notables who favoured constitutional reform. Many of them were Turco-Circassians who had to some extent come to identify themselves with Egypt and the aspirations of its people. But they were also wealthy owners of property who were easily frightened by the spectre of radicalism or a popular uprising.

The third element in the national party consisted of the genuine Egyptian or *fellah* (as opposed to Turco-Circassian) officers in the army. Ismail had blatantly favoured the non-Egyptians, who held all the highest military posts, and the *fellah* officers were in a state of seething discontent. They found a leader in Colonel Ahmed Arabi, the son of a small farmer of lower Egypt. Although poorly educated, he had succeeded in rising to command the Fourth Regiment. Courageous and dignified, he was neither brilliant nor decisive but he appealed to the mass of Egyptians because he remained in touch with them and could express their grievances in terms they could understand.

The unpopular and ultra-reactionary Circassian war minister, Osman Rifky, attempted to have Colonel Arabi and some of his colleagues arrested and court-martialled for mutiny. But Arabi had the support of the key regiments in the capital and the manoeuvre failed. The government was forced to capitulate and dismiss Rifky.

Arabi and his friends became the natural leaders of a movement which rode on a swell of popular support. As *The Times* pointed out on 12 September 1881, 'The army, we must remember, is the only native institution which Egypt now owns. All else has been invaded and controlled and transformed by the accredited representatives of France and England.'

The situation was still capable of peaceful resolution. Neither Arabi nor those like the Islamic reformer Shaikh Muhammad Abduh, al-Afghani's disciple, who joined his ranks, were firebrand revolutionaries. Still less so were the land-owners in the national movement. The British government – now headed by William Gladstone, with his long reputation for anti-imperialism – was still reluctant to intervene. The British representatives in Egypt, although often ill-informed about the true nature of popular feeling in the country, believed that the situation could still be saved if the khedive acted firmly but with wisdom and restraint according to their advice. Unfortunately, Tewfik was quite inadequate for the task. While appearing to show some sympathy for Arabi's demands, such as that the size of the Egyptian army should be increased and that the number of Europeans employed in Egypt should be reduced, together with their inflated salaries, his real objective was to be rid of the rebellious colonel. He even sent an emissary to Sultan Abdul Hamid to tell him that Arabi aimed to form an Arabian Empire with the agreement of Britain. But Abdul Hamid was more than a match for Tewfik in double-dealing. He informed Arabi that he was satisfied with his loyalty and commanded him at all costs to defend Egypt from invasion, lest it should share the fate of Tunisia which had recently been occupied by France.

In fact Gladstone's government would have preferred the sultan to have taken responsibility for restoring the authority of the khedive. But it was also Gladstone's policy to maintain a close *entente* with France in the face of Bismarck's growing ambitions in Europe, and the French were totally opposed to any Turkish intervention, being nervous that Abdul Hamid might, through Egypt, be planning to raise a pan-Islamic resistance movement which would endanger their hold on Tunisia. Nevertheless, Britain was still hoping that no intervention at all would be necessary when, in December 1881, the French government fell and was replaced by one led by Gambetta, the arch-nationalist hero of France's resistance to Prussia in 1871. Gambetta insisted on strong action and forced Britain's lethargic foreign secretary, Lord Granville, into the dispatch of an Anglo–French Joint Note addressed to the British and French consuls-general in Egypt. The menacing Note in effect demanded the restoration of the *status quo ante* and the maintenance of the khedive on the throne 'on the terms laid down by the Sultan's Firmans and officially recognized by the two Governments, as alone able to guarantee, for the present and future, the good order and development of prosperity in Egypt, in which France and Great Britain are equally interested.'

The consequences of this high-handedness were predictable. National feeling in Egypt was further aroused. Arabi was appointed under-secretary of state for war and the quasi-parliament (the Chamber of Notables) demanded some control over Egypt's budget, which was in the hands of the Anglo–French financial controllers. Gambetta fell from power after only two months and was replaced by the more moderate De Freycinet, but the damage had been done.

The Egyptian army now dominated the nation, and the mass of the people gave it their enthusiastic support. The *fellahin* naïvely hoped that Egypt would henceforth be ruled by Egyptians and they would no longer be squeezed for taxes. Some of the notables shared these feelings, but many were alarmed by the threat of social upheaval and wavered in their support. Meanwhile the nervous and resentful khedive continued to intrigue against Arabi but did not dare to confront him openly, and Sultan Abdul Hamid maintained his policy of giving both sides the impression that he supported them.

As Egyptian national feelings hardened, so too did those of the British and French governments and their representatives in Egypt. The latter reported that the country was dissolving into anarchy, although this was far from being the case – Egypt was effervescent but not in chaos. Members of the British cabinet, preoccupied by a state of near rebellion in Ireland, convinced themselves that native Egyptians were incapable of governing themselves – only the Ottoman Turks were considered a natural governing race – and that vital

British interests were at stake. Even Gladstone – anti-imperialist and notoriously anti-Turk – accepted this view. Later he told the House of Commons, 'It has been charitably believed, even in this country, that the military party was the popular party, was struggling for the liberties of Egypt. There is not the smallest rag or shred of evidence to support that contention.' This blatant untruth was an apparent attempt to satisfy his conscience.

Still hoping for Turkish intervention, although under Anglo-French supervision, Britain and France sent a powerful joint naval force which stood off Alexandria. Shortly afterwards an event took place which seemed to justify all the fears of the alarmists: a major riot in Alexandria left several hundred killed or injured, including some fifty Europeans. Relations between Europeans and Egyptians had certainly deteriorated as the oratory of Muslim shaikhs whipped up national feeling and every European came under suspicion of hoping for a European invasion, but that the riot had been instigated by the military, as European officials on the spot at first claimed, was highly improbable if only because it would have provided justification for European occupation. In fact the rioting started with a brawl and then spread, but it was the presence of the Anglo-French squadron which inflamed the situation. The action of the interventionists was self-justifying. Fearful Europeans evacuated Alexandria in thousands.

The attitude of the British government was now harder than that of the French. British suspicions that De Freycinet was planning a secret deal with Arabi were confirmed when the French premier refused a British proposal for Anglo-French protection of the Suez Canal on the ground that the only danger to the Canal came from outside intervention. When, on 19 July 1882, the British admiral issued an ultimatum to Arabi that Alexandria would be bombarded unless he dismantled the fortifications he was erecting around the city, De Freycinet withdrew the French fleet. A joint Anglo-French invasion of Egypt no longer remained a possibility.

The cabinet council, presided over by the khedive and attended by the sultan's representative, decided it would be dishonourable not to reject the ultimatum. Both Tewfik and Abdul Hamid were still uncertain whether Arabi's forces could resist and were hedging their bets. The British fleet bombarded Alexandria for ten hours, destroying all the forts and part of the city. Arabi evacuated his forces, leaving Alexandria in flames.

Sultan Abdul Hamid at last accepted the principle of sending Turkish troops to restore order, but he still prevaricated as he bargained with the British ambassador about the terms under which he would intervene. As he had not abandoned all hope of appearing to the Egyptians as their protector against the infidel, he failed to declare Arabi a rebel. Arabi still enjoyed popular support in the country and was maintaining a reasonable degree of order and security.

Meanwhile the mood in Britain was becoming increasingly jingoistic. Gladstone and some of the cabinet were still against invasion, fearing the consequences. France and the other European powers were not unhappy with the bombardment of Alexandria but they were totally opposed to any unilateral British occupation of Egypt. In the end the imperialists in the cabinet, supported by the British public, prevailed. Gladstone's request for funds for an expeditionary force was overwhelmingly endorsed by the House of Commons. He justified his action by claiming that Arabi and his followers were anti-Christian militarists who cared nothing for the liberties of the people. The insecurity of the Suez Canal was only a symptom, for 'the seat of the disease is in the interior of Egypt, in its disturbed and its anarchical condition.'

Arabi was no great military leader and he was dilatory in manning Egypt's defences – partly because he still believed that Britain would come to terms. Also he honestly believed that Britain would respect the neutrality of the Suez Canal, and he accepted the urgent appeals of the aged de Lesseps that he should do the same. He failed to cover his eastern flank. British warships appeared at Port Said and Suez and closed the Canal. Arabi's 10,000 regular troops and a rabble of hastily recruited *fellahin* were no match for the 30,000 troops of the British expeditionary force. At the battle of Tel el-Kebir, on 13 September 1882, the Egyptians were surprised and routed. Ten thousand Egyptians were lost, compared with the fifty-seven British dead and twenty-two missing. The British commander wrote in his official report on the battle, 'I do not believe that in any previous period of our military history have the British Infantry distinguished itself more than upon this occasion.'

British troops occupied Cairo. Arabi and his associates surrendered, and the khedive's authority was formally restored as the council of ministers made submission. In a laconic decree, Tewfik announced that the Egyptian army had been disbanded. But it was not possible to return to the previous *status quo*; for all his failings, Arabi had permanently changed Egypt through his unsuccessful movement. For the first time, a subject oriental people had attempted to throw off the domination of a privileged minority to establish its own form of constitutional representative government in defiance of the European powers. As one of his admirers, General Gordon, remarked, 'He will live for centuries; they will never be "your obedient servants" again.'

The fact that most of Arabi's former political allies now deserted to the khedive could not disguise the reality that the khedive was now a British puppet. The National Party had been destroyed, but his real authority had gone with it. He was not even allowed to shoot Arabi without trial as a rebel: Britain insisted that the colonel should have a fair trial, and his costs were paid for by liberal-minded British sympathizers. (He was eventually sentenced to exile in Ceylon, where he spent eighteen years.)

Britain now faced a dilemma. Despite dark French and Ottoman suspicions that it had always intended to seize control of the Suez Canal and the lower Nile, Britain knew that the acquisition of Egypt and its incorporation into the empire was out of the question. For one thing it would almost certainly have provoked a European war for which the British government, with its small army and its continued preoccupation with Irish affairs, was quite unprepared. A month after Tel el-Kebir, in response to a question in the House of Commons as to whether Britain contemplated an indefinite occupation of Egypt, Gladstone replied, 'Undoubtedly, of all things in the world, that is a thing which we are not going to do.' On the other hand, immediate evacuation was also out of the question, as the puppet khedive's regime could hardly have survived and vital British interests were at stake. The Gladstone government sent Lord Dufferin, a sophisticated statesman (a former governor-general of Canada and a future viceroy of India), to Cairo to recommend a solution. He roundly concluded that 'The Valley of the Nile could not be administered from London as it would arouse the permanent hatred and suspicion of the Egyptians.' He rejected both direct rule as in the colonies and indirect rule through a British resident as in the princely states of India. But Dufferin's own well-intentioned solution was vague: it was a matter of persuading the Egyptians that all Britain wanted was to help them to govern themselves 'under the uncompromising aegis of British friendship'.

In the end the Egyptians got neither direct nor indirect rule but a unique and curious hybrid. Egypt was not incorporated into the empire but it became the most important link in Britain's imperial system – a situation which lasted until the Second World War. British power in Egypt was overwhelming, but it always had to be exercised with apparent restraint. For one thing the other European powers, led by France, were bitterly jealous of Britain's control of the Nile and the Canal and retained important rights. Anglo-French dual control was abolished but the Caisse of Public Debt, the Capitulations and the international status of the Canal remained.

The person chosen to manage this unprecedented type of relationship between two countries was Evelyn Baring, who had returned to India after his first service in Egypt on the Caisse but was now brought back with the misleadingly modest title of British agent and consul-general in Egypt. Despite his unusual position, Baring – later Lord Cromer – was to become the archetype of the British imperial proconsul at the zenith of the empire. He was upright and dedicated, if quietly arrogant (being nicknamed 'over-Baring'). His genuine sympathies for the Egyptians – especially the *fellahin* – were always patronizing. In his twenty-four years as the real ruler of Egypt, he never learned any Arabic (leaving that to his oriental secretary). He had no love for Egyptian nationalists who believed that their people were capable of governing themselves. He acquired extraordinary influence in London – British foreign secretaries came and went, but Cromer remained.

When Cromer (as he will now be called) arrived in 1883, he believed he could set up a stable regime with British advisers which would make it possible for British troops to be withdrawn – provided the British government could end all interference by other European powers. But this was quite impractical, as he soon realized. Moreover, Egypt was under serious military threat from the south. Muhammad Ali's quasi-empire in the Sudan had remained under Turco-Egyptian rule for some sixty years until in 1881 it was destroyed by a rebellion under the inspired politico-religious leadership of Muhammad ibn Abdullah – 'the Mahdi'. Egyptian garrisons were overwhelmed and then in the spring of 1883, just as Cromer was arriving in Egypt, an entire Sudanese Egyptian force led by British officers was wiped out by the Mahdi's troops. Egypt itself was under threat.

The Gladstone government was now fully aware of what it had taken on in Egypt. Britain had not only to stabilize the regime but also to protect it. There was no question of recovering the Sudan from the Mahdi with the forces available so, with Cromer's approval, an evacuation policy was forced on the reluctant khedive and his ministers. Cromer did not, however, approve of the government's decision to send the eccentric General Gordon to oversee the orderly evacuation of the remaining scattered Egyptian garrisons. This had huge public support in Britain – Gordon was a popular hero who had served in various parts of the empire as well as acting as governor-general of Sudan in the time of Ismail, vainly attempting to put down the slave trade. 'Chauvinists and humanitarians', in Cromer's words, now combined to pursue a more forward Sudanese policy. As Cromer had suspected, when Gordon was appointed, rather than carrying out the evacuation policy, he stayed on in beleaguered Khartoum in the belief that he could come to terms with the Mahdi and end his rebellion. A relief expedition from Egypt failed to reach him in time, and in January 1885 Khartoum was overwhelmed by the Mahdist forces and Gordon was speared to death on the steps of Government House.

The Mahdi himself died during the siege, but Sudan now came under the rule of his successor, the Khalifa, for thirteen years until it was slowly and painfully recaptured by an Anglo-Egyptian army under General Kitchener.

The Sudanese question was now temporarily shelved. The Mahdist forces were unable to penetrate upper Egypt, as had been feared. The British troops in Egypt, who had begun to reorganize the Egyptian army, were capable of seeing to the country's defence, but there could be no question of their immediate withdrawal. However, the British government – now led by the cool and calculating Tory Lord Salisbury – was still prepared to try to reach an agreement with the sultan and the European powers which would allow a British evacuation within a few years provided Britain's interests were safeguarded. Salisbury sent Sir Drummond Wolff as his representative to Istanbul to negotiate with the Sultan, and Wolff and the sultan's envoy went to Egypt to arrange a settlement which would allow the British troops to withdraw from Egypt 'in a convenient period'. But the other powers, led by France and Russia, were bitterly opposed to Salisbury's insistence that Britain should have the right to return to Egypt whenever it pleased. As Sultan Abdul Hamid characteristically prevaricated, Salisbury's attitude hardened. While he continued to give priority to the maintenance of a European balance of power, he foresaw the coming scramble for Africa and also Egypt's crucial importance as both the gateway to India and the outlet of the Nile. While he had not abandoned the belief he had inherited from Disraeli that the survival of the Ottoman Empire was the best protection against Russian encroachment in the eastern Mediterranean, he was beginning to look on it as fatally diseased and to consider Egypt as a substitute.

In May 1887 Wolff and the Turkish envoys provided for the evacuation of the British garrison, leaving Egypt a neutral territory. However, Article 5 of the draft Anglo-Turkish Convention stipulated that British troops would not withdraw 'if there was any appearance of danger in the interior or without'. Abdul Hamid was faced with a dilemma. If he ratified the Convention it would set a precedent for other powers to occupy parts of his empire and then claim the right of re-entry before leaving. If he refused to ratify it he would in effect be abandoning even his nominal suzerainty over Egypt. In the event he decided to reject the Convention, and the most important part of the Arab world was lost to his empire.

Cromer was delighted with the sultan's decision – he felt he had managed to obtain a grip on Egyptian affairs and was restoring the country to solvency. As he characteristically wrote in his retirement, 'All history was there to prove that when once a civilized Power lays its hand on a weak State in a barbarous or semi-civilized condition, it rarely relaxed its grasp.' The British occupation of Egypt, which was to last seventy-four years, had happened almost by accident – it was neither planned nor foreseen. However, although Britain periodically affirmed its intention to withdraw (one calculation was that various ministers declared withdrawal to be imminent no fewer than seventy-two times during those years), the British came increasingly to take Egypt for granted. It was not coloured red on the map, but every British schoolboy somehow perceived that it was. It was inconceivable that Britain should give up control of the gateway to its empire in Asia and Africa.

However, as we have seen, Britain's control over Egypt was far from absolute. Annexation was out of the question as the European powers, led by France, had made clear that this could lead to war. The Caisse of Public Debt and the Capitulations remained the instruments of international control over Egypt's finances. It was twenty-two years before the 1904 Entente Cordiale between Britain and France settled a number of outstanding differences between the two colonial powers in Africa and Asia (and also prepared the way for the Anglo-French alliance against Germany in the First World War). In particular, the Entente provided that Britain would renounce its rights and interests in Morocco (preparing the way for France's occupation of Morocco a few years later) while the French did the same for Egypt, accepting that no time-limit should be fixed for the British occupation. The Caisse of Public Debt was not abolished but its authority was much reduced.

Lord Milner, another great British imperial proconsul, called British rule in Egypt 'the Veiled Protectorate' – a system by which Cromer ruled from behind a screen provided by the khedive and his cabinet, whose members all had British advisers in their ministries. There were two main strands to Cromer's thinking: in politics he was an arch-imperialist, and in financial and economic matters he was a Gladstonian *laissez-faire* liberal. Fortunately, in Egypt the two ideologies were easy to combine. He had no belief that the Egyptians were capable of governing themselves, or ever would be. To use one of his own favourite phrases, they were a natural 'subject race', in contrast to the supreme Anglo-Saxon example of a 'governing race'. The Turkish aristocracy had the remnants of a capacity to rule, but its members were hopelessly decadent and corrupt. Like many of his colleagues, he had a patronizing affection for the hard-pressed *fellahin*, but he saw no point in training them to manage their own affairs – money spent on their education above the very lowest level was a dangerous waste. He had no doubt that Egypt would benefit from the europeanization of every aspect of life, although he realized with regret that this was impossible.

Egypt's commitments to repay Ismail's debts absorbed more than half its revenues, requiring the utmost financial prudence (which in any case fitted Cromer's Gladstonian principles). Fortified by his experience in India, Cromer believed in the thesis of John Stuart Mill, which had been adopted by Gladstone, that taxation should be as low as possible, to allow money to 'fructify' in the pockets of the producing classes. Accordingly there were no tax increases (the public could hardly have borne them) with the significant exception that, on the free-trade principle, countervailing duties were imposed on the products of Egyptian industries to equalize their prices with those of foreign imports. This virtually wiped out the Egyptian tobacco industry.

Slowly and painfully the economy recovered, and by the 1890s the budgets were showing small surpluses. The mainstay of the recovery was the increase in the output of agricultural crops – principally cotton, but also cereals, beans and rice. This was greatly assisted by one of the only kind of public works that Cromer was prepared to countenance – irrigation. British engineers, most of them with previous experience in India, set about repairing the great Delta barrages and canals built under Muhammad Ali and Ismail and expanding the system. Their crowning achievement was the building of a new dam at Aswan in upper Egypt. Completed in 1902 and raised further in 1907 and 1912, this saved vast quantities of water by evening out the flow of the Nile between the autumn flood season and the rest of the year.

Unable to reduce taxes, as they would have wished, Cromer and his advisers set about improving the lot of the *fellahin* by replacing the corvée with paid labour and preventing the use of the *kurbaj*. This was gradually achieved during the first decade of British rule.

There was no doubt that Egypt was now better administered than before. Government decisions were normally carried out; an effective and reasonably uncorrupt civil service was being created. One of the most important factors in this was that the British officials in the Anglo-Egyptian service were collecting the kind of statistical information without which effective government is impossible. In this respect Egypt was unique in the Ottoman Empire.

With the exception of a few Liberal and Radical MPs at Westminster, the British people, encouraged by the evidence of the tens of thousands of tourists who poured into Egypt every winter, had no doubt that the Egyptians should be wholly grateful for Cromer's efforts on their behalf. The reaction of the Egyptians was inevitably more various and complex. The khedive and his ministers, together with the Turco-Circassian ruling class from which they almost exclusively came, were happy that their power had been restored and that a radical nationalist upheaval had been averted. Their view was shared by those who had been temporarily swept by enthusiasm for the Arabi revolt. Shaikh Muhammad Abduh, the most important of Arabi's civilian supporters, decided to collaborate with the British occupiers when he was allowed to return from exile in 1884. He agreed to become a judge and began to work for the reform and modernization of Islamic education in Egypt. Cromer liked and respected him but felt that his task was impossible.

If the Egyptian ruling class temporarily accepted the presence of British troops, however, it was much less enthusiastic about what Nubar Pasha, the first prime minister after 1882, called the 'administrative occupation'. Nubar tried to retain Egyptian control over the civil police, but failed. His successor, Riaz Pasha, was equally unsuccessful in preventing European supervision of the legal system – European inspectors were appointed to the native courts. On both these matters Cromer was adamant. The truth was that inside every Egyptian, however much he had benefited materially from the British occupation, there was some degree of resentment against rule by a Christian European power. Inevitably, this resentment would grow over the years.

In the early years of the British occupation there was a remarkable growth in rural unrest and acts of brigandage. This both alarmed and mystified Cromer, who had a passion for good order. It was partly a grass-roots rejection of the occupation but it also reflected the breakdown of the traditional system whereby the *omdehs* or village mayors, appointed by the government, maintained law and order in the countryside in collaboration with the Islamic *qadis* or judges. Although the *omdehs* were sometimes arbitrary and cruel, they generally reflected the local viewpoint. It was a system that the *fellah* could understand.

It is true that European secularist principles of law had already been introduced into Egypt long before the British occupation. Muhammad Ali had started the process, which was extended by the introduction of the new Ottoman penal code, based on French law, in 1863. By 1880 the Islamic *sharia* law was confined to matters of personal status (divorce, inheritance etc.) and homicide. The trouble was that these principles were now being applied much more widely – to matters of government as well as law – under the aegis of a Christian colonial power. At least this was the theory.

In 1883 Lord Dufferin actually persuaded Tewfik to issue an

Organic Law granting the right of universal suffrage to male Egyptians over twenty years of age. But Cromer saw to it that the elected legislative and provincial councils remained powerless. As we have seen, he had no faith in the capacity of Egyptians to govern themselves, and he considered representative institutions to be entirely unsuitable for the government of a 'subject race'.

Nor did Cromer believe there was any purpose in training an élite of native Egyptians to take over the higher executive positions – in fact, during his twenty-four years in Egypt, their numbers in the higher ranks of the government service actually declined, while those of Englishmen and other Europeans increased. Accordingly, he had little interest in the spread of education above the elementary level. From his experience in India he had concluded that the expansion of Western-style higher education manufactured a class of discontented and place-seeking demagogues who were divorced from their own people. As he wrote shortly before his retirement, 'I am doing all I can to push forward both elementary and technical education. I want all the next generation of Egyptians to be able to read and write. Also I want to create as many carpenters, bricklayers, plasterers etc., as I possibly can. More than this I cannot do.' Unfortunately, even these efforts were not very successful. On his retirement, about 1.5 per cent of the population was receiving primary education as compared with 1.7 per cent in 1873, and the vast majority remained illiterate.

Cromer reversed Muhammad Ali's and Ismail's policy of providing free education in state schools and colleges. His *laissez-faire* principles told him that it was not the state's duty to provide education, and this also accorded with his general aim to economize. The result was that higher education became the prerogative of the wealthy. Like the great majority of his British colleagues in Egypt, Cromer was unsympathetic towards proposals to establish a university, which he believed would foster dangerous nationalism. However, he did not interfere with the higher institutes of learning which had survived from Ismail's reign: the schools of medicine, engineering and law. Since the reformed Egyptian legal system was based on French law, the teachers in the law school were French and it was this, in the absence of a university, which became the focus of nationalism.

The obverse side of the neglect of education under Cromer was that there was no systematic attempt to impose English culture on Egypt in the manner in which the French aimed to produce a

Gallicized élite in their North African possessions. The educational system was only partially and gradually brought under British control and Anglicized. Although the use of English inevitably became more widespread, and ambitious young Egyptians needed to acquire it, the Egyptian upper classes remained francophone. This was partly because of the limitations of the Veiled Protectorate and partly because Cromer would have regarded the effort to turn the native Egyptians into pseudo-Englishmen as futile; he had nothing but contempt for the few Egyptians who managed to acquire a university education abroad and became europeanized.

It was therefore natural that Cromer should make no attempt to interfere with the Islamic system of education which existed in the village *kuttabs* or Koranic schools and the *madrasahs* attached to the mosques which served for secondary education. This would have provoked a most hostile reaction. Again the principle of *laissez-faire* served all his purposes. But while he respected the laws of Islam, he expressed the view that as a progressive social system it was a total failure. He often said that Egypt could never have a genuinely civilized society under Islam – the position of women alone making this impossible – but he had no wish to see Egyptians abandon their religion. He felt that the europeanized Egyptian he so despised was 'generally an agnostic'. But while he sympathized with the efforts of Muhammad Abduh – who had become grand mufti of Egypt – to reform and modernize the education system at the great al-Azhar mosque in Cairo, he was sure they were fruitless because 'reformed Islam is Islam no longer.'

Cromer's authoritarianism was so often negative rather than positive in its expression. He favoured *laissez-faire* rather than firm government action. He considered that Egypt was a natural agricultural country and that the *fellah* was a good farmer – better than his Indian equivalent – who with enough land and low taxation would produce well. He considered Muhammad Ali's ambition to turn Egypt into a manufacturing country as unrealistic, as it would have required heavy protective tariffs and an expensive programme of industrial training for Egyptians, to which he was naturally opposed.

With prudent financial management Egypt was prosperous at the turn of the century, and real *per capita* income was probably higher than at any subsequent period. But this concealed some real weaknesses. The level of dependence on a single crop – cotton – was dangerous, and there were technical problems in overflooding from irrigation through lack of drainage and a variety of cotton pests which the parsimonious government was hesitant to tackle. Moreover, although Cromer hoped for the creation of a large class of Egyptian small farmers who would act as a conservative bulwark to society, only the most vigorous government action could have prevented the new prosperity from accruing to those who were already economically powerful – the big land-owners – while the *fellahin* sank deeper into debt. After twenty-four years of Cromerism, 80 per cent of those who owned land in Egypt possessed less than 25 per cent of the whole, while at the other end of the scale 1 per cent owned more than 40 per cent of the whole.

Egyptian nationalists would later claim that Cromer deliberately planned to make Egypt a vast cotton plantation, producing cheap raw material for the Lancashire cotton mills. But he had no such conscious intention – to him this was a natural role for a 'subject race'. Moreover, although he would not have liked to admit it, he was in many respects continuing the policies of Ismail.

In 1892 Khedive Tewfik died and was succeeded by his 17-year-old son Abbas Hilmi, who was being educated in Europe. Cromer at first thought that Abbas would be as pliable as Tewfik, but he was intelligent and forceful – more in the mould of his grandfather Ismail than his father. Soon he attempted to assert himself by rejecting Cromer's choice of ministers and criticizing the standard of the British-trained Egyptian army. Since his succession coincided with the first new stirrings of nationalist feeling since the collapse of the Arabi revolt, Abbas began to see himself as leading a challenge to British rule. Cromer was thoroughly alarmed.

His fears were unnecessary. Abbas was hoping for help from Istanbul – Egypt was still nominally part of the Ottoman Empire. But, as usual, Sultan Abdul Hamid gave no more than verbal promises of support, as he was quite unprepared to risk his relations with Britain or the other European powers, which might have no love for the British occupation but equally had no wish to see any revival of Egyptian independence. Abbas had also hoped that the return to power of Gladstone's Liberal government in Britain would help him, because the Liberals professed greater understanding of Egyptian nationalism than the Tories. Unfortunately, Gladstone's foreign secretary was Lord Rosebery, a Liberal imperialist who gave his full support to Cromer. Seeing that he could be forced to abdicate, the humiliated Abbas capitulated. The Veiled Protectorate continued, with Cromer pulling the strings behind his screen.

When Abbas challenged the quality of the Anglo-Egyptian army, a furious Kitchener, its *sirdar* or commander-in-chief, threatened to resign. Since the army's dissolution in 1882, British officers had trained a new force of some 15,000 which included five black battalions of southern Sudanese tribesmen. (The cost was borne by the Egyptian budget, with an additional contribution towards the stationing of the British occupying troops.) The first purpose of the new army was to help defend Egypt's borders, but by 1892 both Cromer and the British government had come to regard the reconquest of the Sudan as vital. Italy had penetrated Ethiopia and was threatening to gain control of the waters of the upper Nile, and, as Cromer wrote to London, 'Whatever Powers hold the Upper Nile Valley must, by the mere force of its geographical situation, dominate Egypt.'

Reconquest began in 1895. Cautiously and economically, Kitchener's army, strengthened by 8,000 British troops, advanced up the Nile and finally routed the Mahdist forces outside their capital, Omdurman.

The difficult question arose as to the future status of the Sudan. The reconquest had been directed by Britain but it had been carried out in the khedive's name mainly by Egyptian troops at Egypt's expense. But there was no question of restoring the *status quo* of before the Mahdist revolt. In Salisbury's words, the British government had every intention of keeping 'a predominant voice in all matters connected with the Sudan'. The result was the decision to establish an Anglo-Egyptian condominium. Hailed as a masterpiece of British pragmatism, this worked reasonably well for some years. One advantage was that it prevented the system of Capitulations from being extended to the Sudan. But the theoretical equality of Britain and Egypt in the government of Sudan was no more than a façade: the higher levels of the administration were all in British hands, and the governor-general, who was appointed by the khedive on British advice, was always an Englishman. Egyptians had not abandoned their claim to rule Sudan and as they recovered their independence from Britain this became the most contentious issue between Britain and Egypt.

The nationalist renaissance in Egypt, on which Khedive Abbas had vainly hoped to capitalize, gathered strength in Cromer's last years, before his retirement in 1907. It found its leader in a slender and passionate youth named Mustafa Kamel who, like several other nationalists, had studied law in Cairo and in France, where he had received encouragement for his views. Cromer was inclined to dismiss the nationalists as insignificant, and it was true that they had all the characteristics of salon intellectuals – powerfully eloquent but weak in practical proposals to meet the needs of ordinary Egyptians, from whose feelings they were divorced. These weaknesses were partly due to their style of education but also arose because the Veiled Protectorate denied them any prospect of taking a part in government.

The nationalists were also confused in their aims. Kamel was attracted to the pan-Islamic movement as the best weapon against the British occupation, and he received some secret encouragement and funds for his National Party from the sultan. But the illogicality of combining pan-Islamicism with Egyptian territorial nationalism was exposed in 1906 when Abdul Hamid, who was building a railway across Arabia to Medina, landed a force at the head of the Gulf of Aqaba and laid claim to the whole of the Sinai peninsula. Kamel and his party launched a vigorous campaign in his support. It was left to Cromer to insist that Sinai belonged to Egypt. His concern was to protect the Suez Canal from the Turks, but it was he rather than the nationalists who championed the cause of Egyptian territorial integrity.

Cromer allowed a free press to flourish in Egypt. He had a liberal streak, but principally he did not think that fiery nationalist editorials (Kamel founded his own paper in 1900) were a threat to his order. The ironic consequence was that there was greater freedom of the spoken and written word in Egypt than in the Arab Ottoman provinces. Two leading newspapers were founded in Cairo by Arab Christians from Syria.

The press was by no means exclusively anti-British, nor were all politically active supporters of Mustafa Kamel nationalists – some were mere collaborators, who were doing well out of the British occupation and saw no advantage in bringing it to an end. But there were moderates to whom Cromer gave headmasterly approval as 'the Girondists of the Egyptian national movement'. These included Shaikh Muhammad Abduh, who died in 1905, and his spiritual disciples in the Umma or People's Party. They doubted Kamel's political judgement, especially during the Aqaba incident. Another moderate was Saad Zaghloul, a young lawyer. Cromer allowed him to become head of the newly created education department and, when Cromer left Egypt, warmly commended him as the ideal type of moderate nationalist. But Zaghloul was to become the representative of uncompromising nationalism and Britain's implacable enemy.

In 1906, despite Kamel's powerful charisma, his movement was losing ground. Then an event occurred which united the national feelings of all Egyptians. Although hardly momentous in itself, it was a turning-point in the British occupation and its effects may be compared with the effect on the Indian independence movement of the Amritsar massacre in 1919. At Denshawai, a small Delta village, a shooting-party of British officers was set upon and beaten by outraged *fellahin* who believed that the British were killing the pigeons which were the local staple diet. An officer who went for help died of concussion and heat-stroke. A *fellah* who tried to help him was found by a party of British soldiers who, assuming he had murdered the officer, beat him to death.

Cromer and his colleagues, backed by the British press, saw the incident as a symptom of the xenophobic fanaticism that was sweeping the countryside, fanned by the nationalists. Exemplary punishment was required. A special tribunal sentenced four to hang, seventeen more to prison or flogging. The sentences were carried out on the site, and the villagers were compelled to watch.

This was not an atypical act of colonial repression – the horrified reaction of educated Egyptians may be taken as a tribute to the general physical mildness of the British occupation. But the shock and outrage, even among those who had come to accept the British presence, gave a lasting impetus to the national movement. When Cromer retired in the following year, the silent Egyptian crowds watched him on his route to Cairo station from behind British troops with fixed bayonets.

Cromer's reputation remained high in Britain and his own self-congratulatory account of his achievements was generally accepted, although some close observers felt that he had become increasingly out of touch, surrounding himself with nonentities like any autocrat. In 1906 a reforming Liberal government had swept to power in Britain, however, and it was clearly time for a change.

The choice of successor fell on Eldon Gorst, a senior diplomat who had spent nearly twenty years in Egypt and, as financial adviser to the Egyptian government, had led the negotiations with France over the 1904 Entente Cordiale. Small, highly ambitious and academically brilliant, his outward sense of superiority concealed an inner lack of self-confidence. He lacked Cromer's presence but, unlike Cromer, he spoke excellent Arabic. He was not much liked by other Anglo-Egyptian officials.

Gorst was thrilled with his appointment. He wrote, 'Throughout the British Empire there is no place in which the occupant enjoys greater freedom of action than that of British Agent and consul-general in Egypt. The consul-general is *de facto* ruler of the country, without being hampered by a parliament or by a network of councils like the viceroy of India . . .' But, having stepped into Cromer's shoes, he felt that a change of direction was needed:

I wanted [he said] to render our rule more sympathetic to the Egyptians in general and to the Mohammadens in particular by preventing the British element riding roughshod over the Egyptians, by putting a check on the annual British invasion of new recruits, by giving great encouragement to the Egyptian official class, and last, but not least, by giving a more national character to the educational system.

Gorst was trying not to end the British occupation but to make it more acceptable and, by so doing, to subdue the nationalist ferment. To the fury of his British colleagues he set about reducing their powers in favour of the Egyptian *mudirs* (district officers) and he tried to blow life into the moribund provincial councils to act as the *mudirs'* advisers. But Gorst's principal strategy was to restore the authority of the khedive, which had been emasculated by Cromer. His rapprochement with Abbas allowed the khedive to replace the ministers who had been subservient to Cromer with others more to his liking. But the khedive was no democrat: he shared Gorst's aim of reducing the influence of the nationalists who challenged his authority. As happens so often, however, the modest degree of liberalization merely fuelled the nationalist demands. Agitation increased, and the press heaped an avalanche of abuse on Egyptian ministers as well as the English occupiers. Gorst found himself restoring the repressive press law of 1881 which Cromer had never found it necessary to use because he despised the native press and regarded it as a useful outlet for young Egypt to let off steam. In the countryside there was an alarming new crime wave which partly reflected the rebellious spirit of the nation. Gorst introduced a Relegation Law allowing suspected brigands to be imprisoned without trial in a new penal colony in the Kharga Oasis.

In common with not a few of the academically brilliant, Gorst lacked political imagination. His next error, in 1910, was to attempt to extend the Suez Canal Company's original ninety-nine-year concession, due to expire in 1968, by forty years in return for an annual share of the profits. He persuaded the shadowy general assembly to approve the Company's offer, but even this gathering of elderly and conservative notables was unable to accept something which so outraged Egyptian public opinion. The Canal Company was already regarded as a foreign 'state within a state'. Only one assembly member dared to vote in favour of acceptance. Gorst was obliged to let the matter drop.

Two days later Boutros Ghali, the Coptic grandee whom the khedive had chosen as prime minister, was assassinated by a young Egyptian nationalist. Ghali was unfairly regarded as a British stooge and, as minister of justice, he had presided over the Denshewai trial. When Gorst refused to reprieve him from execution, the assassin became a hero in the streets of Cairo.

Gorst's policies appeared to be in ruins, and there was uproar in Britain. Arthur Balfour, leader of the Conservative opposition in the House of Commons, used the occasion to deliver a philosophical address on the general unsuitability of self-government for 'orientals'. The former US president Theodore Roosevelt, who passed through Egypt on his return from an African hunting-trip, told the British to 'govern or get out'.

Although he did lack political flair, the well-intentioned Gorst was also unlucky and he faced the obstructive opposition of most of his British colleagues. His term of office began with a financial collapse and an acute recession. He might have recovered the situation if he had retained his energy and interest, but he was facing an agonizing death from cancer of the spine. In 1911 he had to go.

In some respects Kitchener, the hero of Omdurman, was the obvious successor. Deprived by the Liberal government of his ambition to become viceroy of India, where he had been commander-in-chief, he was glad to accept what he regarded as the almost equally important post of British agent in Egypt. He was soon entertaining visions of the annexation of Egypt to Britain, with himself as the first viceroy of Egypt and Sudan. He shared the dream of Cecil Rhodes – an Africa coloured red on the map from Cairo to Cape.

The British government warned that, while order must be restored, there must be no simple replacement of civilian rule by the military. Kitchener's style was much closer to that of Cromer than that of Gorst. He once again emasculated the role of the khedive, his old opponent. He restored the power of the British advisers and increased their numbers. His personal ascendancy – semi-regal in style – was even greater than that of Cromer, who expressed alarm from his retirement. The proctorate's veil had virtually been removed.

With a series of repressive measures, Kitchener succeeded in scattering the nationalists (whose morale had not recovered from Mustafa Kamel's premature death in 1908), but he did not rely merely on coercion. Like Cromer, he showed sympathy with the *fellahin*, but he took more practical steps to try to help them, attempting to familiarize himself with their problems in a series of quasi-royal visits to the countryside. He ordered the belated establishment of Egypt's first Ministry of Agriculture. He tried to tackle the problem of acute overflooding in the Delta by means of drainage, and that of *fellahin* indebtedness with a new law which made it impossible to recover in the courts any money lent to a *fellah* who owned less than five *feddans* (a *feddan* being about one acre), that is 90 per cent of all *fellahin*. The economics of this measure were doubtful, as it undermined the new Agricultural Bank which had been founded to relieve the *fellahin* from the grip of the usurers. But it at least temporarily raised the morale of the *fellahin*, who showed reasonable content with Kitchener's policies.

Having pacified the countryside – the Egypt which mattered in the view of both Kitchener and Cromer – he felt he could ignore the despised urban intelligentsia. In 1913 he even felt confident enough to allow some constitutional changes, to satisfy both the Liberal government at home and the moderate nationalists in Egypt. A new partially elected legislative assembly was given some powers over taxation and the right to interrogate ministers. This was a cynical exercise, because Kitchener had no more belief than Cromer or Balfour in the value of representative institutions for orientals, but he felt it would be a useful palliative and that those he dubbed the 'noisy extremists' would be excluded. But he was wrong. Saad Zaghloul, now emerging as a truly intransigent nationalist, was elected first vice-president of the new assembly. Zaghloul showed himself a skilled parliamentarian and under his leadership the assembly so criticized and discredited government ministers that they were delighted when the parliamentary session ended. The start of the First World War before the next session was due to begin brought the tentative exercise in constitutional government to an end.

Kitchener claimed credit for restoring order to Egypt, but later experience shows that he was fortunate and his luck would not have lasted. If it had not been for the war, which gave Britain the excuse to clamp down on political activity, the new nationalist ferment could not easily have been contained.

When the First World War brought Britain, France and Russia into conflict with Germany and Austro-Hungary, Britain hoped that Turkey would remain neutral and that Egypt could be kept out of the war. Britain's sole strategic concern was the security of the Suez Canal. When Turkey decided to join the Central Powers – Germany and Austro-Hungary – in November 1914, Egypt's status became a problem for it was still nominally part of the Ottoman Empire. There were strong voices in the cabinet (in which Kitchener became minister of war) in favour of annexing Egypt and abolishing the Muhammad Ali dynasty. But the remaining British officials in Egypt demurred at the prospect of direct rule and, at a time when Germany was being accused of tearing up international treaties, the Foreign Office was opposed to breaking the countless undertakings not to annex Egypt.

The typical British compromise was to declare a protectorate, in December 1914, and simply to remove the figment of Ottoman suzerainty. The pro-Ottoman Khedive Abbas was conveniently on a European tour and was informed that he had abdicated. A replacement was found in his elderly and amiable uncle Hussein Kamel. There were still problems: Hussein Kamel could hardly be given the same title as his new suzerain King George V of England, so a compromise was reached on 'Sultan', to be addressed as 'Hautesse' instead of 'Majesté'. The new sultan died in 1917 and was replaced by his younger brother, Prince Ahmed Fuad. Fuad was not satisfactory, however – although no Anglophobe, he had been educated in Italy, where he lived with his exiled father Khedive Ismail, he spoke little Arabic and he made no attempt to hide his lack of sympathy for Egypt and its problems.

Still unresolved was the question of whether Egypt had become part of the British Empire and the Egyptians British subjects. Cromer, in retirement, considered that Egypt was now in the empire, but in fact the matter was left in abeyance. The protectorate declaration merely said that all Egyptian subjects 'will be entitled to receive the protection of His Majesty's government'. Egypt remained officially neutral, with Britain responsible for its defence, but Egyptians were expected to contribute to the war effort. Egyptian troops helped to defend the Suez Canal against the first and only Turkish attack. Over 20,000 Egyptians served in the camel transport and labour corps in Palestine and in France, and suffered heavy casualties.

The disadvantage of failing to annex Egypt was that Britain was unable to abolish the Capitulations and all the other international commitments. On the other hand, the fact that Britain never colonized Egypt as France colonized Algeria meant that the eventual Egyptian independence was not bought at the cost of a long and bloody war.

The British remained ambiguous about the concept of an Egyptian nation – as did many Egyptians, although for different reasons. Cromer had described Egypt as a 'nondescript country'. Since a 'true Egyptian' was indefinable, an 'Egypt for the Egyptian' policy was nonsense. When Egypt ever achieved a self-governing body, he said, all the communities should have to have representation, and since the Europeans and Levantines (Italians, Greeks, Maltese etc.) – those whom Cromer called the 'Brahmins of Egypt' – contributed by far the most to the country's wealth, these should be represented out of proportion to their numbers. During the war, these ideas were codified by the British judicial adviser in a proposed constitution which would have given the British advisers and the foreign communities permanent control over all legislation. But by then such ideas were not only insensitive but quite unrealistic. The spirit of Egyptian nationalism, although forced underground during the war, emerged with renewed vigour when the war ended. The existence of an Egyptian nation became undeniable.

6. Turks and Arabs

Greek independence followed by the enforced Turkish withdrawal from most of the Balkans during the nineteenth century, caused the centre of gravity of the Ottoman Empire to shift inexorably eastwards. Because the sultan/caliph no longer ruled over millions of Christian Europeans, he was no longer a threat and a challenge to the powers of Europe. But he could aspire to leadership in Asia.

The shift towards Asia was increased by the loss of control over Arab North Africa, which had already achieved a large degree of independence. Algeria and Tunisia went to the French in 1830 and 1881. The great prize of Egypt, whose al-Azhar mosque/university underpinned the caliph's spiritual authority, was lost almost unnecessarily to the British in 1882. Tripoli, the last Ottoman foothold on the North African coast, was seized by the Italians in 1912, as Lord Kitchener in Cairo ensured Egypt's neutrality in the Turkish–Italian war.

However, Sultan Abdul Hamid still controlled the Arab heartland and the first great centres of Arab/Muslim civilization, from Mecca and Medina to Baghdad, Jerusalem, Damascus and Aleppo. Turkey controlled most of the hinterland of the Arabian peninsula – although the British had a colony in Aden, dominated the waters of the Persian Gulf and were establishing special treaty arrangements with the coastal shaikhdoms. Ironically, the opening of the Suez Canal had made it easier to send troops to re-establish the Ottoman Empire's hold on Yemen.

The Ottoman hold over this vast territory, with its plains, mountain ranges and river systems, varied in form and intensity. In many areas hereditary local dynasties, strengthened by their geographical remoteness in mountains and valleys, were allowed substantial autonomy in return for maintaining adequate forces, pacifying the surrounding countryside and collecting taxes. In some cases, as in northern Mesopotamia, they were needed to protect the empire's frontiers against the rival Persian Empire. In others, as in Mount Lebanon where they were indigenous rather than a Mamluke military caste, they were the most effective rulers because they had the loyalty of their people. But there were also large areas of steppe and desert which were dominated by powerful groups of nomadic tribes, such as the Shammar or Bani Sakhr, who could not be prevented from plundering the traditional trade and pilgrimage routes.

Life in the great cities was fairly stable and secure, but in the countryside it changed considerably and frequently according to the competence and authority of the local governors. It was into this variegated system that, from 1820 onwards, an attempt was made to introduce the reforms of the *Tanzimat* in order to centralize and streamline the administration of the state. The overall aim was to modernize and strengthen the empire in the face of the European threat.

Being based on an ideal rather than on reason, these reforms inevitably had indifferent results. They changed much over fifty years and they also disrupted. Since they introduced modern secular ideas, such as citizenship and universal equality before the law, they were opposed by the powerful religious authorities. They undermined delicate relationships which had stood the test of time between the many minorities which composed the Asian empire. Moreover, the disruption allowed the European powers, which were steadily increasing their economic influence throughout the Levant and Mesopotamia in the nineteenth century, to extend their political influence too. Two processes were therefore at work which were ultimately bound to conflict – Ottoman centralization and European penetration.

Mount Lebanon, with its large Maronite Christian population, provided the most suitable theatre for European intervention. The local rulers – the Shihabi amirs – had converted from Sunni Islam to become Maronites at the end of the eighteenth century. The outstanding Amir Bashir II played off the Maronite peasantry against the Druze peasantry and allied himself with the Egyptians during the period of Ibrahim Pasha's rule (1831–40).

When Ottoman rule was restored, the Shihabi princes were removed and, in the face of open Maronite/Druze conflict, Mount Lebanon was divided by the Ottomans, with strong encouragement from the European powers, into two administrative units – one for the Maronites and one for the Druze. Lebanon had its first government on a confessional basis. But this did not work. For one thing, the Maronites formed a majority in the Druze 'qaimaqamate'. More-

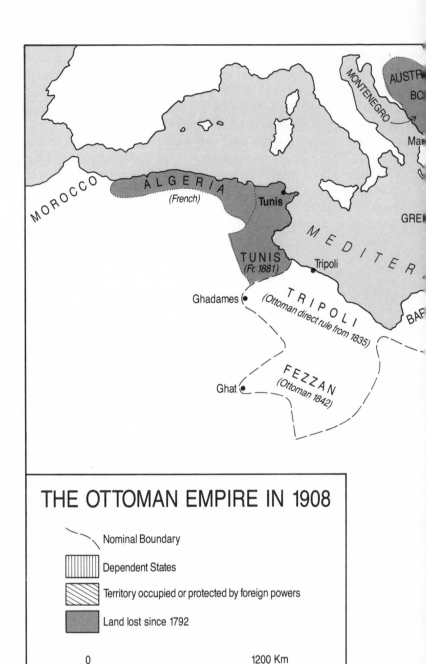

MOROCCO

ALGERIA
(French)

Tunis

TUNIS
(Fr. 1881)

Tripoli

Ghadames

T R I P O L I
(Ottoman direct rule from 1835)

F E Z Z A N
(Ottoman 1842)

Ghat

MONTENEGRO

AUSTR
BC

Ma

MEDITER

GRE

BAR

THE OTTOMAN EMPIRE IN 1908

Nominal Boundary

Dependent States

Territory occupied or protected by foreign powers

Land lost since 1792

| 0 | | | 1200 Km |
| 0 | | | 800 Miles |

Source: Bernard Lewis, *The Emergence of Modern Turkey*, Oxford University Press, 1961

over, the whole region was in a state of disruption, as the traditional economy disintegrated under the invasion of Western products which began under Ibrahim Pasha.

The instability and tension increased until civil war broke out in 1860. The Druze landlords of Mount Lebanon wished to curb their Maronite tenants, who were increasing in numbers and wealth, and attacked and massacred them in thousands. This sparked off a wave of persecutions of Christians in other parts of Syria. France, which with varying degrees of encouragement from the Ottoman sultan had long regarded itself as the protector of its Maronite fellow-Catholics, landed troops in Beirut and invaded the Druze stronghold of the Shuf. A conference of European powers which had signed the Treaty of Paris following the Crimean War – which included the Ottoman Empire – met in Beirut to consider how Lebanon should be governed. The conclusion was the creation of the autonomous *sanjak* or province of Mount Lebanon, with a Christian governor chosen by the sultan from outside Lebanon and assisted by a Maronite-dominated council chosen on a confessional basis. This was to be under the protection of the six powers – Britain, France, Russia, Prussia, Austria and Italy.

Autonomous Lebanon covered only part of the present-day Lebanese Republic. It excluded Beirut, Tyre and Sidon on the coast and the Bekaa Valley to the east, and it was heavily dominated by the Maronites who formed 90 per cent of the population. Although it prospered for the next half century, its creation was a first step towards undermining the *millet* system – the ancient network of communities through which the religious minorities shared in the administration of the empire.

France was the chief patron of the Roman Catholics in the Arab Levant, and Russia of the Orthodox Christians. Britain was left as protector of the Druze and of the small community of Jews, who formed about 4 per cent of the people of Palestine. The unfortunate Armenians in the heartland of the empire lacked any effective outside patron. There were hardly any Protestant Christians in the empire, but American Protestant missionaries played a crucial role in the penetration of Western cultural influence. The founding in 1866 of the Syrian Protestant College – later the American University of Beirut – helped to stimulate alarmed French Catholics to found the Université Saint-Joseph in 1874. The two institutions would play a leading role in the cultural renaissance of the region.

In Palestine – the region known to the Christian West as the Holy

Land, which in the twentieth century was to be given defined borders
– European rivalries were peculiarly intense, as might be expected, but
their effects tended to neutralize each other. Arab Christians were a
minority, although a substantial one, and intercommunal relations
between Muslims, Christians and Jews were generally harmonious.
From the ending of Egyptian rule in Syria in 1840, the Ottomans
were able to pursue their centralizing reforms of the *Tanzimat*. These
meant reimposition of Turkish military control and the reduction of
the powers of the local feudal lords, who had become virtually
independent – levying their own taxes and fighting among themselves.
The effects of the reforms were generally beneficial. Security
improved, the population increased and the economy prospered.
Jaffa became a household name in Europe through exports of oranges
from the great plantations around it.

Although the direct power of the feudal families had been reduced,
many of them were allowed to retain considerable influence. With
economic progress and expansion, the trend was to increase the
importance of the towns, and town councils were dominated by
representatives of these families – Nimrs, Tuqans, Khalidis and
Husseinis. Despite the centralizing policies of Istanbul, the Palestinian notables retained considerable freedom to manage their affairs. Jerusalem, because of its crucial importance, was in 1874 made
an 'independent' *sanjak*, with the result that the governor of Jerusalem
was directly answerable to the sultan in Istanbul.

It was not only in Palestine that improved security helped the
economy to prosper as the population increased. In the vast plains of
western and northern Syria, European late nineteenth-century travel-
lers reported seeing limitless fields of golden corn where only a few
years earlier had been barren waste.

The progress was not without setbacks, however. Even the lands of
the ancient Fertile Crescent were dependent on an uncertain rainfall,
and the 1870s saw a series of disastrous harvests. Ottoman bankruptcy
affected the ability of the wealthier classes to invest. Finally, many
able-bodied young Syrians and Palestinians were forcibly recruited
into the Ottoman armies during the Russian and Balkan wars. However, by the 1880s the situation had improved. The Ottoman Empire
had turned eastwards from the Balkans, and the coming of the
railways vastly improved communications. Exports of silk, fruit and
wool from Syrian ports steadily increased at the turn of the century.

Mesopotamia, or Iraq, remained the most backward and ill-governed of the Arabic-speaking provinces of the Turkish Empire. Its vast resources were left untapped. After 1831, when direct rule from Istanbul was reimposed under the *Tanzimat* reforms, the Ottoman *walis* or governors were unable to make much headway in pacifying the rebellious tribes and Kurdish hill-chiefs to settle the countryside and improve communication. The most was achieved by the enlightened Midhat Pasha, who arrived in 1869. He enforced conscription, founded municipal authorities and established schools and hospitals. He attempted to dredge the Shatt al-Arab waterway – the joint outlet of the Tigris and Euphrates rivers to the Gulf – and to open the Tigris and Euphrates to regular steamer navigation. But there was a limit to what he could do in the three years of his governorship. Baghdad, once the glory of the Golden Age of Islam, remained a squalid and impoverished city compared with Cairo, Aleppo or Damascus, which retained much of their former greatness.

In spite of Mesopotamia's poverty and backwardness, however, the powers of Europe were fully aware of its potential importance. In particular, Britain – which already dominated the waters of the Persian Gulf – saw it as the gateway to India and helped to establish telegraph and postal services linking Baghdad with Istanbul, the Gulf and India. Gradually it came to regard central and southern Mesopotamia as a British sphere of influence. But other powers were probing the region. France had an interest in Mosul in northern Mesopotamia; Russia looked towards the warm waters of the Persian Gulf; and, by the end of the century, imperial Germany, the sultan's new ally, had appeared on the scene.

Britain already controlled the waters of the Gulf and in 1861 it established a land base when it signed a treaty with the ruler of Bahrain to protect his island from external claims (from Persia and Turkey) in return for British suzerainty and the exclusion of all other powers. But from the mid nineteenth century the Ottomans set out to absorb into the empire and its reformed administrative system all the independent Arab principalities of Nejd (central Arabia) and the Gulf coast. Ottoman suzerainty had lapsed in this region since the withdrawal of the Turkish fleets in the seventeenth century. In 1819 the Egyptian forces of Muhammad Ali had conquered the Saudi/Wahhabi state in Nejd on behalf of the sultan, and Turco-Egyptian authority was extended to the coastal region of al-Hasa. But the

Egyptian forces remained only until 1840, when Muhammad Ali's own quasi-imperial ambitions were cut short. The Saudi state, based on its new capital, Riyadh, revived.

A new opportunity for the Ottoman Turks arose in 1865, when the long and peaceful reign of the Saudi amir Feisal bin Turki came to an end and a violent feud over the succession broke out between his two sons. Midhat Pasha accepted the offer of vassaldom from one of them in return for Ottoman support, and in 1871 a Turkish force was dispatched by sea to establish garrisons along the Gulf coast. However, the principal result was thoroughly to alarm the British government. Britain did not at this stage interfere in the internal affairs of the Arab shaikhdoms, but it had come to regard the Gulf as a British lake, and the reappearance of the Turkish navy in however modest a form was a cause for concern. The British-controlled government of India, which was especially involved, wondered whether the local Arab chiefs or the Persians might be stimulated into acquiring their own naval force to challenge British supremacy. But there was little need to worry: the Turks confined their attention to the mainland, and Britain strengthened its treaty with the ruler of Bahrain to forestall both Turkish and Persian ambitions.

The status of the emirate of Kuwait, with its great natural harbour at the strategic head of the Gulf, was a cause for concern. Since its foundation by the Sabah family from Nejd in the mid eighteenth century, it had grown and prospered as a pearling and trading centre under a succession of able rulers and it was a strong focus of British interest. However, the Sabahs were able to remain virtually independent in return for a nominal acceptance of Turkish suzerainty. It was only in 1899 that Britain finally accepted the request for formal British protection from the Kuwaiti amir, Mubarak the Great (1895–1916), and this was not to repel the Turks but to forestall the German plan to extend the Berlin–Istanbul–Baghdad railway to Kuwait. Under the Anglo-Kuwaiti Treaty, Mubarak accepted, in terms similar to other agreements with Arab Gulf rulers, not to 'cede, sell, lease, mortgage or give for occupation or any other purpose any portion of his territory to the government or subjects of any other power'.

The most prized of all the Arabic-speaking provinces of the Ottoman Empire was the Hejaz in western Arabia. It was the least developed economically, but it contained the Holy Cities of Islam – Mecca and Medina. Here Turkish control was maintained after the expulsion of the Wahhabis in 1811–19 but it was far from secure, even after the opening of the Suez Canal made it easier to dispatch troops from Istanbul. The Ottoman *walis* shared power with the prestigious Arab Grand Sharifs of Mecca, who by long tradition came from the Bani Hashem, the most noble of Arab clans, who traced their descent from the Prophet's daughter. Public order was badly maintained, foreign consuls were frequently murdered and the unfortunate Muslim pilgrims had little defence against marauding bandits.

As we have seen, Sultan Abdul Hamid, after the loss of most of his Christian subjects in the Balkans and the better part of his North African empire, determined to assert his leadership over what was still the greatest Muslim power in the world. He was prepared to make use of the *Tanzimat* reforms where they served his purposes in improving the administration of the outlying provinces, but the concepts within these reforms of the rights of citizens and equality before the law were even more distasteful to him than to his predecessors. He aimed at unfettered autocracy, but he pursued his aims by skilful diplomacy, intrigue and manipulation rather than brute force.

The Ottoman sultans in the eighteenth century had revived the title of caliph, and although it had little of its original meaning – the Prophet's successor and spiritual/political guide and leader of all Muslims – the world had generally acknowledged the title, as a form of diplomatic politeness. Abdul Hamid set out to assert himself as the sultan/caliph and world leader of Sunni Islam and to spread the doctrines of pan-Islam. This would serve the double purpose of strengthening his position within what was left of his empire and mobilizing its human resources against the increasing penetration by the Christian West. Unlike many of his predecessors, he was naturally pious and sober, and he emphasized these aspects of his court. He lavished money on mosques and Islamic foundations throughout the empire. He surrounded himself with the most learned Muslim scholars, and he established a missionary school to spread the news of Istanbul's rejuvenated faith and piety throughout the Muslim world.

Abdul Hamid had little need to worry about the loyalty of the mass of Anatolian peasants to their sultan/caliph, but his suspicious nature caused him to doubt the wholehearted acceptance of his leadership by his more numerous Arabic-speaking subjects. He became convinced that there was a movement to restore the Arab caliphate. There was little evidence for this. It was true that some non-Turkish Muslim thinkers in the empire blamed the last centuries of Ottoman domination for the current decadence of the Islamic world. Disciples of Jamal al-Din al-Afghani, like the Egyptian Muhammad Abduh and the Syrians Rashid Rida and Abdul Rahman al-Kawakibi, were passionately concerned with the revival and reunification of the Muslim *umma* or nation as a means of resisting the domination of the West and its ideas. They felt that this regeneration could come only through the Arabs among which Islam originated. But although these men founded newspapers and published pamphlets in Paris or Cairo (where they were under British protection), they were intellectuals rather than political activists.

Political dissent within the empire at that stage scarcely followed national/racial lines. The Egyptian nationalist leader Mustafa Kamel in the 1890s looked to the sultan as the natural leader of the pan-Islamic movement which he espoused against the British. Arab resentment and hostility against the Turks was only beginning to stir; indeed, the term 'Arab' was still generally reserved for the semi-nomadic people of the Arabian peninsula. Men like Rashid Rida believed that it was in Arabia that the movement for the regeneration of Islam would have to start, and in fact the first practical effort to oust the Ottomans as unfit rulers of the Islamic homeland was made by the Saudi Wahhabi forces at the beginning of the nineteenth century. But they had been defeated, and their challenge was to be renewed only when the empire was on the point of collapse.

Sultan Abdul Hamid's fears and suspicions of subversion among his non-Turkish subjects caused him to pursue a twin-headed policy. He promoted some to high positions in his government and lavished gifts and hospitality on visiting Arab dignitaries; at the same time, he constantly intrigued to prevent local political leaders from becoming too powerful. When necessary, he encouraged rivalry and antagonism between clans and tribes. He kept himself informed through his vast network of spies and the new telegraph system, installed by French and British engineers, which reached the most distant provinces. Any potentially dangerous local leader or possible trouble-maker was eliminated, if necessary by force. One of these was Hussein Bin Ali, a member of the family of the Grand Sharifs of Mecca – that is, a Hashemite. Because of his eminence, he had to be treated politely.

Accordingly, in 1893 Abdul Hamid issued him with an invitation which he could not refuse: to come to settle with his three small sons, Ali, Abdullah and Feisal, in Istanbul. Abdul Hamid's instinct was correct, for Hussein and his sons would become one of the principal instruments for the downfall of the empire.

The most outstanding of the Arabs whom Abdul Hamid promoted was the Syrian Izzet Pasha. In the later years of the sultan's reign he rose to a position of great power and influence in which he was the principal force behind the single most important instrument of Abdul Hamid's pan-Islamic policy – the building of the Hejaz Railway. This ran from Damascus to Medina, but a planned extension to Mecca was never completed. Built by engineers from the sultan's new ally Germany between 1901 and 1908, the railway cost some £3 million and, because it was presented as a supreme instrument of Muslim piety – to reduce the dangers and arduousness of the pilgrimage to Mecca – a third of the cost was raised by volunteer contributions from throughout the Muslim world, to which were added special taxes imposed in the empire. The project added immensely to the pious sultan/caliph's prestige as the leader of Sunni Islam, but it had the important additional political/strategic advantage of bypassing the British-controlled Suez Canal and making it possible to send troops from Syria to the Hejaz within a few days.

Despite all Abdul Hamid's efforts to secure the loyalty of the Muslim faithful, in the Arab provinces there were stirrings of opposition to Ottoman Turkish rule. Some local leaders or clans had specific cause for resentment when the sultan favoured their rivals, and there was more general dislike of his despotic and unprincipled methods of government. Among the Arab Christian communities centred on Maronite Lebanon there was especially powerful anti-Ottoman feeling, fostered by cultural and commercial contacts with the West, the spread of literacy and education and the knowledge of French protection. But precisely because Arab Christians were a minority and their resentment arose from their sense of holding permanent second-class status in the empire, there was no question of their combining forces with their Muslim fellow-Arabs in a movement of rebellion. The concept of an Arab nation was confined to a few intellectuals, while that of a common Ottoman citizenship based on the principle of equal rights, which had originated in the *Tanzimat* reforms, had made little headway under Abdul Hamid's pan-Islamic order. Religious loyalties were still much stronger than Western secularist ideas. Syrian Arabs did not think in terms of overthrowing the empire which had been the champion and protector of the Islamic *umma* for four centuries.

The real rebellion against Abdul Hamid came from a wholly different source, which lay much closer to Istanbul. The most genuine and effective body of reforms which Abdul Hamid had taken over from his predecessors was the improvement and expansion of civil and military education. This had produced a substantial new educated middle class. The Young Ottomans who wished to end the sultan's despotism were effectively scattered and suppressed in the first years of his reign, but their ideals survived and re-emerged towards the end of the century in a revolutionary movement known as the Young Turks. This spread rapidly among the students in the military, medical and law colleges in the capital and the provinces. Talaat Bey, a law student who was also chief clerk at the Salonika post office, and Rahmi Bey, a local notable, together with a few associates, founded a secret society which they called the Committee of Union and Progress (CUP) to emphasize the ideal of the unity and equality of all races and creeds within the empire. This ideal attracted the support of Freemasons and Jews, who came to play a leading role in the movement. Links were established with the Turkish exiles in Paris.

Although the Young Turks staged an abortive coup in 1896, this was easily suppressed. The sultan had little idea of the danger that threatened, and his spy network seems to have been less effective close to home. The revolutionaries were appalled by the sultan's mishandling of the affairs of Macedonia, the last substantial Ottoman province in Europe, and outraged by the empire's abject weakness in relation to the powers of Europe. In 1908, provoked by reports that Edward VII of England and Tsar Nicholas of Russia were planning the partition of Turkey at their meeting in Tallinn, army officers such as Enver Bey, Jemal Pasha and Mustafa Kemal (the future Kemal Atatürk) joined the new movement, bringing to it the command of military units in the Macedonian army. It was in the spirit of saving the fatherland that in 1908 the Young Turks raised the standard of revolt in Salonika, the Macedonian capital, which had become the headquarters of the CUP. The rebellion spread rapidly, even to the Albanian units which Abdul Hamid had regarded as securely loyal.

The Young Turks, led by Major Enver Bey, demanded the restoration of constitutional rule. Discovering that both the Shaikh ul-Islam – the senior religious authority – and a majority of his own ministers sympathized with the revolutionaries, Abdul Hamid was forced to give way. The short-lived constitution he had abolished forty years previously was restored.

On behalf of the Young Turks, Enver Bey proclaimed the end of arbitrary government and the principles of the new order: 'Henceforth we are all brothers. There are no longer Bulgars, Greeks, Romanians, Jews, Muslims; under the same blue sky we are all equal, we glory in being Ottomans.'

The announcement was received with wild popular rejoicing in Istanbul. The wily Abdul Hamid did not lack resource. Affecting enthusiasm for the liberal constitutionalism he had so speedily discarded after his accession, he reopened the parliament which had been closed for forty-one years. The crowds lining the streets cried 'Long live the constitution', but they also chanted 'Long live the sultan.'

The Arabs in Istanbul and the notables in the Arab provinces also welcomed the new era. They hoped that the declared spirit of racial equality would mean the end of Turkish domination and of the imposition of Turkish language and culture on the Arabs in the empire.

A brief Turco-Arab honeymoon ensued, but for several reasons it could not last. In the first place the spirit of Ottomanism enshrined in Midhat Pasha's constitution took no account of racial equality among Muslims. Enver Bey in his declaration had referred to 'Muslims' rather than Arabs or Turks. The electoral system ensured the massive predominance of Turks in parliament – where they numbered 150 out of a total of 243, compared with 60 Arabs – despite the fact that Arabic-speaking Ottoman citizens almost certainly outnumbered the Turks in the Empire. Secondly, the army officers who had taken over the leadership of the Young Turks were no liberal democrats. Their professions of faith in unity and equality as the spirit of Ottomanism were not hypocritical, but they did not go deep. They detested Abdul Hamid's rule for its corruption and inefficiency rather than its despotism. Faced with his appalling legacy of misgovernment – the empty treasury, the relentless pressure of the European powers in the Balkans and later the Italian invasion of

Libya, the last Ottoman province in Africa – the Young Turks had little time to apply the principles of constitutional freedom. Moreover, unlike the Young Ottoman intellectuals, they had no interest in political theories – their approach to government was practical and empirical and their overriding aim was to strengthen the empire's defences. If they paid tribute to the ideals of the French Revolution, it was because they believed that the slogans of 'Liberty, Equality and Fraternity' had welded the people of France into the potent force which overwhelmed the Revolution's enemies. The citizens of the Ottoman Empire would no doubt behave similarly.

Their immediate problem was an attempt at counter-revolution. While avowedly accepting the new constitution, Abdul Hamid secretly encouraged the disgruntled and reactionary elements who opposed the new order. In April 1909, troops of the Istanbul garrison mutinied, massacred their officers and raided parliament. When Abdul Hamid pardoned the leaders of the revolt and formed a new cabinet, the Young Turks sent an army from Salonika to restore order, punish the insurgents and restore the authority of the CUP. Three days later parliament met and announced the abdication of Abdul Hamid. His brother Reshad was proclaimed sultan, with the title of Mohammed V. This mild and self-effacing 64-year-old was quite prepared to accept the role of constitutional monarch.

The CUP wisely decided to spare Abdul Hamid's life, and he was interned in a private villa in Salonika. His former subjects have extraordinarily mixed impressions of his long reign. For Turks, the record of the modernizing reforms he achieved in some limited areas is outweighed by his inability to prevent the final humiliation of the House of Ottoman which had once been a great European power. But a different impression has remained among the non-Turkish Muslims in the empire. In some cases they were peoples or tribes whom he had favoured over their rivals – Kurds against Armenians, Sunnis against Shiites in Mesopotamia. But over a longer period it is the record of his pan-Islamic policies which has survived. It matters less that these were often used to further his despotic ends than that he is seen as the last ruler to champion the cause of the Islamic *umma*. In the late twentieth century, Arabs will almost invariably refer to the fact that it was Sultan Abdul Hamid who refused the request of the Austrian Dr Theodor Herzl, the founder of political Zionism, to lease part of Palestine as a national home for the Jews. In fact Abdul

Hamid was inclined to accept the request in return for substantial loans from international Jewry, but he was persuaded by his ministers that this would be disastrous for his pan-Islamic policies and his prestige among his Arab subjects. It is the sultan's refusal which is remembered.

If in 1908 there were scarcely any Arabs who thought of separation from the Turkish heart of the empire which remained the sole protector of Sunni Islam, there were undoubtedly many who hoped for decentralization, autonomy for the Arab provinces and the acceptance of Turco-Arab equality. The Young Turks, on the other hand, did not so much insist on Turkish domination as take it for granted. It was only when they felt threatened by increased national feeling among the remaining non-Turkish elements in the empire – Greeks, Armenians and Kurds as well as Arabs – that they turned to a specifically Turkish nationalism. In its narrower form this aimed at the consolidation of the Turkish nation within Anatolia (or approximately the borders of the present Turkish Republic). But there was also a wider movement – the pan-Turanian – of which the ideologist was the writer Zia Gokalp. This called for the union of all Turkish-speaking peoples, including those of central Asia where the Turks had originated. Although the CUP did not formally adopt the pan-Turanian programme, the concept was highly attractive to some of its leaders such as Enver Bey. Romantic and historically dubious in its expression, it was essentially racist. It was also anti-Islamic, in that it called for a return to an era before the Turks adopted Islam.

The dominant outlook in the CUP was therefore secular and nationalist, rather than pan-Islamic. Most of its leaders were Freemasons, and they were closely associated with the Jews of Salonika, who played an important role in the Young Turk movement. But this did not mean that they were either able or willing to abandon the empire's role of leadership of the Islamic world which, after four centuries, was still acknowledged by both its Christian and its Muslim subjects.

Talaat Bey recognized the problem that this presented for the Young Turks' objective of an empire which would be both centralized and 'ottomanized' to a far greater degree than under Sultan Abdul Hamid. In a secret speech to the Salonika CUP in August 1910, he said that, while the constitution provided for equality of 'Mussulman and Ghiaur [i.e. non-Muslim]', they all knew that this was an unrealizable ideal.

The Sheriat [i.e. *sharia*], our whole past history and the sentiments of hundreds of thousands of Mussulmans and even the sentiments of the Ghiaurs themselves, who stubbornly resist every attempt to ottomanize them, present an impenetrable barrier to the establishment of real equality. We have made unsuccessful attempts to convert the Ghiaur into a loyal Osmanli and all such efforts must inevitably fail, as long as the small independent States in the Balkan Peninsula remain in a position to propagate ideas of separatism among the inhabitants of Macedonia.

These independent states – Greece, Serbia and Bulgaria – were indeed afraid that an Ottoman Empire rejuvenated by the Young Turks might try to recover its hold over the Balkans. Without any encouragement from the European powers – except for Russia – they formed a secret alliance, and in October 1912 they launched a war against Turkey. By December, they had seized Salonika and western Thrace, forcing the CUP to move its headquarters to Istanbul. The Turkish army retreated to lines defending the capital. When the Balkan allies fell out over the division of the spoils and fought each other, Turkey was able to recover a portion of Macedonia and the key city of Edirne, but Crete and most of the Aegean islands were ceded to Greece. Turkey's role in Europe had almost been eliminated.

The Young Turks did not expect ottomanization of the empire's Muslim subjects to present the same problems. The trouble was that, for them in their newly invigorated spirit of Turkish nationalism, ottomanization really meant 'turkification'. (It hardly needs to be said that pan-Turanian ideas were unlikely to appeal to Ottoman Arabs.) Turkish had always been the language of Ottoman officialdom, but Arabic held its place among the mass of Ottoman Arabs. As the language of religion, Arabic was also predominant in education. The Young Turks now aimed to turn the heterogeneous empire into a nation with a single language. Turkish was made a compulsory subject in every school. It was required to be used in the law courts, and even the street names in the cities were turned into Turkish, although it was incomprehensible to the vast majority of the population in the Arab provinces.

The result of these turkification policies was a profound stimulus to the consciousness of their Arabism among the Ottoman Arabs. This was still a long way from the secular Arab nationalism which emerged later: it was rooted in their pride in Arabic as the language in which God spoke to the world through the Prophet, and in the unique place of the Arabs in the history of Islam. This Arab awareness had been submerged but in no way eliminated by the acceptance of Turkish and military leadership during many centuries.

One of the Arab responses to the concept of a Turkish master race was the founding of various societies or parties dedicated to the protection of Arab rights and the achievement of Arab autonomy within the empire. In Beirut, Baghdad and Basra these societies had to remain underground, but the most important of them – the Young Arab Society or al-Fatat – was established by a group of Arab students in Paris, and this secretly gathered support throughout the Arab provinces.

Within the empire, the Arab leader who was best placed to challenge Ottoman domination was the Grand Sharif of Mecca. As custodian of the holy places of Islam and supervisor of the Muslim *hajj* or pilgrimage, he was hardly a subject for 'turkification'. The powers in Istanbul had to treat him with a certain respect. The post was now occupied by Hussein Bin Ali, the troublesome member of the hereditary sharifian Hashemite family whom in 1893 Sultan Abdul Hamid had 'invited' to settle in Istanbul, where his activities could be kept under observation. As a gesture of goodwill during the brief Turco-Arab honeymoon after the 1908 revolution, the CUP appointed him Grand Sharif, ignoring the shrewd warnings of Sultan Abdul Hamid. They soon had cause for regret. Now in his mid-fifties, the venerable, white-bearded Sharif Hussein was powerfully ambitious. His mild and courteous manner concealed a will of steel which sustained his sense of his own destiny. But he was also naturally cautious, and he did not immediately cause trouble with the Turks. He even conducted a successful expedition on their behalf to suppress a rebellion in the Asir province of south-western Arabia. In return, the Ottoman government encouraged him to extend its authority into the interior. This involved him in conflict with a formidable Arab rival – the House of Saud – which would cause the downfall of his Hashemite family in Arabia, just as the Hashemites would be the instrument for the overthrow of Turkish rule in the Arab provinces of the empire.

The House of Saud had recovered from its internal divisions in the 1860s, which had allowed the Turks to occupy eastern Arabia, but had then suffered defeat at the hands of its long-standing rivals in northern Nejd. In 1891 Abdul Rahman, the head of the House of

Saud, was forced to flee from Riyadh and take refuge with the amir of Kuwait. He was accompanied by the eldest of five sons, the ten-year-old Abdul Aziz, commonly known by his patronymic Ibn Saud, who was to prove to be one of the outstanding figures in the modern history of the Middle East.

By the time he reached manhood, Ibn Saud dominated his companions with his physical presence and personality. In 1902 he succeeded in recapturing the Saudi capital of Riyadh with a tiny force, and he set about restoring the former Saudi/Wahhabi state. Rashidi power was in decline; he reconquered Nejd and in 1913 went on to occupy the eastern Arabian province of al-Hasa, which had been barely held by the Turks. He was recognized by Britain as 'Sultan of Nejd and its Dependencies', but he could not go further as the entire Persian Gulf coast from Kuwait to Oman was under Britain's exclusive influence.

In western Arabia, he suffered a setback. Sharif Hussein succeeded in taking Ibn Saud's favourite brother, Saad, hostage and Ibn Saud was forced to accept a nominal Ottoman suzerainty in order to ransom him. He swore revenge against the Hashemites.

Sharif Hussein, having made himself indispensable to the Turks, set about asserting the rights and dignity of his office against the Ottoman *wall* of the Hejaz. But he was looking further – to making the Hejaz an autonomous Arab province which could then be the nucleus for the independence of all the Arab provinces within the empire.

Hussein's sons, by now grown to manhood, shared his ambitions. Abdullah, the second and cleverest, was deputy for Mecca in the new Ottoman parliament, and he caused the CUP the greatest suspicion. They tried to win him over by offering the post of governor-general of Yemen, where Ottoman authority had recently been reasserted, but he cannily refused. Less cautious than his father, in February 1914 he visited Cairo to sound out the British agent, Lord Kitchener, and his oriental secretary, Sir Ronald Storrs, on the possibility of the British government supporting his family's ambitions on behalf of the Arabs. But although Britain by this time did not see how war with its great rival imperial Germany could be avoided, it did not see an Ottoman alliance with Germany as inevitable. The traditional policy of regarding the survival of the Ottoman Empire as favourable to British interests remained. Kitchener was therefore non-committal to the point of being discouraging, and Abdullah came away disappointed.

After Sultan Abdul Hamid's unsuccessful counter-coup in 1909, the CUP were in sole command in the empire and free to pursue their illiberal and centralizing policies. They at once prohibited the formation of political associations based on ethnic or national groups and closed down minority clubs and societies. They made much wider use of the death penalty than Abdul Hamid would have considered. The CUP's policies did not, however, go unchallenged. In the Young Turks movement there had always been a different, liberal, tendency which favoured decentralization of power and saw ottomanization not as the imposition of Turkish political and cultural dominance but as the creation of a pluralist and multi-denominational empire in which the autonomous rights of the religious and national minorities would be respected. In its most explicit form, this tendency was represented by the Ottoman Decentralization League of Prince Sabah al-Din, a nephew of Abdul Hamid, who had gone into exile in Paris to escape his uncle's despotism. With his programme for the devolution of power to autonomous provinces under the Ottoman flag and for protection of the Ottoman army, he appealed to Arabs as much as to liberal Turks. Branches of his League sprang up throughout the empire. It was dissolved as subversive by the CUP shortly after the 1908 revolution, but it continued to survive underground and in 1912 it emerged as the Ottoman Administrative Decentralization Party, which was formed in Cairo under British protection by a group of prominent Syrian *émigrés*.

Although the Prince's League was suppressed by the CUP, there were many more in the new Ottoman parliament who favoured both constitutional government and some degree of decentralization. They feared that the CUP was proving even more despotic in its methods than Abdul Hamid. They received support from respected liberal elder statesmen from the Hamidian era.

All these groups and individuals combined in 1911 to form a single opposition front: the Liberal Union. This soon demonstrated that it had widespread popular support. The CUP acted promptly by dissolving parliament and using all means of pressure in the subsequent election – known as the 'big-stick election' – to ensure that out of 275 members only six belonged to the opposition.

This high-handed action only provoked a more dangerous opposition to the CUP from within the armed forces. A group called the

'Saviour Officers' demanded the withdrawal of the army from politics and, with the support of Albanian units, used threatening troop movements to carry out a bloodless coup which forced the resignation of the CUP-controlled government and its replacement by one led by the veteran liberal Kamel Pasha.

The liberal interregnum lasted only a few months. The Balkan War was reaching its most disastrous stage, with the enemy at the gates of Istanbul. It was the occasion for the CUP to recover power. On 23 January 1913, Enver Bey and a group of officers forced their way into the cabinet room and shot dead the minister of war. A CUP government was restored, and Turkish liberalism went underground for a long period.

The empire was now effectively ruled by a triple dictatorship of Enver, Talaat and Jemal Pashas. Enver, the youngest of the three, was brave, vain and flamboyant – still the popular hero of the Young Turks. He commanded adoration in the army and concentrated on the revival and improvement of the Ottoman military forces, whose morale was at a low ebb following the Balkan disasters. His admiration for the military power of Germany, which was helping to train the Ottoman army, made him the most pro-German of the triumvirate. In contrast to Enver, Jemal Pasha was cool and calmly self-assured, but his aristocratic politeness concealed a streak of coarse ruthlessness. Talaat, the only civilian, was the ablest and most intelligent – a man of ideas. He was charming and humorous, but quite uncompromising in his fierce Turkish patriotism.

By 1914 the CUP had been in charge of the empire for barely six years. The liberal interregnum had been too brief to affect its policies. In the Arab provinces these had caused a serious deterioration in Turco-Arab relations, but in the Turkish homeland there were some substantial achievements of the kind that are often associated with effective modernizing dictatorships which are little concerned with constitutional liberties. Provincial and municipal government were greatly improved; the cities were made cleaner and safer and public transport was organized. Javid Pasha, the brilliant finance minister, of Jewish origin, was able to do little to ease the empire's burden of foreign debt – especially as costly wars were being fought – but he successfully reformed the tax system to improve revenues. (The CUP failed in its efforts at liquidating the Capitulations; that had to wait until Turkey joined the Great European War.)

Perhaps the Young Turks' greatest achievement was in expanding education. Building on the efforts of the nineteenth-century reformers, they went much further in creating a modern progressive system at all levels, with new teacher-training colleges and specialized institutes. They were the first rulers of an independent Muslim country to create a state education system which was open to girls; previously the daughters of only the wealthiest classes had been educated, privately. The way was opened for Turkish women to enter public life as lawyers, doctors and administrators.

Enver Bey's degree of success in rejuvenating the Ottoman armed forces is difficult to evaluate. The armed forces were of enormous size; one million men were under arms when the Young Turks came to power, and this number was increased by the introduction of military conscription. But it was the raising of military standards and the modernization of weapons which were most required. The German general Liman von Sanders was appointed inspector-general of the Ottoman army, and the British Admiral Limpus was given the task of reorganizing the navy. When war came, Turkey's opponents, who had never doubted the courage of the Turkish soldiers, certainly found them better prepared for modern warfare than they had expected.

In its foreign policy the CUP was by no means unresourceful. The overriding aim, as in everything else, was the preservation of Turkey's Asian empire and the strengthening of its defences. The intense rivalry between the European powers left opportunity for manoeuvre. Both Talaat and Jemal were anxious to secure an alliance with the Triple Entente of Russia, France and Britain which aimed to hold the balance of power in Europe against the ambitions of the Central Powers – imperial Germany and Austro-Hungary. Russia was the most eager to respond, as it was by now thoroughly alarmed by the dominant position Germany had acquired in Istanbul and feared that it would gain control of the Dardanelles straits. Although Britain and France had shown some benevolence towards the Young Turks' Revolution, they were unprepared to include the Balkan states in any territorial guarantees for Turkey's remaining position in Europe. They both expected Turkey to remain neutral in any forthcoming war and that their interests would thus remain secure. Britain no longer regarded the survival of the Turkish Empire as a matter of great concern; the alliance with Russia provided sufficient protection for vital British interests in the Persian Gulf.

Despite Talaat's and Jemal's repeated efforts, they were unable to achieve an alliance with the Triple Entente. Feeling that there was an urgent need for protection from one of the powers, they accepted Enver Pasha's view that this should be Germany. On 2 August 1914 – five days after the assassination of the Austrian archduke Francis Ferdinand at Sarajevo, which led directly to the First World War – Turkey signed a secret alliance with Germany which allowed Turkey to remain neutral unless Russia intervened in the Austro-Serbian conflict which had just broken out. On 4 August Britain declared war on Germany. Yet even then all was not lost. Talaat still favoured neutrality. Diplomatic relations with Britain were satisfactory. The British naval mission headed by Admiral Limpus and the British ambassador Sir Louis Mallet were of high standing. In London the Ottoman ambassador, Hakki Pasha, had by the summer of 1914 succeeded in negotiating a series of agreements which satisfactorily resolved all the outstanding differences between Turkey and Britain, France and Germany over their railway interests in Mesopotamia and Syria and navigation on the Tigris and Euphrates. An Ottoman–British agreement defined the borders between Kuwait, Nejd and Iraq.

Turkey ultimately abandoned neutrality because Enver – the dominant member of the triumvirate – was convinced that Germany would win the coming war. Any doubts about taking Germany's side were removed when Britain commandeered two Turkish battleships which were on the point of completion in British shipyards. This high-handed action caused a wave of anti-British feeling throughout Turkey. As Germany poured ships and men into Istanbul, the British fleet blockaded the Dardanelles and demanded that Turkey affirm its neutrality by expelling the German mission. On 28 October the German admiral took the Turkish fleet into the Black Sea to bombard Russian ports, and on 3 November the British fleet shelled the Turkish ports at the entrance to the Dardanelles. Although they had been reluctant to join the war before having time to mobilize, Enver and his colleagues could not retreat. Turkey declared war on the Allies on 5 November.

7. The Persian Factor

The only great schism in Islam – between Sunnis and Shiites which followed the death of the Prophet – led to a prolonged struggle for dominance in the Muslim world between the two branches of the religion. For some four centuries it was possible or even probable that Shia Islam would prevail, and it reached the height of its power in about AD 1000. But first the Seljuk Turks who came to dominate the Islamic heartlands in the eleventh century and then their Ottoman successors four hundred years later were fiercely Sunni. Shiism continued to survive and flourish in Persia and Mesopotamia, but henceforth it constituted a declining minority of the Islamic *umma*.

There is no great doctrinal difference between Sunni and Shiite Islam: they agree on the absolute centrality of the Prophet in the religion and on most of the historical details of his life; there are no major differences in ritual; and on theological matters there is a broad consensus. The division is historical and political. The Shiites believe that the Prophet should have been succeeded by his cousin and son-in-law Ali and that the succession was then reserved for the direct descendants of Muhammad through his daughter Fatima and her husband Ali. The successor, or imam, who was also the infallible interpreter of Islam, was generally nominated by the previous imam from among his sons. Most Shiites believe that there were twelve imams – Ali, his sons Hassan and Hussein, and nine in line of descent from Hussein. The last was Muhammad, born in 873, who disappeared mysteriously or went into occultation. The 'twelver' Shiites, who in the twentieth century form the great majority of Shiites in the world, believe that Imam Muhammad is only hidden and will reappear as the Mahdi or 'rightly guided one' to restore the golden age. (Another Shiite sect, the Zaidis, is confined to Yemen, while offshoots of Shiism, such as the Druze, Alawites and Ismailis, are numerically small although they may have strong local political importance.)

Shah Ismail I of Persia, who ruled from 1501 to 1524 and founded the Safavid dynasty (1501–1736), established Shiism as the state religion. It is probable that a majority of his subjects were Sunnis, but he skilfully used the new faith to bind his disparate peoples together. Shia Islam became the foundation of a proud and even xenophobic Persian nationalism which still flourishes in the modern age, as for the past four centuries Persia (renamed Iran in 1935) has been the only nation-state of significance in which Shiism is the official religion.

Ismail had wider aspirations for his religion, and when the ardently Sunni Ottoman sultan Selim I persecuted his Shiite subjects, he attempted to come to their aid. His ill-trained troops were no match for the Ottoman Janissaries and he was defeated, but he was able to prevent the Turks from seizing any of his territory and he even held on to the districts of Mosul and Baghdad which he had won in earlier campaigns. He also held off the Sunni Uzbeks in Turkestan to the north-east. Persia was on the defensive, but the menace of Sunni enemies helped the process of welding the nation together.

The struggle between the rival Sunni Ottoman and Shiite Persian empires lasted more than two centuries along their common frontier which stretched for some 1500 miles from the Black Sea to the Persian Gulf. The battle for Mesopotamia wavered back and forth and was finally decided in the Ottoman favour only at the end of the seventeenth century. Even then, Mesopotamia was far from secure from Persian attack. Persia's western frontiers have remained roughly unchanged until the present day.

The need to guard against the hostile Persian presence on the Ottoman Empire's eastern borders acted as a brake to Turkish western expansion, earning Persia the gratitude of the Christian states of Europe. Equally, the Ottoman Empire served to isolate the Persian Empire from the West.

Except for relatively brief periods of recovery, the Safavid dynasty went into a long secular decline on the death of its founder. The apogee of the dynasty was the reign (1587–1629) of Shah Abbas the Great. With the help of the English adventurer Sir Robert Sherley, he carried out much-needed reforms of his army, establishing an élite cavalry corps which was comparable to the Turkish Janissaries, and his reign was a period when the stuggle went against the Ottomans. He was a capable administrator, and a builder of genius. He made his capital the city of Isfahan, which became one of the masterpieces of Islamic architecture. He fostered trade and industry and, although an ardent Shiite Muslim, encouraged Christian Armenians to inhabit a quarter of the capital. Isfahan grew until his English visitors noted that it rivalled London in size.

When Shah Abbas died, he left his country immeasurably stronger than when he had come to the throne at the age of sixteen. European penetration of the Persian Empire had hardly begun. With the help of the fleet of the British East India Company in the Gulf, he was able to evict the Portuguese who, a century earlier, in the time of Shah Ismail, had obtained a foothold on the island of Hormuz and on the adjoining mainland. In return for its help, he granted the Company valuable privileges at the port of Bandar Abbas, which was named after him. But British domination of the Gulf still lay well in the future.

Envoys of the European powers to Abbas's court were politely received but he resisted their suggestions that he form an alliance with them against the Ottoman Turks – Persia's isolation from the West was the best guarantee of its empire's integrity.

Abbas left his country one fatal legacy: he instituted the practice, which closely resembled that in the Ottoman court, of immuring the heir apparent and other royal princes in the harem, for purposes of security. The result was that the heir and princes were physically weakened and totally inexperienced in the art of government. His successors were not only cruel and despotic but also incompetent, and the court eunuchs secured excessive power and influence.

In 1709 the Sunni Afghans rose in rebellion, and, repeatedly defeating the badly led Persian forces sent against them, succeeded in capturing Isfahan and forcing the shah to flee. The Afghans controlled only part of the country, and a majority of the people remained loyal to the Safavids.

Persia was in a gravely weakened condition. Tsar Peter the Great of Russia had for long been seeking ways of establishing a trade route to India across the Caspian Sea and beyond. Using as a pretext the attacks on some Russian merchants in northern Persia during a tribal uprising, he invaded the country in 1722. His action alarmed the Ottoman Turks, who now also invaded Persia, to prevent Russia from gaining control over territories on their borders. War between Russia and Turkey was avoided by the settlement of 1724, under which the two powers agreed to partition northern and western Persia between them, leaving the rest to the Afghan usurpers in the centre and the Safavids in the east. Russian pressure was henceforth a permanent feature of Persia's existence.

In 1729 the Safavids were restored to the throne. However, this was accomplished only with the help of Nadir Quli Beg, a member of the Asfar tribe, who had formerly been a leader of a gang of robbers but turned out to be a brilliant general. In 1736 he deposed the young Shah Abbas III, bringing the Safavid dynasty to an end, and placed himself on the throne with the title of Nadir Shah.

Before he ascended the throne, Nadir Shah's military skill had already succeeded in forcing both the Ottoman Turks and the Russians to relinquish their conquests. He recaptured Kandahar from the Afghans and thus restored Persia's previous borders. But this enormously ambitious man was not content with this. He turned eastwards with his armies to invade India, which, under the Mogul dynasty, was sunk in corruption and decline but still vastly wealthy. Bypassing the well-defended Khyber Pass, he defeated the Mogul emperor Mohammed Shah and in March 1739 entered Delhi in triumph. The booty was on a gigantic scale. An Indian historian remarked that 'the accumulated wealth of 348 years changed owners in a moment.' One captured item was the Peacock Throne, which Nadir removed to Persia where it served for the coronation of future shahs.

Nadir had succeeded where Alexander the Great had failed. However, he did not attempt to hold India but restored the bulk of Mohammed Shah's lands to him, while keeping the provinces on the southern banks of the River Indus which had belonged to the Persian Empire of Darius the Great.

His appetite for conquest was still unsatisfied. He turned against the Uzbek states of Turkestan to the north-east and captured Samarkand and Bokhara. He drove into the Caucasus to hold back the advancing Russians. By 1740 he had not only restored and extended the borders of Persia but also established the country as a great military power. However, his genius was purely military; he had no concern with the just and efficient administration of the empire. He was a Persian Bonaparte without a Code Napoléon. Harsh, cruel and suspicious, he came to be hated by his subjects, and in 1747 his murder by a group of his own officers was little mourned. Some fifty years of relative chaos ensued as the throne was disputed between rival claimants. In 1794 Agha Mohammed of the Qajar tribes defeated his enemies and made himself shah. Although a eunuch (he had been made one when taken captive as a youth), he was the founder of the Qajar dynasty which lasted until 1925. After capturing the city of

Tehran he made it his capital. On his assassination in 1797, Agha Mohammed was succeeded by his nephew Fath Ali who reigned until 1834.

By the beginning of the nineteenth century Persia's long isolation from the West had come to an end. The Ottoman Empire, which though hostile had acted as a barrier of protection from the West, was in irreversible decline. Britain was in possession of India, and its navy controlled the waters of the Gulf. The Russian Empire was continuing the great colonial expansion eastwards into Asia that had begun under Peter the Great. Throughout the nineteenth century Persia was caught in the pincer-like pressure of these two powers.

However, it was France – and specifically the remarkable ambitions of Napoleon Bonaparte – which was instrumental in bringing Persia into the orbit of European politics. Having failed in his attempt to use Egypt as a springboard for an attack on the British in India, in 1800 Napoleon planned an invasion of India via Afghanistan in alliance with Tsar Paul of Russia. The plan may have been wholly impractical, but it thoroughly alarmed the British rulers of India. It was aborted by the assassination of Tsar Paul in 1801, but the French menace remained. When the advancing Russians annexed two provinces of Georgia and in 1805 declared war on Persia, seizing Derbent and Baku, the Persian shah Fath Ali turned to France for help. By the Franco-Persian Treaty of Finkenstein in 1807, Bonaparte undertook to recover the territories Russia had seized. But Bonaparte almost immediately made peace with Tsar Alexander, and Persia was left to face Russia alone.

By the 1813 Treaty of Golestan, which ended a hopeless war, Persia ceded Georgia, Baku and other territories to Russia. But the struggle was not ended: three frontier districts remained in dispute, and when Russia arbitrarily occupied them in 1827 the shah was compelled by outraged public opinion to declare war. After initial successes, this war also ended in disaster for Persia, mainly because the shah refused to pay his troops during the winter. Under the humiliating Treaty of Torkaman in 1828, Persia not only gave up all claims to Georgia and other territories lost in the earlier war but also paid a heavy indemnity and granted extraterritorial rights (similar to the Ottoman Capitulations) to Russian citizens on Persian soil. This and a simultaneous commercial treaty providing for free trade between Russia and Persia provided the basis for future relations between Persia and other European powers.

Britain's principal concern in the region in the early nineteenth century was to maintain Afghanistan as a barrier to French and Russian ambitions towards India. In 1800 Britain sent a mission to Persia, the first since the time of King Charles II. Headed by a young Scots officer, Captain Malcolm, it aimed to persuade the shah to bring the ambitious Afghan amir of Kabul under control to counteract any possible designs of the French or Russians and to sign a political and commercial treaty. The mission was successful, but the treaty lapsed in 1807 when Britain refused to provide help against Russian aggression on Persia's north-western borders. The British interest remained, however, and in 1814 another treaty was signed whereby the shah agreed not to sign treaties or co-operate militarily with countries hostile to Britain; in return, Persia was to receive a subsidy of £150,000 a year which would lapse if Persia engaged in any war of aggression. The subsidy was withdrawn in 1827, when Persia was technically the aggressor in its second disastrous war with Russia.

When Fath Ali died, he was succeeded by his grandson Mohammed Shah (1834–48). The young shah was determined to win fame by recovering some of Persia's lost territories. He was wise enough to see he could do nothing to stem the Russian colonizing drive through Turkestan which, only temporarily halted by the Crimean War, was pursued relentlessly throughout the mid nineteenth century. Instead, with Russian encouragement, he turned eastwards to try to conquer the province of Herat in north-western Afghanistan and territories beyond. Britain was instantly alarmed. France was no longer a threat to India, but expansionist Russia seemed highly dangerous. The Persian–Russian treaty of 1828 gave the Russians the right to appoint consuls throughout Persian territory. Britain gave help to the Afghan rulers of Herat and exerted pressure on the shah by occupying Kharg Island in the Gulf. Mohammed Shah was forced to abandon his siege of Herat.

Nasir al-Din Shah, who succeeded his father Mohammed in 1848 at the age of seventeen and reigned for forty-eight years, pursued the same policy of attempting to recover territories to the east, with Russian encouragement. Britain protested and imposed a treaty on Persia under which the shah undertook to refrain from any further interference in Afghanistan. When, despite the treaty, in 1856 Nasir al-Din obtained control of Herat through an Afghan nominee, Britain again seized Kharg Island and, near Bushire, landed troops which advanced inland to defeat a strong Persian force. The British then withdrew and sailed up the Shatt al-Arab waterway at the head of the Gulf to capture the port of Mohammereh. Under a treaty concluded in Paris in 1857, Persia then agreed to withdraw from Herat and to recognize the kingdom of Afghanistan.

In the 1870s and 1880s, Russia completed its conquest of central Asia and bordered Persia on the north-east as well as the north. The 1200 miles of common frontier stretched from Mount Ararat and around the Caspian Sea to the borders of Afghanistan. Given its weakness, Persia's only means of resisting Russian pressure was to seek Britain's backing, and this required the granting of a series of concessions to British commercial interests.

Throughout the nineteenth century the Persian shahs ruled as despots with little restraint on their personal power. Only the nomadic tribes – about a quarter of the population, who inhabited the mountain ranges along Persia's eastern and western borders – retained a sense of independence, regarding the monarchy with some disdain. The great majority of the rest of the population consisted of illiterate peasant farmers living close to subsistence level in small mud villages. Although legally free, in practice they were tied to the land. Most of the landlords (who measured their wealth by the number of villages they owned) were absentees, living in the larger cities and leaving the management of their villages in the hands of an agent. Despite their wealth and power over the peasantry, they did not form a cohesive feudal class which was capable of challenging the absolutism of the throne, and, as the ultimate owners of the land, the shahs did not hesitate to confiscate an individual landlord's property when they were in need of funds.

There was no European type of bourgeoisie or professional class. In Shiite Persia, the religious hierarchy, made up of mullahs, with a better-educated upper class of *mujtahids*, learned in Islamic law, was much larger than its equivalent, the *ulama*, in Sunni Islam. But, despite its influence with the people, it rarely chose to defy the authority of the throne. The nearest equivalent to a middle class was formed by the *bazaaris* or merchants, who ranged from itinerant pedlars to wealthy exporters of the carpets and textiles which were virtually Persia's only manufactured goods. However, their lack of cohesion meant that their political influence was very limited.

The most serious challenge to the shahs came from the leaders of religious sects. In the 1840s a rebellion broke out led by the Agha

Khan, spiritual head of the Ismailis, and then another by the Babi movement, created by Mirza Ali Mohammed, son of a Shiraz merchant, who after making the pilgrimage to Mecca declared himself to be the *bab* (gateway) to the divine truth. His movement spread and became so strong that in 1850 Nasir al-Din Shah was obliged to have him executed. Two years later a Babi attempt to assassinate the shah led to the fierce persecution of the sect, and most of the survivors fled the country. However, an offshoot of the Babis – the Bahais – continued. This never threatened the shahs but was still held in suspicion.

The closest equivalent to a reform movement in nineteenth-century Persia was instituted by Mirza Taqi Khan, the capable and honest vizier appointed by the young Nasir al-Din when he came to the throne. Impressed by the *Tanzimat* reforms in Ottoman Turkey, he persuaded the shah to reorganize the armed forces and ensure that they were properly paid and to end the sale of titles and offices and various other abuses. He was also responsible for the founding of the École Polytechnique or Dar al-Fanun in Tehran and the first Persian newspaper. But the reforms were short-lived. The shah's formidable mother persuaded him that Taqi Khan was becoming too powerful, and Nasir al-Din ordered his execution.

Despite his occasional acts of cruelty the shah was generally a humane ruler, but his liberal and reformist inclinations, which had been encouraged by Taqi Khan, did not last. He was affected by the failure of the constitutional movement in Ottoman Turkey and Abdul Hamid II's speedy reversion to autocratic rule in 1878. In the last years of his reign he ruled as despotically as any of his predecessors. His greatest achievement was to establish security throughout the empire. There was some very limited modernization in the form of paved roads and the electric telegraph (installed by the Indo-European Telegraph Company, acting on behalf of the British government of India to serve its imperial interests). The Dar al-Fanun in Tehran taught science and engineering on modern lines, and there was a modest growth in the publishing of newspapers and books. In general, however, the systems of administration, education and justice (which applied both Islamic and customary pre-Islamic law) remained on medieval lines. The shah enjoyed travelling to Europe but prevented the Persian upper class from educating their children abroad, in case they should be infected with Western ideas.

The shah and his court were extravagant and demanding. To protect the throne, he maintained substantial armed forces which, although ill-paid, corrupt and inefficient, were costly. Since there was so little economic growth or development, and the returns from the sale of government offices were limited, state revenues were minimal. The shah therefore had recourse to the granting of concessions to foreign interests. The most remarkable of these was the concession awarded to Baron Julius de Reuter, a naturalized British subject, in 1873. Covering all Persia, this gave the Baron a seventy-year monopoly on the construction and operation of all Persian railroads and streetcars and on the exploitation of all mineral resources and government forests, including all uncultivated lands; an option on all future enterprises connected with the construction of roads, telegraphs, mills, factories, workshops and public works of every kind; and the right to collect all Persian customs duties for twenty-five years. In return, de Reuter was to pay the Persian government 20 per cent of the railway profits and 15 per cent of those from other sources. Lord Curzon commented that this represented 'the most complete and extraordinary surrender of the entire industrial resources of a kingdom into foreign hands that has probably ever been dreamt of, much less accomplished in history'.

The shah naïvely believed that he had both ensured some revenues and delegated his country's economic regeneration to Britain. Russia's furious reaction forced him to cancel the concession, but in 1899 British pressure forced him to grant a more limited concession which enabled de Reuter to establish the Imperial Bank of Persia, with the right to issue its own banknotes, and to search for oil.

Largely because of his willingness to mortgage the country's resources in this way, Nasir al-Din lost popularity in his later years and a liberal reformist movement began to emerge. Although Persia was much more isolated from the West than Ottoman Turkey, there was some penetration of Western ideas and methods via the foreign military missions, consular and bank officials and the Christian missionaries who were permitted to found schools and hospitals. The reform movement had a more potent stimulus from another source – the reformer and preacher of pan-Islamic ideals Jamal al-Din al-Afghani. The shah was attracted by al-Afghani's writings in his Paris exile and in 1886 he invited him to Persia, where he became an honoured member of the Royal Council. However, he soon began to preach subversive and revolutionary ideas – to the alarm of the shah and his ministers – and, when in 1890 he led the popular denunciation of the granting of a tobacco concession to a British group, he was deported from Persia. His movement survived, and in 1896 one of his disciples assassinated Nasir al-Din.

The reform movement gathered strength during the reign of Nasir al-Din's weak and ailing son Muzaffar al-Din, who exceeded his father in extravagance. A new reformist leader was Malkom Khan, the Persian ambassador in London, who campaigned against the shah's chief minister. When dismissed, he published a newspaper *Qanun* ('Law') calling for a fixed code of laws and the assembly of a parliament. Although banned in Persia, the paper nevertheless had a wide circulation in the country.

In 1903 the shah appointed his able but ultra-reactionary son-in-law Prince Ayn-u-Dula to assume control of government affairs. His actions provoked further opposition, and matters came to a head in 1905. A group of merchants, outraged by the extravagance and corruption of the court and the country's increased indebtedness which had led the government to introduce an onerous new customs tariff, took *best* or sanctuary in a Tehran mosque, in accordance with an ancient custom, in order to voice their protests. They were joined by some prominent mullahs. When the shah promised to meet some of their demands but then prevaricated and intensified the repression, a larger group combining many of the country's notables – merchants, bankers and clerics – took *best* in the grounds of the British legation to persist with their demand for the introduction of a legal code and also, for the first time, a constitution. In October 1906, now in desperately bad health, the shah complied – with extreme reluctance. A Majlis or parliament was convened which drafted a Fundamental Law of the constitution.

The Constitutional Revolution, as it is known, received the support of virtually the whole nation and was a milestone in Persian history. Subsequent shahs attempted to reverse it, but none was wholly successful and some form of constitutional and representative government has survived to the present day.

The constitutionalists received some inspiration from the attempt by their Russian counterparts in 1905 to end the autocratic role of the tsar. A different kind of stimulus came from the Russo-Japanese War of the same year, in which for the first time a modernizing Asian state defeated one of the great European powers. (This was also an inspiration for the Egyptian nationalist leader Mustafa Kamel in the same period.) However, with its blend of the secular and clerical, the reform movement had a strongly Persian character.

Muzaffar al-Din was succeeded in 1907 by his son Mohammed Ali, who reigned for only two years, amid continuing unrest. Like his father, he repeatedly promised to accept reforms only then to ignore them. At one point he bombarded the Majlis, which he had attempted unsuccessfully to dissolve, and killed or wounded many deputies. This led to a serious uprising in Tabriz which his troops were unable to quell. Russian troops intervened, ostensibly to protect Russian nationals. The nationalist forces gathered strength and marched on Tehran. Unable to resist, the shah took refuge in the Russian legation. As he went into exile in Russia, the Majlis decided that his 11-year-old son Ahmed Mirza should succeed him.

Popular feeling had been stirred up not only by the shah's action but also by the Anglo-Russian agreement of August 1907, which was designed to settle all outstanding differences concerning Persia and Afghanistan between Russia and Britain. The two powers were already expecting the coming struggle with imperial Germany, in which there were strong chances that Ottoman Turkey would be Germany's ally. In effect the agreement divided Persia into Russian and British spheres of interest, with Russia taking the north and centre, Britain the south-east, and the south-west remaining a 'neutral' zone. Persian opinion was dismayed and angry when the agreement was made known. Britain especially had been thought to have sympathized with the constitutionalist revolution. The European powers' wider strategic interests did not concern the Persians: Russia and Britain were henceforth regarded as the two imperial powers which sought to destroy Persia's independence.

Britain might be said to have had the worst of the 1907 agreement, because south-eastern Persia consists mainly of desert. However, British interests in Persia were about to receive a powerful boost. De Reuter had abandoned his mineral concession after two years, having failed to find oil, but in 1901 Shah Muzaffar al-Din granted an Englishman, William Knox D'Arcy, a sixty-year petroleum and gas concession covering the whole of the Persian Empire. The British government had lobbied strongly in D'Arcy's favour through the legation in Tehran, and the Persian grand vizier, who had been won over, successfully kept the deal secret from the Russians until it was signed.

D'Arcy looked for oil for several years without success, until his funds were nearly exhausted and he began to look around the world for new investors. At this point the British Admiralty intervened. The First Sea Lord, the dynamic and independent-minded Admiral John Fisher, had long ago determined that the British navy should convert its ships from the use of coal to oil. This, he reckoned, would increase its fighting capacity by 50 per cent. But 90 per cent of the world's oil was then produced in the United States and Russia, and the rest was already covered by concessions. The world market was dominated by Standard Oil and Royal Dutch Shell. It was urgently necessary to find an independent source under British control. In 1905 the Admiralty persuaded the British Burmah Oil Company to link up with D'Arcy and provide new funds. In 1908 D'Arcy's engineers, at the point of abandoning the search in despair, drilled into one of the world's largest oilfields at Masjid-i-Sulaiman in south-western Persia. The Anglo-Persian Oil Company was formed, and shares were sold to an enthusiastic public.

There were still difficulties. The oilfields were situated not in the British sphere of influence but in the neutral zone. The semi-independent Arab shaikh of Mohammereh regarded the area as his territory. Marauding tribes threatened the pipeline needed to export the oil to the Gulf. Accordingly Britain signed an agreement recognizing the shaikh and his successors as the lawful rulers of Mohammereh in return for an annual rental. The shaikh undertook to protect the oil installations.

In 1911 the young Winston Churchill became First Lord of the Admiralty in Britain's Liberal government, and a huge and expensive three-year development programme for the navy was launched. In addition to Persia's vital strategic significance for the British Empire, Persian oil was of crucial military importance. In June 1914, just two months before the outbreak of the First World War, Churchill presented the House of Commons with an agreement under which Anglo-Persian would guarantee oil supplies for twenty years while the British government would buy a controlling interest in the company (later the Anglo-Iranian Oil Company and ultimately British Petroleum) for £2.2 million. Despite a few members' misgivings that this would provoke the Russians and further weaken the Persian government, the agreement was overwhelmingly approved. Churchill later estimated that the investment brought savings of £40 million and paid for the gigantic expansion of the British navy without any cost to the British taxpayer.

With the 11-year-old Ahmed Mirza on the throne, Persia's internal situation became more chaotic. The victorious nationalists split into two parties – revolutionaries and moderates. The Russians sent troops to Kazvin in Tehran province, against British protests, on the familiar pretext of protecting their nationals. The lack of administrative experience of the new regime showed the urgent need of foreign advisers but, since neither Britain nor Russia would agree to the appointment of the other's nationals, it was necessary to look elsewhere for these. Belgians were placed in charge of the customs. An appeal was made to the United States, and President Taft recommended an experienced lawyer and civil servant William Shuster, who in 1911 was placed in charge of Persia's finances with full powers for a three-year period. Although the United States was in no way an imperial power in the Middle East at that period, the Russians vigorously protested, and persisted with their opposition to the point of threatening to occupy Tehran. The regent Nasir al-Mulk thereupon carried out a *coup d'état*, dissolved the Majlis and acceded to the Russian demands by expelling Shuster and his colleagues in January 1912. Shuster's efforts had just begun to show results, but the country was now left in even greater confusion.

Protests from the US government and liberal opinion in Britain were in vain – the need to accommodate Russia in the face of the expected war with Germany was paramount for Britain's Liberal government. When the war did break out and Turkey allied itself with Germany, the Turkish threat to Russian territory and to the oilfields in the south caused Russia and Britain to occupy part of Persia in spite of its declaration of neutrality.

8. The Sick Man Dies: 1918

In November 1914 the fate of the Ottoman Empire was sealed when Turkey joined Christian Europe's civil war in alliance with the Central Powers of Germany and Austro-Hungary against Britain, France and Russia. As we have seen, the powers of Europe, with the intermittent exception of Russia, had preferred to maintain the integrity of Asiatic Turkey and its Arab dominions. They interfered to bring pressure on successive sultans to further their interests, but they did not consider partitioning the empire. Britain's single-handed occupation of Egypt in 1882 was reluctant and almost accidental – the restoration of Ottoman authority in Egypt would have been preferable but was impractical. However, once the action was taken, Egypt became a vital link in Britain's world-wide imperial system which could not be abandoned.

Apart from their war strategy, all three Allies had to consider the reactions of the millions of Muslim subjects in their empires – Arabs in French North Africa and Muslim peoples in British India and in Russian central Asia. Would they be willing to fight for their Christian rulers against the sultan/caliph? It was a popular belief that any Muslim was only waiting for the call to *jihad* or holy war to slaughter the infidel. The triumvirate who ruled Turkey hastened to issue such a call.

Britain had two immediate strategic concerns in the Middle East – the protection of the Suez Canal and the protection of the Gulf. Both were vital links with India: the Canal had to be kept open for the transport of Indian troops to Europe, and the Gulf region now had the additional value of the oil installations at Abadan.

Jemal Pasha was the member of the Ottoman triumvirate who took command in Syria. As he stepped onto the train in Istanbul he declared, 'I shall not return until I have entered Cairo.' Jemal was an able general and he was assisted by a brilliant German chief of staff, von Kressenstein. Egypt was denuded of British troops, who had been sent to France, and was defended only by hastily assembled Australian and Indian units supported by Egyptian artillery and two

French cruisers which happened to be in the Canal. Jemal's first assault on the Canal, in January 1915, was repelled. His hopes that the Egyptian populace would rise against the British occupiers were belied. However, with the help of Sinai beduin tribesmen, von Kressenstein kept British forces tied to the Canal for two years. The Germans also succeeded in stirring up the warlike Senussi tribesmen in Cyrenaica and, although they posed no serious military threat, these also kept substantial British forces tied to the frontier.

As soon as the war with Turkey broke out, an Indian brigade was landed at Basra, which it took without difficulty, and began the advance towards Baghdad. Britain suffered a dangerous setback when a large Anglo-Indian force was surrounded at Kut and was forced to surrender, but Baghdad fell in March 1917 and by the end of the war British troops were in control of most of modern Iraq.

The war began disastrously for the Turks as, contrary to German advice, Enver Pasha, who was both commander-in-chief and minister of war, launched his troops against Russia in the Caucasus in the hope of raising a revolt among the Muslims of central Asia to help fulfil his pan-Turanian dreams. The Russians recovered from the initial onslaught and the Turkish troops suffered from the fearsome cold. Moreover, throughout eastern Anatolia the Turks were threatened by the insurrection of their embittered Armenian subjects, who disrupted communications and formed volunteer groups to help the Russians. Others joined the Russian Armenian forces. The Turks took a terrible revenge by ordering the deportation of the entire Armenian population from eastern Anatolia to northern Syria. Hundreds of thousands were killed, and many more died of hunger, exposure and disease. Between one and a quarter and one and a half million perished. Armenian nationalists still seek revenge against representatives of the Turkish state.

Despite the reverses on the Caucasus front, Turkey was far from defeated. With the war bogged down in France and the Russian advance held by Germany and Austria, Britain attempted to eliminate Turkey from the war by landing a large force (including Australasian contingents) on the Gallipoli peninsula to threaten Istanbul. The German inspector-general Liman von Sanders was in command of the Turkish defences, and his second in command was Mustafa Kemal (the future Kemal Atatürk). Despite a munitions shortage, the Turks fought tenaciously and neither side succeeded in dislodging the other. But by the winter it was Britain which accepted failure and withdrew its forces. Turkey's morale improved; by a huge recruitment drive, its forces were increased to fifty-two divisions or 800,000 men. However, successes against Britain in Mesopotamia were offset by continued advances of the Russians into eastern Anatolia. The Turkish forces were widely spread over several fronts.

The role of Egypt in the Gallipoli campaign was as a vast military camp and hospital for the Allies. The Egyptian people responded with their customary stoical friendliness to the invasion of tens of thousands of uninhibited Allied troops, even though the troops provoked a crippling rise in prices. An auxiliary labour corps of some three thousand Egyptians was sent to the Dardanelles, where they proved an outstanding success at digging trenches.

In the summer of 1916, von Kressenstein launched his final offensive against the Suez Canal. He was beaten back, and the British forces under General Murray were then in a position to sweep the Turks out of Sinai. By December 1916 they had reached El Arish before Gaza.

The Egyptian people were forced into political quiescence by the vast weight of British military power. The *fellahin* could show only passive resistance to increasingly insistent demands by the military government that they should surrender their firearms and volunteer for camel transport or the auxiliary labour corps. Several thousand did eventually serve in Palestine and France and suffered casualties.

The pro-Turkish and pan-Islam feeling which Britain had feared was almost non-existent. The oriental secretary in Cairo, Sir Ronald Storrs, wrote, 'Pious Muslims shake their heads and say, "We wish the Turks all success – from afar."' In the Canal zone it was only some Muslims in two Indian battalions of the Canal Defence Force who deserted to the Turks. They were caught and shot and the trouble was prevented from spreading. A succession of Indian Muslim ruling princes was brought in to help stiffen the morale of the troops.

That pro-Turkish feeling was subdued did not mean that Egyptian nationalism was dead. Although leaderless and confused, the students were fervently nationalist and their clubs seethed with bitter opposition to the occupation. Secretly they applauded two unsuccessful assassination attempts on the life of Sultan Hussein Kamel. However, the British government handled the situation with some skill. When the sultan died in the summer of 1917, it resisted the demands that

Britain should annex Egypt which came from some MPs and which were supported by Sir Reginald Wingate, the new high commissioner in Cairo; Britain was still concerned with the reaction of other Mediterranean powers. Instead the 49-year-old Prince Ahmed Fuad, a son of the khedive Ismail, was brought in to replace Hussein Kamel.

While pro-Turkish sentiment presented little problem for Britain in Egypt, there was a possibility that anti-Turkish feeling could be encouraged in the Ottoman Arab dominions. It was known that the Arabs had good cause for resentment against their rulers – especially in the aftermath of the brief Arab–Turkish honeymoon which followed the Young Turks revolution – but detailed intelligence was lacking.

Six weeks before Turkey entered the war, Lord Kitchener, at Ronald Storrs' suggestion, approached Sharif Hussein in Mecca to find out which way the Arabs would turn if Turkey allied itself to Germany. The sharif was as cautious as Kitchener himself had been with the Amir Abdullah eight months earlier. He hinted that he might bring the Hejazis out in revolt against the Turks if he was ensured of enough British support. A further message from Kitchener (who by now was minister of war in the British cabinet) promised Hussein that, if he would come out against Turkey, Britain would guarantee his retention of the title of Grand Sharif and defend him against external aggression. It hinted that if the sharif were declared caliph he would have Britain's support, and it included a general promise to help the Arabs obtain their freedom.

The message was enough to cause Sharif Hussein to contemplate the much wider objective of a general revolt against the Turks, under his leadership. But for this he required much more specific assurances from the Allies, and the year 1915 was spent trying to elicit them from Cairo while he continued to sound out the other leading Arabs in the peninsula with whom he was in contact.

The British cabinet for its part had no clear policy towards the Arabs or for the future of the Ottoman provinces in Asia after Turkey's defeat. It was obviously desirable that Turkey should be knocked out of the war as soon as possible, but this was primarily to give Britain and France access to Russia and Romania to encircle the Central Powers. This was the strategy behind the Gallipoli campaign. There was an assumption that the Turks would have to give up

Constantinople/Istanbul and the Dardanelles strait and that 'in the interests of Islam' (according to the foreign secretary, Sir Edward Grey) there should be an independent Muslim political unit somewhere else. Its centre would naturally be the Muslim holy places and Arabia, but it remained to be settled what else it would include.

Britain's Arab policy evolved in a way that the British considered pragmatic but which the Arabs came to regard as unprincipled. Sir Percy Cox, the chief political officer of the Mesopotamian Expeditionary Force, which occupied Basra at the beginning of the war, was aware of the importance of winning Ibn Saud, the new power in central Arabia, to the British cause. He sent Captain W. H. I. Shakespear as British representative at the Saudi court. Shakespear had already made friends with Ibn Saud during his heroic journeys of exploration in Arabia, and he was the Englishman whom the Wahhabi ruler most admired. However, Shakespear was killed in a skirmish with the Saudis' Rashidi enemies in January 1915. His death eliminated the possibility that Britain might invest in the Saudis, who had long demonstrated their independence from the Turks, as the leaders of an Arab revolt.

To the Arab Bureau – the group of high-level British experts gathered in Cairo – there were sound political reasons for looking to the Hashemites from the Hejaz to lead the Arabs. Sharif Hussein's position as keeper of the Islamic holy places made him the obvious person to counter the Ottoman call for a *jihad* against the infidel. But at that stage Britain had little knowledge of the state of opinion in Mesopotamia (Iraq) and Syria, although it was in a position to sound the feelings of leading Arabs in Cairo. Moreover, Britain had to consider the interests of its principal allies, Russia and France. In 1915 there was already a fear that huge Russian losses were causing the Russian people to lose enthusiasm for the war. France, which was bearing the brunt of the war on the western front, had a claim to a special position in Syria, based on long-standing cultural and political ties that had been acknowledged by Britain before the war. During 1915, Britain began secret negotiations with its two allies on the future of all the Ottoman lands. Although British, the government of India also had its own interests and means of pressure on London, and it regarded Mesopotamia, the Gulf and the Arabian peninsula, as its special concern. It is hardly surprising that Britain lacked a coherent policy towards the Arabs.

The British government negotiated the agreement with Sharif Hussein to launch his revolt against the Turks by a correspondence which took place between July 1915 and February 1916, being conducted through Sir Henry McMahon, the British high commissioner in Egypt.

The sharif's aim was to secure British support for Arab independence in all the Arab provinces of the Ottoman Empire from Mersin in the north, the Persian frontier in the east, the Mediterranean in the west, and the Red Sea and the Indian Ocean in the south. The only temporary exception he was prepared to make was Aden. Doubtless he knew that Britain would not accept all his demands, but he was setting out his maximum negotiating position.

McMahon's crucial letter is his second, dated 24 October 1915, in which he pledged British support for Arab independence in the areas proposed by the sharif subject to certain reservations:

The districts of Mersin and Alexandretta, and portions of Syria lying to the west of the districts of Damascus, Homs, Hama and Aleppo, cannot be said to be purely Arab, and must on that account be excepted from the proposed delimitation.

Subject to that modification, and without prejudice to the treaties concluded between us and certain Arab Chiefs, we accept that delimitation.

As for the regions lying within the proposed frontiers, in which Great Britain is free to act without detriment to the interests of her ally France, I am authorized to give you the following pledges on behalf of the Government of Great Britain, and to reply as follows to your note:

That subject to the modifications stated above, Great Britain is prepared to recognize and uphold the independence of the Arabs in all the regions lying within the frontiers proposed by the Sharif of Mecca.

In other passages in the same letter, McMahon said it was understood 'that the Arabs have already decided to seek the counsels and advice of Great Britain exclusively; and that such European advisers and officials as may be needed to establish a sound system of administration shall be British'. He added that he considered it was agreed that

as regards to the two Vilayets of Baghdad and Basra the Arabs recognize that the fact of Great Britain's established position and interests there will call for the setting up of special administrative arrangements to protect those regions from foreign aggression, to promote the welfare of their inhabitants and to safeguard our mutual interest.

The ambiguity in some of these phrases was no doubt deliberate, and the shrewd sharif was aware of the reasons. He protested vigorously about the exemption of the Syrian Mediterranean coast from the area of Arab independence, saying that the vilayets of Aleppo and Beirut could not be regarded as anything but Arab provinces. He reluctantly agreed to shelve the problem for the duration of the war but declared his trust that Britain would subsequently persuade 'her ally France' to hand them over to the Arabs. He was more ready to compromise on the Iraqi provinces, recognizing the existing reality of the British military occupation, but he pointed out that, because they were part of the former Arab Empire, the seat of the caliphs and the first centre of Arab culture, it would be 'impossible to persuade or compel the Arab nation to renounce the honourable association'. He agreed that the end of the occupation would be determined by negotiation, but 'without prejudice to the rights of either party or the natural wealth and resources of these parts'.

The ambiguity which sowed most trouble for the future concerned Palestine. The name was not mentioned in the correspondence because Palestine was not an Ottoman administrative division, although it was a geographical expression employed throughout the Christian world. British cabinet ministers certainly referred to Palestine in their discussions. By no stretch of the imagination could McMahon's exemption of 'portions of Syria lying to the west of the districts of Damascus, Homs, Hama and Aleppo' – which was a vague attempt to accommodate French interests in Lebanon – have referred to the *sanjak* of Jerusalem, which covered two-thirds of Palestine and lay well to the south. It may be argued that the sharif either understood or should have been aware that Palestine was excluded, but there is no proof and he never accepted it. Britain could easily have clarified the situation by saying that Palestine must have a special status because it was sacred to Judaism, Christianity and Islam, but it chose not to do this. Clarity was not an objective.

The sharif's weakness lay in the fact that his claim to leadership was far from being acknowledged by the Arabs outside the Hejaz. Apart from the imam of Yemen (who remained pro-Turkish), the Arab shaikhs on the fringes of the Arabian peninsula (who were in treaty relationship with Britain) and Ibn Saud in the interior (who was the sharif's hostile rival), the Arabs of Mesopotamia looked forward to their own independence, while the sharif had little contact with the Arabs of Syria, who were under iron Turkish rule. When Jemal Pasha first arrived in Syria to command the Fourth Army, he curbed his naturally despotic nature and declared a policy of 'clemency and tolerance towards the Arabs'. 'I am in a position to assure you that the Turkish and Arab ideals do not conflict,' he said in Damascus in January 1915. 'They are brothers in their strivings, and perhaps their efforts are complementary.' However, after his failure to invade Egypt and his intelligence services reported the scale of Arab anti-Turkish activities, he resorted to a policy of repression. First he took every opportunity to send Arab units of the Ottoman Army out of Syria and replace them with Turks, and then he put on trial a number of prominent Arab civilians who had been implicated in treasonable activities by documents seized in the French consulates. Eleven were publicly executed in August 1915 and twenty-one more the following May in the central squares of Damascus and Beirut.

However, if the Syrians were feeling increasingly anti-Turkish, they by no means saw their salvation in France. Hostility towards the possibility of French rule surprised even British intelligence, which attributed it to aspects of French colonial policy in north-west Africa. Only the Maronites of Mount Lebanon looked to France as a protector.

By the spring of 1916, Sharif Hussein knew that he had to act, as a large Turco-German force was about to arrive in the Hejaz on its way to Yemen. On 16 June he raised the flag of the Arab Revolt and seized Mecca from its small Turkish garrison. He had hoped for a simultaneous landing by Allied troops at Alexandretta (Iskenderun) to promote an uprising against the Turks in Syria, but this was rejected by the British war cabinet, despite strong support from the military, because of French opposition to any landing in Syria other than by French troops. For the time being the Arab Revolt remained confined to the Hejaz. On 2 November 1916 Sharif Hussein was proclaimed 'King of the Arab Countries' by his followers, but this was not acceptable to Britain and France. A compromise was reached, and in January 1917 they both recognized him as king of the Hejaz.

Britain had never specifically promised to acknowledge Sharif Hussein's claim to leadership of all the Arabs, although it had encouraged him to believe that it would. The truth was that Britain's secret negotiations with France on the future of the Arab Ottoman dominions had already resulted in an agreement early in 1916. The two allies had previously accepted, with some misgivings, that Russia should have Constantinople and the Dardanelles. The task of negotiating had been delegated to Georges Picot of France and Sir Mark Sykes of Britain, and the Sykes–Picot agreement which they concluded partitioned the whole of Syria and Iraq and a large part of southern Turkey into spheres of direct or indirect French and British influence. France's area corresponded to the future states of Syria and Lebanon, and Britain's to Iraq and Transjordan. France's area of direct control would be the Mediterranean coastal regions, and Britain's the vilayets of Basra and Baghdad (in addition to the ports of Haifa and Acre). In the hinterland, which would be under the indirect control of the two powers, France and Britain were prepared 'to recognize and uphold an independent Arab state or confederation of Arab states under the suzerainty of an Arab chief'. In addition there was an area including Jerusalem and most of Palestine which was to be under some form of international control. Only the area comprising the present-day Saudi Arabia and the Yemen Arab Republic was to be left independent. (Britain had Aden and retained its exclusive relationship with the Arab Gulf shaikhdoms.)

For understandable reasons, Britain and France chose to keep the details of their agreement secret. Sharif Hussein had some suspicions of the Allies' intentions, and in early 1917 Sir Mark Sykes was sent to Jedda by the British Foreign Office to allay his fears. But although they discussed the question of French arms in Lebanon and the Syrian coastal regions, with Hussein maintaining the principle that these regions were as much Arab in character as the interior, Sykes did not inform him of the broader aspects of the Sykes–Picot agreement.

Meanwhile, although the Arab Revolt launched by the sharif aroused little response in Mesopotamia and Syria, which were still firmly under Turkish control, it made an important contribution to the war in the Middle East. It immobilized some 30,000 Turkish troops along the Hejaz railway from Amman to Medina and prevented the Turco-German forces in Syria from linking up with the Turkish garrison in Yemen. There could have been the most serious consequences for the Allies if the enemy forces had made contact with the Germans in East Africa and succeeded in closing the Red Sea to Allied shipping. The Arab forces, who were mainly armed tribesmen with only a small core of regular troops, were under the command of Amir Feisal, the sharif's third son. Feisal lacked the subtle intelligence of his elder brother, Amir Abdullah, but with his imposing appearance and restrained dignity he seemed to Colonel T. E. Lawrence, one of the British officers sent by the Arab Bureau in Cairo to help the revolt, to possess the right qualities for leadership.

In the spring of 1917 the British offensive against Turkey in Syria/Palestine was going badly. In April, General Murray's expeditionary force was heavily repulsed in Gaza and held up for three months. Then, at the end of June, Murray was replaced by General Allenby, a brilliant and forceful commander (nicknamed 'the Bull') who at once moved GHQ from Cairo to Palestine and speedily raised morale. At the end of October he launched his offensive and drove on towards Jerusalem.

Morale was also high in Amir Feisal's camp. In July his forces captured the port of Aqaba with a daring stroke. The Arabs were making an important contribution to Turkey's defeat. However, as Allenby was advancing, the Bolsheviks seized power in Russia, discovered documents referring to the Sykes–Picot agreement among the imperial archives, and informed the Turks about these. Jemal Pasha lost no time in passing the details on to the Arabs, as proof of treachery against the Muslim peoples of the Ottoman Empire by the Christian powers. Sharif Hussein at once asked for an explanation from Sir Reginald Wingate (who had succeeded McMahon in Cairo). Wingate represented the Petrograd documents as referring to provisional exchanges between the British, French and Russian governments, rather than to any hard agreement, and suggested that the success of the Arab Revolt and the withdrawal of Russia from the war had created an entirely new situation.

This last point was true, but its principal consequence was to relieve the Allies of their promise of Constantinople and the straits to Russia. The success of the Arab Revolt had scarcely improved Sharif Hussein's bargaining position *vis-à-vis* the Allies. Their mutual and independent interests remained unchanged. With its huge base in Egypt, Allenby's armies in Palestine and control of Mesopotamia (Baghdad had fallen in March 1917), Britain was much the stronger power in the region. Its priority was the security of the British Empire, both in the present and in the future. But France was Britain's only major partner in the total war with Germany. It had suffered colossal casualties in Europe – far greater than Britain's – and in 1917 its determination was wavering. Britain was not going to frustrate the Middle East ambitions of its ally for the sake of the Hashemites, who were heavily dependent on British money, arms and military advice.

Allenby drove on to take Jerusalem on 9 December. Tactfully he walked rather than rode into the Holy City. He was then held up by the severity of the winter and the stiffening of the Turco-German forces under the command of General Liman von Sanders, who were benefiting from Russia's removal from the war. But in September 1918 Allenby resumed his advance to drive the Turks out of Syria. Damascus fell on 1 October. The first Allied troops to reach the city were a body of Australian cavalry, but Lawrence arranged for Feisal's Arab forces to make the triumphant entry and install their own governor.

Liman von Sanders was recalled, and it fell to Mustafa Kemal, who had halted the Russian advance in Anatolia in 1916, to extricate the Seventh Army. He brought it back to Aleppo and finally managed an orderly retreat across the Taurus Mountains. Aleppo fell to the Allies on 26 October, and two days later the Ottoman government abandoned the struggle and signed the armistice agreement at Mudros.

The revelation of the Sykes–Picot agreement was not the only reason for Arab doubts about Britain's intentions for the future of the Arab provinces of the Ottoman Empire. On 2 November 1917 – a few days before Jemal Pasha informed Sharif Hussein of the secret Anglo-French accord – a letter from the British foreign secretary, Arthur Balfour, to a leading British Zionist Jew, Lord Rothschild, was published:

His Majesty's Government view with favour the establishment in Palestine of a National Home for the Jewish people, and will use their best endeavours to facilitate the achievement of this object, it being clearly understood that nothing shall be done which may prejudice the civil and religious rights of existing non-Jewish communities in Palestine or the rights and political status enjoyed by Jews in any other country.

This apparently unsensational document, known as 'the Balfour Declaration', planted the seeds of a conflict which has lasted almost to the end of the century and is unlikely to be resolved before another century has passed. Although few were aware of this at the time, it was the result of a compromise between British and Zionist aims. Its consequences have been greater than those of the Anglo-French agreement, which were eliminated by the demise of British and French imperial power within a few decades.

Since the failure of the last attempt to restore Jewish independence in Palestine in AD 134, the Jews had become scattered throughout the world. Only a few thousand religious Jews remained in Jerusalem, and there were tiny communities elsewhere in the Holy Land. The Jews in the rest of the world experienced varying degrees of persecution and prosperity, discrimination and tolerance, but from the eighteenth century they benefited from the economic expansion of western Europe and the movement towards religious toleration. During the nineteenth century, liberalism and assimilation appeared to be steadily gaining ground in western Europe, particularly in Russia and Russian Poland, where the concentration of Jewish population was greatest. Just as anti-Jewish movements, influenced by the nationalist temper of the nineteenth century, began to emphasize race rather than religion, so the Jews themselves, under the influence of their environment and the pressure of persecution, began to think in terms of a new Jewish nationalism. However, it took nearly two thousand years to develop the idea of a mass return of the 12 million Jews in the world to Palestine to re-create a Jewish state – the Jewish prayer 'Next year in Jerusalem' was the expression of a spiritual or Messianic ideal rather than a political slogan.

In the second half of the nineteenth century, there was a steady movement of Jews from eastern Europe to settle in Palestine. Supported by Jewish philanthropy, they went mainly to found colonies to work the land. They were the pioneers of 'practical Zionism'. They were very much fewer than those who went to western Europe and the United States, but by 1914 there were about 80,000 Jews (including the indigenous communities) in Palestine, compared with about 650,000 Arabs.

'Political Zionism', or the concept of turning Palestine into a national Jewish state, was founded by Theodor Herzl, a prominent Austrian political journalist who in 1896 published his book *Der Judenstaat* (*The Jewish State: An Attempt at a Modern Solution of the Jewish Question*), in which he declared that the Jewish question was neither social nor religious but national. Although himself an assimilated agnostic Jew, he maintained that assimilation had not worked.

Anti-Semitism was growing. He did not believe that all Jews should be forced to go to the new Jewish state; the important thing was that Jews should enjoy sovereignty over a piece of territory to suit their national requirements. If it were in Palestine, the European Jews would help to civilize the surrounding region.

Herzl organized the first Zionist Congress, at Basle in 1897, where the delegates called for the colonization of Palestine by Jewish agricultural and industrial workers and *the organization and binding together of the whole of Jewry*.

For tactical reasons, the early Zionists spoke of a 'home' rather than a 'state' in Palestine, although they still had to secure Ottoman consent for this. As we have seen, Herzl's request was rejected by Sultan Abdul Hamid. Herzl then considered Sinai and Cyprus (inhabited by Greeks and Turks), but these were denied him by Cromer of Egypt and the British Colonial Office. In 1903 the British government made a lukewarm offer of territory in Uganda, which Herzl reluctantly agreed to consider, but this was rejected by the sixth Zionist Congress shortly before his death in 1904.

There followed a decade of frustration for political Zionism. The World Zionist Organization, based in Vienna, was established on a sound footing, and it was possible to step up the process of practical Zionism as the Young Turks allowed some relaxation of Jewish immigration into Palestine. A Jewish National Fund to buy land in Palestine was founded in 1901. But the objective of turning Palestine into a national home for all the Jews seemed as far away as ever. World Jewry had still to be won over to Zionism. Many of the most prominent and wealthy Jews in central and western Europe were opposed to what they saw as a disruptive movement. American Jews still showed little interest. Religious leaders were divided, with the chief rabbi of Vienna declaring that Zionism was incompatible with Judaism.

The weight of support for Zionism came from the mass of east-European Jews. However, in the years leading up to the First World War the Zionist organization moved the focus of its attentions to Britain, where it could act most freely and where, according to Herzl, there was least anti-Semitism. Two of Herzl's leading east-European lieutenants – Chaim Weizmann and Nahum Sokolov – were now living in England. By 1914 Weizmann, as president of the English Zionist Federation, was familiar with half the British cabinet. Such

Zionists fully understood the importance of securing the support of the most powerful Gentiles as well as world Jewry. In some important cases they had little or no need to persuade.

Many different individuals contributed to the genesis of the Balfour Declaration. The British Gentiles among them were guided by a remarkable mixture of imperial *Realpolitik* and romantic/historical feelings. It was a Jewish member of the British government, Herbert Samuel, who in January 1915 first proposed to the cabinet the idea of a Jewish Palestine which would be annexed to the British Empire. But it was not until after David Lloyd George took over the conduct of the war at the end of 1916, as the leader of a National Coalition of Liberals and Conservatives, that the Zionist cause made real headway. The prime minister, a close friend of the Gentile Zionist editor of the *Manchester Guardian* – C. P. Scott – was an easy convert, as were other members of his cabinet – Balfour, the foreign secretary; Lord Milner, the former imperial consul in Africa; and a large group of Foreign Office officials and government advisers which included Sir Mark Sykes. These were non-Jews who saw huge advantages in a Jewish Palestine as part of the empire. But underpinning their imperial convictions was the romantic appeal of the return of the Jews to Zion, which, founded on Old Testament Christianity, was part of their Victorian upbringing. (Zionism also had this twin attraction for Churchill, who was not in the cabinet in 1917 but would return to it.) The British cabinet had already veered away from the commitment in the Sykes–Picot agreement to international control for Palestine. 'Britain could take care of the Holy Places better than anyone else,' the prime minister told C. P. Scott, and a French Palestine was 'not to be thought of'.

It was ironical, but in the circumstances not surprising, that the only Jew in the cabinet, Sir Edward Montague, secretary of state for India, should also be the most outspoken opponent of the Balfour Declaration. Montague was a member of the highly assimilated Anglo-Jewish aristocracy, many of whom feared the effect of Jewish nationalism on their own position. Montague had his counterparts in other countries – Henry Morgenthau Sr, a former US ambassador to Turkey, was a pronounced anti-Zionist, for example. Nevertheless the British cabinet was convinced that world Jewry was overwhelmingly in favour of Zionism and gave credit to Britain for supporting the cause. It believed that this had helped to bring the United States into the war in April 1917 and to maintain its enthusiasm thereafter. The British may have had an exaggerated view of the wealth and influence on Washington of American Jews at that period, but it was their belief in these that mattered. Moreover, the Germans were aware of the possibilities to be gained by winning Jewish sympathy, especially among the many American Jews of east-European origin who hated the Russian government. Germany was trying to persuade the Turks to lift their objections to Zionist settlement in Palestine, although so far without success. Finally, it was hoped that Britain's adoption of Zionism would win over the Russian Jewish socialists who were trying to influence the Kerensky government to take Russia out of the war.

All these strands of practicality and idealism came together in making the Balfour Declaration. The British cabinet believed it was a finely balanced document. When Balfour asked Rothschild and Weizmann to submit a draft, it said that 'Palestine should be reconstituted as the National Home for the Jewish people.' This was too strong and the final draft, as we have seen, said only that the British government favoured 'the establishment *in* Palestine of a National Home for the Jewish people'. It also added the provisos concerning 'the civil and religious rights of non-Jews in Palestine' and 'the rights and political status enjoyed by Jews in any other country'.

Even this cautious wording greatly increased Sharif Hussein's alarm about the Allies' intentions. This time Commander D. G. Hogarth, the head of the Arab Bureau, was dispatched to see him in Jedda. Hogarth pressed the case for the return of the Jews to Palestine, but Sharif Hussein – now king of Hejaz – was already showing perceptive anxiety that the Balfour Declaration might foreshadow a Jewish state in Palestine. Hogarth reported, 'The King would not accept an independent Jewish State in Palestine, nor was I instructed to warn him that such a state was contemplated.' Hussein accepted the assurances and ended by showing enthusiasm for the advantages that Jewish immigration would bring to the Arab countries.

The British government lost no time in implementing the terms of the Balfour Declaration. Soon after Jerusalem's capture from the Turks, Weizmann arrived at the head of a Zionist Commission and established its headquarters there. The Commission found that the Arabs of Palestine were already thoroughly alarmed – they took it for granted that Palestine should remain a purely Arab country. Before the war they had begun to resent the activities of the Zionist colonists and their establishment of exclusive Jewish communities, but these had not presented a serious threat as the Ottoman authorities had kept their expansion to a minimum. Now, in 1918, the Arabs believed the Zionists aimed to take over the country and place them in subjection. After all, although the Arabs formed about 90 per cent of the people of Palestine, the Balfour Declaration referred to them as the 'existing non-Jewish communities' whose civil and religious rights – but not political rights – were not to be prejudiced.

Weizmann and the Commission felt that the British military authorities were not doing enough to bring home to the Palestinian Arabs Britain's determination to implement the terms of the Balfour Declaration. British officials in Palestine, for their part, thought the Zionists should do much more to reassure the Arab majority of their real intentions. The question is, what were these real intentions?

Although the Zionists were prepared to make tactical compromises of the kind which produced the Balfour Declaration, there can be no doubt that their true aim was to turn Palestine into the national home for the Jews to which most of the Jews in the world would want to emigrate. They might have differed over its precise borders, but in their view Palestine was to become a Jewish national state with a substantial Jewish majority. However, they had come to realize how difficult it might be to achieve this. Weizmann was surprised by how 'non-Jewish' Jerusalem and Palestine had become. He left after a few months, believing that it might be impossible to prevent Palestine from becoming an Arab state.

The attitudes of British ministers were more complex. Although they had more than an inkling of the true Zionist objectives, most of them were quite ignorant of the real situation in Palestine and the sentiments of its people although few regarded these as of great importance compared with the interests of the British Empire. They certainly could not foresee that they were helping to create one of the least soluble political problems of the century. Some were disturbed when the incompatibility between Zionist aspirations and the overwhelming feelings of the indigenous Arabs became apparent from the reports of British officials on the spot. The author of the Balfour Declaration had no such doubts. A year after the war he wrote, 'The four great powers are committed to Zionism and Zionism, be it right or wrong, good or bad, is rooted in age-long tradition, in present needs, in future hopes, of far profounder import than the desires and prejudices of the 700,000 Arabs who now inhabit that ancient land.'

The doubts that had been raised about the intentions of the Allies did not prevent the wild Arab rejoicing which greeted the liberation of Syria. The civil population had suffered fearfully from the war, because a plague of locusts, combined with the normal disruption of war and the corruption of Turkish officials and Syrian merchants, had caused widespread famine. Between 300,000 and 500,000 people died, out of a total population of 4 million.

Although it was Allenby's policy wherever possible to allow Amir Feisal's troops to enter the captured cities in triumph and to take over the administration, the entente with France was clearly Britain's first consideration, and when France objected to the display of Feisal's flag in Beirut Allenby ordered its removal. The French hastened to land troops in Beirut at the end of the war, and the whole coastal area from Tyre to Cilicia in Asia Minor came under French military administration. The British Occupied Enemy Territory Administration South (OETA South) covered Palestine, while the main towns in the Syrian interior were under Feisal's authority but with an attachment of British officers (OETA East) on whom the Arabs, with their limited experience in administration, were heavily dependent. Mesopotamia was maintained as a single unit under an Anglo-Indian administration. The Sykes–Picot agreement, modified to reflect the realities of the situation, was already being applied.

Allenby and his military administrators faced a prospect of immense difficulty, which was not helped by the frequently conflicting instructions they received from Whitehall. Apart from France and the Zionists, with their demands, the new American ally had entered the scene. The fact that the United States had no imperial ambitions towards the Middle East greatly added to the moral force of President Wilson's sermon-like speeches about the post-war settlement. He chose to take Britain at its word. When a group of seven prominent Arabs living in Cairo presented a memorandum asking for a clear definition of British policy, Britain's reply – known as the Declaration to the Seven, and given wide publicity – was that the future government of Arab territories liberated by the action of Arab armies would be based on the principle of the 'consent of the governed'. Wilson included this phrase among his Four Ends of Peace which, under his influence, were later incorporated in the Covenant of the League of Nations. It was later given even greater force by an Anglo-French declaration of 7 November 1918 – that is, in the week between the signing of the armistice agreements with Turkey and Germany – which said that the goal of the British and French governments was the complete and final liberation of peoples oppressed by the Turks and the setting up of national governments and administrations which should derive their authority from the free exercise of the initiative and choice of the indigenous population.

Even allowing for American pressure, it is difficult to see why Britain and France should have felt that such barefaced hypocrisy was necessary. Turkey had already been defeated, and there was no need to sustain the Arab Revolt. There was no intention in London or Paris of allowing the indigenous population in the former Ottoman territories the free choice of their rulers. Even 'the consent of the governed' was an empty phrase.

9. The Anglo-French Interregnum, 1918–1939

Partition of the Arab East

The end of four centuries of Turkish rule in the Middle East was sudden and complete. Since Turkish rule had been accepted as the natural order for so long, it is hardly surprising that its removal left the vast majority of the population feeling confused and disorientated. The Ottoman ruling class had provided the leaders of Arab society – even in Egypt, which had been under British control for nearly forty years.

As we have seen, Ottoman governments and their representatives in the Arab provinces sometimes gave reason for them to be detested, but this did not mean that Turkish political leadership of the heart of the Islamic world had come to seem unnatural. Despite some later rewriting of history, the concept of a separate Arab nation – still less the doctrine of secular Arab nationalism – had scarcely begun to develop. The Hashemite claim to Arab leadership had been born almost haphazardly in the circumstances of war. It was far from being accepted by all the Arabs and would always suffer from its sponsorship by Britain. But the total Ottoman collapse did give Britain and France a brief period in which they felt that they could act largely as they pleased. This was something that would otherwise have been unimaginable for two invading Christian powers.

The Turkish heartland of the Ottoman Empire only narrowly avoided its own dismemberment – largely through the indomitable leadership of one man, Mustafa Kemal. After the signing of the Mudros armistice agreement, the new sultan, Mohammed VI (Mohammed V had died in July 1918), dissolved the Turkish parliament and formed a new government of men who were ready to accept the terms of the Allies. Apart from an Allied administration of Istanbul, the French were occupying Cilicia and Adana, British forces had taken over the Dardanelles strait and the Italians, the fourth of the western Allies, had landed at Antalya. Only the Russians had no claim. Under the Treaty of Brest-Litovsk (9 March 1918,

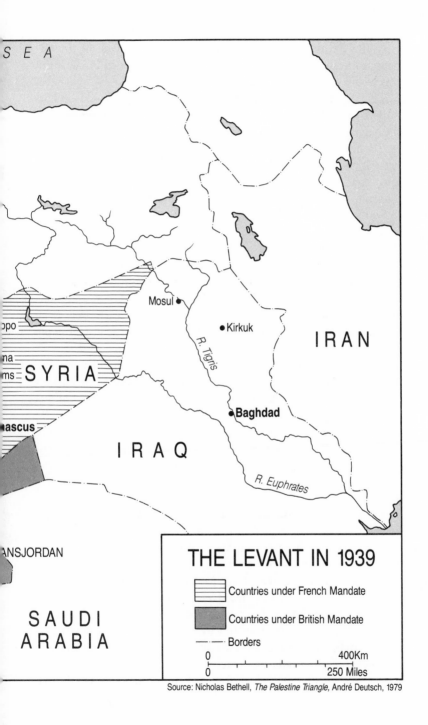

_S E A_

Mosul

●Kirkuk

opo

na

ms

SYRIA

I R A N

R. Tigris

Baghdad

ascus

I R A Q

R. Euphrates

ANSJORDAN

SAUDI
ARABIA

THE LEVANT IN 1939

Countries under French Mandate

Countries under British Mandate

–·–·– Borders

0   400Km

0   250 Miles

Source: Nicholas Bethell, _The Palestine Triangle_, André Deutsch, 1979

after the Bolshevik Revolution), Turkey had regained all the territories lost to Russia in the war, as well as those ceded in 1877. But
this would mean little if Turkey ceased to exist.

The Committee of Union and Progress had collapsed and its
leaders had fled. The sultan then decided to crush the remnants of
the Young Turks. Mustafa Kemal, who already enjoyed high prestige
in Turkey, was causing the sultan and his government trouble by
organizing resistance to the Allies in Istanbul, so Mohammed VI
appointed him inspector-general of the Ninth Army, based on
Samsun, with orders to disband the remainder of the Ottoman
forces.

Mustafa Kemal landed at Samsun on 9 May 1919, but instead of
disbanding the army he gathered supporters for the declaration of a
Turkish state free from foreign control. The Allies, determined to
fight resurgent Turkish nationalism, allowed a large Greek force to
land at Izmir and occupy the surrounding district. Greek ambitions
extended to the whole of western Anatolia, in which there were large
Greek minorities – the former Christian Empire of Constantinople
might be restored.

While the sultan ordered the Turkish troops not to resist the
Greeks, Kemal was rapidly gathering support for the cause of Turkish
independence. Although exhausted by eight years of almost continuous warfare, the Turkish people were roused to pursue the struggle
by the Greek advance into the Anatolian heartland. They rejected the
harsh terms of the Treaty of Sèvres of August 1920, which would
have left Turkey helpless and deprived of some of its richest provinces, and the sultan, now little more than a puppet, was increasingly
discredited.

The Graeco-Turkish war lasted two years, from 1920 to 1922. At
first the Turks were unable to halt the Greek advance, but in 1921
the tide turned with a great Turkish victory on the River Sakayra. In
1922 the Greeks, weakened by dissension at home, were in headlong
retreat, and in September 1922 Mustafa Kemal occupied Izmir.
When his forces crossed the Dardanelles to drive the Greeks out of
European Turkey too, a direct clash with Britain was only narrowly
averted. The Allies gave way and by the terms of the armistice, to
which Greece also adhered, they recognized Turkish sovereignty
over Istanbul, the straits and eastern Thrace.

The peace conference which followed culminated with the Treaty of Lausanne of 24 July 1923. This recognized full Turkish sovereignty in nearly all the territories which are now those of the Turkish Republic. The long-suffering Armenians lost their hopes of independence in the process. After the Bolshevik Revolution, eastern or Russian Armenia declared its independence. Hopes of the western or Turkish Armenians of joining the new republic were destroyed by the advance of Mustafa Kemal's forces, and in December 1920 the government in the Armenian capital, Yerevan, handed over power peacefully to the Bolsheviks. The remnants of the Turkish Armenians fled mainly to Lebanon and Syria, where after a few years they were offered citizenship.

The Kurds suffered a similar bitter disappointment. The Treaty of Sèvres recognized an independent Kurdish state of Kurdistan, but this was cancelled by the 1923 Treaty of Lausanne. The Kurdish problem remained to destabilize the politics of the three countries in which Kurds form important minorities – Turkey, Iran and Iraq.

Although a considerable body of Turkish opinion favoured the retention of a constitutional monarchy, Mustafa Kemal was determined to get rid of the sultan, and his prestige and authority were such that he had his way. On 1 November 1922 the National Assembly passed a law abolishing the sultanate, and Mohammed VI fled into exile. On 29 October 1923 Turkey was proclaimed a republic, with Kemal as president.

The Islamic caliphate attracted as much loyalty as the sultanate and, although Mustafa Kemal would have liked to abolish the offices of sultan and caliph together, he bowed to the popular will in this matter. He agreed that Mohammed VI's nephew Abdul Mejid should become the spiritual head of Islam. But, although the caliph was shorn of all political power, his court became the centre of monarchist intrigue, and when two prominent Indian Muslims, Amir Ali and the Agha Khan, published a declaration calling upon the Turkish people to preserve the caliphate, Mustafa Kemal took advantage of the unfavourable Turkish reaction to this foreign interference and abolished it. A bill to this effect was passed by the National Assembly on 3 March 1924.

The title of caliph has not since been revived. In May 1926 a caliphate congress, held in Cairo, was attended by delegates from thirteen Muslim countries (not including Turkey), but its deliberations were inconclusive. Since then, the caliphate has not been an issue in the politics of the Muslim world.

Mustafa Kemal was a secular nationalist who believed that all the inheritance of the Ottoman Empire should be abandoned and Turkey should be transformed into a modern European state. This involved less of a sudden break with the past than might appear. The *Tanzimat* reforms had laid the foundations of a secular state, and the Young Turks, even while attempting to preserve the empire, had given a powerful impetus to the cause of Turkish nationalism. During the war years, the secularization of education had proceeded and the universities and public positions had been opened to women. Certain of the law courts under the control of the religious authorities had been placed under the Ministry of Justice. A law in 1916 had reformed marriage and divorce.

Mustafa Kemal carried the process much further. A new legal code, based on a variety of European systems, was substituted for the Islamic *sharia*. In 1928 the constitution became officially secular with the deletion of the clause reading that 'the religion of the Turkish state is Islam' and 'laicism' was established as one of the six cardinal principles of the state. A Latin-based alphabet replaced the Arabic script of Ottoman Turkish and finally, in 1935, surnames on the European model were introduced. Mustafa Kemal took the name of Atatürk or 'Father of the Turks'.

Because of Kemal's extraordinary ascendancy over his people, these reforms were profound and far-reaching; however, they did not mean that the Turkish people as a whole renounced Islam. Though the authority of the *ulama* was destroyed, the Turkish masses, who remained peasant farmers, preserved their Islamic faith. Even the intelligentsia would have ridiculed the idea that they had ceased to be Muslims – in their view there had only been a Turkish reformation of Islam.

What the creation of the Turkish Republic and the abandonment of the empire did mean was that Turkey abruptly ceased to be a factor in the political development of the Middle East (only territorial disputes involving vilayets of Mosul and Aleppo remained, and these were settled in the 1920s and 1930s – with Britain and France). Atatürk's success in developing a strong national state capable of dealing with the European powers on equal terms influenced both Arab and Persian nationalists – especially the latter – but their differing circumstances meant that Turkey was more of an inspiration than an example. They neither wished nor could hope for their countries to become part of Europe, although Turkey could nurse this aspiration, even if to some it appeared unrealistic.

After the abolition of the sultanate and caliphate, Atatürk organized the new republic as a secular parliamentary democracy. The 1924 constitution guaranteed equality before the law and freedom of thought, speech, publication and association. In theory sovereignty lay with the people and was exercised in their name by the single-chamber parliament – the Grand National Assembly – which elected the president of the republic, who chose the prime minister. Ministers were supposed to be responsible to parliament.

Democracy remained severely restricted, however. Atatürk used his immense prestige to override the constitution whenever he chose. In 1924 he organized his supporters as the Republican People's Party (RPP). This dominated political life, as all members of the Assembly belonged to it, and the RPP ruled Turkey for twenty-seven years. Yet, despite his authoritarianism and arbitrary methods, Atatürk planted the seeds of liberal constitutional government. The Assembly had real powers, and Atatürk tried to have his way by persuasion rather than by force.

In the economic field, Atatürk concentrated on developing Turkey's rich mineral resources, industry and communications. With a lively memory of Ottoman Turkey's subservience to European financial and economic control through the Capitulations, he instituted an *étatist* policy of large-scale state enterprises to exercise close control over planning and development. Although increasingly bureaucratic and inefficient, these enterprises made considerable progress towards industrializing Turkey between the two World Wars and, because they had no Marxist ideological basis, their eventual liberalization did not present insuperable difficulties.

After Atatürk's death in 1938, opposition to the elected dictatorship gained ground and his successor, Ismet Inönü, partly under the influence of the democratic ideals of the Western Allies in the Second World War, allowed the establishment of a multi-party system. The Democratic Party emerged as the chief rival to the RPP, advocating free enterprise and a multi-party system, and it steadily gained popularity until it won a resounding victory in the 1950 elections. The genuineness of Turkey's secular democracy was demonstrated when Inönü allowed a peaceful transfer of power.

*

The experience of Turkey's former Arab subjects was wholly different.

At the end of the First World War the principal concern of the four Western Allies, as they prepared for the peace conference to be held in Paris, was the post-war settlement in Europe following the defeat of Germany and the Austro-Hungarian Empire. The future of the Middle East was not high on the conference agenda. As a consequence of its defeat of Turkey, Britain had acquired supreme power in the region, subject only to its obligations to its French ally. The war in the desert had caught the imagination of the British public, as the well-publicized romantic exploits of T. E. Lawrence provided relief from the squalid horrors of the trench warfare on the western front.

The possibility of annexing the former Ottoman Arab provinces as colonies was not seriously entertained except by a few Arabist officials – the age of European imperial expansion was already at an end. But the Arabs, who for so long had been ruled by Turks, were regarded as one of the 'subject races' rather than a 'governing race', to employ Cromer of Egypt's categorization of humanity. (The 'noble and independent' Arab beduin were different, but they did not occupy territory of political or economic significance.) The conflict between the undertakings to Sharif Hussein and to France concerned only a small minority of specialists, such as T. E. Lawrence himself, who were almost unanimously Francophobe. In general it was felt that the Arabs should be grateful for their liberation from the Turks – as indeed most of them were. Although in theory the new doctrine of self-determination, based on President Wilson's ideals, was the guiding principle of the post-war settlement, its effect was quite underestimated.

It was Egypt – the country which had already been under British control for nearly forty years – which provided the first shock. Compared with the Syrians, the Egyptians had suffered little from the war. With the huge rise in cotton prices, Egypt's natural wealth had actually increased. Large profits were made from the supply of goods to the Allied troops. But the prosperity concealed powerful social grievances. Although supposedly voluntary, recruitment of the *fellahin* and their camels and donkeys to the labour and transport corps was in effect compulsory under martial law, and was deeply resented. The new wealth accrued to the big and medium-sized land-owners, who possessed 75 per cent of the cultivated area, and to a small new capitalist class in the cities. The reality for the rest of the population was a steep rise in the cost of living. The government's lack of any social and economic policy allowed the large land-owners to abandon food-growing for cotton-growing, thus creating a near-famine and a sharp rise in the death rate, which actually exceeded the birth rate during the war.

The fermenting nationalism which had merely been submerged by martial law came to the surface. The British high commissioner, Sir Reginald Wingate, had allowed the formation of a commission headed by the British judicial adviser to consider legislative reform and Egypt's political status after the war. This reached the conclusion that Egypt should have a legislature of two chambers, of which the Upper House would be the more important. This would include Egyptian ministers, British advisers and representatives of the foreign communities elected by special electorates. The judicial adviser's view was that, since Egypt's financial interests were largely in foreign hands, the Egyptians had no right to a dominant voice in legislation affecting them.

These proposals, when leaked in November 1918, were a provocation to Egypt's nationalist leadership. They were fully aware that the Wilsonian doctrine of self-determination for the people freed from Turkish rule had been endorsed by the Allies. Already the Arabs of Arabia, whom the Egyptians regarded (with some justice) as being more backward than themselves, were preparing to send a delegate to the Paris peace conference. Two days after the Armistice, Zaghloul Pasha presented himself at the British Residency at the head of a delegation (*wafd* in Arabic – the name that was to become attached to Zaghloul's supporters) to say that the Egyptian people wanted their complete independence and to request proceeding to London to present their case. Zaghloul had been kept out of the government by Wingate, but he was the undoubted leader of the nationalist movement. Balfour, Britain's foreign secretary, who was already looking forward to the Paris peace conference, brusquely rejected the visit and when Rushdi Pasha, the prime minister, proposed that he should come to London instead he repeated the refusal, saying in a dispatch to Wingate that while the British government 'desire to act on the principle which they had always followed of giving the Egyptians an ever-increasing share in the government of the country . . . As you are well aware, the stage has not yet been reached at which self-government is possible.' Britain had no intention of abandoning its responsibilities for order and good government in Egypt 'and for protecting the rights and interests both of the native and the foreign populations of the country'.

Zaghloul seized his chance. Pointing out that even Egypt's prime minister had been spurned, he organized a nation-wide campaign of protest to back his claim to be Egypt's true representative. Balfour relented to the extent of inviting Rushdi to London, but he rejected Rushdi's insistence that Zaghloul should accompany him. Rushdi and his cabinet then resigned on 1 March 1919, with the full approval of Sultan Fuad.

Although Zaghloul stepped up his agitation, the high commission believed the trouble would die down and recommended that Zaghloul be deported. Balfour agreed, and Zaghloul and three of his colleagues were bundled on a train to Port Said and taken on a British destroyer to Malta.

The public reaction was immediate and severe. Rioting students in Cairo were supported by strikes among government officials, doctors and lawyers and the capital came to a standstill. To British astonishment, the trouble spread to the provincial towns and the countryside, to take the form of a national uprising which Egyptian nationalists later called their 1919 Revolution.

Stern military action, with the use of flying columns into the countryside and bombing raids on suspect gatherings, brought the uprising to an end in a few weeks. But the British government understood that repression would not suffice. News of the uprising had been as unwelcome as it was unexpected at a time when the government was concerned with the Irish troubles nearer home as well as involved in the affairs of the Paris conference. The prime minister, Lloyd George, with one of his rare intuitive flashes, decided that General Allenby, who had arrived in Paris to give his views on Syria, was the right man to restore the situation in Egypt, and in March 1919 Allenby was instantly dispatched to replace Wingate.

Allenby's brief was to restore law and order and do anything required 'by the necessity of maintaining the King's protectorate over Egypt on a secure and equitable basis'. However, behind the bluff and sometimes brusque military exterior of Allenby 'the Bull' lay an acute political mind with liberal tendencies. He had already, in Paris, argued against the imposition of French rule in Syria against the clearly expressed wishes of the inhabitants, and he at least half-believed in the principle of self-determination – which was 50 per cent more than the British and French politicians who had publicly adopted it.

Immediately on his arrival, Allenby assured the Egyptians of his intention to redress their justifiable grievances. Using all his prestige he forced a reluctant Lloyd George to agree to the release of Zaghloul and his colleagues – an action which horrified Anglo-Egyptian officials. Zaghloul unrepentantly resumed his demand for an end to the protectorate, and some of the strikes and agitation were resumed. Allenby acted firmly, as London expected, but he already understood, as the British government did not, that the protectorate would have to go. He now welcomed the decision to send out a high-level mission headed by the colonial secretary, Lord Milner, although again the mission's brief was to study the cause of the disorders and to recommend the form of the constitution which *under the protectorate*, 'will be best calculated to promote [Egypt's] peace and prosperity, the progressive development of self-governing institutions and the protection of foreign interests'. In prescient words, Balfour told the House of Commons on 17 November that '. . . the question of Egypt, the question of the Sudan, and the question of the Canal, form an organic and indissoluble whole' and England was not going to give up any of its responsibilities. 'British supremacy exists,' he said; 'British supremacy is going to be maintained.'

The truth was that the course of the First World War had appeared to justify the British occupation of Egypt and the change in focus of British Middle Eastern policy from Istanbul to Cairo which had occurred almost accidentally in the nineteenth century. It was hardly surprising that in 1919 no British statesman was prepared to contemplate abandoning control of Egypt.

When the British government's intentions were made known, Zaghloul ordered a boycott of the Milner mission which spent three disheartening months in Egypt and was everywhere met by hostile demonstrations and demands for Egypt's complete independence. However, the mission reached some firm and realistic conclusions; that, since it had never been part of the British Empire, Egypt could not be annexed in the post-war world and had to be recognized as an independent constitutional monarchy. The preservation of British rights and interests would have to be secured by an Anglo-Egyptian treaty to replace the protectorate. This raised the question of who would sign on Egypt's behalf. Adly Pasha, the prime minister, was a politician of standing but he knew he could not carry the nation without Zaghloul's support. Adly persuaded Zaghloul to go to London with his mission to work at the details. After several weeks' discussion, during which both sides made concessions, the basis for a treaty had been reached. Egypt would be independent, with its own diplomatic representatives. Britain would defend Egypt in case of war and, although it would have the right to keep forces on Egyptian soil for the protection of its 'imperial communications', this 'would not constitute in any manner a military occupation of the country or prejudice the rights of the Government of Egypt'.

Zaghloul and his Wafd had achieved most but not all of their aims. Now Zaghloul showed his fatal lack of statesmanship. Unwilling to admit that he had failed to achieve Egypt's total independence, he refused to urge the mass of his supporters in the country to accept the terms of the treaty. When, as prime minister, Adly Pasha went to London in July 1921 to conclude the treaty (without Zaghloul, who had insisted that he should lead the delegation), he did not dare to make the concessions demanded by Lloyd George's cabinet, which was hardening its position. Adly knew that Zaghloul could bring out the street to denounce him for treachery. When Adly returned from England empty-handed, Zaghloul and his followers stepped up their protests with strikes and violent demonstrations.

Allenby now acted firmly by ordering Zaghloul's second deportation – this time to the Seychelles – having ensured with a heavy use of force that there would be no repeat of the 1919 uprising. He then proposed that Britain should make a unilateral declaration of Egypt's independence while reserving its vital interests. The British cabinet was divided between moderates led by the foreign secretary, Lord Curzon, and hardliners represented by Winston Churchill, the new young secretary of state for the colonies. Allenby stormed into London threatening to resign if his proposals were not accepted. Lloyd George gave way, and on 28 February 1922 Britain published a declaration recognizing Egypt as 'an independent sovereign State' but reserving to its discretion four points to be the subject of Anglo-Egyptian negotiations in the future. These were 'The security of the communications of the British Empire in Egypt; the defence of Egypt against all foreign aggression or interference, direct or indirect; the protection of foreign interests in Egypt and of minorities; and the Sudan.'

Two weeks later Sultan Fuad assumed the title of King Fuad I. A constitutional commission produced a constitution based on the Belgian model, providing for a Senate and an elected Chamber of Deputies. Although this gave the king considerable powers – including the right to dissolve parliament and to appoint some of the senators – these were not as great as the king would have wished, and Allenby had to intervene to prevent the establishment of a royal dictatorship. The ultimate consequence was that for the next thirty years Egypt was governed by an uneasy and ultimately unworkable balance of forces: the palace, where the powers of the Muhammad Ali dynasty had been partially restored; parliament and the politicians, among whom the Wafd party was usually but not always dominant; and the British residency (which, despite independence, was still not an embassy). Repeated efforts to negotiate an Anglo-Egyptian treaty to settle outstanding differences broke down because Britain's minimum demands were unacceptable to Egyptian national pride. The most enduring of these differences concerned the Sudan, which the monarch and the Wafd united in claiming for Egypt – a claim which Britain resolutely rejected. Indeed it was the Sudan problem which caused a final break between Britain and Zaghloul. The 70-year-old leader, allowed back from exile, won a sweeping victory for his Wafd in the first parliamentary elections. As prime minister, he pressed Egypt's claim to the Sudan. There was a full-scale mutiny by Sudanese military cadets, who were Sudanese nationalists but ready to co-operate with their Egyptian counterparts against Britain. Anglo-Sudanese officials naturally blamed Egypt for the disturbances. In this fevered atmosphere in the summer of 1924, Sir Lee Stack, *sirdar* of the Egyptian army and governor-general of the Sudan, was murdered by a group of ninety Egyptian terrorists. An outraged Allenby drove to the Egyptian parliament with a cavalry escort to deliver a harsh ultimatum which included the banning of all demonstrations, the payment of a heavy indemnity and – most important – the withdrawal from the Sudan of all Egyptian troops. Rejecting the ultimatum, Zaghloul resigned. Although still Egypt's national leader, he never regained power. He died in 1927. The king dissolved parliament and was able for a time to establish a royal semi-autocracy with weak ministers, but his powers were insufficient for this to last and the unstable façade of parliamentary democracy survived.

In Egypt, Britain had already been effectively governing the country for nearly forty years, but it was there dealing with a people who had constituted a nation for some 5,000 years, even while under the rule of a series of empires. In the rest of the former Ottoman provinces the victorious Allies were confronted with a very different situation. With the exception of the remote and mountainous kingdom of Yemen, there were no nation-states. Sharif Hussein's ambitious claim to become ruler of a unified kingdom was summarily rejected by the Allies and he was confined to the weak and impoverished kingdom of the Hejaz.

Despite strong French opposition, Hussein's son, Amir Feisal, secured a place at the Paris peace conference, although it was made clear to him that he represented only the Hejaz and not the Arabs as a whole. From this weak position in Paris, he attempted to retrieve what he could of Arab aspirations. Taking his stand on the various declarations by the Allies in favour of self-determination, he proposed that a commission of inquiry be sent to Syria and Palestine to examine the wishes of the inhabitants. President Wilson enthusiastically accepted the proposal, and his suggestion that the commission should consist of French, British, Italian and American representatives was endorsed by the conference. But in reality the French were strongly hostile to the commission, while the British were lukewarm, and eventually all the parties except the Americans withdrew. The American appointees, Henry King and Charles Crane, decided to go on their own, and their report fully explains British and French hostility towards the commission.

They found that the inhabitants of Syria/Palestine overwhelmingly opposed the proposal to place them under great-power mandates which were a thinly disguised form of colonial administration. They acknowledged the need for outside assistance, provided it came from the United States or, as second choice, from Britain. On no account did they want assistance from France. The King–Crane commission started out strongly favourable towards Zionism but soon concluded that the Zionist programmes would have to be greatly modified if the promises of the Balfour Declaration to protect the rights of the non-Jews in Palestine were to be upheld. After discussion with Zionist leaders in Jerusalem, they had no doubt that the Zionists looked forward 'to a practically complete dispossession of the present non-Jewish inhabitants of Palestine'.

The King–Crane report was ignored by the Allies. It was clearly repugnant to Britain and France; and the United States, after raising so many expectations, was about to retreat into twenty years of isolationism. But a serious rift between the Allies also seemed possible, as the British government regarded French ambitions in Syria as excessive – a view that was strongly held by all the leading British Arabists, such as T. E. Lawrence. Britain also felt some obligation towards the Hashemites – a sentiment that was in no way shared by the French. When France wanted to garrison Syria with French troops, Britain refused to agree.

Meanwhile, after Amir Feisal's return from Paris in May 1919, his supporters organized elections wherever they were possible throughout Syria (although they were blocked by the French in the coastal regions). A General Syrian Congress, meeting in Damascus, called for recognition of the independence of Syria (including Palestine) and Iraq and for the repudiation of the Sykes–Picot Agreement, the Balfour Declaration and the mandatary system. But the realities of power soon reasserted themselves. Britain persuaded Feisal that he must compromise with France. In November 1919 he went to Paris and reached an agreement with the French premier, Clemenceau, providing for French occupation of the coastal areas and a French monopoly of assistance to the fledgeling Arab state in the interior.

Feisal was quite unable to persuade his followers to accept the dismemberment of Syria, and on 8 March 1920 the General Syrian Congress in Damascus passed a resolution proclaiming the independence of Syria/Palestine with autonomy for Lebanon. At the same time a similar meeting of Iraq's leaders declared Iraq's independence, with Amir Abdullah as king.

Britain and France responded swiftly. Refusing to recognize the Damascus resolution, they hastily convened a meeting of the Supreme Council of the League of Nations, which announced its decision on 5 May 1920. Syria was to be partitioned into the two French mandates of Lebanon and Syria and the British mandate of Palestine, while Iraq was to remain undivided as a British mandate. The British mandate for Palestine carried with it the obligation to carry out the terms of the Balfour Declaration.

Aroused by these decisions, the Arabs of Syria urged Feisal to declare war on the French. Aware of his military weakness, Feisal allowed his hot-headed younger officers to attack French positions on the Lebanon border. The French commander-in-chief, General Gouraud, sent an ultimatum on 14 July demanding that French forces be allowed to occupy Aleppo, Homs, Hama and the Bekaa plain. Feisal accepted the ultimatum but the action was pointless because the French had already decided to seize Syria. A French column, including Senegalese and North African Arab troops, advanced and took Damascus on 25 July. Brave resistance by Feisal's ill-trained troops could do little against French tanks and planes. France invited Feisal to leave Syria, and he was received in exile by an embarrassed British government. The colonial secretary, Winston Churchill, told the Imperial Conference in 1921 that French operations against Syria had been 'extremely painful' but 'we have these strong ties with the French and they have to prevail, and we were not able to do anything to help the Arabs in the matter . . .'

Having been awarded the mandates for Syria and Lebanon, one of France's first acts was to enlarge Lebanon at Syria's expense. France's intention was to make Lebanon the headquarters for its Middle Eastern operations. The Maronites of Lebanon traditionally looked to France as their protector, whereas Syria had become a focus of Arab nationalism. In his decree of 31 August 1920, General Gouraud declared the creation of le Grand Liban, consisting of the former autonomous sanjak of Mount Lebanon plus the Bekaa plain to the east and the coastal towns of Tripoli to the north and Sidon and Tyre to the south. The population of le Grand Liban had a small Christian majority, but this was threatened by the stronger Christian tendency to emigrate and the higher Muslim birth rate.

The Allies' decisions on the partitioning of the Ottoman Empire were not carried out peacefully. Apart from the fighting in Syria, there was an uprising against the Jews by the Arabs in Palestine, whose alarm intensified as the objectives of the Zionist leaders became clear. In Iraq, where Arab hopes had been thwarted by the establishment of an Anglo-Indian administration on colonial lines with virtually no Arab participation, the tribes of the middle Euphrates rose in a rebellion which was put down only at heavy cost.

The urgent need for post-war economy caused the British government to act. Churchill, with T. E. Lawrence as adviser, held a conference in Cairo in March 1921. No Arabs were present, but the meeting was attended by the high commissioner for Iraq, Sir Percy Cox, and the newly appointed high commissioner for Palestine, Sir Herbert Samuel, who had first put forward the Zionist idea to the British cabinet. It was decided to carry out the arrangement already prepared in London to make Feisal king of Iraq. The future of Amir Abdullah created a problem. Disappointed in his hopes of becoming king of Iraq, he had arrived from the Hejaz at Maan near Aqaba in November 1920 at the head of tribal forces, declaring his intention of attacking the French in Syria to avenge his brother Feisal.

From Cairo, Churchill travelled to Jerusalem, with the joint purpose of reassuring the Palestinian Arabs that there was no intention of allowing Palestine to become a Jewish state and of conferring with Abdullah. He rejected Abdullah's various proposals for the incorporation of Transjordan (that is, the east bank of the River Jordan) into either Iraq or Palestine under an Arab administration, but a provisional arrangement was reached whereby Britain agreed to recognize Abdullah as amir of Transjordan with an annual British subsidy until Britain could persuade France to restore an Arab state in Syria with Abdullah at its head. Since the French were adamant against this, the provisional arrangement became permanent, and the state of Transjordan came into existence until, following the first Arab–Israeli war (1948–9), it was incorporated with the West Bank of Jordan to form the Hashemite Kingdom of Jordan.

The mandates for Palestine, Syria, Lebanon and Iraq were formally approved by the Council of the League of Nations in July 1922 and became effective in September 1923. In 1924 the United States, which was not a member of the League of Nations, gave its approval to them. Transjordan was added to Britain's Palestine mandate, but the mandatary was permitted to exclude it, and in fact did exclude it, from the area of Jewish settlement.

The dismemberment of the Ottoman Empire thus resulted in the creation of five new states – Syria, Lebanon, Transjordan, Iraq and Palestine. All of them were under the tutelage of Britain or France, which had also been chiefly responsible for establishing the shape of their frontiers. With the Treaty of Mudros (1918), Turkish suzerainty over Yemen, which had never been very effective, finally came to an end. The country's remoteness and inaccessibility, reinforced by the wishes of its rulers, ensured that it remained backward but independent. Another new state – the kingdom of Hejaz, the residue of King Hussein's dream of an independent Arab federation under Hashemite rule – was short-lived. In the rest of Arabia, Ibn Saud, 'Sultan of Nejd and its Dependencies', was extending his rule. Having finally subdued his Rashidi enemies to the north, in 1920 he sent his 15-year-old son Feisal to the south-western Arabian highlands of Asir to secure the allegiance of its people. He did the same with the Jawf region on the borders of the newly created emirate of Transjordan. But Ibn Saud was faced with a recurring problem: his undisciplined and ferocious tribal warriors, who had no regard for international frontiers, launched raids deep into the territory of Transjordan and Iraq. British planes and armoured cars joined the local tribesmen to drive them back with heavy losses.

The boundaries between Nejd and both Kuwait and Iraq were still not properly defined. Ibn Saud regarded border demarcation as ludicrous in an area where the nomad inhabitants lacked any sense of nationality and were accustomed to wander over huge stretches of desert to find pasturage for their flocks. But the British protectors of Iraq and Kuwait were determined to establish a frontier beyond which Wahhabi power would not be allowed to expand. At Uqair, the sea-port of al-Hasa on the Gulf, Sir Percy Cox, high commissioner of Iraq, reached an agreement with Ibn Saud whereby a large slice of territory claimed by Iraq was allocated to the new kingdom of Iraq. In order to placate Ibn Saud, some two-thirds of the land that had been considered to belong to Kuwait at the time of the 1913 agreement with the Ottoman government became part of the Nejd. An embarrassed Cox later explained to the amir of Kuwait that nothing could be done to prevent Ibn Saud from taking the territories if he wished.

Britain was less successful in arranging an accommodation between Ibn Saud and his old rival and enemy King Hussein of the Hejaz, to which all Wahhabi ambitions were now directed. The embittered old king refused to sign the 1921 draft treaty, which would have meant accepting the accomplished fact that Syria, Lebanon and Palestine were all lost to the rule of his family. His annual subsidy from Britain had been discontinued. However, he still aimed to assert himself. He demonstrated his authority over his family by making a state visit to Aqaba, where he was received with due deference by his son Abdullah, the new amir of Transjordan. He then made a fatal error. Since

Mustafa Kemal of the new Turkish Republic had just abolished the institution of the Islamic caliphate, Hussein declared himself to have assumed the title of 'Prince of the Faithful and Successor of the Prophet'.

Early in the war Britain had supported the idea of a restored Arab caliphate, but now it was no longer interested. In the Muslim world as a whole, apart from some Hashemite loyalists in Palestine and Syria, reaction to Hussein's declaration ranged from indifference to anger. Among Ibn Saud's Wahhabi warriors there was rage. It was at this moment that Britain decided to end the £60,000 subsidy it had been paying Ibn Saud since 1915. He therefore no longer had any motive for restraining his warriors, who at once fell upon the Hejaz. Hussein, who, whatever his faults, remained dignified and courageous to the last, wanted to fight to the end, but the Hejazis persuaded him to abdicate in favour of his eldest son, Ali, who had retreated to barricade himself with his forces in Jedda and might be able to sue for better terms from the Wahhabis. Hussein sailed away to an embittered exile in Cyprus, taking with him what remained of his treasures.

Ali held out in Jedda for a year until he surrendered and abdicated. Ibn Saud's forces soon overran the rest of the Hejaz, but he took care to restrain his Ikhwan warriors, reports of whose excesses terrified the local population. Ibn Saud gave priority to security. He reopened the Islamic pilgrimage route and set out to demonstrate that he could ensure the security of the holy places after centuries of disorder. An English Muslim who made the *hajj* (pilgrimage) in 1925 wrote of Ibn Saud, 'He is probably the best ruler that Arabia has known since the days of the four Khalifas.'

With Ali's abdication in December 1924, Ibn Saud became ruler of the whole Hejaz, except that in the extreme north-west the British authorities in Palestine retained some territory by sending troops and armoured cars to occupy the strip of land between Maan and Aqaba, on the grounds that, as part of the former Ottoman vilayet of Damascus, it should now be included in the British mandate for Palestine. The reality was that it was considered essential for Amir Abdullah's emirate of Transjordan to have an outlet to the sea. Ibn Saud never accepted the *fait accompli*, but he was unable to prevent it.

Ibn Saud now controlled the holy places of Islam. The question was, how would the Muslim world respond? The great majority of Muslims, who were not Arabs, were likely to be sceptical that a tribal leader from central Arabia should succeed in protecting and securing the holy places when the sharifian rulers and Ottoman Turks had so manifestly failed. Already they were alarmed by the Wahhabi destruction of the tombs of Muslim saints.

Ibn Saud acted with skill and caution. He appointed his second son, Amir Feisal, as his viceroy of the Hejaz and Abdullah Damluji, an experienced Iraqi in his service, as director of foreign affairs. Delegates of eminent Persian and Indian Muslims visited the Hejaz and reported favourably. The people of the Hejaz were also impressed by Ibn Saud's ability to maintain security and by his willingness to adjust to their more sophisticated urban ways. On 8 January 1926 the Hejaz notables approached him with a formal request to accept their loyalty as king of the Hejaz, and he agreed to rule, with God's help, through the holy *sharia*.

As well as being their king, Ibn Saud was the people's imam, which meant that he led them in prayers and set them an example in religious devotion. But he went no further than this – unlike Sharif Hussein, or King Farouk of Egypt at a later date, Ibn Saud never aspired to the title of caliph; he was only resolutely opposed to anyone else taking the title.

The Soviet Union was the first of the powers to recognize the new Saudi regime, followed rapidly by Britain, France and the other European powers. The United States was to wait another decade before it showed any interest in Arabia. The Soviet Union saw Ibn Saud as an independent anti-imperialist force and hoped to use his new state as a channel for political and commercial penetration of the Middle East, which was otherwise under British or French control. By 1938 the Soviets realized their error and the Soviet legation in Jedda was closed. Most of the staff were liquidated in the Stalinist purges.

Problems with Britain remained, as Ibn Saud refused to recognize the British mandates in Iraq, Palestine and Transjordan until his claim to the Maan–Aqaba territory was accepted. Under the 1927 Treaty of Jedda this matter was shelved, but Britain recognized 'the complete and absolute independence of the dominions' of Ibn Saud, who in return agreed to respect all the British treaties of protection with Arab Gulf shaikhdoms.

He was still faced with the task of unifying and administering his vast but thinly populated territories – some two-thirds the size of India. He had appointed his eldest son, Saud, viceroy of Nejd with Feisal as viceroy of the Hejaz, but he also needed outside help and this he confined to Muslim Arabs – Iraqis, Syrians and Egyptians. His policy was to make each tribal chief responsible for security in his own area and accountable to him, while the Wahhabi army remained in the background as the ultimate sanction. He also contracted several dynastic marriages with the daughters of the leaders of important tribal confederations, which partially explains why forty-four sons survived him and today there are some four or five thousand Saudi princes in direct line of descent from the king.

He showed wisdom in many respects. Although he remained the supreme ruler, with overwhelming prestige, he never ignored public opinion. He was determined that his kingdom should have those Western inventions which would make life easier for his people, provided these did not undermine their way of life. He did not try to force the pace but used persuasion where possible. A gathering of religious shaikhs was convinced that the telephone was not the instrument of the devil when they heard on it a voice reciting the Holy Koran. (A generation later his son, King Feisal, used the same methods to overcome objections to television and to girls' education.)

Despite his tact and political skill, in 1929–30 Ibn Saud was faced by a full-scale revolt among some of his Ikhwan warriors, who denounced his Western innovations and demanded the right to raid across the borders into Transjordan and Iraq, whose people they regarded as infidels. Eventually Ibn Saud took the field against them and put down the rebellion. His authority was now unchallenged throughout his territories, and on 8 September 1932 the kingdom of Hejaz and the sultanate of Nejd were officially united as the kingdom of Saudi Arabia.

The desert boundaries of the new kingdom with the Arab Gulf shaikhdoms remained unsettled, but this would only present problems later, in the oil era. On the other hand, a dispute with the Imam Yahya, ruler of the ancient kingdom of Yemen, concerning the Asir coastal region on the Red Sea, led to a brief Saudi–Yemeni war in 1934. After a Saudi force under Amir Feisal had occupied the Yemeni port of Hodeida, Ibn Saud ordered a halt. In the peace negotiations he behaved with generosity and magnanimity, abstaining from any demands on Yemeni territory. A treaty of 'Muslim Friend-ship and Arab Fraternity' was the basis of untroubled relations between the two countries for the next thirty years.

In the first three decades following the break-up of the Ottoman Empire, Saudi Arabia and Yemen were the only states of the Mashreq or Arab East which were fully independent. Under its imam Yahya, who ruled from 1904 to 1948, mountainous Yemen kept itself vir-tually impenetrable to the outside world and hardly impinged on the politics of the region. Saudi Arabia, because it included the holy places of Islam and had in Ibn Saud a ruler of unique prestige, exerted more influence. However, it remained the least developed part of the region – proud but intensely poor. The improved admin-istration of the *hajj* pilgrimage increased revenues in the 1920s, as the number of pilgrims increased to 100,000 a year and each pilgrim paid a fee of £5 in gold. However, the number of pilgrims declined drastically in the 1930s as a consequence of the Great Depression, falling to only 20,000 in 1933. In 1931 Ibn Saud's finance minister was forced to declare a moratorium on all the kingdom's debts and to commandeer for ready cash the gasoline stocks of two private com-panies in Jedda. With some reluctance, in 1933 Ibn Saud granted an oil concession for the kingdom's eastern territories to Standard Oil of California. Oil was discovered in commercial quantities in 1938, in what was to prove to be one of the largest oilfields in the world, but, because the Second World War intervened, it was only in the 1950s that the kingdom became the major producer in the region and began to acquire vast wealth.

The Inter-war Years

(a)   Egypt

Britain's unilateral declaration of Egypt's independence in 1922, with significant reservations protecting British imperial interests, gave Egypt an unstable and anomalous political framework. The British residency was no longer the only real centre of power in the country but one of three, alongside the palace and the Wafd. As long as British troops remained in occupation, British power could always be exerted, but it was exercised with increasing difficulty and diminishing effectiveness.

The same pattern of events was repeated several times. The king, who had considerable powers under the constitution but wished that they were greater, would dissolve parliament and try to rule without it. When he could do so no longer, an election would be held in which, provided the elections were substantially free, the Wafdists always won a sweeping victory. In later years the Wafd was seen to have lost its cohesion and sense of purpose as it became riddled with faction and corruption, but in the 1930s it was undoubtedly the political expression of Egypt – comparable to the Congress Party in India during the years of struggle for independence from British rule.

In 1925 Britain's Conservative government replaced Allenby as high commissioner with Lord Lloyd, a close friend of Winston Churchill who, like Churchill, refused to acknowledge that the empire was in decline. Lloyd accepted the constitutional position in Egypt and used his influence to prevent King Fuad from attempting to exclude the Wafd from power. But he was adamant on maintaining Britain's reservations to Egypt's independence, and for this he considered it necessary that the numbers and authority of both civilian and military Anglo-Egyptian officials should not be reduced beyond the point which he considered to be the essential minimum. In particular he resisted Wafdist efforts to expand the armed forces and replace the British high command with Egyptian officers. Fearing a repeat of the Arab revolt, Lloyd was always prepared to summon a British warship to Alexandria in times of crisis.

In general Lloyd had his way, but he felt angrily frustrated. As he wrote to a friend,

> ... our present position is impossible ... We cannot carry on much longer as we are. We have magnitude without position; power without authority; responsibility without control. I must insure that no foreign power intervenes in education, aviation, wireless communications, railways or army (where all seek to do so), and I must achieve this without upsetting the parliamentary regime which we forced upon the country against the king's wishes ...

Lloyd's analysis of the anomalies of the British position in Egypt was correct. The British government's aim remained to secure an Anglo-Egyptian treaty of alliance in which, in return for some concessions, Egypt would accept the limitations to Egyptian independence which Britain considered essential – including the abandonment of Egyptian claim to sovereignty over Sudan. When King Fuad paid a state visit to London in 1927, the British Foreign Office attempted to initiate negotiations for a treaty with the Egyptian prime minister, Sarwat Pasha, without Lloyd's knowledge. Lloyd had the satisfaction of seeing his prediction vindicated that any Egyptian prime minister would be either unwilling or unable to sell such a treaty to the Egyptian parliament. When Zaghloul Pasha died later in the year, Nahas, his successor as leader of the Wafd, was anxious to show that he was as fervent a champion of unfettered Egyptian independence as his predecessor. After weeks of aimless political manoeuvres, the Egyptian parliament rejected the proposed treaty.

When Ramsay MacDonald came to power in Britain at the head of a Labour government, Lloyd was replaced. His romantic right-wing brand of Toryism had been too much even for Stanley Baldwin's Conservative government. Another attempt was made to reach a treaty agreement, and this time success seemed in sight as Britain was even prepared to withdraw its troops from the Suez Canal zone, but – not for the last time – negotiations broke down over Egypt's demand for the revision of the 1899 Anglo-Egyptian condominium agreement on the Sudan. The Sudan was a question which was capable of arousing the whole country, as even the illiterate *fellahin* were aware of the importance of the Nile flood on which their lives depended.

King Fuad had not given up hope of reducing the Wafd's domination of Egypt's political life. When he refused to give his assent to two bills presented to parliament by the Wafd, Nahas resigned in the belief that the king would be unable to resist the Wafd's popular strength. The king turned to Sidky Pasha, an autocratic millionaire who had held office with ability in various governments but always followed his own path. Sidky was not a king's man, but he was quite prepared to inaugurate a quasi-dictatorship under royal auspices. With the help of British troops he suppressed public demonstrations and went on to amend the 1923 constitution and the electoral law to increase the king's powers and ensure the defeat of the Wafd in the 1931 elections.

Sidky's position was immeasurably strengthened by the fact that he was clearly no puppet of Britain, the palace or anyone else. He muzzled the press and deflated the Wafd by preventing it from using its most powerful weapon – control of the streets. At the same time he used the political moratorium to exhibit his talent for finance. Sidky had been one of the original promoters of Egyptian capitalist enterprise during the First World War; his abilities were suited to dealing with the consequences of the world depression and shielding Egypt from them as far as possible. His regime marked the beginning of the move away from free-trade liberalism, installed under Cromer, towards the Egyptianization of the economy.

In opposition, the Wafd was more than ever the popular party. When in 1933 Sidky was forced to abandon the premiership after a stroke and was succeeded by lesser men, the Wafd was able to rouse the country with demands for the restoration of the 1923 constitution which would inevitably restore the party to power.

Britain faced a dilemma. The popular mood in Egypt was becoming dangerous. In November 1935 there was a huge pro-Wafd demonstration by students in Cairo. (The grave 17-year-old leader of the secondary students, named Gamal Abdul Nasser, was grazed on the forehead by a police bullet.) But Britain was still reluctant to see the return of a Wafdist government.

However, a solution was at hand. Although the Wafd had lost none of its appetite for power, it was now more prepared to compromise to achieve it. The Wafd had learned that it could never hold power for long against British opposition. At the same time, it shared Britain's growing alarm at Italian imperial ambitions in Africa, manifested by Italy's invasion and seizure of Ethiopia. Egypt was dependent on Britain for its defences.

As the Wafd abandoned its demand for an immediate and total British evacuation, its relations with the British high commission improved. Nahas became on good terms with the formidable Sir Miles Lampson, who, with more than a trace of the qualities of Cromer, had been appointed high commissioner in 1933 and was to remain in Egypt for thirteen years.

Even King Fuad, although still detesting the Wafd, was prepared to envisage its return, as this would give him some much needed popularity. In December 1935 he agreed to the restoration of the 1923 constitution. Four months later he died and was succeeded by his handsome and affable 16-year-old son Farouk, who returned from a brief and inadequate period of schooling in England.

The first important event of the new reign was the signing, on 26 August 1936, of the Anglo-Egyptian treaty of alliance, at which no fewer than six unsuccessful attempts had been made over the previous fourteen years. If the 1922 declaration had given Egypt semi-independence, the 1936 treaty went some of the rest of the way. Sir Miles Lampson became ambassador instead of high commissioner, and Britain sponsored Egypt's entry into the League of Nations. Britain undertook to bring the Capitulations to a speedy end and at the Montreux Conference in 1937 obtained full rights of jurisdiction and taxation over all residents from the Capitulatory powers.

The treaty was for a period of twenty years and both parties were committed to a further alliance in 1956, although Egypt would then have the right to submit to third-party judgement the question of whether British troops were any longer necessary in Egypt. The British occupation was formally ended, but British troops would only gradually be withdrawn to the Canal zone and Sinai, as Egypt's defence capability improved. Egypt gained control over its security forces for the first time since 1882. The British inspector-general of the Egyptian army was replaced by an Egyptian, and military intelligence was Egyptianized. The numbers of Europeans in the police force were scaled down, although Russell Pasha remained at the head of the Cairo police force until his retirement ten years later. Egypt had to abandon most of its ambitions to recover control over the Sudan, though it is true that the terms of the Allenby 1924 ultimatum were reversed. Egyptian immigration into the Sudan was no longer restricted, and Egyptian as well as Sudanese troops were to be placed at the disposal of the governor-general. Egyptian officials were to be employed where no Sudanese were available. However, this did not mean that the pre-1924 situation in Sudan had been restored, because by this time a Sudanese national movement had developed and more Sudanese had become qualified. The Anglo-Egyptian condominium in Sudan was a fiction as Britain remained unequivocally the dominant partner.

As events turned out, all the treaty's concessions to Egyptian nationalist demands were largely nullified by the clause which gave Britain the right to re-occupy the country with the unrestricted use of Egyptian ports, airports and roads in the event of Britain's involvement in war. Only three years passed before this clause was invoked. However, in 1936 the immediate reaction of the Egyptian crowds was favourable. The young king was wildly cheered in the streets – even Sir Miles Lampson was applauded. There were hopes of a new era, as the king gave the impression that he would take a special interest in the plight of the impoverished *fellahin*. Under his guidance the Wafd would institute some true reforms.

The reality was rather different. Farouk did not lack either intelligence or good intentions, but he had been badly trained for his task. Also, he shared his father's detestation of the Wafd and his taste for political intrigue.

The Wafd remained the party of the masses and the true expression of political Egypt. However, before the treaty, its 'anti-Britishness' was the only real plank in its political platform. Its ranks contained a whole spectrum of views, from arch-conservative to extremely radical, but its centre of gravity was well to the right. The vast majority of those who voted for it lived in the rural areas which were dominated by the large and medium-size land-owners. Very few Wafdist members of parliament wanted any serious changes in Egypt's social or economic system; above all they did not want any reform in the fantastically unequal holdings of land, which meant that 6 per cent of the proprietors owned 63 per cent of the cultivated area. On the other hand, Egypt's small but growing industrial sector was the creation of a few wealthy Egyptians outside the Wafd, such as Sidky Pasha and Talaat Harb, who co-operated with a number of European industrialists and financiers in establishing an Egyptian Federation of Industries in 1924.

In one field – education – the Wafd could claim to have instigated reform to repair the neglect of the Cromer era. One of the first acts of the Zaghloul government in 1923 had been to declare education free and compulsory. The education budget was steadily increased in the 1920s and 1930s, and the number of pupils of both sexes rose rapidly. The expansion was most remarkable in secondary and university education. But there were serious defects. Since few new schools were built, the classes became overcrowded and standards declined. Also, no attempt was made to adapt the system to Egypt's needs and, as later became characteristic of many newly independent countries, a growing body of graduates from the state secondary schools and universities was unable to find employment. The problem was compounded by the existence of an entirely separate network of foreign secular and religious schools alongside the Egyptian state system. These had high prestige but they greatly accentuated class divisions, as the sons and daughters of the Egyptian upper class who were sent to them grew up speaking French and feeling little in common with the mass of their fellow-countrymen.

The students began to show increasing impatience and discontent with the Wafd and with Egypt's handicapped form of parliamentary democracy in general. Many of them regarded the Anglo-Egyptian treaty as a betrayal, and some of them looked to a new leader – an eloquent and charismatic former schoolteacher named Hassan al-Banna, who founded his Muslim Brotherhood in Ismailia in 1928.

In his early years al-Banna appealed most to the poor and illiterate, but in 1934 he moved his headquarters to Cairo and began to attract supporters from the better educated – students, teachers, civil servants and army officers. Branches of the Brotherhood sprang up throughout the country. Al-Banna's appeal was simple and idealistic. He called for an Islamic state based on the Holy Koran, the traditions of Islam providing everything that was needed for the new social order. But if the Brotherhood lacked a political programme, it had organization through its network of branches. Its youth groups began to receive paramilitary training.

The Brotherhood had rivals in its appeal to Egyptian youth. There was the Young Egypt (Misr al-Fitat) party of Ahmad Hussein, which was nominally socialist but which, with its uniform of green shirts modelled on Mussolini's Black Shirts, had a strongly fascist character. In response the Wafd organized a rival group of Blue Shirts who fought a series of pitched battles with the Green Shirts in the universities. It was not long before a fascist-type royalist youth movement was formed and joined the fray. Egyptian political life was speedily deteriorating.

Although the Anglo-Egyptian treaty was unpopular with those who wanted to end all traces of the British occupation, it had one side-effect which helped their cause. The Egyptian army was now theoretically an ally of the British, so Britain was anxious to improve it; at the same time the Wafd needed to gain popularity. For the first time the Military Academy was opened to young men from classes other than the land-owning aristocracy. Gamal Abdul Nasser, Anwar al-Sadat and a score of other ambitious young Egyptians were able to take up a military career and so play their part in the Free Officers movement which seventeen years later launched the 1952 revolution which brought both the monarchy and the British occupation to an end.

The Wafd was, however, in a slow but inexorable decline and no longer had the unrivalled control over the masses of Zaghloul's day. King Farouk, who now enjoyed the advantage over his father of being in control of his own secret police as well as the paramilitary youth movement, made the active independent politician Ali Maher his *chef de cabinet*. In December 1937 he felt strong enough to dismiss the Wafd 'for having violated the spirit of the constitution', and in the subsequent elections, which were partially rigged, the Wafd was heavily defeated. In August 1939, barely two weeks before the outbreak of the Second World War, the king felt able to appoint Ali Maher prime minister.

However, although the Wafd's power was in decline, the king still had to reckon with the British embassy, and this was now in *de facto* alliance with the Wafd. Although Lampson in theory no longer enjoyed Cromer's degree of authority, he behaved as if he did, and his treatment of the young king recalled Cromer's handling of the rebellious Khedive Abbas Hilmi forty years earlier. Lampson referred to him contemptuously as 'the Boy' and assured the Foreign Office that he was perfectly capable of dealing with him. Farouk, who had detested Lampson from the moment when Lampson arrived in Egypt, lacked the courage and strength of character to stand his ground against the British Embassy on questions of genuine political importance; he could only irritate and provoke Lampson in minor matters, such as keeping him waiting for appointments.

Nevertheless, a *modus vivendi* would probably have been reached if it had not been for the outbreak of war in 1939. This vastly increased Egypt's importance to Britain as a military base and, at the same time, strengthened Lampson's hand in his dealings with the king.

(b) The Mandates

The system of mandates set up by the League of Nations under Article 22 of its Covenant was unprecedented. It was also a form of compromise. While the victorious powers in the First World War wished to retain the former German colonies and the territories of the Ottoman Empire which in most cases they had made great sacrifices to conquer, they had made frequent pledges that their inhabitants would not be handed back to their former masters. They had also made solemn undertakings that the annexation of territory was not their aim in war. The outstanding example was the Anglo-French declaration about the former Ottoman provinces of 5 November 1918.

The mandates were not colonies but a form of trust in which the mandatary power administered the territory under the supervision of the League of Nations through a Permanent Mandates Commission. The supreme council of the League defined the terms of the mandates and the boundaries of the territories. The United States was not a member of the League but, as one of the former Allies, insisted that its consent to the mandates was necessary, and all mandate proposals were therefore submitted to the United States, which approved them on condition that 'free and equal treatment in law and in fact was secured to the commerce of all nations.'

It must be said that some British and French statesmen regarded the distinction between mandates and colonies as no more than a fiction. One of the frankest was the British foreign secretary, Lord Curzon, who told the House of Lords on 25 June 1920,

It is quite a mistake to suppose . . . that under the Covenant of the League or any other instrument, the gift of the mandate rests with the League of Nations. It does not do so. It rests with the Powers who have conquered the territories, which it then falls to them to distribute, and it was in these circumstances that the mandate for Palestine and Mesopotamia was conferred upon and accepted by us, and that the mandate for Syria was conferred upon and accepted by France.

The mandated territories, which included the former German colonies in Africa and the Pacific, were at varying stages of political and social development. Since the mandate principle was that they should be brought to independence as soon as was practically possible, they were divided in three classes. The former Turkish vilayets of Mesopotamia (Iraq), Palestine and Syria, were included in class A, for which early independence could be most easily foreseen. The mandates for them were issued to Britain and France only when the Treaty of Lausanne came into force in August 1924, by which time the two Allies had already made various *de facto* arrangements for the establishment of boundaries and forms of administration which the League of Nations was in no position to reverse. Many *faits accomplis* had to be accepted.

The League was supposed to enjoy an unqualified right of supervision, and the mandatory powers were obliged to submit annual reports on the exercise of their trusteeship. In addition the League could receive petitions from inhabitants of the territories and other interested parties. The weakest point in the system lay in the impossibility of independent verification of the mandataries' reports, which varied in completeness and accuracy.

(i) Iraq

The new kingdom of Iraq suffered from many problems related to its national unity. The centrifugal forces were powerful. The large and rebellious Kurdish minority in the north felt that it had been deprived of its hopes of self-determination by the post-war settlement. There were also substantial Turkoman and Christian Assyrian minorities. The Arab population was divided between Sunnis and Shiites, the latter being more numerous but the Sunnis being politically dominant.

However, Iraq was perhaps the most successful of the mandatary regimes. Although King Feisal I had been imposed on the country from outside, he proved to be an effective unifying force. Kurdish and tribal beduin lawlessness was gradually overcome, and the Shiite *mujtahids* or religious authorities (who were mainly Persian) were brought under control. Relations with Persia were not cordial but remained peaceful. The boundary disputes with Ibn Saud, exacerbated by Hashemite–Saudi rivalry, were more bitter, but a measure of reconciliation was achieved through British mediation. The relationship with the former Turkish suzerains was the most difficult. At the 1923 Lausanne Conference, the Turkish Republic demanded the return of most of the vilayet of Mosul, which was widely believed to be rich in oil. After two years of wrangling within the League of Nations, Turkey reluctantly but unequivocally accepted the award of Mosul to Iraq.

Following the defeat of those British officials in the immediate post-war period who favoured Iraq's incorporation into the British Empire, relatively liberal policies were pursued. The initially extensive powers of British officials were gradually reduced. A constituent assembly was convened in 1924 which, in the following year, approved an Anglo-Iraqi treaty and an Organic Law which made Iraqi ministers responsible to a two-chamber parliament. However, the treaty, which maintained important exclusive British rights in Iraq, was approved only under heavy British pressure against the radical opposition which demanded unfettered independence.

By the late 1920s Britain was prepared to end the mandate,

provided British interests could be maintained, but a new treaty was long delayed because of the continued nationalist opposition to any British tutelage in a concealed form. Some League of Nations members also insisted that Iraq was not yet ready for full independence. (France, in particular, was alarmed by the possible precedent for its own mandates.) Finally, an Anglo-Iraqi treaty was concluded in 1930, providing for a twenty-five year alliance during which the two countries undertook to consult each other in order to harmonize their common interests in matters of foreign policy. Britain would have the use of certain air bases in Iraq and existing means of communications and in return would provide a military mission to help train the Iraqi army.

In 1932 the British mandate formally ended; Iraq became independent and joined the League of Nations under British sponsorship. Only a strong body of Iraqi opinion remained dissatisfied, believing that the country was still under British hegemony. In their view this was aggravated by the power of the Iraq Petroleum Company, which monopolized Iraq's oil resources. In August 1933, an ominous prelude to independence was the massacre by an army unit of three hundred Assyrian villagers in northern Iraq. The massacre was applauded by most Iraqi opinion and the soldiers were never punished. A large part of the Assyrian community left for Syria.

King Feisal I died suddenly in 1933 and was succeeded by his son Ghazi. Handsome and popular, Ghazi had the reputation of being an Arab nationalist, but he lacked his father's authority. In 1927 oil had been discovered in commercial quantities near Kirkuk in the north, and production bringing in the first substantial revenues began in 1934. Irrigation, communications and the public services all made progress – the development of the country's vast potential resources had begun. However, the absence of King Feisal made the development of a viable political system more difficult. The country was served by some able and devoted ministers and officials who survived from the Ottoman period, of whom the most outstanding was Nuri al-Said. But parliamentary democracy failed to take root. No authentic political parties developed. Elections were largely controlled, with conservative personal and class interests remaining dominant. A series of incompetent, reactionary and increasingly authoritarian cabinets succeeded each other in office. Politicians had no hesitation in organizing a tribal uprising, which could never be fully controlled, against the government of their rivals in office. The old-style politicians were opposed by an alliance of reformist middle-class intellectuals and young nationalist army officers inspired by the example of Kemal Atatürk. In 1936 these seized power under the leadership of General Bakr Sidqi. The movement ended, ten months later, as it had begun – with assassination and a military coup. It had failed because the reformist elements were soon set aside; the army was divided and the bulk of the population was alienated from the new rulers. But the coup was an event of great significance, because it established a precedent for military coups in the Arab world. Despite its failure, the Iraqi army had gained a new self-assurance and a taste for interference in political life.

The army faction which overthrew Bakr Sidqi remained in power behind the scenes, capable of making or unmaking cabinets. However, in 1938 this group, known as The Seven, was instrumental in bringing a civilian – Nuri al-Said – to power. Pro-British and conservative, Nuri was to dominate the Iraqi state for the next twenty years through his strong personality and political finesse.

(ii) Syria and Lebanon

Having enlarged Lebanon at Syria's expense, France based its policy in the two mandates on the strengthening and promotion of the traditionally Francophile Maronite Christian elements as against the Muslim Arab population. In both countries in the early years of the mandates France behaved in the manner of a colonial government backed by superior military power. The press was controlled, and nationalist demonstrations were instantly suppressed.

The terms of the mandates promised a constitution for both countries in three years. But France considered the creation of an independent unitary state in Syria to be a very distant goal. The French army regarded strategic control of the region as essential, and French politicians were always concerned with the potential effect of concessions on France's North African possessions.

Some members of the minorities and a small proportion of the Sunni Muslim majority accepted that French rule might bring advantages. But the vast majority, especially the educated élite, demanded immediate independence, and many went further to insist that the independent state should also include Palestine and Transjordan. France, on the other hand, with the unmistakable purpose of dividing

Syria in order to rule it more easily, partitioned the country into separate autonomous districts: one in the Alawite (Nusairiyah) mountains in the north-east inhabited mainly by the sub-Shia Alawite sect, one in the Jebal Druze in the south where most of the people were Druze, and one in the rest of Syria with Damascus as the capital. Within the last a special status was given to the district of Alexandretta (now Iskenderun) with its mixed population of Arabs, Turks and Armenians. All three districts had autonomous administrations with French advisers, but there was an overall supervisory administration under the high commissioner for Syria and Lebanon in Beirut.

The fragile framework was soon shaken when in 1925 a revolt in the Jebal Druze, due to local grievances, led to an alliance between the Druze and the nationalists of Damascus, who had begun to organize themselves in the People's Party.

The Druze warriors penetrated Lebanon and even the suburbs of Damascus, provoking a two-day French bombardment. The rebellion continued sporadically for two years, leaving much bitterness, but the French were constrained to pursue a more conciliatory policy. In 1928 they allowed elections to be held for a Constituent Assembly. These were clearly won by the nationalists, who formed a cabinet. The construction drafted by the assembly was, as expected, unacceptable to the French because it spoke of the unity of geographical Syria and failed to recognize French control.

In 1930 the French high commissioner unilaterally promulgated a new constitution which made Syria a parliamentary republic with France retaining control over foreign affairs and security. Desultory and unsuccessful negotiations followed to draw up a Franco-Syrian treaty which would be acceptable to both sides. However, by 1936 a new situation had arisen. A left-wing Popular Front government had come to power in France, and Britain had created precedents by granting independence to Iraq and reaching a treaty agreement with Egypt. Like their Egyptian counterparts, the Syrian nationalists, now organized in a National Bloc coalition, were concerned by the rising tensions in the Mediterranean region created by Italian imperial ambitions.

Negotiations now made progress, and in 1936 a treaty was signed providing for Syrian independence, with Franco-Syrian consultation on foreign policy, French priority in advice and assistance, and the retention by France of two military bases. The Druze and Alawite districts would be incorporated into Syria.

However, although the treaty was ratified by the Syrian parliament, it was never ratified by the French Chamber of Deputies and so remained inoperative. The Popular Front government fell from power and was replaced by a more right-wing cabinet which insisted on keeping control over the Levant states for strategic and economic reasons. There were prospects of the discovery of oil in north-eastern Syria, and Syria and Lebanon lay across the air-routes to the Far East. With the renewed threat of war with Germany, the potential effect of Syrian independence on French North Africa had become even more important – France, with its 40 million population, could hope to balance Germany's 80 million only by drawing on the manpower of North Africa.

The prospect of war with Germany also led France to conciliate Turkey over the question of the district of Alexandretta, which was claimed by Turkey. In 1937 France gave the district a fully auton-omous status, and after a Franco-Turkish commission had ensured a Turkish majority in parliamentary elections (although Arabs and Armenians outnumbered Turks in the population) France agreed to the absorption of the District of Alexandretta into Turkey in June 1939. The district was renamed the Hatay. Turkey in fact remained neutral during the Second World War but at least it did not become Germany's ally as in the First. To the present day, official maps of the Syrian Arab Republic show Alexandretta as part of Syria.

By 1939 it had become clear that the French government had no intention of ratifying the Franco-Syrian treaty. On the eve of the Second World War the Syrian president resigned and the constitution was suspended.

France expected Lebanon, with its dominant Francophile majority, to be easier to govern than Syria. However, the creation of *le Grand Liban*, which included many Muslims and non-Maronite Christians, caused the balance of the population to change. Although the Maron-ites remained the largest single community, their narrow majority in the population was eroding as a result of their lower birth rate and higher tendency to emigrate than other communities. A constitution, which was drafted in Paris with little consultation with the Lebanese, was imposed in 1926. It provided for a bicameral parliament and a president. In an attempt to ease sectarian tensions, the principle was

established that seats in parliament and the cabinet should be distributed on the basis of religious affiliation. The president was a
Maronite, the prime minister a Sunni Muslim and the president of
the Chamber of Deputies a Shiite. There would always be a Greek
Orthodox and a Druze member in the cabinet. However, the president, who was elected for a six-year term and had the right to choose
the prime minister, enjoyed the strongest powers and the Maronites
remained politically and socially dominant in the country.

Emotionally, a large part of the Lebanese population both rejected
French control and saw themselves as part either of Syria or of a
wider Arab nation. The growth of a Lebanese national identity
focused on the land within the borders of *le Grand Liban* was fragile
and made more difficult by the sectarian basis of the political system,
but it would be an error to suppose that such a national identity did
not exist. The people of Tripoli, Sidon and the Bekaa were not
unanimous in wishing to secede from the Lebanese Republic. The
unity of the Lebanese nation could have been greatly strengthened
and much more trouble avoided in the future if the Maronites had
agreed to a more equitable sharing of power – by allowing, for
example, the presidency to alternate between Christians and Muslims.
Nevertheless, the prosperity of Beirut as a centre of trade and
services helped towards the growth of a middle class of both Muslims
and Christians with some common sense of a national interest which
partly transcended sectarian loyalties. A nascent movement for independence, critical of excessive and undiminishing French interference
in government, was joined by a number of prominent Maronites. In
1936 the Maronite patriarch published a collection of memoranda
voicing these criticisms in detail. In the same year the French
government proposed a Franco-Lebanese treaty similar to the one
with Syria, but, just as with Syria, although this was promptly
ratified by the Lebanese parliament, it was never ratified by the
right-wing governments which succeeded the Popular Front in
France.

Outside the political sphere, the achievements of the French mandatary in Lebanon and Syria were far from negligible. It introduced a
relatively modern administrative system, customs organization and
land registration based on a pioneering cadastral survey. It built
many roads and improved urban amenities. In Damascus and Aleppo
it initiated city planning. One of its finest achievements was the

creation of a department of antiquities to preserve and administer the Levant states' unparalleled archaeological heritage. Some encouragement was given to agriculture, especially in north-eastern Syria's Jazirah region, but the economic effects of the mandate were affected by the chronic weakness of the French franc on which the Syrian and Lebanese currencies were based. Also, considerable resentment was caused by the policy of granting monopolies to French companies whose profits were repatriated to France.

Education received a powerful stimulus, although in some respects the policy was controversial. The French language and culture were promoted. Arab children were taught a French interpretation of history and even learned to sing '*La Marseillaise*'. Foreign mission schools were protected and in Lebanon much of the educational system and almost all higher education remained in their hands, with teaching mostly in French or English. As a consequence the educational standards of the Lebanese people as a whole were higher than anywhere in the former Ottoman Empire. On the other hand, the lack of an adequate state education system did nothing to promote national unity. In Syria, where the mission schools were much less important, a state educational system was constructed under the mandate and the University of Damascus was established, with its teaching mainly in Arabic.

(iii)   Palestine and Transjordan

When the British government undertook the mandate for Palestine in 1919, it was unaware that it was taking on an impossible task. Its failure to solve the problems was to infect Britain's relations with the Arabs for a generation.

Article 6 of the Balfour Declaration, which was incorporated within the terms of the mandate, stated:

The Administration of Palestine, while ensuring that the rights and positions of other sections of the population are not prejudiced, shall facilitate Jewish immigration under suitable conditions and shall encourage co-operation with the Jewish Agency referred to in Article 4, close settlement by Jews on the land, including State lands and waste lands not required for public purposes.

Britain's first high commissioner for Palestine, from 1920 to 1925, was Sir Herbert Samuel, a Jew who had been the first to propose the idea of a Jewish Palestine to the British cabinet in 1914. But he had never been an active member of the Zionist movement, and as high commissioner he made strenuous efforts to be fair to the 'other sections of the population', ultimately incurring the disappointment and even odium of the Zionists. He set up an administration including Muslims, Christians and Jews and for a time worked with an advisory council of similar composition which he hoped would lead ultimately to a partly elected legislative council for a joint community. But the Arabs, who fundamentally rejected both the mandate and the Balfour Declaration, boycotted the elections and demanded a national government. Severe rioting ensued. On Samuel's insistence, the British government issued a White Paper declaring Britain's intention to hold the balance between the Arab and Jewish communities. However, the Arabs were convinced by this that the true intention was to wait to grant self-government until the Jews in Palestine had grown sufficiently in numbers and power to become dominant, and they continued to demand an immediate national government, citing the promises made to the Arabs during the war. They rejected Samuel's proposal for the formation of an Arab Agency to match the Jewish Agency.

One of Samuel's actions with good intentions towards the Arabs had fateful consequences. To maintain the balance between the two leading families in Jerusalem, he overturned the elections for mufti of Jerusalem in favour of a young nationalist, Hajj Amin al-Husseini. From this position, Hajj Amin, an uncompromising nationalist who singularly lacked political wisdom, was able to gain the leadership of the Arabs of Palestine.

However, the years 1923 to 1929 were relatively quiet, mainly because Arab fears were reduced by the drop in Jewish immigration. In 1927 there was nil Jewish immigration into Palestine and in 1928 the net immigration was only ten persons. The Zionists continued to consolidate their settlements and their political presence, but their hopes of dominance receded. The British mandatary authorities became complacent and drastically reduced the garrison, despite the warnings of the Permanent Mandates Commission.

In 1929 the situation sharply deteriorated. In August, Britain consented to the creation of an enlarged Jewish Agency in which half the members were recruited from Zionist sympathizers outside Palestine. The Zionists acquired a new sense of confidence. In the same month a dispute concerning religious practices at the Wailing Wall in Jerusalem led to widespread communal clashes, with severe casualties. Troops were rushed in and order was restored. Arabs massacred Jewish colonists in Hebron. Arab casualties were mainly caused by British soldiers.

Britain was fully confronted with the contradictions in the mandate. The new high commissioner, Sir John Chancellor (1928–31), proposed that the mandate should be reshaped to remove the special privileges of the Jews, restrict their land purchases (which were proceeding apace with the help of Zionist funds and sales by absentee Arab landlords) and give the Arabs a measure of self-government. A British technical report established that there was no margin of land available for new immigrants without substantial development funds which, at a time of world depression, the British government was quite unready to provide. In 1930 the colonial secretary in Britain's Labour government issued a White Paper which gave some priority to Britain's obligations to the Arabs by restricting Jewish immigration and ending Jewish land purchases. In the ensuing uproar the Zionists, who naturally saw their hopes of a Jewish Palestine vanishing, were able to use their sympathizers among all parties in the British parliament to cause Ramsay MacDonald's weak and nervous cabinet to rescind the White Paper. The Palestinian Arabs became convinced that recommendations in their favour would always be annulled at the centre of power. They began to attempt to organize their own international support. In December 1931 a Muslim Congress was called in Jerusalem, attended by representatives of twenty-two Muslim countries, to warn against the danger of Zionism. But although fellow-Arabs in neighbouring countries were beginning to be aroused by the plight of the Palestinian Arabs, there was little practical support they could provide. A boycott of Zionist and British goods called in 1933 was largely ineffective.

In the first half of the 1930s there was a sharp rise in Jewish immigration, from 4,000 in 1930 to 30,000 in 1933 and 62,000 in 1935. This was due partly to fears of Hitler's rise to power in Germany but much more to growing confidence in Palestine's future which, in spite of world depression, was enjoying something of a boom based on its citrus industry. In 1935 the Arab parties, although far from united, collectively demanded the cessation of Jewish immigration, the prohibition of land transfer and the establishment of democratic institutions. The British offered a legislative council of twenty-eight members on which the Arabs would have fourteen seats and the Jews eight, with the remaining six reserved for British officials. Most, although not all, Arabs rejected the proposal because they would not be represented in proportion to their numbers. The Jews bitterly denounced it because they believed it would provide the Arabs with a permanent stranglehold on the development of the Jewish national home. For this reason some Palestinians later came to regret their rejection.

The Arab rebellion of 1936–8 against the mandate, which at first smouldered and then burst into flame, was provoked by continuing fears that Jewish immigration would lead to Zionist dominance and the certainty that Britain would not effectively prevent it. The spark was provided by the knowledge that the Zionists were smuggling in arms for self-defence. In April 1936 the Arab political parties formed an Arab Higher Committee, under Hajj Amin, which called a general strike. This was maintained for six months. At the same time Arab rebels, joined by volunteers from neighbouring Arab countries, took to the hills and a full-scale national uprising began.

For not the first nor the last time, Britain sent out a commission of inquiry. Lord Peel's commission of 1937 concluded that Britain's obligations to Arabs and Jews were irreconcilable and the mandate unworkable. It therefore for the first time recommended the partition of Palestine into Jewish and Arab states, with Jerusalem and Haifa remaining under British mandate and with a 12,000 annual limit to Jewish immigration for the next five years. The tiny Arab state would be joined to Transjordan under Abdullah. The Zionists' response was ambivalent. Britain had for the first time spoken of a Jewish state and had proposed the forcible transfer of some of the Arab population. But they disliked the limitation on the size of the Jewish state, which would exclude Jerusalem, and the limit on Jewish immigration. They still hoped to become dominant in an undivided Palestine. The Arabs, on the other hand, were unanimously outraged (except for Amir Abdullah of Transjordan, who urged acceptance) and their rebellion intensified, in spite of the heavy use of British force and the outlawing of the Arab Higher Committee. Most of the Committee's members were deported to the Seychelles, but Hajj Amin escaped to Baghdad from where he continued to exert some influence in favour of the maximum Arab demands.

The League of Nations then authorized the preparation of a detailed partition plan. However, the technical commission which reported in November 1938 declared the Peel commission's proposal to be unworkable. The British government agreed and called for a round-table conference, which was held in London during February and March 1939. This was a failure, as were the two bilateral conferences with Jews and Arabs which followed. (The conference with the Arabs included representatives of the Arab states, as an acknowledgement that Palestine was of interest to all the Arabs.)

The Arab rebellion gradually died down in the early months of 1939. Following the Munich crisis in 1938 and the postponed threat of immediate war, Britain had been able to pour in extra troops. The long and unsuccessful struggle left the Palestinian Arabs exhausted and demoralized.

The British government, however, was primarily concerned with the approaching world war, which now seemed inevitable. The priority was to secure at least the passive support of the Arabs who formed the vast majority of the population in the strategically vital Middle East region (including Palestine, where they were still some 70 per cent). It was assumed that the Jews would inevitably be on Britain's side in any war against Hitler. A new British government White Paper in May 1939 provided for the limitation of Zionist immigration to 75,000 over the next five years, with further immigration subject to Arab 'acquiescence'. The White Paper said that the object was the establishment 'within ten years of an independent Palestine State in such treaty relations with the UK as will provide satisfaction for all commercial and strategic interests of both countries'. It was clear that the Arabs would still then be in substantial majority.

Although this new policy was more favourable to the Arabs, the Mufti's party rejected it – mainly on the grounds that experience showed that the British government could not be trusted to carry it out against Jewish opposition. More moderate Arabs shared these doubts. The Zionists, on the other hand, were appalled and angered because they considered it a death blow to their aspirations and a betrayal of the Balfour Declaration. They became even more determined to establish their own state in Palestine. Already the Jewish community in Palestine was largely self-governing through an elected assembly which levied its own taxes. Purely Jewish trade unions were united in a confederation, the Histadrut, which performed numerous other functions as banker, entrepreneur and land-owner. Between 1922 and 1939 Jewish colonies had increased from forty-seven to two hundred and Jewish land-holdings had more than doubled. The Hebrew University on Mount Scopus in Jerusalem, opened in 1925, was playing the leading role in the training of the country's intellectual and academic leadership. The most significant development for the future was the creation of the Haganah, the secret but officially tolerated Jewish army. This gained experience in defending Jewish settlements against Arab attacks, and some of its members assisted British forces in suppressing the Arab rebellion.

The Jews in Palestine were a formidable force and they were determined to oppose Britain's new policy. But the odds seemed heavily weighted against them.

East of the River Jordan in the newly created emirate of Transjordan under the rule of Amir Abdullah, the problems were infinitely less complicated. Having secured the League of Nations' approval for Transjordan's exclusion from the policy of the Jewish national home, on 25 May 1923 Britain recognized Transjordan as an independent state, subject to British obligations under the Palestine mandate. Under French pressure, Syrian leaders who had taken refuge in Transjordan were ordered to leave.

All troops were placed under the command of a British officer, and with British help the fledgeling Jordanian forces were able to deal with some internal tribal dissension and the incursions of Wahhabi warriors from the Nejd in the early 1920s.

The country was poor, undeveloped and thinly populated, but it acquired a social and political cohesion which Palestine lacked. Britain virtually dictated the terms of the 1928 treaty under which, through a British resident appointed by the high commissioner for Palestine, Amir Abdullah was to be guided by British advice in such matters as foreign relations, finance and jurisdiction over foreigners. There were a score of British advisers and a modest British subsidy (£101,000 out of a total state budget of £257,000 in 1925–6) and, in spite of the poverty, some slow and steady progress was made. Roads and schools were built, although it was fifteen years before the country had more than one secondary school.

In 1931, after ten years' experience in Iraq, Captain John Bagot Glubb (or Glubb Pasha, as he was later known) arrived to found the Desert Patrol as a special branch of the Transjordanian army (the

Arab Legion) entrusted with the task of keeping order in the desert. Its novel aspect was that it used tribesmen to maintain security among their fellow-beduin. Glubb had remarkable success in gaining the confidence of the beduin and persuading them of the advantages of stability and order. In this way they became loyal to the Transjordanian state and many of them came to serve in the regular armed forces.

Faced with the problem of Palestine, Britain was happy to allow Abdullah increasing independence as the undisputed leader of Transjordan. Although his claim to rule was based on his Hashemite family's version of pan-Arabism, his remarkable political skills enabled him to secure the fierce loyalty of most of the local tribal leaders to himself and his family. In 1934 Britain agreed that the amir could appoint consular representatives in other Arab states, and in 1939 it approved the formation of a council of ministers in charge of government departments and responsible to the amir. In 1946 Transjordan became formally independent, although still relying heavily on British subsidy and support. Amir Abdullah took the title of king.

Although Transjordan was developing separately and differently, it was far from insulated from events in Palestine west of the River Jordan. There were many ties of blood between the people of the two banks, and the higher levels of education among Palestinians resulted in some of them being recruited as officials for the fledgeling administration in Amman. Transjordanians felt emotionally involved in the unfolding tragedy of Palestine. However, an element of territorial nationalism was growing up in Transjordan as it did elsewhere in the former Arab provinces of the Ottoman Empire. (Here it was given some historical validity by the feeling that the Transjordanians were descended from the Nabataeans of Petra.) A feeling of 'Transjordan for the Transjordanians' was eventually translated into a law confining government posts to Transjordanians. This was opposed by Arab nationalists, who maintained that nothing should intensify the artificially imposed divisions between the Arabs, but in practical terms the separate development of Transjordan had the support of the great majority of the country.

Abdullah concentrated on building up his power base in Transjordan, which, though smaller and poorer than Palestine or Syria, had the advantage that he could rule it through his personal authority. But this did not mean that he had abandoned his Hashemite pan-

Arab aspirations. These did not include Egypt or the Arabian peninsula, which by 1925 had been lost by the Hashemites to Ibn Saud,
but he had never abandoned his family's claims in Greater Syria. He
had little chance in French-ruled Syria, but Palestine was different.
At the beginning of the British mandate he made a shrewd and
realistic assessment of the Zionists' power and aspirations and was
quite prepared to negotiate with them. He foresaw a time when the
Palestinian Arabs might seek his protection and be prepared to accept
his rule. It was for this reason that he urged acceptance of the 1937
Peel commission's proposal for partition and the joining of Arab
Palestine to Transjordan.

Inevitably Abdullah's stand gave him many enemies among Arab
nationalists who opposed the Hashemites, ranging from Hajj Amin's
Husseini family in Palestine to republicans in Syria. He had his
supporters in both these countries, but they did not predominate. His
Hashemite cousins in Iraq were more friendlily disposed but were
not prepared to accept his leadership. He was prepared to await
events in Palestine.

Persia/Iran

Although Persia declared its neutrality at the outbreak of the First
World War, it did not escape involvement. Turkey's violation of
Persian territory in order to attack Russia and the Turkish threat to
the Anglo-Persian Oil Company's oilfield and refinery in the south of
the country led to the occupation of large areas of Persian territory by
Russian and British troops. This increased sympathy among the
Persian people for the German and Turkish side in the war. At the
end of the war, Persia joined the League of Nations as an independent
state, but the country was in chaos. Its armed forces were divided
and the treasury was empty.

The defeat of Russia in the war and the subsequent Bolshevik
Revolution helped to relieve Persia from Russian pressure for a time.
This tempted Britain to bring Persia into its sphere of influence. The
foreign secretary, Lord Curzon, wrote in 1919,

Now that we are about to assume the mandate for Mesopotamia, which will
make us coterminous with the western frontiers of Persia, we cannot permit

the existence, between the frontiers of our Indian Empire . . . and those of our new Protectorate, of a hotbed of misrule, enemy intrigue, financial chaos and political disorder. Further . . . we possess in the south-western corner of Persia great assets in the shape of the oilfields, which are worked for the British Navy and which give us a commanding interest in that part of the world.

Curzon instigated the Anglo-Persian agreement of 1919 which, while reaffirming Persia's independence and territorial integrity, provided for the appointment of British military and civil advisers, co-operation in the development of transport and a loan of £2,000,000. The agreement would have ensured British ascendancy in Persia and was strongly criticized by the United States. However, in consequence of the strength of feeling aroused in the country, the Majlis refused to ratify the agreement and the British advisers who had taken up their posts were sent home.

In contrast, on 26 February 1921 a Soviet-Persian treaty was signed by which the Soviet government renounced 'the tyrannical policy' of tsarist Russia, remitted all Persian debts and abandoned extraterritorial privileges for Russian nationals. The treaty also gave up all concessions then held by the Russian government or nationals, although the Soviet government secured under pressure the valuable concession of the Caspian fisheries, which had previously belonged to Russian nationals but had lapsed. This treaty was promptly ratified by the Majlis. Little attention was paid to a clause authorizing Russia to send troops into Persia if it judged that it had become a base for military action against Russia.

With a weak and corrupt government and an incompetent young shah, the internal situation further deteriorated. At this point the forceful and outstanding commander of the Persian Cossack brigade, Colonel Reza Khan, was persuaded by a group of reformers to march with his men on Tehran. He entered the capital on 21 February 1921. The cabinet resigned and a new government was formed with Reza Khan as minister of war and commander-in-chief. Shortly afterwards he took full control of the government as prime minister.

Reza Khan's first task was to reunite and build up the armed forces. He commandeered state funds to ensure that the troops were regularly paid. In this way he gradually created a relatively efficient and disciplined army of 40,000, through which he aimed to establish the authority of the central government throughout the country. In 1924 he suppressed a rebellion by the autonomous shaikh of Mohammereh (renamed Khorramshahr), in whose territory the Anglo-Persian Oil Company's concession lay. To help reorganize the country's disastrous finances he invited in a US financial expert, A. C. Millspaugh, who with a small group of advisers made considerable progress. In the inter-war years Persia became a major oil producer. Production rose from 12 million barrels in 1920 to 46 million in 1930, making Persia the fourth largest producer in the world, after the USA, Russia and Venezuela.

Because of public disillusion with the long experience of corrupt and incompetent monarchy, there was widespread support for a republic. The religious leaders, who feared the consequences of Kemal Atatürk's abolition of the caliphate and institution of a secular republic, opposed such a change, however. Reza Khan therefore decided to retain the monarchy and make himself shah. On 31 October 1925, by a large majority, the Majlis declared the end of the Qajar dynasty. A new constituent assembly then vested the crown in Reza Shah, with the right of succession to his heirs. He took the name of Pahlavi for his dynasty. In 1935 he officially changed the name of the country from Persia to Iran.

Although it was the mullahs who had helped to make him shah, he regarded most of them as backward and reactionary. In fact in many respects he modelled his regime on that of Atatürk as he embarked on a policy of westernization. He introduced a French judicial system which challenged the competence of the religious courts. Civil offices were opened for marriage, education was reorganized on Western lines and literacy steadily increased. The University of Tehran was established in 1935, with a number of Europeans on the staff. In 1936 women were compelled to discard the veil and European costume was made obligatory for both sexes. Reza Shah pursued his policy of pacifying and unifying the country – a task which had been beyond the competence of the Qajar shahs – by subduing the semi-independent tribes. The Bakhtiaris and Kashgars were placed under the rule of military officers.

Improved communications were vital for the unification of the empire's extensive territories. The German Junkers company organized an internal air service. Postal services and telecommunications were vastly improved. American and European engineers helped to build roads and railways. The construction of a Trans-Iranian Railway from the Caspian Sea to the Gulf was a project for which the shah aroused the enthusiasm of the whole nation.

Progress meant industrialization, and a range of new textile, steel, cement and other factories were established. Some of them were profitable.

Reza Shah's firm rule and national assertiveness raised Iran's international standing and increased its bargaining power. He denounced all treaties which conferred extraterritorial rights on the subjects of foreign powers. In a dispute with the Soviet government over the Caspian fisheries, he secured a compromise in the formation of a Persian-Russian company to exploit the fisheries. To achieve his aim of improving the meagre revenues from the Anglo-Persian Oil Company, he was prepared to take the risk of cancelling the concession in 1932. Britain referred the matter to the League of Nations, and the dispute ended in 1933 with a compromise under which Persia received substantially better terms.

Reza Khan's vigorous assertion of Persian national rights forced Britain to remove the seat of its authority in the Gulf to Bahrain on the western coast. Two British coaling stations on Persian territory were removed, and the Royal Air Force switched its route for flights to India from the Persian to the Arab shore. However, friction continued as Reza Khan periodically reasserted Persia's claim to Bahrain.

Reza Khan's successes had negative aspects. His lavish and authoritarian military rule left little room for personal freedom or initiative. The Majlis was preserved but became little more than a façade. Some of the economic policies were misconceived and wasteful. Agriculture was seriously neglected, and the policy of settling the nomads was an outright failure because no adequate provision was made for them to maintain their flocks in the areas of their settlement. Most seriously for Reza Khan's reputation, he acquired huge areas of the best land for himself either by confiscation on political charges or by methods of purchase which amounted in effect to expropriation.

Oil and the Middle East

The first oil to be discovered in the Middle East was in Persia, and for the first three decades of the twentieth century Persia remained the only oil-producing country in the region. Lord Curzon may have slightly exaggerated when he declared that 'the Allies floated to victory on a wave of oil' in the First World War, but nevertheless for Britain, with its controlling interest in the Anglo-Persian Oil Company, Persian oil was the major strategic and economic interest in the region alongside the Suez Canal.

However, even before the First World War there was little doubt that northern Mesopotamia was another potentially oil-rich area. Oil from surface seepages was taken by donkey to provide domestic fuel in Turkey. In 1904 Calouste Gulbenkian, a wealthy Armenian financier, wrote a report on the commercial possibilities of the oil of northern Mesopotamia which caused Sultan Abdul Hamid to transfer these state lands to his own privy purse. On the eve of the First World War, the Ottoman government granted a concession to the Turkish Petroleum Company (TPC) in which the Anglo-Persian Oil Company had a half interest together with Royal Dutch Shell and the German Deutsche Bank. The participants in TPC pledged themselves not to be interested directly or indirectly in the production or manufacture of oil in the Ottoman Empire in Europe and Asia except through the TPC with the exclusion of certain areas delimited on a map by a red line. This became known as 'the Red Line agreement'. Hence at the end of the war, Britain, with its troops occupying Mosul and having expropriated the German interest in TPC, was in a commanding position to control Mesopotamian oil. However, Britain had obligations to France under the secret 1916 Sykes–Picot agreement which, in its original form, included Mosul in the French zone of influence. In 1919 Britain persuaded France to transfer Mosul to the British zone, in return for a guaranteed role in the development of Mosul oil.

France also agreed to the construction of two separate pipelines for the transport of oil from Mesopotamia and Persia through the French spheres of influence to the Mediterranean.

It was at this point that the United States government intervened. Although the USA was retreating into the political isolation which lasted until the Second World War, it was determined that, while accepting the Anglo-French mandates, an 'open-door' policy should be maintained in commercial matters in the mandated territories. This meant equal treatment 'in law and in fact to the commerce of all nations', but oil was the chief concern. The British government, on the other hand, felt that the USA already had enough oil of its own in Texas. A prolonged and sometimes acrimonious correspondence between the US State Department and the British Foreign Office ensued. The final upshot was that Iraq's oil industry became a monopoly of the Iraq Petroleum Company (IPC), the successor of the TPC, which was owned jointly in 23.75 per cent shares by the Anglo-Persian Oil Company (later BP); Royal Dutch Shell; an American group which was ultimately reduced to Standard Oil of New Jersey and Socony-Vacuum (later Mobil); and the Compagnie Française des Pétroles (CFP), with Calouste Gulbenkian holding the remaining 5 per cent. The US State Department had achieved an entrée for American companies into the Middle Eastern oil arena, but in doing so it was in fact accepting the provisions of the Red Line agreement which Britain considered to be still in force, excluding all other than IPC participants.

A major oilfield was discovered near Kirkuk in 1927, and by 1934 production was contributing substantially to Iraq's revenues.

Throughout the 1920s the Anglo-Persian Oil Company, which continued to dominate the Middle East oil scene, showed little interest in the oil potential of the territories on the western shores of the Gulf – that is in Kuwait, Bahrain or the Eastern Province of the future kingdom of Saudi Arabia. This was partly because the company's geologists were convinced that, despite the seepages of bitumen in Kuwait, only the eastern side of the Gulf would yield oil in commercial quantities. The western shores of the Gulf lacked the Oligocene–Miocene rock formations found in Persia and Iraq. However, this did not mean that either the British government or APOC was happy to see a concession granted to a non-British company on the western shore. On APOC's behalf the British government resisted US pressure to allow the amirs of Kuwait and Bahrain to grant concessions to non-British companies. In 1931 the amir of Bahrain granted a concession to Standard Oil of California, which organized the Bahrain Petroleum Company (Bapco) as a Canadian-incorporated subsidiary to maintain the fiction that it was British.

When Bapco found oil in commercial quantities in May 1932, after only six months' drilling, the situation was transformed. The potential of the western shores of the Gulf was apparent. Standard Oil approached King Ibn Saud for a concession and the king, in desperate need of funds, responded. Anglo-Persian sent a representative to make a counter-bid but, since the company already had more than enough oil on its hands and its primary concern was only to exclude competitors from the region, he was authorized to offer an advance payment of only £5,000, whereas Standard Oil, after some hard bargaining, offered £50,000. On 29 May 1933 Standard Oil of California's concession was signed, covering all the eastern parts of the kingdom.

In this way the foundations were laid for the close relationship between Saudi Arabia and the United States which has profoundly influenced the modern history of the Middle East. The king, although far from being anti-British, was probably inclined to favour the US company, apart from its more generous offer, because the United States had no imperialist record in the Middle East. As the ruler of an entirely independent state, he was fortunate in being able to make a free choice.

Standard Oil of California later sold shares in its concession to the Texas Company, and in 1944 the company operating the concession took the name Arabian-American Oil Company (Aramco). The fact that American oil companies developed Saudi Arabia's major natural resource had an important influence on the kingdom. Aramco was never a simple instrument of US foreign policy – in fact it was often at loggerheads with Washington – but the company helped to train young Saudis and a trend began which led to the great majority of a new Saudi élite receiving at least part of their education at American universities. It was natural that US companies, among which Bechtel Corporation was outstanding, should play the major role in the development of the kingdom's new infrastructure. As it came to be realized that Saudi Arabia possessed about one quarter of the world's proved oil reserves, the Saudi–US connection became even more significant.

Kuwait's shrewd ruler, Amir Ahmad, had been conducting prolonged negotiations over an oil concession with both APOC and the American Gulf Oil company. But the bargaining had become desultory because the oil companies were cutting back on their investments during the world depression. Britain's insistence on excluding non-British companies was also a stumbling-block. However, in 1932, following the precedent set in Bahrain, Britain finally succumbed to intensive US pressure to an 'open-door' policy for US oil companies in Kuwait. With the discovery of oil in Bahrain and the conclusion of the Saudi agreement with Standard Oil in the following year, the pace quickened. After lengthy negotiations behind the scenes, APOC and Gulf Oil agreed to bury their differences and form an alliance to negotiate jointly as equal partners for a concession. For this purpose they formed the Kuwait Oil Company (KOC) on a fifty–fifty basis. After further negotiations, in which Amir Ahmad fought successfully to limit the amount of political control which Britain insisted on maintaining over KOC through a separate agreement it reached with the company, a concession agreement for seventy-five years covering all Kuwaiti territory was signed in December 1934.

The remaining Arab shaikhdoms on the western side of the Gulf all had exclusive treaty agreements with Britain. But the British government was still alarmed at the possibility that the precedent of King Ibn Saud granting a concession to a purely American company might be followed by one of the fiercely independent rulers. A company called Petroleum Concessions Ltd, in which Anglo-Dutch, US and French companies held shares in the same proportion as in the Iraq Petroleum Company, was therefore formed to negotiate. The ruler of Qatar granted it a concession in 1935, but the rulers of the six Trucial States (so called since the 1853 truce with Britain under which they undertook to abjure sea warfare) proved more difficult. They bargained and prevaricated for better terms, and various forms of pressure – including threats to confiscate their pearling fleets, on the grounds that they were still engaging in the slave trade – had to be used until they gave in. The last to succumb – in 1939 – was the eccentric but wily ruler of Abu Dhabi, Shaikh Shakhbut, who had become something of a legend in the Gulf since, after his succession in 1928, he succeeded in restoring stability to Abu Dhabi following twenty years of fierce family strife. He was convinced that there was oil in his territory – bubbles of oil had been seen around some of Abu Dhabi's two hundred islands – and the oil men agreed that it was the most promising of the Trucial States. He therefore drove a hard bargain for the concession. He had to wait twenty years before he was proved right, but oil was then found in enormous quantities.

In Saudi Arabia, Kuwait and Qatar, oil on a commercial scale was discovered shortly before the Second World War but its development had to be postponed until after the war. However, in 1939 it was already apparent that the territories surrounding the Persian Gulf would become of enormous strategic and economic importance. In fact by the second half of the century their reserves of oil and natural gas amounted to some two-thirds of all those that had been discovered.

10. The Second World War and its Aftermath

The Middle East was as heavily involved in the 1939–45 conflict – the culmination of what has been aptly described as Europe's thirty-year civil war – as in that of 1914–18. The Turkish Republic was neutral. The new semi-independent nation-states which had been formed from the Arab provinces of the Ottoman Empire were non-belligerent, but they were under British or French occupation and therefore lay within the zone of war. Political life was largely frozen for the duration of hostilities.

As in the First World War, the retention of India was of supreme strategic and political importance to Britain. The protection of oil supplies from Iran was also a considerable secondary concern. Once again Egypt became Britain's great Mediterranean base. With a neutral Turkey and Iran, the Middle East region seemed fairly secure. The British realized with relief that, as a result of the 1939 White Paper on Palestine, the Palestinian Arabs were not going to embarrass them while they were at war with Germany.

The situation was transformed by Italy's entry into the war on Germany's side in June 1940. British forces in Egypt were engaged against the Italians in Libya, and British forces in the Sudan fought the Italian garrisons in Eritrea. Italian aircraft raided Egypt, and the country expected a full-scale Italian invasion. As in 1915, reinforcements were brought in from Australia, New Zealand and South Africa. Britain's determination to keep the Axis powers out of the eastern Mediterranean caused it to divert tanks from the home front to Egypt even when the danger that Hitler would invade Britain was at its height.

The battle in Egypt's Western Desert rolled backwards and forwards. In September 1940 the Italians entered Egypt and reached as far as Sidi Barrani; by the end of the year some spectacular British victories had driven them back into Libya. But, with German reinforcements, the Axis forces, now commanded by General Rommel, re-entered Egypt in April 1941. In the following month the Germans captured Crete, and the British hold on the eastern Mediterranean became perilous.

The danger for Britain was compounded by the situation in Syria and Iraq. Although Iraq broke off relations with Germany in September 1939, an Anglophobe nationalist group of civilians and military became increasingly dominant, encouraged by Germany's victories over France. In March 1941 they seized power in a putsch, and Rashid Ali al-Gailani became prime minister in a government with pro-Axis leanings. The regent, Nuri al-Said and other leading politicians had to flee the country. The government's refusal of a British request to move troops across Iraq under the terms of the Anglo-Iraqi treaty led to open, if subdued, hostilities. Iraqi troops surrounded the British base at Habbaniyah. But Iraqi opinion was divided and uncertain, and promised Axis help for the rebels was too little and too late.

A small Indian force was landed at Basra, to be joined by Arab troops from Transjordan under Glubb Pasha. The revolt collapsed after a few weeks; the Rashid Ali government fled and the regent returned. Successive Iraqi governments co-operated with the Allies for the rest of the war.

Following the fall of France in 1940, Syria and Lebanon came under the control of the Vichy government. Britain promptly declared that it would not allow a German occupation of the two Levant states, but the Vichy government – anxious to secure as many concessions as possible from Germany – instructed the high commission in Beirut to collaborate fully with the Axis. The climax came in June 1941 when German aircraft *en route* to help Rashid Ali in Iraq were allowed to use Syrian airfields. On 8 June 1941 a mixed force of General de Gaulle's Free French and British troops launched a three-pronged invasion from Palestine. Despite some stiff resistance by the Vichy forces, the fighting lasted only six weeks, at the end of which an armistice agreement was signed. Vichy troops were given the choice of joining the Free French or of repatriation to France.

The Soviet Union's entry into the war in July 1941, followed by that of the United States in December, provided reassurance that the Allies would prevail in the end. In the winter of 1941–2 the Axis forces were again pushed back into Libya. But the darkest hour for the British in the Middle East was still to come. With Japanese victories in the Far East threatening Malaya and India, it became the turn of the British forces in the Western Desert to be deprived of tanks, which were diverted eastwards. In January 1942 Rommel again began to advance towards Egypt.

Among the Egyptian people, attitudes towards the war were mixed. The great majority of the politicians were against declaring war on Germany, either because they felt it was not Egypt's war or because they were far from certain that the Allies would win. On the other hand, Egypt more than fulfilled its obligations under the terms of the Anglo-Egyptian treaty. German nationals were interned and German property was placed under sequestration.

King Farouk had no special affection for Germany, but many of his closest circle were Italian, and Ali Maher, his favoured prime minister, was known to have pro-Axis sympathies. When Maher failed to take action against Italian nationals, Britain's ambassador Sir Miles Lampson pressed the king to dismiss him. Farouk reluctantly complied and replaced Maher with two successive prime ministers who were much more sympathetic to the Allied cause. In August 1941 Egyptian troops took over guard duties in the Suez Canal area.

However, there were many in Egypt, apart from the king, who remained so doubtful about the outcome of the war that they felt Egypt should have a more neutral government as an insurance against an Axis victory. Others went further, believing that Egypt should entirely assist such a victory – these included General Aziz al-Masri, the Egyptian chief of staff, and a young captain, Anwar al-Sadat. Sadat was caught working for the pro-German underground by British Intelligence and was interned.

The British prime minister, Churchill, had never had much patience with Egyptian nationalist feelings and had none in time of war. He complained continually that the Egyptians were taking insufficient action against enemy agents who 'infested' the Canal zone. As soon as Churchill became aware of the doubtful loyalty of the Egyptian army to the Allied cause, he insisted that Egyptian troops be sent back from the Western Desert to the Delta and that General Aziz al-Masri should be dismissed. Any possibility of allowing King Farouk to bring Ali Maher back to power was ruled out.

The crisis between Britain and the king reached its climax early in 1942. Under Allied pressure the government decided to break off relations with Vichy France. The king, who was absent from Cairo and not consulted, was furious and forced the prime minister to resign. To have replaced him with Ali Maher would have been too provocative, but he showed his intention of having Maher as a member of a cabinet in which he would hold the real power. Lampson, on the other hand, wanted to see a Wafdist government installed. Rommel was advancing in Cyrenaica, and the cry of 'Long Live Rommel' was heard in the streets of Cairo. Lampson knew that, while it still enjoyed widespread popularity, the Wafd would provide the most effective support for the Allies. He also knew that Farouk would resist the return of the Wafd he detested.

Lampson secured the support of the British government and military chiefs for the use of force. He delivered the king an ultimatum that if he refused to ask Nahas Pasha to form a government by 6 p.m. the following evening (2 February) he would have to 'face the consequences'. When the ultimatum expired with no reply, Lampson had the Abdin Palace surrounded by British troops and armoured cars and forced his way in to see the king, bearing an instrument of abdication. After hesitation, the king capitulated at the thirteenth hour and agreed to call Nahas. Lampson was dismayed because he had hoped to be permanently rid of Farouk.

This humiliation of the monarchy was a seminal event in the modern history of Egypt. For all his faults, the king still personified Egypt, and nationalist opinion was outraged. One senior officer, General Muhammad Neguib, requested the king's permission to resign from the Egyptian Army. The 24-year-old Lieutenant Gamal Abdul Nasser, then stationed in Sudan, was one of a group of young officers who began to dream of taking action to restore Egypt's army.

At this crucial point in the desert war, Britain was concerned only with securing the Egyptian domestic front. Rommel's forces continued their advance, to reach within sixty miles of Alexandria. Exhausted and low in morale, some thousands of British troops deserted and hid in the Delta. As the British embassy burned its files, the British civilians in Egypt came close to panic. Women and children were sent by train to Palestine. But Nahas and his government, having thrown in their lot with Britain, kept their nerve. They interned all suspected Axis sympathizers, including Ali Maher, and refused to accept the inevitability of German occupation even when Rommel's radio was triumphantly announcing his imminent arrival in Cairo.

In August 1942 Churchill came to Cairo and it was agreed that General Montgomery should take over the Eighth Army. On 23 October the battle of Alamein, a turning-point in the war, marked the beginning of the Axis decline in the Middle East. Within seven months the remaining German and Italian forces had evacuated

North Africa. The war receded from Egypt, but the country became an even vaster war base for the Allies, with some 200,000 troops either stationed, in transit or on leave in Egypt. An American presence made itself felt, and the Anglo-American Middle East Supply Centre made Egypt the focus of the Allied war effort in the Middle East and North Africa.

Reza Shah of Iran was less fortunate than Farouk. His country was strategically as important as Egypt to the Allies, and the huge German advances after the invasion of the Soviet Union in June 1941 raised the possibility of a German occupation of Iran and its oilfields. Since Russia and Britain had long been the aggressive imperialist powers in Iranian eyes, nationalist sentiment, especially among the ruling class and senior army officers, tended to be pro-German. The Nazi regime had begun seizing the advantage before the war. German companies played a leading role in Iranian industrialization, German propaganda was vigorous and Nazi agents were active throughout the country.

As soon as the Soviet Union entered the war, it began to demand that German agents and saboteurs should be curbed. Reza Shah appealed to the United States to support Iran's neutrality but the United States, although still not a belligerent, was already bound by the Lend-Lease Act of 1941 to help Britain to supply the Soviet Union with arms through Iran. Washington was unsympathetic and urged Reza Shah to help the Allies 'to stop Hitler's ambition of world conquest'.

The crisis came to a head when the Iranian government officially rejected a joint Soviet and British request to send arms supplies across the country to the Soviet Union. On 25 August 1941 Soviet and British troops invaded Iran simultaneously from the north and south. Iraq provided a convenient base for the British invasion following the replacement of the Rashid Ali government by a pro-British regime. Iranian troops could offer little resistance, and on 16 September Reza Shah abdicated in favour of his 23-year-old son, Mohammed Reza Pahlavi. In January 1942 a tripartite treaty of alliance was concluded with Britain and the Soviet Union, both of which undertook 'to respect the territorial integrity, sovereignty and political independence of Iran' and 'to defend Iran by all means at their command from aggression'. Britain and the Soviet Union defined their respective zones, with the British occupying the south, centre and west and the Russians holding the three northern provinces of Azerbaijan, Gilan and Mazandaran.

The Russians claimed the right of intervention under the terms of the Persian–Soviet treaty of 1921. However, the new agreement stated that the Soviet and British forces permitted to remain on Iranian soil did not constitute an occupation and would be withdrawn not later than six months after the end of the war. In return, Iran undertook to render non-specified military assistance to the Allies. In September 1943 Iran declared war on Germany. In December, Stalin, Roosevelt and Churchill, after holding their first joint meeting in Tehran, issued a declaration expressing their desire for the maintenance of the 'independence, sovereignty, and territorial integrity' of Iran.

The US role in Iran steadily increased during the war, and by 1945 there were 30,000 American troops in the country, although they were non-combatants employed in dispatching supplies to Russia and managing the Trans-Iranian Railway, and they operated as part of the British forces, who were responsible for law and order.

Middle East Reactions: Nationalism, Pan-Arabism and Islam

Italy's surrender in 1943 and the removal of the threat of a German invasion of the Middle East enhanced Britain's position in the region. However, the new situation also meant that Britain was less able to use the overriding exigencies of the war to maintain control over political developments. The minority of Middle Easterners – Arabs and Iranians – who had calculated on an Axis victory to secure their nationalist demands had been disappointed. This did not mean that the majority abandoned their aim of securing the removal of European domination.

The situation in Syria and Lebanon was unusual in that Britain had helped Charles de Gaulle's Free French to oust the Vichy regime in 1941 on the understanding that France would recognize the two countries' independence. This was declared by General Catroux, de Gaulle's representative, before the invasion of the Free French force and was underwritten by Britain with the somewhat ambiguous formula that Britain would recognize that France had a predominant position over the other European powers once the promises of independence had been carried out.

De Gaulle, however, did not believe that the Free French had liberated Syria and Lebanon in order to give them up. He wished to secure treaties based on the 1936 agreements which fell well short of independence. The Syrians almost unanimously rejected the idea of a treaty, hoping to bring matters to a crisis while British troops were still present.

Even in Lebanon, in spite of the traditional Maronite reliance on French protection, the desire for independence was dominant. The new mercantile classes, both Christian and Muslim, felt strong enough to stand by themselves without French protection and they disliked the mandate's limitations on their activities. In 1943 an unwritten 'National Pact' was reached between certain Christian and Muslim leaders to the effect that Lebanon should remain independent within its existing frontiers but should follow an independent Arab foreign policy. Elections held in the same year led to the victory of those opposed to the mandate, and the new government proposed to remove from the constitution those clauses which safeguarded French control. The French replied by arresting the president of the republic and most of the government. Faced with popular disturbances, world-wide protests and a British ultimatum, the French gave in. The ministers were released and the constitution amended.

Elections in Syria in 1943 also produced a clear victory for the nationalists. Gradually and reluctantly, the French began to transfer the mandates' powers to the two governments. But they had not given up all hope, keeping the local Lebanese and Syrian armed forces under the control of the French high command as a means of securing post-independence treaties. When in May 1945 a contingent of Senegalese troops landed in Beirut, the Syrians correctly concluded that France aimed to maintain military control after the departure of the British. Fighting broke out in Damascus and the French bombarded the city. Another British ultimatum forced the French troops to return to barracks. Although these troops remained for one more year, France's rule in the Levant had come to an end. In 1946 Syria and Lebanon joined the United Nations as independent states.

The United States and the Soviet Union, having recognized Syrian and Lebanese independence, were not prepared to accept France's continuing predominance, but it was Britain that France held responsible for its exclusion. Twenty years later General de Gaulle secured some measure of revenge by vetoing Britain's entry into the European Economic Community.

Egypt was the centre of Britain's power in the Middle East but, following the installation of the Wafd government, the country's internal politics were not a major British concern. The Wafd, although still confident that it was the expression of the popular will, was sensitive to charges that it had been placed in power by the British. It claimed to champion the cause of the egyptianization of the state. To the extreme irritation of the British and other foreign communities, it made the Arabic language compulsory for all official correspondence and commercial accountancy. But the reality was that Nahas was still dependent on Lampson's support to prevent the vengeful king from dismissing him. In fact the Wafd, riddled with corruption and public scandal, was losing its mastery. Extra-parliamentary forces, of which the Muslim Brotherhood was the most significant and dangerous, were growing in strength. Rampant inflation, exacerbated by the presence of Allied forces, caused increasing public discontent with the government. The land-owning class was growing richer and, as in the First World War, a new wealthy class of merchants and industrialists had grown up by supplying the foreign forces with goods and services. But the great majority of Egyptians were sinking further into poverty.

In October 1944 the king seized the chance of Lampson's absence from the country to dismiss Nahas and replace him with Ahmed Maher, Ali Maher's genial and very different brother. The new prime minister insisted that Egypt should at last declare war on Germany, in order to ensure its membership of the projected United Nations Organization. On 24 February 1945 Ahmed Maher announced Egypt's declaration of war to parliament; as he left, he was assassinated. Almost certainly the act was planned by the new terrorist wing of the Muslim Brotherhood. Political murder was about to become a feature of Egyptian life.

Egyptians of all political parties felt that, as a reward for Egypt's contribution to the Allied war effort, Britain should evacuate the country entirely and accept the unity of Egypt and the Sudan. But although they hoped that the Labour Party, which had just come to power in Britain, would be more sympathetic to Egyptian national aspirations, the new Labour government was chiefly concerned with maintaining Britain's dominant military position in the Middle East and was not prepared for a revision of the 1936 treaty, which it felt had stood the test of time. Ubiquitous British troops in Cairo reminded the Egyptians of the continuing occupation. The Wafd, in opposition, anxious to renew its nationalist credentials, encouraged anti-British agitation. In February 1946 strikes and demonstrations led to violent rioting in which Muslim Brothers and communists as well as the Wafd all played a role.

The aged but still formidable Sidky Pasha was recalled to power. He acted to control the demonstrations, although some attacks on British soldiers and civilians continued. He insisted that Britain should negotiate, and by now the Labour government was ready to respond. The British military and the Conservative opposition, led by Winston Churchill, maintained that Egypt was an essential Western base for a regional defence system. A crisis with the Soviet Union over Iran had already marked the onset of the Cold War. But the foreign secretary, Ernest Bevin, was prepared to agree to the principle of total evacuation provided the Suez base could be reactivated in the event of renewed war in the Middle East (which by now to the Western powers meant a Soviet invasion of one of the countries in the region). Field Marshal Montgomery, who visited Egypt in the summer of 1946, agreed that Britain could evacuate the Suez base provided it maintained troops in Palestine, Libya and Cyprus. But he also ominously insisted that Britain 'must remain strong in the Sudan, in case of difficulties with the Egyptians'. It was necessary 'to control the Nile, the life-blood of Egypt'.

The old obstruction to the ending of the British occupation of Egypt remained. Although Sidky swiftly reached agreement with Bevin on a total British evacuation in three years, they glossed over the Sudan issue, saying that the 1899 condominium agreement would remain until, after consultation with the Sudanese, a new common agreement could be reached on the Sudan's future status 'within the framework of the unity between the Sudan and Egypt under the common Crown of Egypt'.

The Egyptians understandably interpreted this as meaning that Britain had accepted Farouk as king of Egypt and the Sudan. But the British government, with strident support from British officials in the Sudan, soon made it clear that it had no such intention. Instead it began to institute moves towards Sudanese self-government. Anglo-Egyptian relations remained as bad as ever. Britain did unilaterally fulfil part of the terms of the Sidky–Bevin agreement, as all troops were withdrawn from the Delta to the Suez Canal zone; however, there were over seven times as many as the 10,000 stipulated in the 1936 treaty.

In March 1945 the League of Arab States had been established, with Britain's blessing. It had its headquarters in Cairo and an Egyptian secretary-general. But the founding members, who were the seven Arab states which had achieved independence – Egypt, Iraq, Saudi Arabia, Transjordan, Yemen, Syria and Lebanon – ensured that the League was in no way a federation. Each member retained its full sovereignty, and decisions taken by the Arab League Council were binding only on those members which had voted for them.

Although the League was theoretically inspired by the doctrine of pan-Arab unity, this remained a fragile and undeveloped ideology. As long as the Ottoman Empire remained in existence, the great majority of Arabs, whatever their grievances against the Turks, assumed that the empire would remain the leader of the Muslim world. Only Christian Arabs of the Levant, who felt no such loyalty, thought seriously of secession, but they found little response among their Muslim fellow-Arabs. A few intellectuals such as Rashid Rida or al-Kawakibi argued that the Turks had forfeited their right to Muslim leadership and that Islam would be best served by a return to an Arab caliphate. But this hardly amounted to a programme for political action.

The pan-Arabism preached by Sharif Hussein when he launched his Arab Revolt was haphazard and rudimentary and derived strongly from his personal and family ambitions. His claim to be king of the Arabs was recognized by no more than a few. In the exultant but brief period when Amir Feisal was established as king of Syria, he attempted to keep the pan-Arab idea alive. 'We are one people,' he said in May 1919, 'living in the region which is bounded by the sea to the east, the south, and the west, and by the Taurus mountains to the north.' Most significantly, he was also fond of saying 'We are Arabs before being Muslims, and Muhammad is an Arab before being a prophet.' This was the germ of a secular Arab nationalism. But within a year Feisal was expelled from Syria and, although the British installed him in Iraq, the Arab peoples of whom he spoke were divided by new national frontiers.

In the years following the First World War, therefore, there were two contrary trends among the eastern Arabs. One of these trends was the development of territorial nationalism in the new nation-states as they became involved in a struggle for full independence from Britain and France. This required the creation of a national identity, and it was sustained by the ambitions and rivalries of the national leaders. The House of Saud was hostile and suspicious towards the Hashemites, and there was rivalry between the Hashemites of Iraq and Transjordan.

The opposing trend was the aspiration towards Arab unity based on the feeling, to which all Arabs subscribed to some extent, that they had been artificially divided in order to weaken them and keep them under Western tutelage. Unity was necessary for Arab self-protection and renaissance. This tendency received a powerful impetus from the events in Palestine. The growing awareness that the Zionists, with the help of the West, aimed to seize as much of Arab Palestine as they could was the strongest factor in mobilizing Arab opinion, which was frustrated but not restrained by the fact that so little that was effective could be done to help the Palestinian Arabs.

Islam was and remains a uniquely potent element in Arab nationalism. Muslim militants, such as the Muslim Brotherhood, maintained that nationalism and Islam were incompatible since all Muslims of all races from China to Morocco were members of the same great Islamic nation or *umma*. Pan-Arab intellectuals attempted to demonstrate to the contrary that Arabism and Islam are mutually inclusive. As Abdul Rahman Azzam, the Arab League's first secretary-general, said in a lecture in 1943, the ideals of Islam were the same as those of modern Arab nationalism and of the Arab nation which aimed to take its rightful place in the world and resume the mission which Muhammad had inaugurated. But the debate was largely artificial. Muslim militants in the Arab countries made their appeal for Islamic revival to their fellow-Arabs. Arab nationalism, on the other hand, could never be secular in the style and to the degree of Atatürk's Turkish Republic (or even the Iran of Reza Shah) for the simple reason that Islam is an integral part of Arab civilization and culture. Hence Michel Aflaq, the young Syrian Christian school-teacher who was the ideologist of the Arab Baath (Renaissance) Party which he founded in Damascus in the 1940s, maintained that Islam was a permanent tendency in the life of the Arab nation. 'Muhammad was the epitome of all the Arabs, so let all Arabs today be Muhammad,' he told his followers. On the other hand, the representative of the House of Saud, keepers of the holy places of Islam, have never had any problem about reconciling their Arab and Islamic aspirations, invariably mentioning them in the same breath.

In the 1920s and 1930s, Egypt largely excluded itself from any pan-Arab movement, with the approval of its fellow-Arabs. There was a conflict between the patriotism of an ancient nation-state (in Egypt known as 'Pharaonism') and the ideals of pan-Islam. An extreme view was put forward by the great Egyptian writer Taha Hussein, who said that though Egypt might be part of Europe by virtue of its present culture, it was Pharaonic in its traditions – it was certainly not part of the Muslim East. But most Egyptians had mixed feelings and managed to remain Egyptian patriots while finding inspiration in the concept of Islamic unity at the same time. Mustafa Kamel, Egypt's nationalist leader at the end of the Cromer era, was of this kind. But pan-Arabism did not appeal. Zaghloul interrupted Azzam Pasha, who was speaking to him of Arab unity, with the question 'If you add one zero to another, and then to another, what sum will you get?'

The situation gradually changed from the late 1930s onwards. A growing body of Egyptians, among whom Azzam was outstanding, could see the potential role in the Middle East for Egypt once it was freed from British control, and there were other Arabs who were reaching the same conclusion. Sati al-Husri, an Aleppo-born writer who had followed Amir Feisal from Syria to Iraq and was to do more than anyone to popularize the idea of Arab unity, argued in 1936 that nature had endowed Egypt with all the qualities which made it incumbent upon the country to assume the leadership of the Arab national movement.

The shift towards a view of Cairo as the nucleus of pan-Arabism was not shared by Arab leaders or the Arab masses, including the Egyptian people themselves. It was by no means agreed that the Egyptians should even be regarded as Arabs. In December 1942 Nuri al-Said put forward a scheme for the unification of Syria, Lebanon, Palestine and Transjordan with 'semi-autonomy' for the Jews in Palestine, as a first step towards Arab unity. Egypt was not included. Another scheme, which was proposed by King Ibn Saud's friend and adviser the British Arabist H. St John Philby, was for the Saudi monarch to head an Arab federation with an autonomous Jewish state in Palestine. This found favour with the Gentile Zionist Winston Churchill and the Zionist leadership. Again Egypt was excluded. However, despite Ibn Saud's high prestige, which caused both Churchill and Roosevelt to imagine him as 'king of the Arabs', all such schemes were impractical because of the enmity between the Saudis and the Hashemites – neither would ever accept the others' leadership.

However, the British Foreign Office was in favour of closer ties between the Arab states, provided that Western interests could be maintained. A major factor was the hope that it would be easier to solve the Palestine problem within a broader Arab framework. From May 1941 onwards, Anthony Eden, the British foreign secretary, made repeated statements that Britain favoured any scheme that commanded general approval among the Arabs for strengthening the cultural, economic and political ties between the Arab states. Britain now accepted that Egypt – the site of the Middle East Supply Centre and focus of the Allied war effort in the region – would make the best headquarters for any Western-sponsored Arab federation. Moreover the Wafd government led by Nahas, in wartime alliance with Britain, had begun to be attracted by the concept of an Egyptian-led Arab union. King Farouk was equally determined that Egypt should not be left out. Reluctantly Nuri al-Said and the other Arab leaders came to accept the inevitable: there was no alternative to Egypt. The last act of the Wafd government before it was driven from office in October 1944 was to sign the Protocol of Alexandria with the six other independent Arab states which led to the foundation of the Arab League in the following year.

While Arabs and Iranians in their overwhelming majority sought the removal of European tutelage and domination in the aftermath of the war, there was one group in the Middle East which had different priorities: the Zionist Jews. When the war began, their dream of an independent Jewish state in Palestine had faded as a result of the change in British policy embodied in the 1939 White Paper. Their anger and bitterness were deep. Yet there could be no question of not helping Britain in the war against the Nazis. David Ben Gurion, the Zionist leader who was to become Israel's first prime minister, coined the slogan that the Jews would fight the White Paper as if there were no war and the war as if there were no White Paper. Some 27,000 Palestine Jews enlisted in the British forces during the war, but others believed they could best serve their cause by building up the Haganah, the semi-secret Zionist army in Palestine. The war gave a powerful impetus to the development of a Jewish munitions industry, which supplied the British forces in 1942–3 but could strengthen the Zionists in the future. The British continued to reject Zionist demands for the formation of a Jewish army, flying the Zionist flag, to fight alongside the Allies.

As the danger of German invasion passed with Rommel's defeat at Alamein, and at the same time news began to leak out from Europe of Hitler's unspeakable atrocities against the Jews, the Palestine Zionists turned decisively against Britain. Enraged by Britain's deportation of the few illegal immigrants who managed to reach Palestine, they blamed Britain alone for the failure to rescue European Jewry. Anti-British acts of resistance multiplied. A splinter group from the mainstream Haganah joined hands with the even more extreme Stern Gang in widespread attacks which culminated in the murder of Lord Moyne, British minister of state in Cairo, in November 1944. An outraged Churchill, a close friend of Moyne, temporarily abandoned his long-standing pro-Zionism.

The war also marked a decisive move of the headquarters of international Zionism from Britain to the United States. Chaim Weizmann still believed that the Zionists' best hopes of achieving their aims lay in Britain, but he was overtaken by a new generation, represented by David Ben Gurion, which looked to the coming American superpower to force Britain's acquiescence. At a conference, in which all shades of Zionist opinion were represented, at the Biltmore Hotel in New York in May 1944, a programme was adopted providing for unrestricted Jewish immigration and the establishment of Palestine as a Jewish commonwealth 'integrated in the structure of the new democratic world'.

The Palestine Arabs, on the other hand, remained largely quiescent during the war. Some 12,000 joined the British forces. Hajj Amin al-Husseini escaped from Baghdad after the fall of Rashid Ali and went to Germany, where he tried to mobilize Muslim world opinion for the Axis cause. But he had little impact.

The coming to power of a Labour government in Britain in 1945 raised the hopes of the Zionists, because the Labour Party had opposed the 1939 White Paper and in conference in 1944 it had passed a resolution suggesting that the Arabs should move out of Palestine as the Jews moved in. But once in power the Attlee government was faced with complex and daunting realities. Britain was nominally one of the Big Three which had won the war, and the Labour government had no more intention than the Conservative opposition that Britain should relinquish its position at the top table. In the Middle East region, where it had been the undoubted victor, Britain appeared to be the paramount power. In fact, exhausted and impoverished by the war, Britain was already facing a decline in its role, and the Labour government's momentous decision to grant independence to India in 1947 would undermine Britain's position as a global power. At the same time it was beset by problems in Europe, caused by the expansion of the Soviet empire in eastern Europe and by the breakdown of the wartime alliance with Stalin, which marked the outbreak of the Cold War. In the Middle East, Britain was confronted by Egypt's demands for an end to the British occupation. Alternative military bases could be found in the eastern Mediterranean, but this was no answer to the by now insoluble problem of Palestine.

The prospect offered by the 1939 White Paper – that Palestine would become an independent binational Arab/Jewish state with the Arabs dominating the government – had been destroyed by Hitler. He had been defeated, but there was no overwhelming pressure that the survivors of the Holocaust should be allowed to take refuge in Palestine. Neither the Western countries, such as the United States, nor the Zionist leadership wanted them to go elsewhere.

The British foreign secretary, Ernest Bevin, still believed that a solution might be found by negotiation. He unwisely told the House of Commons that he would 'stake my political future' on solving the Palestine problem. But he wanted to make the United States share responsibility. As soon as the war ended, President Truman cabled the British government to demand the immediate entry of 100,000 Jews into Palestine. The US Congress wanted unrestricted immigration. In November 1945 Bevin announced the formation of an Anglo-American commission of inquiry. In April 1946 this recommended the continuation of the mandate and a unitary state, repeal of restrictions on land sales and the immediate admission of 100,000 Jews – in effect a return to the 1922 policy. The commission criticized the existence of the Jewish underground forces, which it estimated at 65,000, and it recommended that they should be disarmed.

The British government found these proposals impracticable as they stood but approved some discussions on Jewish and Arab autonomy. As Britain continued trying to prevent illegal Jewish immigration, the Zionist underground stepped up its activities, which reached a peak with the blowing up in July 1946 of the King David Hotel in Jerusalem, containing British civilian and military offices.

Meanwhile, the seven independent Arab states were attempting to act to prevent an Arab disaster in Palestine. Their heads-of-state meeting in Egypt in May 1946 reaffirmed the Arab character of Palestine, and another meeting in June in Syria passed secret resolutions threatening British and US interests in the Middle East if Arab rights in Palestine were disregarded.

The British government faced an impossible dilemma. Public opinion in Britain was divided between Zionist sympathizers and those outraged by Zionist atrocities. In the Middle East, all British interests in the Arab world would be threatened if the Zionists were allowed to seize Palestine, but Britain was under relentless pressure from the US to allow massive Jewish immigration and, in the aftermath of the war, Britain was financially dependent on Washington. (In support of the so-called Truman Doctrine of overseas US involvement, set out in an address to Congress on 12 March 1947, President Truman asked Congress for aid, which Britain could no longer afford, to enable Greece and Turkey to maintain their independence against the Soviet threat.) After one more futile attempt to obtain Arab and Jewish agreement on a joint plan, Britain handed the problem over to the United Nations in February 1947.

In August 1947 a majority report of a UN Special Commission on Palestine (UNSCOP) recommended the partition of Palestine into Arab and Jewish states, which would still be economically unified, with Jerusalem and its environs to be international. By a vote of 33 to 13 with 10 abstentions, these recommendations were substantially adopted by the UN General Assembly in its Resolution 181 of 29 November 1947. This resolution was passed because both the USA and the Soviet Union, which then dominated the UN, voted in favour and were prepared to use pressure. The Soviet Union at that time regarded the Zionist struggle in Palestine as one of liberation against imperialism. Only the Islamic Asian countries voted against the resolution. An Arab proposal to question the International Court of Justice on the competence of the General Assembly to partition a country against the wishes of the majority of its inhabitants (there were 1,269,000 Arabs and 678,000 Jews in Palestine in 1946) was narrowly defeated.

The Zionists welcomed the partition because it recognized a Jewish state which, although including a large area of desert in the south, the Negev, covered 55 per cent of a country in which Zionist land-holdings still amounted to less than 8 per cent of the total. The Arabs, as always, bitterly opposed partition but they were especially outraged because the proposed Jewish state would include almost as many Arabs as Jews.

Britain had already, in September 1947, announced its intention to give up the Palestine mandate on 15 April 1948. The United Nations had made no proposals as to how the partition of Palestine should be carried out or financed, and Britain refused to implement a policy which was not acceptable to both sides or to participate in the UN Palestine Commission which was supposed to supervise the transitional period. Britain merely handed over power to whichever community was locally in the ascendant and, since Arab cadres, in contrast to Jewish cadres, were generally lacking, order was better maintained in the Jewish areas. Communal fighting broke out immediately and soon developed into full-scale civil war as the British administration was dismantled.

Faced with this disaster, the US retreated and declared its opposition to forcible partition. On 30 March 1948 it called for a truce and the further consideration of the problem by the UN General Assembly. But the Zionists, anxious about the American shift in policy, redoubled their efforts to establish their state. The extreme Zionist Irgun and the Stern gang were now collaborating with the Haganah, and the master-plan, known as Plan Dalet, for the seizure of most of Palestine was put into effect. Operations were launched against strategically situated Arab villages. An Arab Liberation Army of some 3,000 volunteers from outside Palestine had some initial successes but could do little against greatly superior Zionist forces. Arab civilian morale crumbled in the face of the onslaught and a psychological offensive which exploited reports of the massacre on 10 May by Irgunists of 250 inhabitants of the village of Deir Yasin. Tiberias, Haifa, Acre, Jaffa and much of Arab Jerusalem fell, and some three to four hundred refugees streamed in terror towards the neighbouring Arab countries.

On 14 May the last British high commissioner left Palestine and the mandate formally ended. The Zionists immediately proclaimed the state of Israel and within hours they had received the *de facto* recognition of the Soviet Union and the United States.

Early on 15 May, units of the regular armies of Syria, Transjordan, Iraq and Egypt crossed the frontiers of Palestine in the hope of restoring the situation for the Arabs.

This apparently determined action by the independent Arab states masked their fatal disunity. It was a unanimous decision of the Arab League to intervene in Palestine, but the unity was no more than a façade. There was no effective liaison between the Arab armies and they did not act in concert. Their military capacity did not reflect the overwhelming Arab superiority in numbers, with 40 million Arabs confronting some 600,000 Zionist Jews. In fact to take the field Egypt had some 10,000 regular troops, Transjordan's Arab Legion 4,500, Syria 3,000, Lebanon 1,000 and Iraq 3,000. Their arms were British or French and, in the case of Transjordan, the commander-in-chief General Glubb and senior officers were British. One surviving Arab statesman recalls that the Arab armies were useful only to perform ceremonial parades. They were confronting some 60,000 Jewish troops who, although never officially recognized by the mandate, were armed and trained and many of whom already had battle experience.

Some of the Arab leaders, especially in Syria and Iraq, were so ignorant of the situation that they expected a walk-over. King Abdullah had the most realistic appreciation of Zionist strength. For some time he had been in secret negotiation with the Zionist leaders and he had formed with them what amounted to a strategic alliance which would enable him to take over the Arab part of Palestine and exclude the Palestine nationalist leaders, such as the Husseinis, who were hostile to the Hashemites. The Egyptian prime minister Nokrashy Pasha, who lacked the flamboyant confidence of the more ambitious Nahas, also had doubts about an Arab victory and had no illusions about the adequacy of the Egyptian armed forces. But Egyptian public opinion had been roused. The Muslim Brotherhood wanted to fight for Palestine, and Hajj Amin al-Husseini, who was now in Egypt, exerted a powerful influence. Of greater importance was king Farouk's determination that the Egyptian army should enter the war.

If Zionist resistance had collapsed there is little doubt that even King Abdullah would have been obliged to continue until the state of Israel had been strangled at birth. But the declared objective of the Arab governments was only to restore order and to protect the 45 per cent of Palestine which had been allotted to the Arabs under the UN partition plan.

At first all went well for the Arabs as they occupied areas which were not yet controlled by the Jews. The Egyptians entered Gaza and Beersheba and linked up with the Arab Legion near Bethlehem. The Legion, with its Iraqi allies, held the central section of Palestine and attempted to blockade Jewish west Jerusalem although, disastrously for the Arabs, they were unable to cut the road from Tel-Aviv to Jerusalem.

The UN mediator, Sweden's Count Folke Bernadotte, secured a four-week ceasefire from 11 June and put forward proposals for a settlement which were rejected by both sides. When the fighting resumed, the Jews broke the siege of west Jerusalem and made lightning gains in nearly all sectors, capturing Nazareth and western Galilee which had been allotted to the Arabs. A second ceasefire called on 18 July was ineffective, and when the fighting finally ended in January 1949 the Jews had occupied all the Negev up to the former Egypt–Palestine border except for the Gaza Strip on the coast. The Iraqis and Jordanians held a slice of territory to the north and south of Jerusalem. Only 21 per cent of Palestine remained in Arab hands. The number of Arabs within the area held by Israel had decreased by between 700,000 and 750,000.

Between February and July 1949 the new UN mediator, the American Ralph Bunche, succeeded in securing separate armistice agreements between Israel and Egypt and the Arab states (except Iraq, which nevertheless withdrew its troops). It was broadly agreed to fix a temporary frontier where the lines had been at the start of the negotiations, while certain border areas were demilitarized. Jerusalem was divided between the Arab east and Jewish west. The Gaza Strip came under Egyptian administration.

No peace treaty was signed. In December 1948 the UN General Assembly appointed a three-member conciliation commission to promote a final settlement and to arrange an international regime for Jerusalem, but all its efforts were frustrated. The Arab states refused to consider a peace treaty unless the Israeli government agreed to accept all Arab refugees wishing to return to Israel. Resolutions demanding that the refugees should be given the option of return or compensation for their property were constantly reaffirmed by the UN General Assembly, and it was on this basis that Israel was admitted to the UN on 11 May 1949. But Israel maintained that the future of the refugees could be discussed only as part of a general peace settlement. The impasse was complete. Half of the Palestinian Arabs had become refugees. Neither the new state of Israel nor its Arab neighbours could expect even a minimum of security and stability.

11. The Entry of the Superpowers and the Nasser Era, 1950–1970

The repercussions of the Palestine disaster (*al-nahda* in Arabic) were felt throughout the Arab East. Blame was divided between Britain, the United States and the Arab leaders whose incompetence and divisive rivalries had contributed to the miserable Arab performance. Arab opinion in general was radicalized. In Syria, a military *coup d'état* took place even before the truce was signed. Although it was soon overturned and a form of constitutional parliamentary government restored, the Syrian armed forces had acquired a taste for political power which was never to diminish. Syria became a byword for political instability.

The Transjordanian monarchy, although at the eye of the storm, survived with the support of a loyal army. King Abdullah was able to carry out his ambition of uniting what was left of Palestine in his newly proclaimed Hashemite Kingdom of Jordan. The majority of the inhabitants of the enclave, defenceless and in imminent danger of being swallowed up by the Zionists, saw no alternative and in December 1948 a conference of some 2,000 Arab notables at Jericho invited King Abdullah to unite Palestine and Jordan. The move was bitterly opposed by the other Arab states, who attempted unsuccessfully to block it. They tried to revive the UN resolution for the internationalization of Jerusalem but, since this was unacceptable to Israel, they failed. King Abdullah remained in control of the Arab Old City.

Jordan had acquired a Palestinian population twice as numerous as the Transjordanians, and half a million of them were destitute refugees. The Palestinians accepted King Abdullah's annexation as the consequence of *force majeure*, but most of them had reservations about being ruled by Transjordanians, whom they regarded as less advanced than themselves. A minority actively detested the Hashemites.

King Abdullah handled this delicate situation with practised ambiguity. He and his government tried to carry out the political integration of the new population and Jordan was the only Arab state to offer the refugees full citizenship, but, like the others, it continued to maintain that the refugees were primarily an international political and economic responsibility and would never abandon their right of return. Thus Jordan aimed both to combat Palestinian separatism and to maintain its right to speak for the Palestinians while proclaiming that one day an Arab Palestine would be restored. This 'Jordanian paradise' was to last for nearly thirty years. It created acute political difficulties but the Jordanian monarchy survived, through a combination of good fortune, external aid, divisions among its enemies and the flexibility and determination of its rulers. Abdullah was assassinated by a Palestinian youth as he entered the al-Aqsa Mosque in Jerusalem on 20 July 1951. His son, Tallal, proved to be mentally unstable and abdicated a year later. Tallal's 17-year-old son Hussein, then at school in England, succeeded and, against all the odds, became the longest surviving Arab head of state.

Egypt was the Arab country in which the Palestine disaster had the most momentous long-term effects. The younger officers who served in the war became convinced of the criminal incompetence of the men ruling Egypt. Food and medical supplies were inadequate, while arms were obsolete and in some cases worthless. Senior officers gave contradictory and meaningless orders, while some showed downright incompetence. (An outstanding exception was Major-General Muhammad Neguib, who was severely wounded in the fighting.) Gamal Abdul Nasser, recently promoted to major, was wounded and distinguished himself in a defensive engagement, but his most vivid memory was the words of one of his most admired superiors shortly before he was killed: 'Remember, the real battle is in Egypt.'

For several years there had been a clandestine movement among the younger nationalist officers. Nasser – grave, thoughtful and reticent in manner, but with considerable charismatic charm – had emerged as its natural leader and organizer. Many of his closest colleagues served with him in Palestine, and on their return they stepped up their activities, more than ever convinced of the urgent need for a radical change in the regime. The military coup in Damascus in March 1949 started a chain reaction which affected all the Arab states. In Egypt the Free Officers, as they now called themselves, formed an executive committee of which Nasser, now a colonel, was formally elected president. They established a chain of cells throughout the armed forces and began to distribute mimeographed tracts denouncing the regime.

Egypt's parliamentary democracy was already crumbling as the extra-parliamentary forces gathered strength. Of these the Muslim Brotherhood was the most visible and had gained new prestige from its members' brave actions as volunteers in Palestine. In November 1948 Nokrashy Pasha made use of martial law to declare the Brotherhood dissolved and its branches closed. A month later Nokrashy was assassinated, and two months after this Hassan al-Banna, founder and Supreme Guide of the Brotherhood, was himself shot down – almost certainly by a wing of the state counter-terrorist police.

King Farouk was steadily losing what remained of his youthful popularity. A combination of glandular disorder and self-indulgence had transformed the handsome boy-king into a cartoon-satire of middle-aged debauchery. His divorce of his popular Egyptian wife Farida at the height of the Palestine war had not helped his reputation, and the frivolous luxury of his life in Mediterranean resorts during Egypt's troubles seemed a callous insult to his impoverished subjects.

Although Farouk's humiliation by Britain had made him increasingly cynical, he had not abandoned his inherited taste for political intrigue or the desire to hold on to power. In January 1950 he recalled his old enemy Nahas and allowed a general election in which the Wafd was still able to gain its customary sweeping victory. Both parties in this improbable palace–Wafd alliance hoped in this way to preserve their share in Egypt's ramshackle system of government.

Britain also hoped for an improvement in Anglo-Egyptian relations, pending the still elusive final agreement, and made some conciliatory gestures. The British government had been working to set up a combined Middle Eastern command with the US, Turkey and France, which it hoped Egypt would join. This was essentially a Cold War move, aiming to keep the Soviet Union out of the eastern Mediterranean, but already it was doomed to failure. Neutralist feeling was nascent in the Middle East, where most of the population regarded the old imperial powers as a more serious threat than Soviet communism. When Britain presented the plan to Egypt in October 1951, it was flatly rejected. In fact the Wafdist government had already decided to abrogate the 1939 Anglo-Egyptian treaty and unilaterally to declare Farouk king of Egypt and the Sudan.

Faced with mounting criticism and exposure of its corruption, the

Wafd was anxious to restore its credentials for uncompromising nationalism. But although its move was wildly popular in the country, it was dangerous because in its struggle with Britain the Egyptian government had to enlist the support of all the forces in the country which were aiming for the overthrow of the constitutional regime. Nahas not only declared a state of emergency and took steps to cut off supplies of food and Egyptian labour to the British troops in the Canal zone but also went further and encouraged the formation of volunteer 'Liberation' squads to carry out sabotage and guerrilla attacks. For these the obvious recruits were Muslim Brothers, communists and any other groups with valuable terrorist experience. Some Free Officers helped to train these groups behind the scenes.

In Britain the Conservatives won the October 1951 elections. They were to remain in power for the next thirteen years. Churchill returned as prime minister and Eden as foreign secretary. Egypt retained its prime importance in their eyes, but there was no obvious solution to the crisis. The Suez base was maintained by importing labour from East Africa, but it had been rendered useless as the 80,000 British were occupied in defending the base against sabotage. The alternative was the reoccupation of Cairo, which was something that even the imperialist Churchill was unwilling to contemplate.

As the guerrilla attacks were stepped up, the British extended their countermeasures and arrested suspects – who included the Egyptian police. Then on 25 January 1952 a strong British force surrounded the police headquarters at Ismailia at dawn and called upon its occupants to surrender. The minister of the interior ordered them to resist, which they did with great courage until some fifty were dead and many more injured.

The next day – since known as Black Saturday – a frenzied mob burned the centre of Cairo. Special attention was paid to British property but also to shops, hotels and restaurants owned by foreigners. Responsibility was never clearly established, but the Muslim Brotherhood, the quasi-fascist Young Egypt organization and other militant groups led the mob. The government may have connived in the first attacks but did not expect them to spread so dangerously. The king, who was entertaining senior officers to lunch, did not attempt to intervene. It was not until the evening that regular troops were called in to bring the city under control. The king and the government subsequently blamed each other for the delay.

The belated move to call in the army was prompted by the very real fear that British troops might intervene from the Canal zone. No Egyptian had forgotten that the British occupation in 1882 had been prompted by riots in Alexandria. In fact the British had a plan to intervene to protect British lives and property, but the rioting had ended before any decision to implement it could be taken.

The king used the government's mishandling of the crisis to dismiss Nahas. He recalled his favourite, Ali Maher, but he only lasted five weeks and Egypt then had four different governments in as many weeks. It was increasingly difficult to find anyone with enough authority to form a cabinet.

The Free Officers realized that the regime was crumbling. Before the crisis, they had planned to move into action in 1954 or 1955. Because they needed a senior officer with a well-known name who would act as their figurehead and give their movement weight and respectability at home and abroad, they had brought in Major-General Muhammad Neguib who was known to be sympathetic, and he became president of the Free Officers' Executive Committee in January 1952. But secrecy was imperative. The king detested Neguib and, in the same month, was enraged by his election as president of the Army Officers' Club against the king's own nominee. Despite their efforts, the Free Officers knew that the state security police were coming close to uncovering their secret organization. But fortunately the king still believed that the great majority of the army remained loyal, and in July he departed as usual to his summer palace in Alexandria.

On the night of 22–23 July, army units loyal to Free Officers seized all the key points in the capital, against only token resistance, and Anwar Sadat announced the success of the revolution over Cairo Radio. Convinced that Britain might intervene to save the king, the Free Officers moved swiftly to take control of Alexandria. Nasser overcame the demands of some of his colleagues that Farouk should be put on trial and executed; instead, the king was allowed to abdicate and go into exile with his new queen, Narriman, and their infant son. This enhanced the reputation of the revolutionaries – not least because the ex-king's behaviour in exile added to the discredit of the monarchy.

The avuncular, pipe-smoking figure of General Neguib was reassuring to interested foreign powers, which were swift to recognize the new regime. The Free Officers transformed their Executive Committee into a Revolutionary Command Council (RCC), with Neguib as its president. It was more than a year before it became apparent to the outside world that the tall, impressive but rather sombre 34-year-old Colonel Nasser was the true leader of the revolution.

The Free Officers had been planning their revolution for a decade and had a clear concept of what they wanted to do – rid the country of foreign (mainly British) influence, eliminate the power of the landlords and the monarchy, and end the corruption of political life. But they had no developed political ideas, let alone a political programme. A few of them had sympathies with the Muslim Brotherhood and a few were Marxists, but the majority could only be described as nationalist. They moved swiftly to consolidate their power. The Wafd remained a threat because, under the old constitution, it could still win any parliamentary election. The leading Wafdist politicians and the ex-king's cronies were put on trial and, charged with plotting with a foreign power and corruption, were sentenced to various terms of imprisonment.

In January 1953 the RCC felt able to dissolve all the political parties and confiscate their funds. A provisional constitution was promulgated which placed supreme power for the next three years in the hands of the RCC. From there it was only one short step to the abolition of the monarchy – the Egyptian Republic was officially proclaimed on 18 June 1953. The old Ottoman titles of bey and pasha were abolished. As Neguib commented, 'The world's oldest monarchy became, for the time being, the world's youngest republic.' Neguib did not regard himself as a figurehead: he felt he had been called upon to command, and he insisted on taking the posts of president and prime minister. Nasser for the time being contented himself with the posts of deputy premier and minister of the interior.

The RCC adopted one important social political measure in the first weeks after the revolution – land reform. In 1952 less than $\frac{1}{2}$ per cent of the landowners between them owned over one third of all cultivable land, while 72 per cent of cultivators owned less than one *feddan* (about one acre) each, amounting to only 13 per cent of the land. Before 1952 several Egyptian economists and politicians had made detailed proposals for land reform, some of which had even reached parliament as draft laws before being quietly quashed. The RCC's agrarian reform limited land holdings to 200 *feddans* and redistributed the confiscated land to the *fellahin* in lots of two to five *feddans*. Legal rents were also drastically reduced. The reform was radical rather than revolutionary, and Marxists called it 'American-inspired'. Only about 10 per cent of the *fellahin* benefited from the redistribution. However, because it was generally successful in avoiding drastic falls in output, it served as a model for other developing countries. Above all, it succeeded in its prime objective of reducing the overwhelming political power of the big landowners who had successfully blocked social and political reforms for generations.

The former regime was not the only threat to the RCC; the principal challenge came from the Muslim Brotherhood and the communists. Of the two the Brotherhood, with its nationwide organization, was much the more formidable and, having played a leading role in undermining the monarchy, it felt it was entitled to at least a share of power in the new regime. But the Brothers were out-manoeuvred and defeated by Nasser, who proved himself a masterly political tactician.

During 1953 Nasser was involved in a power struggle with both Neguib and the Brotherhood. Although honest and popular, Neguib was far from being a natural revolutionary leader. Conservative in temperament, he felt his office entitled him to exercise authority over the hot-headed young officers in the RCC. He was also politically naïve. Nasser appeared to give way to him, and he allowed himself to be placed in a position in which he seemed to be advocating a return to the pre-revolutionary political system, which was something that the army in particular would not tolerate. In April 1954 Neguib capitulated to Nasser, who became prime minister. Neguib lingered on as president, without any real power.

Its tendency to violence was the Brotherhood's undoing. An assassination attempt on Nasser in October 1954 provided grounds for suppressing the organization, and because Neguib was proved to have connections with the Brotherhood, although it was never suggested that he was implicated in the assassination attempt, he was removed from office and placed under house arrest.

By the end of 1954 Nasser was in undisputed control of Egypt, and he would remain so until his death in 1970. He was the first true Egyptian to rule the country since the time of the Pharaohs. His father, who came from a poor *fellah* family of upper Egypt, had earned the primary school certificate which enabled him to enter the

Egyptian white-collar class as a post office official. Nasser had passed through secondary school to enter the military academy when it was opened to the sons of other than pashas and beys as a result of the Anglo-Egyptian treaty. He had shown early his qualities of leadership and his passionate devotion to Egypt. Wide reading of Arab/Islamic and Western history and biography convinced him that the Egyptian people had innate qualities waiting for national redemption after centuries of submission to oppression.

In 1954 Nasser's freedom of manoeuvre was greatly enhanced by the recent settling of the two outstanding political questions which had beset Egypt for over fifty years – the British military occupation and the Sudan. Failure to settle the latter had long prevented a solution of the former, and the RCC's decision on taking power to separate the two went halfway towards resolving both of them.

The Sudan problem was tackled first, and an Anglo-Egyptian agreement for immediate Sudanese autonomy followed by self-determination after three years was reached on 12 February 1953. In a sense both parties were bluffing – neither was able to reject the principle of sudanization and self-government when the other proposed it. The Egyptians hoped and expected that an independent Sudan would opt for union with Egypt. The British were counting on Sudanese elections resulting in a pro-British (and anti-Egyptian) regime under the conservative Umma party. The British were shocked when the pro-Egyptian parties won the elections, but the RCC was equally taken aback when the new Sudanese government decided on complete independence and against union with Egypt. Sudanese independence was declared on 1 January 1956.

The RCC was bitterly disappointed over the Sudan, but the agreement made it possible to begin negotiations over the British Suez base. Talks continued intermittently throughout 1953 and early 1954. A basic obstacle to the agreement was that Britain still regarded Egypt as part of the Western sphere of interest, but negotiations were made easier by the fact that Egypt was no longer the centre of British Middle East policy – Turkey had joined NATO in the autumn of 1952, and the British joint armed forces HQ had been moved from Suez to Cyprus in December 1952.

Nasser rejected a British demand to keep 7,000 servicemen in Suez, but he agreed to the reactivation of the base in the event of an outside attack on any Arab state or Turkey. As the negotiations dragged on, he allowed guerrilla attacks on the base area as a means of putting pressure on Britain. Finally, in July 1954, agreement was reached on the basis of a British proposal to evacuate all British troops and maintain the base on a seven-year lease with a cadre of civilians on contract to British firms. In accordance with the agreement, the last British troops left Egypt on 31 March 1956. *The Times* correspondent wrote on 2 April 1956, 'Their departure was almost as silent and devoid of ceremony as presumably was the nocturnal disembarkation of General Wolseley's forces which captured Port Said 74 years ago.'

At the signing of the agreement in Cairo, Nasser had spoken of a 'new era of friendly relations . . . We want to get rid of the hatred in our hearts and start building up our relations with Britain on a solid basis of mutual trust and confidence which has been lacking for the past seventy years.' These hopes were not fulfilled. The British government – and especially the foreign secretary, Anthony Eden, who replaced Churchill as prime minister in April 1955 – had developed an antipathy towards Nasser during the frequently acrimonious negotiations over Sudan and the Suez base. As Nasser's prestige and popularity grew throughout the Middle East, he seemed to present a threat to all British interests in the region. Britain's hostility was exacerbated by the fact that the Egyptians, despite their noble heritage, were still regarded as one of Lord Cromer's 'subject races' – the leadership of a desert aristocrat such as Ibn Saud was acceptable, but not that of an Egyptian colonel of *fellah* origins.

In his little book *The Philosophy of the Revolution*, published in 1954, Nasser had already shown his awareness of the kind of role that Egypt could play. He wrote of its location at the coincidence of three circles – the Arab Circle, the African Circle and the Islamic Circle. Still in hazy terms, he saw Egypt as the focus of a vast movement of resistance to the imperialism of the West. Initially, he did not see the Arab Circle in terms of pan-Arab unity – indeed, he was suspicious of the Arab League, which he regarded as a fraudulent imperialist conception, and he reduced its influence by removing from office the League's eloquent pan-Arabist secretary-general, Abdul Rahman Azzam. But he did see the Arab states as potential allies in ending Western hegemony. Unfortunately, the only other independent Arab state which had the makings of a stable autonomous power – Iraq – was led by a man whom Nasser regarded as the imperialist West's chief ally – Nuri al-Said. To make matters worse, he was a man of real stature and personality. It was this bitter rivalry with Nuri (which was much more than a mere clash of personalities) that was the main factor in involving Egypt deeply in the politics of Arab nationalism.

Matters came to a head in 1955 with the conclusion of a series of military agreements between Iraq, Turkey, Iran and Britain which became known as the Baghdad Pact. The idea of this patently anti-Soviet alliance had originated with the United States, which had dropped it on realizing that the Arabs were much more concerned about Israel than about any Soviet threat. Britain had joined the pact as a means of maintaining some part of its dominant position in the area. Nasser tried every means to prevent Iraq from joining, because he saw the Pact, with its NATO links through Turkey, as an instrument of continued Western domination. But he failed to persuade the indefatigably pro-Western and anti-Soviet Nuri al-Said. The great mass of articulate Arab opinion was on Nasser's side in this matter, and his influence was enough to prevent Jordan from joining, although the young King Hussein was in favour. But as Nasser's popularity with the Arabs grew, the hostility he aroused in the West increased.

Nasser's horizons were broadening. A crucial influence on his thinking was Pandit Nehru, the figurehead of India's independence, who visited him in Cairo in February 1955 and agreed with him to oppose all military alliances such as the Baghdad Pact. Nasser also developed a warm admiration for President Tito's Yugoslavia. While Nehru had succeeded in pursuing an independent non-aligned policy while remaining a member of the British Commonweath, Tito had defied Soviet leadership of the communist bloc (even under Stalin) and accepted American aid without renouncing communism. Nehru, Tito and Nasser would come to be regarded as the founding members of the club of non-aligned states. In April 1955 Nasser headed Egypt's delegation to the Afro-Asian Conference at Bandung in Indonesia – an event of immense contemporary importance since it symbolized a concerted attempt by the great majority of mankind which is coloured to throw off the hegemony of the white Western nations. The importance of Egypt and its revolution was acknowledged as he was treated as an equal by Asian statesmen such as Nehru and the Chinese premier Chou En-lai. Some of the credit for this was due to his personal qualities – for one so young and inexperienced he acted with remarkable skill and assurance.

Nasser was well on his way to becoming the hero of Arab nationalism; his picture appeared on display throughout the Arab East. But hero status brought new dangers and responsibilities, for he was beginning to arouse huge expectations among the Arabs. Since he was championing the cause of neutralism in the Cold War, he began to arouse the suspicion and hostility of the United States. At the same time Israel was coming to regard Nasser's Egypt as its principal external challenge.

Although Britain appeared to remain the principal Western power with Middle Eastern interests in the decade following the Second World War, in reality its position was being rapidly overtaken by the United States, for two reasons: the onset of the Cold War and US sponsorship of Israel.

US involvement began in Iran. At the end of the war both Britain and the United States withdrew their troops from Iran, as stipulated in the 1942 treaty, but the Soviet Union refused for several months to evacuate the northern provinces. When the Soviet army finally withdrew, the Soviet Union sponsored a puppet socialist regime in Azerbaijan which it aimed should secede from Iran and join the Soviet Union. Unexpectedly firm action by the Iranian government suppressed the Azerbaijani separatists, but the Soviet Union continued to exert pressure on Iran through the autonomy movements in Azerbaijan and Kurdistan and the powerful communist Tudeh Party in Iran. The so-called Truman Doctrine of March 1947, under which the USA offered Greece and Turkey aid (which Britain could no longer provide) to maintain their independence, was soon extended to Iran. In October 1947 the Iranian Majlis plucked up its courage and annulled a highly unpopular Soviet–Iranian agreement for joint exploitation of the oil reserves in the northern provinces.

Britain and the Anglo-Iranian Oil Company remained the principal targets for the powerful force of Iranian nationalism, of which a veteran aristocratic politician, Mohammed Mossadegh, became the spokesman. In 1949 the Iranian government launched an ambitious and much needed seven-year development plan based on the country's revenues. But whereas between 1944 and 1950 AIOC's profits had increased more than tenfold, Iran's revenues had increased only fourfold. Negotiations started with the company in 1948 to increase Iran's share were frustrated by Mossadegh and his followers in the Majlis, who insisted on Iran's right to regain control over the country's principal natural resource. Public opinion was so roused that in May 1951 the young shah was forced to appoint Mossadegh as prime minister and give his assent to a bill nationalizing the Iranian oil industry.

The measure was not only wildly popular in Iran; it inspired the Arab man-in-the-street. Mossadegh's name became legendary in the Middle East as Nasser's would become a few years later. But Mossadegh was unable to carry through his revolution, both because of the strength of the forces opposing him and because of his own inadequacies as a revolutionary leader. The AIOC withdrew from Iran and, in pursuit of their common interest, the major international oil companies successfully imposed a boycott of Iranian oil. Britain resorted to economic pressures and military threats in an attempt to have the nationalization reversed and appealed to the International Court of Justice, which ruled against it, and to the UN Security Council, which refused to intervene. The US government unsuccessfully attempted to mediate. But Iran's revenues dwindled to a trickle.

Mossadegh's popularity among the poor Iranian majority increased with his intransigence against the West. He demanded and received authoritarian powers. He broke off diplomatic relations with Britain and closed its consulates. But in many respects his social and political outlook was reactionary. As a member of the land-owning class, he opposed the breaking up of the large estates in favour of peasant proprietors and he stopped even the shah's modest land-distribution scheme. As the doubts about him grew among Iranian politicians, the shah took courage to challenge his actions and appoint the loyalist General Zahedi prime minister. The shah's attempt failed and he had to flee the country in August 1953, but six days later he returned and Mossadegh was overthrown in a counter-coup which was planned and organized by the CIA, with substantial assistance from British intelligence.

Relations with Britain were restored, but it was the USA which now took over as the principal Western influence in Iran. A group of US, Dutch and British oil companies formed a consortium in which AIOC had a 40 per cent share and negotiated an agreement with the National Iranian Oil Company that had been formed to take over A IOC's assets in Iran to resume operations. The agreement was for twenty-five years. In August 1955 the Iranian government signed a treaty with the United States. With this and its joining the Baghdad Pact in the following year, against strong Soviet protests, Iran indisputably joined the Western camp in the Cold War.

In 1952, when the Eisenhower administration replaced that of President Truman, the United States still had only a peripheral interest in the politics of the Arab world. It had scant sympathy for what remained of the imperial aspirations of Britain and France. It had good relations with the young revolutionaries in Egypt, and it urged Britain to come to terms over the military occupation. But it had no desire to take Britain's place. As we have seen, when Eisenhower's secretary of state John Foster Dulles realized that Egypt and the other Arab states were uninterested in joining an anti-Soviet Middle East Defence Organization, he left Britain as the only Western member of the Baghdad Pact while he concentrated on strengthening the 'northern tier' of states confronting the Soviet Union – Turkey, Iran and Pakistan.

However, the United States did have a close interest in Israel, largely for domestic political reasons. Zionist political influence in the United States went far beyond the American Jewish community. The US Congress was overwhelmingly supportive of the young Zionist state in the Middle East and, although he was the least inclined of any post-war US presidents to relinquish the executive's control of US foreign policy, Eisenhower could not ignore these sentiments.

Although the concept of direct superpower rivalry between the United States and the Soviet Union for influence in the Middle East had come to seem part of the natural order in the 1950s, the history and development of Russian and American interest in the region were totally different. The very concept of the Middle East as a geopolitical entity was new to Russia.

Historically, Russia had more reason for interest in the Muslim world as a whole than any of the Western powers. For 250 years Russia had been ruled by Islamized Mongols. After its restoration to Christendom, Holy Russia absorbed millions of Muslim subjects. By the end of the nineteenth century, following the great tsarist expansion eastwards, the Russian Empire not only contained some 15 million Muslims but also shared some 2,000 miles of frontiers with the only

Muslim states which could be regarded as truly sovereign – the Ottoman Empire and Persia.

The Russian Bolsheviks retained the tsarist empire and created the six Muslim Soviet Republics to form the southern fringe of the USSR. Pre-revolutionary Christian Russia always regarded Islam as hostile but the fact remained that its southern population from the point of view of culture and religion and to a large extent of race remained part of the Middle East. All had belonged to the Muslim East of the caliphates.

This was the reality that the Soviet Union inherited. Lenin's policy was to renounce all tsarist imperial ambitions in the Middle East and to consolidate the Soviet hold on the Muslim republics. The communists were as hostile to Islam as the tsars, regarding it as a counter-revolutionary force. They maintained a fiction that it was being artificially maintained as an anti-Soviet instrument by Western imperialist intrigue, but over the years they could not fail to realize the prevalence and staying power of Islamic culture both outside and inside the borders of the Soviet Union.

Initially, Soviet policy in the Middle East was based on the assumption that the peoples of the region who had been dominated or exploited by Ottoman, British and tsarist imperialism would be attracted by the ideals of the Bolshevik Revolution. The Soviet leaders believed that they had a good chance of gaining control over the secular nationalist movements which were developing in the area. But for the time being the Arab countries remained under British or French control, and the main hopes of the Soviet Union were concentrated on Turkey and Iran, which were always the principal focus of Russian interest. The Soviet misunderstanding of nationalism soon brought disappointment. In Turkey, Mustafa Kemal and his colleagues were quite prepared to accept Soviet arms and money in their struggle against the West, but before long they made clear both that they detested communism and that they still regarded Russia as Turkey's traditional enemy. Moreover, whereas Lenin at least favoured the idea of supporting bourgeois nationalism, even if it meant the collapse of local communist movements, on the ground that nationalism would enforce the retreat of imperialism and hence prepare the way for the eventual downfall of capitalism, his policy was to a large extent reversed by Stalin. Stalin believed that local communist parties should be the spearhead of Soviet policy and that Soviet interests could best be served by a programme of subversion and, where it seemed appropriate, by direct action.

In Iran this policy was especially disastrous. The Soviet Union's support for the establishment of the communist Tudeh Party, its attempt to exploit mutinous movements in the army, and constant efforts at subversion through its consulates, commercial organizations, clubs and propaganda agents served only to rally all the anti-Russian feelings of Iranian nationalism in a way which was no different from the days of the tsars. By 1934 Reza Shah had closed down all the Soviet trade agencies and clubs and all but one of the consulates.

In the Arab countries of the Middle East the communist parties were minuscule and dominated by intellectuals who generally came from the religious and ethnic minorities. The Soviet Union tried to gain a political and commercial entrée into the Arab world through the newly created kingdom of Saudi Arabia, but this was a failure and Stalin closed down the legation in 1938.

Until the Second World War the Arab countries were hardly aware of the existence of the Soviet Union. Its entry into the war in 1941 transformed the situation. The Soviet Union's epic resistance to Hitler's armies gave it new prestige. As an ally of the Western powers, its diplomatic representation, which had hitherto been confined to Turkey and Iran, was extended to most of the Arab states. The Soviet military occupation of northern Iran was made in agreement with Britain and the United States.

However, in the immediate post-war period Stalin's neo-imperialist policies were soon rebuffed. Iran and Turkey remained the focus of Soviet interest, but their hostility was provoked by the disastrous attempt to establish a separatist pro-Soviet Iranian Azerbaijan and by a demand for the return of the provinces of Kars and Ardahan which were ceded to Turkey in 1921. In 1952 the pro-Western government of the kingdom of Iraq broke off relations with Moscow and the moves began which united Iraq with Turkey, Iran and Pakistan in the anti-Soviet Baghdad Pact. Soviet policy in the Middle East suffered a blockade.

The situation began to be transformed with the death of Stalin in March 1953. Under Khrushchev's leadership of the Soviet Communist Party, the Soviet Union, instead of lending support to the small and uninfluential communist parties in the Arab states, reverted to Lenin's policy of backing popular national leaders who were prepared to show independence from the West. Nasser of Egypt was such an Arab leader *par excellence*. Daniel Solod, the exceptionally active Middle East expert who was Soviet ambassador in Cairo, laid the foundations of a *de facto* alliance between the Soviet Union and the Egyptian revolution.

Nasser's growing popularity among the Arabs and his espousal of neutralist policies had two inevitable consequences: one was that his relations with the Western powers deteriorated and the other was that Israel began to regard Egypt as its biggest external challenge. The Zionist state had greatly increased in power and confidence since its birth. Under the 'Law of Return', which gives any Jew the right to emigrate to Israel and settle there, nearly 700,000 Jewish immigrants had poured into the country – first from eastern and central Europe and then from Yemen, Iraq and the Arab Maghreb states. Their absorption, combined with a determination to achieve full employment, a high level of social services and a European standard of living, presented formidable difficulties – especially as the new state was cut off from its natural markets by the total economic boycott which the Arab states attempted to impose and also felt the need to exceed the combined military strength of all its Arab neighbours. Although Israel's economy remained vulnerable, the obstacles were largely overcome through the economic skills and enterprise of the population and the enormous flow of foreign aid, much of it in the form of grants rather than loans, from world Jewry, West Germany (as war reparations) and the United States.

In the absence of any prospect of peace negotiations leading to an Arab–Israeli settlement, Israel from the outset initiated a policy of overwhelming reprisal for any border violations or acts of infiltration – whether these were carried out by individual Palestinian farmers whose lands had been bisected by the armistice lines or by trained *fedayeen* (commandos), the Israeli military response was much the same. In one incident in October 1953, Israeli forces killed some fifty villagers in Qibya on the West Bank.

When Nasser came to power he had every reason to avoid involvement with Israel. Not only was he confronted by major domestic and foreign problems, but also the Palestine war had exposed the weaknesses of the Egyptian armed forces. The West would sell him arms only in tiny quantities, and he was not yet prepared to turn to the East. When Israel's first premier, the militant David Ben Gurion, temporarily withdrew from politics in December 1953 and was succeeded by the moderate Moshe Sharett, there was a period of relative Egyptian–

Israeli *détente*. But in February 1955 the scandal of the Lavon affair – the failure of a plan by the Israeli secret service to force the British to stay in Egypt by simulating Egyptian outrages against British institutions – brought Ben Gurion back to power. One week later the Israeli army carried out a massive reprisal for the *fedayeen* attacks in a raid on Egyptian headquarters in Gaza, inflicting heavy casualties. The action was a milestone in the history of the Arab–Israeli conflict.

Nasser could not ignore this humiliating exposure of Egyptian military weakness. His immediate response was to unleash more *fedayeen*, who tried to penetrate deep into Israel and blow up installations. Egypt suffered world-wide condemnation, but at least Nasser had staved off all demands for an immediate all-out war with Israel, for which he knew that Egypt was not prepared.

It was more important that Nasser began secret negotiations for the purchase of arms, culminating in the announcement on 27 September 1955 – another landmark in recent Middle East history – of a deal with Czechoslovakia for the supply of very large quantities of arms, including Soviet aircraft and tanks, in exchange for rice and cotton. This was the first deal of its kind by any Arab country. The West was outraged, while Arab public opinion was delighted.

Western hostility and Israeli concern reached new heights. France had joined the ranks of Egypt's enemies, mainly because it was convinced (incorrectly) that the rebellion in Algeria which had broken out in 1954 was stimulated and financed from Cairo. A Franco-Israeli alliance which was to last for more than a decade was formed, and news of a secret deal to supply Israel with French weapons added to the urgency of Nasser's search for arms. The British government's detestation of Nasser was approaching its climax. Anthony Eden, the prime minister, held Nasser responsible for every manifestation of Arab anti-Western feeling, including the young King Hussein of Jordan's dismissal of the British commander-in-chief of the Arab Legion, General Glubb. Eden had already decided that Nasser's overthrow was essential. Moreover, Britain and France's colonial empires in black Africa were yet to be disbanded, and Egypt had begun to play the role in the African Circle which Nasser had predicted. Cairo Radio gave vigorous and often vituperative support in various languages for anti-colonial liberation movements throughout Africa. The United States, which still had fewer direct interests in the Arab world than Britain or France, was chiefly concerned with the Cold War aspect of Nasser's neutralism. Pro-Zionist congressmen joined the chorus of those who were saying that Nasser's aim was to unite the Arab states by force and turn them into Soviet satellites. US–Egyptian relations deteriorated further when in May 1956 Nasser recognized communist China, the object of US detestation. Apart from demonstrating his independence, Nasser had the additional motive of evading a possible UN embargo on Middle East arms supplies (China not being a UN member).

The Western powers had, however, not entirely given up hope of keeping Egypt within their orbit. The new Egyptian regime had set its heart on the building of a giant dam on the Nile, near Aswan. By increasing the cultivated area by 30 per cent, providing year-to-year water storage to prevent flooding and drought, and enormously increasing the hydroelectricity supply, this would form the cornerstone of Egypt's development programme. In February 1956 a provisional agreement was reached whereby the World Bank would loan $200 million on condition that the United States and Britain loaned another $70 million to pay the hard-currency costs. The USA and Britain imposed conditions which Nasser found difficult, since they involved some Western control over the Egyptian economy. When he finally made up his mind to accept, however, the USA abruptly announced that the offer was being withdrawn, because Egypt's economy was too unstable for so large a scheme.

The USA and Britain believed that, even if Nasser did not fall from power, he would become more pliable. They were not convinced that the Soviet Union would make good its hints that it was prepared to finance the dam. They were surprised and outraged when Nasser chose the fourth anniversary of the Egyptian Revolution, 26 July 1956, to announce to vast cheering crowds in Alexandria and, via Cairo Radio, to the rest of the Arab world that he was nationalizing the Suez Canal Company and creating an Egyptian Canal Authority to manage the Canal. The entire Third World was thrilled. There existed no more potent symbol of Western colonial domination than the Suez Canal. But there was apprehension about the consequences – the West would surely not allow Nasser to succeed.

Three months of negotiations in London and New York followed, in which Britain took the lead in trying to enforce some international control of the Canal. They failed largely because the US Eisenhower/Dulles administration refused to consider the use of military force to coerce Egypt. But the British and French governments were determined to use force. The secret Franco-Israeli alliance devised a plan for a joint invasion of Egypt with Britain. Eden finally agreed to this, with reluctance due only to his fear that the collusion with Israel would be discovered, with disastrous consequences for Britain's remaining interests in the Arab world.

On 29 October 1956 Israel invaded Sinai, and on the following day Britain and France issued a joint ultimatum (seventy-six years after their Joint Note threatening Arabi Pasha) calling on Egypt and Israel to cease fighting and to withdraw their forces ten miles from the Canal. Israel, as part of the plan, accepted the ultimatum, although its forces were still much more than ten miles from the Canal. Nasser rejected it and ordered his troops which were suffering heavy losses in Sinai to return across the Canal. When the ultimatum expired on 31 October, British and French planes began to bomb Egyptian airfields, destroying almost the entire Egyptian airforce except for those planes which had been sent to Syria for safety. On 5 November an Anglo-French force, assembled in Cyprus, landed near Port Said and, after capturing the city, advanced southwards along the line of the Canal, which the Egyptians had already blocked with sunken shipping.

World opinion was overwhelmingly hostile to the tripartite invasion. The threatened break-up of the British Commonwealth, Soviet warnings and especially the opposition of the United States, which refused to provide help and to relieve the alarming drain on sterling, all contributed to Britain's decision to halt its Suez action. The UN General Assembly decided on 4 November to create a UN Emergency Force (UNEF) to supervise the cease-fire it was calling for and which Britain and France accepted on 6 November. Israel could not continue alone. Britain and France had made two major miscalculations: one was that the Egyptians would be incapable of managing the Canal on their own and the other was that as soon as hostilities began there would be a popular uprising against Nasser. In fact after nationalization the Egyptians showed that they could manage the Canal efficiently, and Nasser's popularity in Egypt and among Arabs elsewhere reached new heights. Egypt suffered military defeat against overwhelming force but scored an almost total diplomatic victory. An angry President Eisenhower compelled the Israelis to withdraw from Sinai and Gaza early in 1957, leaving Egypt in full control of the Canal and its immense quantities of British military stores. With US assistance the Canal was cleared and reopened in April 1957. All British and French property in Egypt was sequestered. About 3,000 British and French nationals were expelled, and many thousands more left because of the loss of their livelihood. Britain and France attempted to retaliate by imposing an economic blockade of Egypt, but the gesture was futile.

The century of Anglo-French domination of the Arab world was finally drawing to a close. Two years later Britain's remaining substantial Arab ally, the Iraqi monarchy, was swept aside by a popular army-led coup and the Baghdad Pact collapsed. The British quasi-colonial role in the Gulf and southern Arabia would last another decade until its dismantlement was forced by financial constraints. France, although apparently more firmly installed in the Arab West, withdrew even earlier when it conceded Algeria's independence in 1962 after a prolonged and futile attempt at repression.

The years 1956 to 1959 marked the high tide of Nasserism as he seemed to sweep all before him. His appeal to the Arabs – and especially to the younger generation, who formed the majority – was overwhelming. They saw him as a modern Saladin who would unite them in order to drive out the Zionists – the crusaders of the twentieth century. The danger for Nasser was that he was raising expectations which neither he nor Egypt could fulfil. He was aware of Arab military weakness, which it would take time for Soviet help to remedy, but he could not regulate the tide of Arab fervour. His personality transcended Arab doubts about Egypt's commitment to the cause of Arab unity, which were shared by the Egyptians themselves.

In June 1956 a new Republican Constitution was promulgated and approved by a 99 per cent affirmative vote. This declared Islam as the religion of the state, recognized Egypt as part of the Arab nation, and provided for government by a president and a council of ministers and a single legislative chamber. Nasser was confirmed as president for a six-year term. Political parties were replaced by a similar political organization, the National Union. Nasser's hold on power was thus formalized. Although he gave high executive positions to some of his outstanding former colleagues in the RCC, he made sure that no rival centres of power developed. The only partial exception, which ultimately proved disastrous, was that he allowed

Abdul Hakim Amer, the defence minister, a large measure of independent control over the armed forces. Amer had charm and
presence but lacked self-discipline and was an incompetent military
commander.

Nasser's political mastery of Egypt could not easily be translated to
the other Arab states. His appeal among the masses was immensely
powerful but the rulers of most independent Arab states, in addition
to Nuri al-Said in Iraq, were basically pro-Western and conservative
and therefore hostile to Nasserism. They used what means they could
to oppose the alarming trend. In Jordan, King Hussein had swum
with the tide in dismissing General Glubb and allowing the formation
of a pro-Nasser government which, in October 1956, terminated the
agreement under which Britain subsidized the Jordanian army. But
when in April 1957 the government proposed to establish diplomatic
relations with the Soviet Union and King Hussein heard that a
nationalist military coup was being planned against him he reacted
with the support of ultra-loyal beduin elements in the army and
dismissed the government. He was helped by the reality that his
overthrow would almost certainly lead to Israel's occupation of the
West Bank. The harsh realities of Jordan's perilous position helped
to develop the king's mastery of political combat. His courage and
shrewdness also played their part.

In Lebanon the ambitious and resourceful President Camille Chamoun used the strong powers of the Maronite presidency to ensure that
an overwhelming majority of his pro-Western supporters were successful in parliamentary elections. Lebanese Arab nationalists – who were
mainly, but not exclusively, Muslims – could only protest.

The Saudi Arabian attitude towards the rise of Nasserism was
more ambiguous. King Saud, who succeeded Ibn Saud in 1953, was
affable and physically impressive like his father but a lesser man in
other respects. He was wildly extravagant and foolish. Although he
delegated some powers to his able and experienced brother, Crown
Prince Feisal, he maintained a system of largely personal rule with
the help of a group of frequently corrupt advisers. He lacked the
wisdom to cope with either the new flow of oil wealth or the
increasingly complex demands of the twentieth century.

His Arab policy was initially guided by the long-standing rivalry
between the House of Saud and the Hashemites. This brought him
closer to Egypt, despite the incongruity between Saudi traditionalism

and the Egyptian Revolution. In 1955 Saudi Arabia agreed to join Egypt and Syria in a joint military command system which was clearly directed against the Baghdad Pact. In 1957 King Saud also accepted that Saudi Arabia should help Egypt and Syria to replace the British subsidy to Jordan.

In the power struggle which was developing in the Arab East, Syria was the key. It was the country in which the desire and need for Arab unity was felt most passionately, but it lacked any strong central authority representing Syria's identity. Since the fall of Colonel Shishakli, who dominated the country from 1950 to 1954, the old political parties from the days of the French mandate contended for power under the parliamentary constitution. Conservative pro-Western Iraq was not without influence, but the trend in Syria was inexorably leftwards, towards the radical neutralist position of revolutionary Egypt. In 1956 Syria followed Egypt in acquiring arms from the Soviet Union and in recognizing communist China. The leftwards tendency was closely associated with the increase in power and influence of the Baath Party. Although founded as little more than a debating society a decade earlier by two Damascus schoolteachers – Michel Aflaq and Salah Bitar – the Baathists succeeded better than any other group in focusing popular feeling. Aflaq, the party ideologist, although shy and uncharismatic, acquired a substantial following for his pan-Arabist ideas among the younger generation. The Baathists won few seats in parliament, but they had supporters in key areas and they were on close terms with a group of officers who were strongly neutralist in feeling and were dominant in the army. From 1956 they were indispensable elements in any government.

The Suez War inflamed popular feeling in Syria and accelerated the leftwards trend. The government multiplied its ties with the Soviet Union.

The possibility that the entire Arab East might be moving into the Soviet camp intensely alarmed the United States, which saw the world in Cold War terms. The credit it had earned among Arab nationalists for its role in blocking the tripartite aggression against Egypt was quickly dissipated when it joined the Anglo-French economic blockade of Egypt. The USA openly and covertly attempted to rally all the pro-Nasser and anti-Western forces in the Arab world. In January 1957 the president issued what became known as the 'Eisenhower Doctrine', which named 'international Communism' as the greatest threat to the

Middle East and promised financial aid to any government which helped to resist it. Iraq and President Chamoun of Lebanon accepted such aid, as did Saudi Arabia, although in ambiguous terms. King Saud was by now thoroughly alarmed by the radical pro-Soviet trend in the Arab world, but he was not yet ready to join the camp of his old Hashemite enemies in Baghdad. He sent some troops to Jordan as a token support for King Hussein's regime following the king's dismissal of his nationalist government. In an improbable attempt to build up the Saudi monarch as a rival to Nasser in the Arab world, or even as an 'Islamic Pope' – a self-contradictory concept – the Eisenhower administration invited him on a state visit to the USA. In Lebanon, assistance by the US embassy and the CIA for the pro-Chamoun forces in the parliamentary elections were a badly kept secret, as were their botched attempts to encourage a pro-Western coup in the Syrian army.

In general, these US actions did more to strengthen the nationalist/neutralist trend in the Middle East than to reassure the pro-Western elements. The Soviet Union, which had undertaken to help build the Nile High Dam and to resist the Western economic blockade of Egypt, gained new friends. Cairo's *Voice of the Arabs* radio programme poured out propaganda, which was often unscrupulous but nevertheless highly effective, against the United States and the 'reactionaries' who were its allies in the Arab world.

As the Middle Eastern Cold War developed, the nervous and vulnerable Syrian regime felt the pressures most strongly. As the United States declared its alarm that Syria was moving into the Soviet camp, the Soviet Union issued a warning to the West against intervening in Syria. In September 1957 Syria accused Turkey of massing troops on its frontier. The threat was insubstantial, but Nasser sent a token body of troops to Damascus to express support.

Although the government was normally dominated by Syrian politicians of the old school, who would have preferred to keep Syria in the pro-Western camp, real power lay in the hands of the Baath. But the tide of pro-Soviet feeling meant that the communists were also gaining ground – especially in the army. Faced with relentless US pressure but also the prospect of sharing power with the communists – or even a communist takeover – the Baath decided that the best policy was a union between Syria and Egypt which would secure Nasser's protection. The conservative politicians were forced to swim with the popular tide. On 2 February 1958 the Egyptian and

Syrian presidents jointly announced the complete merger of their two states into a United Arab Republic.

The West and its Arab allies were predictably hostile and alarmed. In reaction, the Hashemite monarchies of Iraq and Jordan announced their own federal union. On the other hand the ultra-reactionary and isolationist Imam Ahmed of Yemen decided it was a wise insurance to join the United Arab Republic in a shadowy confederation to be known as the United Arab States, which was also declared in February 1958.

From then on events moved swiftly – 1958 was a momentous year for the Middle East. In March, King Saud was forced to relinquish powers to his brother Feisal after the Syrians revealed details of a plot by the king or one of his advisers to assassinate Nasser and so prevent the union of Syria and Egypt. Feisal was regarded as less pro-Western and more pro-Egyptian than his brother. In May the dangerous political polarization of Lebanon between Lebanese and Arab nationalists, which had been intensified by the Suez crisis, developed into a muted civil war which simmered on throughout the summer with Syria, now part of the United Arab Republic, aiding and encouraging the Arab nationalist rebellion against President Chamoun and his pro-Western government.

It was his decision to help Chamoun which in July 1958 led to the downfall of Nuri al-Said of Iraq. Although always a masterly politician, he and his colleagues were dangerously out of touch with popular opinion – especially among army officers. An Iraqi version of Egypt's Free Officers organization had been formed under Brigadier Abdul Karim Kassem. When the government ordered a brigade stationed near Baghdad to move to Jordan – almost certainly with the aim of exerting pressure on Syria to destroy the union with Egypt – the troops used the opportunity to seize the capital, overthrow the regime and declare a republic. Opposition was minimal but, in contrast to Egypt's bloodless coup, the young King Feisal II, his uncle the crown prince and all but one member of the royal family, as well as the premier Nuri al-Said himself, were murdered. A government was formed with Kassem as prime minister and minister of defence and army officers in other key positions. The new republic of Iraq declared its close alignment with Egypt.

Nasser and Nasserism were triumphant. Not only were they ruling in Syria – the vital Arab heartland – but in Iraq their strongest single opponent in the Arab world and the only effective remaining instrument of pro-Western policies had fallen. It was true that the immediate consequence of the Iraq revolution was that the United States, fearing the final collapse of the pro-Western camp in the Middle East, landed 10,000 marines in Beirut at President Chamoun's request, while British troops were flown into Jordan. But the marines did not help to keep Chamoun in power – the US wisely encouraged the compromise whereby the Lebanese settled their crisis themselves. General Fuad Chehab, the army commander who had kept the armed forces neutral in the political struggle, was constitutionally elected to succeed Chamoun. The rebels achieved much of what they wanted, since Lebanon became more neutral and less stridently pro-Western than under Chamoun. The short-lived Jordanian–Iraqi federation had collapsed, and it did not look as if a few British troops would be enough to keep King Hussein on his throne.

Though Nasser was at the apogee of his power in the Middle East, a decline from the summit was almost inevitable. In reality Nasser's extraordinary successes – which were partly due to the mistakes of his opponents and their failure to understand the true nature of his appeal to the Arab masses – had concealed the underlying weakness of his position. Suez and its aftermath had given Egypt an international status which it could not hope to sustain.

Arab expectations of the imminent triumph of the cause of unity were at their highest – like the German or the Italian states in the nineteenth century, the members of the Arab League could unite as a single entity. But there were a host of geographical and political reasons why Bismarck's role could not be Nasser's. The political societies of the Arab nation-states – some of them new, like Syria and Iraq; some of them ancient, like Egypt and Yemen – were vastly different and their common culture and the emotional euphoria of pan-Arabism were not enough to unite them.

Nasser's immediate problem was the government of the United Arab Republic. He said later that when the Syrian leaders came to Cairo to ask for union he felt it would be better to start with a loose federation for a transitional period. When they insisted on a full merger it was his turn to insist that, if he was to have the responsibility, the UAR should be ruled from Cairo. But although Nasser had a remarkable capacity for self-education – and in his lengthy public speeches he always sounded like his people's teacher –

he had not learned enough about Syria. It was wealthier, less populous and more pluralistic than Egypt, and its political society was much less mature. Above all, it was a supremely difficult country to govern.

On their side the Syrian Baathists, who were the force behind the merger, had deceived themselves. They had come to feel that Nasser shared many of their ideals and aims. As they saw it, he had adopted Michel Aflaq's slogans of 'Freedom, unity and socialism' and 'One nation with an eternal mission'. There was some truth in this, but what Nasser was not prepared to do was to allow the Baath to rule Syria under the umbrella of his authority and prestige. He soon brushed the Baathist leaders aside, into sullen exile or bitter opposition. The post-independence parliamentary constitution was replaced by a single political organization on the Egyptian model. Nasser appointed two Syrian vice-presidents for the UAR and several Syrian ministers in the central government, but he kept most of the executive and legislative power in his own hands.

Some of the Egyptian officials who went to work in Syria were of high calibre, but many were not. Inevitably, Syrians began to feel that they were in the position of junior partners to Egyptians whom they were inclined to regard as less able and energetic than themselves. In particular the Syrian army suffered from wounded pride, while Syrian merchants, businessmen and land-owners who had a long tradition of dynamic activity in a generally free economy watched with growing apprehension as Egypt imposed its state socialist principles upon them. In Egypt the move in the economy away from the capitalist West towards the Soviet bloc, the drive towards rapid industrialization and the building of massive public works including the Nile High Dam had made a huge expansion of the public sector almost inevitable. The 'Arab socialism' which Nasser was developing may have been restrained by pragmatism in Egypt, but it was not adapted to Syria. The Syrian left was equally hostile. While the Baath had been ousted, the communists were given short shrift – as they were in Egypt.

To make matters worse, Syria's basically agricultural economy suffered three consecutive years of disastrous drought between 1958 and 1960.

As Syrian disaffection with the union increased, the new revolutionary government in Iraq soon belied the high hopes of the pan-Arabists. Before the end of 1958 Kassem had arrested and jailed his principal collaborator in the military coup, Colonel Aref, who favoured an immediate Iraqi–Egyptian union. He blamed an abortive Arab nationalist revolt in Mosul in February 1959 on Nasser. During 1959 he allowed the Iraqi communists to strengthen their position at the expense of the Arab nationalists (led by the Iraqi Baathists), and for nearly four years he succeeded in maintaining a precarious balancing act by preventing either group from taking over the state. Despite this, Nasser distrusted him and was convinced that Iraqi communism was a danger to the whole Arab world. Kassem, an unstable and inordinately vain man, developed a bitter and jealous hatred of Nasser.

To meet the declining situation in Syria, Nasser in 1960 sent his closest colleague, Field Marshal Abdul Hakim Amer, to Damascus as his proconsul with instructions to alleviate the causes of growing Syrian opposition to the union. But although Nasser retained much of his personal popularity among the Syrian people and drew wildly enthusiastic crowds on his visits, he had manifestly failed to discover a satisfactory method of governing Syria. On 28 September 1961 a group of Syrian army officers rebelled. They arrested Field Marshal Amer, put him on a plane to Cairo and announced Syria's secession from the United Arab Republic. A new government was hastily formed from conservative Syrian politicians.

Nasser initially contemplated intervening, but changed his mind when all resistance to the coup rapidly faded. A few days later he said it was not imperative for Syria to remain part of the UAR but he would not oppose its re-entry into the United Arab States.

It was a time for Nasser's many enemies both in the Middle East and elsewhere to triumph. Western governments were delighted, but equally the leaders of Iraq, Jordan and Saudi Arabia did nothing to conceal their pleasure.

Nasser himself told the Egyptians, 'We must have the courage to admit our mistakes.' But his own analysis was that he should have been more vigorous in imposing Egypt's socialism on Syria. Three months before Syria's secession a series of laws had been decreed in Egypt nationalizing cotton export firms, banks, insurance companies and 275 major industrial and trading companies as well as cutting maximum land holdings by half and sharply increasing income tax. Nasser was convinced that Syria's secession was simply the counter-attack of the Syrian bourgeoisie against such a sharp move to the left. Believing that Egypt's bourgeoisie might be planning similar action, he launched his own precautionary counter-offensive in which the property of more than a thousand of Egypt's wealthiest families was confiscated.

He knew that this was insufficient and that he had to give his Arab socialism a clearer ideological definition. He spent the winter of 1961–2 in preparing his 30,000-word Charter of National Action before summoning a National Congress of Popular Powers attended by labour unions, professional associations and other community groups to debate its terms. Although influenced by Marxism (especially the Yugoslav model) and European welfare-state socialism, he attempted to adapt these to his view of the special needs of Egyptian and Arab/Islamic society. The Charter was secular but not anti-religious. It started from the assumption that Egypt's pre-revolutionary parliamentary democracy based on Western models was a 'shameful farce' because 'political democracy cannot be separated from social democracy.' The vote was meaningless unless the citizen was free from all exploitation, had an equal opportunity with his fellows to enjoy a fair share of the national wealth and was assured of an adequate living-standard. Although the Charter endorsed the nationalization of all public services and most of industry and the export–import trade, it ruled out land nationalization and allowed the private ownership of buildings, subject to supervision. It distanced itself from Soviet practice by rejecting the priority given to heavy industry at the expense of the production of consumer goods.

The Charter provided for a new and unique political organization, to be known as the Arab Socialist Union, with a pyramid form based on 'basic units' in villages, factories and workshops and rising through elected councils at the district and governorate levels to the National Executive headed by the president. The National Assembly was retained as the ASU's legislative branch. In this, as in all the ASU's elected bodies, half the seats had to be reserved for workers or farmers (defined as anyone owning less than twenty-five *feddans*). Nasser believed that his intention was clear: to create a social democracy in which the mass of the Egyptians would for the first time genuinely participate. But such a system can hardly flourish when it is created instantly from above – it was significant that the National Congress approved his Charter without amendment.

Nasser's absorption with his National Charter and the fact that he was no longer concerned with the problems of governing Syria – which he said had taken up three-quarters of his time for three-and-a-half-years – did not mean that he was turning his back on the Arab world or abandoning his claims to Arab leadership. These were not his intentions – even if they had been, circumstances would not have allowed them. He remained by far the dominant figure on the Arab scene, and expectations in him remained high among ordinary Arabs. To symbolize his attitude, he retained the name of United Arab Republic for Egypt.

Hostile Arab governments poured out invective. The Saudis concentrated their attack on Egyptian socialism, which they said was atheistic. Even Imam Ahmed of Yemen – ailing, but still awe-inspiring to his subjects – contributed to the anti-Egyptian chorus; the shadowy United Arab States of the UAR and Yemen was dissolved. The most violent abuse emanated from Syria, where a series of highly unstable governments elected under the old constitution replaced each other in rapid succession. Syrian spokesmen accused Nasser and Egypt of oppressing Syria with a reign of terror, as well as embezzling funds of the Syrian state. Cairo's response was louder and more effective than all these criticisms, because Egypt's propaganda media were more developed than those of any other Arab state. Nasser's theme was that there could be no compromise between Arab socialism and 'reaction'. One of his favourite phrases was that 'unity of ranks is no substitute for unity of aims.'

Yet Egypt was to some extent on the defensive. After a flaming row with the Syrians at an Arab League council meeting in Lebanon, Nasser announced that Egypt was withdrawing from the Arab League. Then, one year after Syria's secession, events in distant Arabia enabled him to regain the initiative. On 28 September 1962 some pro-Egyptian officers in the Yemeni army revolted against Imam Badr, who had just succeeded his father Ahmed, seized the main towns and declared a republic. The royalist cause was not lost, however, because Badr escaped and his uncle, Amir Hassan, returned to Saudi Arabia from the United States to rally support among Yemeni tribesmen against the new republic. Nasser at once decided to answer the revolutionaries' call for help, and a substantial Egyptian expeditionary force sailed up the Red Sea to the Yemeni port of Hodeida. The resulting prolonged involvement in the Yemen – described as 'the Egyptian Vietnam' – cost Egypt dear. Its troops were ill-prepared for guerrilla tribal warfare in mountainous territory. The intervention was unpopular among those of the Egyptian public who were directly affected by it and a matter of indifference to most of the rest. Yet the fact of a Nasserist coup in Yemen raised Egypt's morale at the time and increased its prestige in the rest of the Arab world. In mounting the expeditionary force to Yemen, Nasser showed conclusively that Egypt's armed forces were the only ones in the Middle East about which Israel needed to worry. It was Nasser's opponents who were now on the defensive. The defection to Cairo of seven of Saudi Arabia's precious officer pilots in October 1962, followed shortly by the commander of the Jordanian Air Force and two Jordanian pilots, showed that the loyalty of the armed forces in the two Arab monarchies was dubious.

Pan-Arabist emotion was a powerful factor in a further coup in Iraq, on 9 February 1963. An army revolt, in which Baathist officers played the leading role, overthrew and killed General Kassem. Colonel Aref was installed as president and immediately declared his pro-Egyptian sympathies.

Syria's fragile government could not long resist the joint pressure from Cairo and Baghdad. Exactly one month after the Iraqi revolt, a military coup in Damascus swept aside all the men who had been in power since the break-up of the Syrian–Egyptian union, and a new Revolutionary Command Council pledged itself to support 'the new movement of Arab unity'. The Baathists had not led the coup, as they had in Iraq, but they were the only civilian organization outside the old regime which was capable of forming a government. Within a week, Iraqi and Syrian ministerial delegations were in Cairo to discuss plans for the unity of Syria, Iraq and Egypt.

This seemed like another moment of great triumph for Nasser. But disillusion came even more swiftly than with the Syrian–Egyptian union as the mutual mistrust between Nasser and the Baathists came to the surface. Nasser felt he could get along with the Iraqi Baathists – who had borne the brunt of the struggle with Kassem, were in firmer control than their Syrian counterparts and had no heritage of rancour with Egypt – but he had no confidence in the Syrian Baath. For their part, a few idealistic Baathists in both Syria and Iraq had a genuine doctrinal disagreement with Egypt in their demand for democratic freedoms and collective leadership. But most Baathists simply believed that salvation for the Arabs could come only through the Baath party and to this end were prepared to use methods which were quite as totalitarian as anything in Egypt.

The tripartite unity talks were not helped by the fact that Nasser dominated them with his personality and his long experience of power. (He later made cruel fun of the shy and stuttering Michel Aflaq, who was incapable of expressing his views clearly.) Although a form of agreement on a tripartite federation was reached on 17 April, the union was stillborn. During May and June the Syrian Baathists were purging the army of non-Baathist officers and suppressing Nasserist demonstrations. Following the ruthless suppression of an attempted pro-Nasser coup in Syria in July, Nasser openly attacked the Baath for the first time, describing the Syrian regime as 'secessionist, inhuman and immoral' and revealing that Egyptian intelligence had uncovered an Iraqi–Syrian alliance against him.

As Egypt's relations with Iraq and Syria worsened, Nasser had some satisfaction when in November the Iraqi Baathists, who had already made themselves unpopular by their violent methods and who had renewed the exhausting war with the rebellious Kurdish minority which had so weakened Kassem's regime, split into two factions and were ousted by President Aref (whom they had tried to keep as a figurehead) and some senior non-Baathist officers. True to his simple-minded notions, Aref renewed pressure for an immediate union with Egypt. But experience had made Nasser cautious. He suggested to the Iraqis that they should first ensure their own national unity, which among other things meant finding a solution to the Kurdish problem.

Although Nasser regarded Arab political union as impossible for the foreseeable future, he saw the urgent need for some kind of joint Arab action. The Israelis had completed the diversion of some of the waters of the River Jordan to the Negev Desert, though this was something he and other Arab leaders had rashly sworn to prevent. This was no time to insist on 'unity of aims' before 'unity of ranks'. In the Arabs' divided condition there was little hope of their taking effective common action, but there was a very real danger that one Arab state – Syria, where the most irresponsible ultra-left elements were in the ascendant – would act on its own and plunge the others into a war with Israel for which they were not prepared. Nasser therefore issued an invitation to all Arab kings and presidents, which he knew they would find it difficult to refuse, to meet in Cairo in January 1964, setting a precedent for the holding of regular summit meetings. He used the occasion to mend his bridges with pro-Western

Arab leaders such as King Hussein, the ailing King Saud, and President Bourguiba of Tunisia and to emphasize the isolation of the Syrian Baath. A second summit was held in Alexandria in September. The Arab heads of state agreed to set up a Unified Arab Military Command under an Egyptian general, and also a Palestine Liberation Organization (but not a government in exile), with its own army, to represent the Palestinian people. They all agreed, although with little enthusiasm, on the choice of the verbose and flamboyant Palestinian lawyer Ahmed Shukairy to head the PLO. King Hussein made clear that the PLO would not have any authority inside Jordanian territory. The heads of state also decided on plans to divert the sources of the River Jordan in Arab territory, in order to forestall Israel's irrigation schemes.

The pressing problem of how to satisfy Arab public demands for action over Palestine without provoking a potentially disastrous war with Israel had been postponed rather than solved. Arab opinion was deluded in thinking that some positive action was at last being taken. Lebanon and Syria were reluctant to carry out the diversion of the Jordan tributaries in their territory without more adequate protection than the Arab states could provide, and the mutual trust which was essential if the Unified Arab Military Command was to function was lacking.

During 1965 and 1966 the division deepened between the radical Arab camp (led by Egypt) and the conservative (led by Saudi Arabia). In December 1964, King Saud had abdicated and had been succeeded by his brother Feisal. Although Nasser agreed publicly with Feisal on the need to settle the disastrous royalist/republican civil war in Yemen, neither was prepared to make the necessary compromise.

In Feisal, Nasser for the first time since the death of Nuri al-Said faced a rival star-personality, although one of a very different kind from himself. The most they had in common was the puritanical restraint of their private lives. Reserved, dignified and reflective, Feisal commanded immediate respect. Like Nuri, Feisal made little appeal either to the intelligentsia or to the urban masses, but he was the custodian of the holy places of Islam and the ruler of an Arab state which, however backward and underdeveloped, had never been under imperialist control and therefore lacked the complexes of the colonized. As a diplomat and statesman he was in a different class from his brother Saud: while refusing any kind of liberal constitutional reform, he was encouraging a much more rapid and intelligent social and economic development at home. This made it all the easier for him to rally to his banner those elements in the Arab world afraid of or antagonistic towards Nasserism.

Feisal's appeal was naturally more Islamic than nationalist. In December 1965 he went on a state visit to Iran, and in his address to the Iranian Majlis he suggested the need for Islamic unity against subversive alien influences from outside. Although he was deliberately unspecific, no one doubted that he was referring to Egypt's Arab socialism. Feisal had embarked on creating a conservative 'Islamic Front' against Nasser.

Nevertheless, it was Nasser who continued to play the commanding role on the world stage. His differences with the Soviet Union, which had arisen over Nasser's hostility towards the Iraqi communists, had been overcome and Moscow still regarded Cairo as the focus of its Middle East policy. The relationship was symbolized in the much publicized visit to Egypt in May 1964 by the Soviet premier Khrushchev for the inauguration of the second stage of the building of the High Dam – the gigantic project which not only aimed to change the face of Egypt but was also the flagship of Soviet aid to the Third World. On the other hand, the United States also accepted the inevitability of Nasser's Arab leadership. Towards the end of the second Eisenhower administration, the US State Department came to the conclusion not only that Nasser was not a communist but also that in reality he promised the best defence against communism in the Middle East. This revised attitude was consolidated by President Kennedy, who came close to establishing cordial and confident relations with Nasser and was warmly admired by him in return. Between 1958 and 1964 the USA provided Egypt with over a billion US dollars in aid – mostly in cheap long-term loans.

Kennedy's death came as a shock to Nasser and to all the Arabs, who felt they had lost the first American statesman with some sympathy for their point of view. Nasser was not reassured when President Johnson, who had much less interest in foreign affairs than Kennedy, gave evidence of being much more sensitive to the concerns of US Zionists. Nasser's relations with Washington deteriorated sharply over the question of the Congo (Zaïre), where Egypt was giving increasing support to the rebels against the government of Moise Tshombe which the US wanted to sustain in power. Nasser reacted angrily and defiantly when he concluded that the US was trying to use its supplies of cheap food to Egypt as a means of pressuring him to change his policies. However, when the US House of Representatives passed a resolution to stop all further aid to Egypt, President Johnson and his secretary of state, Dean Rusk, refused to accept that the hands of the United States should be tied in the Middle East in this way. The president exerted all his influence to have the vote reversed in the Senate.

For reasons of language, racial and religious affinity and strategic interest, Nasser had not given the same priority to his African Circle as to his Arab Circle, but Egypt had acquired important influence throughout black Africa, where most of the states had only just acquired independence. In July 1964 Nasser was host to the second conference of the Organization of African Unity. His position as a leader of the non-aligned movement was taken for granted, and in October 1964 fifty-six heads or representatives of heads of non-aligned countries held their summit meeting in Cairo. The concept of non-alignment might have been incapable of precise definition but it had real meaning to most countries in the Third World, which to some extent identified it with Nasser and its policies.

Nasser's function as a world statesman could not solve his domestic difficulties or avert the looming threat of a new war with Israel. Egypt's commitments were dangerously over-extended. Although his policies of industrialization and rapid economic expansion had achieved a commendable growth rate over the past decade, some of the projects had been ill-conceived and the burden of debt had risen to alarming levels. He had successfully exploited Egypt's strategic role to secure aid from East and West, but Western aid was tailing off, the country's credit was being destroyed and foreign exchange was desperately short. Although the Egyptians' acceptance of his leadership still appeared overwhelming, to an extent which could not be explained solely by the police methods which the regime undoubtedly used, in the summer of 1965 Nasser, in uncharacteristically depressed mood, announced the discovery of a nation-wide conspiracy by a revived Muslim Brotherhood, revealing ideological and political dissatisfaction at many levels of society.

The responsibilities of Egypt's assumed role of Arab leadership were more immediately dangerous. The continuing civil war in Yemen not only added to Egypt's economic burdens but also tied down some 40,000 of its best-trained troops. At the same time, events were moving rapidly towards the tragic denouement of a third Arab–Israeli war.

In February 1966 the Syrian regime, which had begun a rapprochement with Egypt, was overthrown by the radical wing of the Baath. The new Syrian rulers had no love of Nasser, but they were more strongly hostile towards the Arab kings and, if possible, even more bellicose than their predecessors towards Israel. While King Hussein was trying to prevent Palestinian *fedayeen* from operating from his territory, Syria gave them encouragement and support and accordingly Israel's threats of heavy retaliation were principally directed against Syria. Nasser could not reject a Syrian appeal for help, and in November 1966 he signed a comprehensive Syrian–Egyptian defence pact. He had a commitment to Syria without the power to control it.

A few days later, three Israeli soldiers were killed by a mine explosion near the Jordanian frontier. Although Syria was clearly the main source of Palestinian sabotage attacks, Israel launched its customary heavy retaliation raid against a West Bank village. Protesting against their inadequate protection by the Jordanian army, the West Bankers rose in a revolt which was quelled only with difficulty. King Hussein angrily attacked Nasser for his criticism of Jordan's handling of the affair and taunted him with hiding behind the protection of the UN Emergency Force (UNEF), which had kept the Egyptian–Israeli front quiet since 1956.

Tension rose to a new height the following spring, as Israeli leaders issued increasingly severe warnings to Syria. Soviet, Syrian and Egyptian intelligence combined to warn Nasser that an Israeli attack on Syria was imminent. Nasser's response on 18 May was to ask the UN secretary-general U Thant to withdraw the UNEF from Sinai (where, on Israel's insistence, it was stationed only on Egypt's side of the border). When U Thant complied, the road to war was wide open. Nasser ordered troops into Sinai and, with the eyes of the Arab world upon him, announced the closure of the Straits of Tiran to Israeli shipping. King Hussein, realizing that he would be unable to stand aside from the inevitable war that was coming, flew to Cairo on 30 May to sign a defence pact with Egypt. Egypt now had defence agreements with both Syria and Jordan, but there was no real co-operation between them and no semblance of an Arab joint command.

The Arab countries were now in a state of emotional self-intoxication as the belief became widespread that final victory over Israel was imminent. Even Nasser abandoned his usual doubts about Arab military capabilities, although he had exaggerated faith in his own military commander, Field Marshal Amer. He also believed that it was possible that the United States would restrain Israel from attacking and that he could score a tactical victory without fighting. He himself promised the Soviet Union that Egypt would not strike first. However, experience should have told him of the high probability that Israel would act if international pressure was not going to reopen the Straits of Tiran to its shipping. Any last doubts should have been removed when the activist General Moshe Dayan joined the Israeli cabinet on 1 June.

On 5 June 1967 Israel attacked all seventeen of Egypt's military airfields, destroying most of its airforce on the ground, and on 6 June Israeli forces advanced rapidly into Sinai. The seven Egyptian divisions in Sinai were defeated, and an estimated 10,000 Egyptian soldiers were killed or died of thirst in the struggle to return across the Suez Canal, which Israeli forces reached on 9 June. After destroying the Egyptian airforce, Israel could turn against Jordan, which had entered the war as Egypt's ally. By the evening of 7 June, with the Old City of Jerusalem and the West Bank occupied, Jordan accepted the UN Security Council's demand for a cease-fire. Egypt accepted on the following day. Israel was now free to turn against Syria, which had confined itself to probing attacks. Israeli troops stormed up the Golan Heights and occupied the key town of Quneitra on the Syrian plateau. Syria accepted the cease-fire on 10 June.

The swift and shattering course of the Six-Day War had many immediate and long-term consequences. The Zionist state of Israel had gained military control over all Jerusalem and the remaining 21 per cent of Palestine. Some 200,000 more Arab refugees crossed the River Jordan to the East Bank. Israel had occupied the whole of Sinai and its forces were on the banks of the Suez Canal, where this time they intended to stay. In seizing the Golan Heights, Israel had removed Syria's strategic advantage.

While Israel's victory had been too swift for the Soviet Union to help its Egyptian and Syrian friends, Western governments and public opinion were almost unanimously hostile towards the Arabs and favourable towards Israel. The only notable exception was France's President de Gaulle, who during both the war and its aftermath showed some sympathy with the Arab position and warned against Israel's domineering tendencies. Egypt's break with Britain and the United States was complete. At the outset of the war, on the basis of information from King Hussein that Jordanian radar stations had detected approaching from the sea a large flight of aircraft which could come only from British and US carriers, Egypt broke off relations with the US and Britain and expelled all US and British citizens.

Nasser's heavy share of responsibility in the disaster was clear, and his position, both in Egypt and among the Arabs, was irreparably damaged. In dark tones on the third evening of the war he announced on Cairo Radio his acceptance of full personal responsibility and his intention to resign and hand over power to his vice-president, Zakariya Mohieddin. He also dismissed his right-hand man Field Marshal Amer. Whether or not Nasser had expected it, the reaction was an overwhelming public demand that he should remain in office. The extraordinary dominance which he had achieved in Egypt, and his position as the generally well-loved father figure of a nation accustomed to paternalistic rule, meant that he was not allowed to abandon the presidency at a time of such desperate crisis. His health was deteriorating – he suffered from 'black diabetes', which caused defective blood circulation – and there is little doubt that the 1967 disaster shortened his life. But in one sense Egypt's situation made his position easier, since those who might have challenged his power were restrained by their lack of any practical alternative to his policies. In August 1967 he was faced with a conspiracy to restore Field Marshal Amer as head of the armed forces, and in 1968 and 1969 there were serious outbreaks of student and industrial unrest, but he overcame these with a mixture of firmness and mild concessions. While there was considerable dissatisfaction, especially among the professional classes and intelligentsia, because the old power structure had not been radically changed, the continuing state of emergency with Israel provided a powerful argument for postponing fundamental reforms.

The Soviet Union at once showed its readiness to repair Egypt's enormous military losses, and Soviet arms and equipment poured into the country. But although Nasser's public speeches were defiant and even bellicose in tone, in reality he accepted that Egypt's military options were extremely limited. In November 1967 he accepted the UN Security Council Resolution 242 calling for an Israeli withdrawal from the occupied territories in return for Arab *de facto* recognition of Israel, and he publicly agreed with the Soviet leaders on the need for a political settlement in the Middle East.

As Egypt's armed forces recovered, in 1969–70 Nasser allowed them to conduct a 'war of attrition' against Israel along the Suez Canal. The Egyptians scored several successes, which raised public morale, but Israel exacted a heavy cost by bombarding Egypt's Canal cities and conducting commando raids deep into Egyptian territory. Nasser asked the Soviet Union to step up its aid, and the number of Soviet military advisers in Egypt was increased from about 3,000 to 10,000. But Nasser still had not abandoned hope that a political solution to the Arab–Israeli conflict could be achieved through US pressure on Israel to withdraw from occupied Arab territories. On 1 May 1970 he made what he called a 'final appeal' to President Nixon to withhold support for Israel so long as it continued to occupy Arab lands, and on 23 July he announced Egypt's acceptance of the Rogers Plan, sponsored by the US secretary of state William Rogers and based on UN Resolution 242, which led to a cease-fire in the Suez Canal area on 7 August.

The burden of Arab leadership had finally proved too heavy for Egypt. It would be an exaggeration to say that the Nasser era in the Middle East came to an end during the six fateful days in June 1967, although it began an irreversible decline then. In fact Arab shame and humiliation caused by the catastrophe intensified the anti-Western trend in parts of the Arab world. In South Arabia (the former British Aden Colony and Protectorate) left-wing extremists took power when Britain withdrew in 1967 and created the People's Democratic Republic of Yemen. In 1969 the conservative parliamentary regime in Sudan was overthrown by radical socialist army officers led by Colonel Jaafar Nimeiry, who moved the country leftwards towards closer relations with Egypt and the Soviet Union. A few months later the aged King Idris of Libya was ousted in a coup led by a passionately Nasserist young beduin colonel named Muammar Qaddafy. The events in Sudan and Libya were a boost for Nasser in his decline; they offered the prospect of strategic depth for Egypt's armed forces and of economic help through Libya's oil wealth. On Qaddafy's insistence, Libya, Sudan and Egypt began to discuss plans for a federation. But Nasser's experience could not make him enthusiastic about such a prospect, and in 1969 neither Sudan or Libya could be of much help in Egypt's immediate difficulties.

The support of Sudan and Libya could not outbalance two greater realities which tended to diminish Egypt's role in the Arab world. One was the fact that Egypt's defeat greatly enhanced the position of King Feisal, the leader of the conservative and fundamentally pro-Western oil states of Arabia. At the Khartoum summit meeting which followed the 1967 war, Feisal secured Nasser's agreement to withdraw all his troops from Yemen. Although the Arab leaders at the summit reached the apparently intransigent conclusion that there should be no peace, no direct negotiations and no recognition of Israel, the reality was that, in return for substantial economic aid which would continue 'until the traces of aggression are removed', Nasser agreed that the Arab oil states could lift the half-hearted boycott they had imposed on Britain and the United States during the Six-Day War.

King Feisal was now in a stronger position to press his view that Islamic unity was at least as important as Arab unity. In 1969 he secured the holding of the first conference of Islamic heads of state at Rabat, before the Arab summit for which Nasser was pressing. The Islamic summit was a triumph for Feisal as it agreed to the founding of the Islamic Conference Organization with its permanent headquarters in Jedda. When the Arab summit did take place a few months later, Nasser failed to secure Feisal's agreement that the Arabs should devote all their resources to supporting Egypt in its struggle with Israel. It was a tired and disillusioned Nasser who accepted the US-sponsored cease-fire on the Suez Canal a few months later.

The other major consequence of Egypt's defeat was that the Palestinian Arabs no longer looked to the Arab regular armies led by Egypt to liberate Palestine. Neither the Palestine Liberation Organization created by the Arab heads of state nor the Palestine Liberation Army, excluded from Jordan, played any role in the Six-Day War. On the other hand, al-Fatah, the largest of the unofficial Palestinian guerrilla organizations, had since 1965 been carrying out operations against Israel from Jordan and Syria. After the 1967 war it chose one of its leaders, the small and dynamic Yasir Arafat, as its spokesman. Guerrilla operations against Israel faced formidable difficulties and made little military impression, but in the wake of the war they aroused enormous public enthusiasm. In 1969 al-Fatah and its allies succeeded in ousting the discredited Ahmed Shukairy from the leadership and Arafat was elected chairman of a new PLO executive. The PLO could never be wholly independent of the Arab states as it could only operate in their territory, but it was not controlled by any one of them. A genuine new political entity in the Arab world – the embryo of a future Palestinian state – had emerged.

The radical anti-Western trend among the Arabs which followed the Six-Day War ran counter to the increased influence of Saudi Arabia. But the Palestinian guerrillas, and the Baathists who controlled Syria and Iraq, were no more inclined to accept Egyptian leadership than King Feisal. Nasser could still act as a mediator, however. When in Jordan in September 1970 a civil war broke out between the Jordanian armed forces and Palestinian resistance organizations, which had bitterly criticized his acceptance of the US peace plan, he was able to call the Arab heads of state to an emergency summit in Cairo at which he succeeded in bringing Yasir Arafat and King Hussein together. It was his last political act. On 28 September, as his guests departed, he died – exhausted – of a heart attack.

Gamal Abdul Nasser has sometimes been compared to Muhammad Ali. Like the pasha, for a time he dominated much of the Middle East from Cairo and gave Egypt a power and influence in the world beyond its natural strength. He also for a time successfully exploited the rivalries of stronger powers, but ultimately ended in failure. But the comparison does not go very far. Unlike Muhammad Ali, Nasser was a native Egyptian – the first to rule Egypt for more than 2,000 years – with a passionate love for his country. But he was an Egyptian who developed a genuine belief in the movement to unite the Arabs, of which he saw Egypt as the natural leader. His attempts to modernize and industrialize Egypt and to carry out social and economic reforms were as much intended to create a better educated and fairer society for the mass of Egyptians as to add to the country's strength. After their long period of humiliation, he gave them a new sense of pride and dignity which by no means entirely disappeared after his downfall.

Yet Nasser was essentially a man of his time – that of the decolonization of the Arab world – who, as he perceived himself in his early tract *The Philosophy of the Revolution*, fulfilled a role that was waiting to be filled. His influence was in decline before his early death at fifty-two, and 'Nasserism' – a term he personally disliked – could not long survive his disappearance. In a sense, the way in which he came to personify the Arabs in the eyes of the world gave the Arab East an unnatural and temporary unity following the dismemberment of the Ottoman Empire. After his death, underlying forces came to the surface and soon revealed how fragmented the Middle East had become.

12. The Years of Turbulence

With the ending of the Nasser era, the trends which had been apparent since the Arab disaster of 1967 asserted themselves more strongly. There was a further shift in power and influence towards the oil-producing states of the Middle East. At the same time, Israel, which had suffered a period of economic crisis and self-doubt before the Six-Day War, gained new confidence as the indisputably dominant military power in the region. On the other hand, the Arabs of Palestine, whose suffering and oppression had intensified, began the process of asserting their own national identity.

In the two key states of the Arab East – Syria and Iraq – younger leaders emerged in Hafez al-Assad and Saddam Hussein who, against powerful opposition, succeeded in dominating their country's affairs for at least two decades. Neither could hope to don Nasser's mantle of Arab leadership, if only because of intense rivalry between them, but they were able to make the Syrian and Iraqi nation-states become regional powers of significance. They were helped by the fact that Anwar Sadat, Nasser's successor, effectively abandoned Egypt's claim to Arab leadership by setting out on his own course which led to a separate peace with Israel. The tragic victim of the variety of conflicting religious/political and socio-economic forces in the Middle East was the tiny republic of Lebanon, which from 1975 was devastated by a seemingly endless civil war.

The post-Nasser era was marked by a sharp decline in the influence of the Soviet Union in the Middle East and some improvement in relations between the United States and most of the Arab regimes, although these relations were always endangered by the virtually unswerving US support for Israel. By the end of the 1960s Britain had withdrawn from the Gulf and southern Arabia, and the quasi-imperial British role in the Middle East had been finally liquidated.

The Rise of the Oil States

Before the Second World War, the Middle East countries – principally Iran and Iraq – produced less than 5 per cent of the world's output of crude oil. By 1949, as Kuwait and Saudi Arabia joined the ranks of the big producers and western Europe was ravenous for oil to fuel its post-war recovery, the proportion rose to 12 per cent and a decade later to 25 per cent. As Middle East oil was uniquely plentiful and easy to produce and the economies of the rich industrialized states continued to expand, the upward trend seemed inevitable. By 1970 the Middle East was producing half the oil of the non-communist world.

The Middle Eastern oil-producing states began to become relatively wealthy in the post-war period. In 1950 the oil companies' practice of making modest royalty payments for each tonne of crude oil extracted was abandoned by a new system of a fifty–fifty division of net profits between the oil companies and the ruler or government of the producing state. Since output was also increasing steadily, government revenues rose rapidly. In Iraq they went from £13.9 million in 1951 to £51.3 million in 1953. In Saudi Arabia, where revenues were barely half a million dollars before the Second World War, they reached $56 million in 1950 and over $200 million by 1956.

This new wealth transformed the outlook for these previously impoverished countries and enabled them to embark on the building of schools and hospitals and the creation of an economic infrastructure. But their needs were great and their income was still limited in relation to their population and extensive territories. Iran, which had enjoyed some oil income for two generations, had the largest population – about 20 million in 1960. The exception was Kuwait, whose population of fewer than 200,000 was gathered mainly in Kuwait City at the head of the Gulf. Kuwait's oil revenues increased astronomically – from £3 million in 1949 to £60 million in 1952 – making it the first of the oil city-states (to be followed a decade later by the emirates of Abu Dhabi and Dubai), and it was possible for the modest but exceptionally wise Amir Abdullah Salem al-Sabah (1950– 65) to envisage Western living standards for his people within a generation.

In the 1950s Kuwait was still tied to Britain by the Anglo-Kuwaiti treaty of 1899. To the outside world, and especially to the other Arab states, it appeared as little more than a British colony. For Kuwait to become fully independent was difficult, because of the lack of educated Kuwaitis who would be capable of running the administration. However, in 1961 the Kuwait government asked for the abrogation of the treaty, and Britain complied. The risks were immediately apparent when the unstable Iraqi dictator Abdul Karim Kassem revived a long-standing claim to Kuwait and threatened to occupy it by force. The amir appealed to Britain, which landed troops – the Macmillan government seeing an opportunity to redeem the shame of the Suez episode – but two months later they were withdrawn and replaced by an Arab League force. Kuwait had skilfully demonstrated that, though the other Arab states might formerly have regarded Kuwait as an artificial entity, they now wanted its independence. This was the best guarantee for the country's future.

The Kuwaitis wisely adopted a position of resolute neutrality between the conservative and radical camps in the Arab world. They declared their non-alignment in the Cold War by immediately establishing diplomatic relations with the Soviet Union.

Nothing did more to enhance Kuwait's position than efforts it made to share its new wealth with its less fortunate fellow Arabs. In the year of independence it set up the Kuwait Fund for Arab Economic Development to provide long-term low-interest loans for vital development projects in the other Arab states. The Fund was a pioneer of its kind in the developing Third World.

The rulers of the other Arab Gulf states who were in treaty relationship with Britain – Bahrain, Qatar and the tiny emirates of the Trucial Coast – still saw neither the need nor the possibility of abandoning British protection for full independence. In 1958 oil had been found in vast quantities in Abu Dhabi, which was called a 'new Kuwait', but its population was less than a quarter of Kuwait's and it seemed too small even to become another oil city-state. When the British Labour government decided in 1966 to abandon South Arabia, including the Aden military base, it was assumed that it would reinforce its military base in Bahrain. The British prime minister Harold Wilson still dreamed of a British quasi-imperial role east of Suez. However, in 1968 a drastic British financial crisis caused a sudden volte-face and Britain informed the ruling Arab amirs that it would be finally withdrawing from the Gulf by 1971. This so concentrated the rulers' minds that for the first time they discussed subsuming their rivalries in a federation. Bahrain and Qatar, with the bare minimum of income and population to remain unattached, opted for independence, while the seven shaikhdoms of the Trucial Coast formed the federation of the United Arab Emirates with their capital in Abu Dhabi, the largest and richest of the members. Abu Dhabi's shrewd and able ruler Shaikh Zaid became president of the federation, which has survived for two decades in the face of considerable scepticism.

The wealth of the Arab Gulf states and their role in the international oil industry has given them a significance in the affairs of the Middle East and the rest of the world out of all proportion to the size of their populations. However, this does not mean that the oil-producing states of the Middle East – including those like Iran or Iraq with much larger populations – acquired any significant role in world affairs in the 1950s and 1960s as a consequence of their increasing revenues. They had only a minor share of control over the export and marketing of their crude oil and gas – their largest, and in some cases their only, national resource. Control remained in the hands of the major international oil companies, and the example of the failure of Mohammed Mossadegh's attempt to acquire full control of Iran's oil industry through the act of nationalization served as a potent warning. In 1956 and 1967, attempts by the Arab oil-producing states to use oil as a bargaining counter against Western support for Israel were half-hearted and ineffective and were speedily abandoned. However, this did not mean that these countries abandoned all hope of acquiring more power over their major national resource by means other than nationalization – they all felt a strong sense of grievance. In the 1950s and 1960s, the great flow of cheaply produced oil from the Middle East actually caused the price of oil to fall in absolute terms and even more in real terms. In 1959 the major oil companies twice cut crude oil prices in Venezuela and the Middle East without consulting their host governments. The exasperated reaction of the governments of Iraq, Iran, Kuwait, Saudi Arabia and Venezuela was to form the Organization of Petroleum Exporting Countries (OPEC), which was pledged to restore prices and to force the oil companies to consult OPEC members before any future price changes.

As all the major producing countries joined OPEC, its members accounted for 90 per cent of oil exports outside the communist world. But OPEC was in no way an effective cartel, as its members lacked both the means and the determination to impose pro-rationing – that is, the limiting of production on a quota system – which would have been the only way to raise prices. This still did not mean that they had abandoned their objective of gaining sovereignty over the development of their natural resources. They soon realized that the key was the acquisition of knowledge and experience in the oil industry by their own nationals. Despite the failure of Mossadegh's adventure, Iran, with much the oldest oil industry in the Middle East, had the advantage of a surviving National Iranian Oil Company which from 1957 onwards gained valuable experience in partnership with the Italian state oil company AGIP outside the principal oil-producing areas controlled by the consortium of major American, British and French companies. Iraq, Kuwait and Saudi Arabia all followed Iran's example by establishing their own national oil companies in the 1960s. In 1961 Kassem of Iraq made an ill-advised attempt to make a short cut to control of the country's oil resources by issuing Law 80 expropriating without compensation all the Iraq Petroleum Company's concession area except for the 0.5 per cent of this area in which it was already operating. The company refused to accept the unilateral decision and drastically cut back production and exports so that Iraq, like Iran in 1952, lost its position among the major Middle East oil producers.

However, the oil companies were not to remain triumphant and contemptuous of OPEC for long. In the late 1960s there was the first complete reversal in the international oil market in favour of the oil-producing countries. The closure of the Suez Canal (from 1967 to 1975) and the intermittent closure by the Syrians of the pipeline across their territory caused a shortage of some 25 million tonnes of oil for Europe. This placed a premium on the oil of Libya, where the young anti-Western Colonel Qadaffy replaced the elderly and conservative King Idris in 1969. Libya could exploit the fact that it was dealing with small 'independent' US oil companies outside the magic circle of the major companies. Libya secured an increase in price; it was modest, but a new trend had been set. As the oil companies feared most, what they called a 'leap-frog' effect took place as the three biggest Middle East producers – Iran, Saudi Arabia and Iraq – negotiated through their experienced and Western-trained oil ministers the Tehran agreement of 1971, which secured a further small increase. The agreement was supposed to run until 1976, but in 1973 the third Arab–Israeli war broke out (see below, page 294), the Arab states declared an oil boycott of countries supporting Israel – the first remotely effective use of the 'oil weapon' – and in the ensuing sellers' market caused by a panic fear of shortages among the industrialized nations the price of oil increased at a pace that previously would have seemed unimaginable. By the end of 1974 the price had quadrupled – from about $3.5 a barrel to $15.

This huge shift in income – and hence of power and influence – to a few Middle Eastern states had important political and economic consequences. The symptoms appeared immediately, as within a few days of the ending of the war the nine countries of the European Economic Community and Japan issued a joint declaration on the Arab–Israeli problem which was unprecedentedly favourable to the Arab standpoint.

The shift in power was most immediately apparent in the case of Iran, with its ambitious westernizing shah and its population comparable only to that of Egypt in the region. Although Iran was not involved in the Arab–Israeli war or the Arab oil boycott which triggered the new price rises, it took the lead in exploiting the situation within OPEC, demanding even higher increases in oil prices to compensate for the inflation (partly caused by the price increases themselves) in the prices of industrial goods imported from the West. The shah greatly extended his aim of establishing Iran as a regional superpower, declaring in various press interviews that Iran would become one of the half-dozen leading industrial powers in the world by the end of the century. He dramatically increased the already high spending on Iran's armed forces (the USA having none of the reservations about supplying weapons to Iran that it felt about Israel's Arab neighbours). As part of his determination to impose a 'Pax Iraniana' on the Gulf region and to exclude radical pro-communist elements, he sent some 3,000 troops to Oman to help its sultan against left-wing rebels in Dhufar supported by the quasi-Marxist state of South Yemen. At the same time the original estimates for state expenditure under Iran's fifth five-year plan, for 1973–8, were more than doubled, with the emphasis on the development of the infrastructure and industrialization.

The effect of the price rises on Saudi Arabia was equally spectacular, if somewhat different. Before the oil boom Saudi Arabia, like Iran, had been spending heavily on economic infrastructure, education and health, while about a quarter of its revenues were devoted to defence. Under King Feisal's wise and prudent leadership, the kingdom had moved in a decade from being in debt to having a large surplus. Although it still had huge development needs and much of the population was still living on the edge of poverty, there was no way in which the pace of development could keep pace with the increasing revenues. Similarly, despite the high spending on the armed forces, Saudi Arabia was still a long way from being a significant military power. The kingdom was faced with the novel problem of having to dispose of its surplus income. The quadrupling of oil prices in 1973 raised this problem to a quite different level. Revenues rose from $2.7 billion in 1972 to just under $25 billion in 1975. The Saudi state was receiving every hour as much as its revenues for an entire year in the 1930s.

The pace of Saudi development was enormously accelerated. The second five-year plan, for 1975–80, called for the spending of $142 billion, or ten times that envisaged by the first plan in real terms. The prospect of completing all the main infrastructure projects – roads, airports and sea-ports and power stations – by the end of the decade was now attainable. But the fundamental objective, which had already been decided in the early 1960s, was to make use of the country's gigantic oil and gas resources as the basis for a variety of other industries. The centrepiece of this plan was the creation of two entirely new industrial cities – one at Jubail on the Gulf and the other at Yanbu on the Red Sea. The cost was initially estimated at $70 billion, which was more than that of putting a man on the moon. It was undeniably the biggest single industrial project in history.

Despite these astronomical costs, it was still possible to bring immediate benefits to the Saudi people through a variety of subsidies and the abolition of the few existing taxes.

Saudi Arabia also became one of the world's biggest aid donors, through either its own Saudi Development Fund, created in 1974, or a variety of international agencies. In the 1970s the Saudi Arabian aid programme accounted for more than 10 per cent of the kingdom's GDP – a far higher proportion than that of any of the major industrialized countries. But, despite this massive spending, Saudi Arabia by 1975 had accumulated greater financial reserves than those of the United States and Japan combined.

In less than a generation the impoverished desert kingdom had acquired immense international responsibilities as a financial super-power. It was a key member of the International Monetary Fund and the World Bank. Because it was by far the biggest non-communist oil exporter, with one-third of the proved reserves in the non-communist world, it became OPEC's 'swing' producer, which meant that by raising or lowering its level of output it could influence the international price of oil. The Saudi oil minister, Ahmed Zaki Yamani, became in the 1970s one of the best-known personalities on the world scene.

The assassination of King Feisal in April 1975 by a deranged nephew was a tragic loss for the kingdom which he had brought through a period of peculiar difficulties into an era of international prominence which brought new problems. However, the succession of his brother Khaled was smooth. The new king was in poor health and had little appetite for government. Crown Prince Fahd, an able man with an easy-going temperament but a powerful appetite for administration, took over the main responsibility for running the government (as he continued to do when he succeeded on King Khaled's death in June 1982). The replacement of the austerely aristocratic Feisal by the affable Fahd meant a change of style rather than substance; essentially, Saudi policies remained the same. At home the breakneck pace of economic development was combined with extreme conservatism in social mores. Abroad, Saudi diplomacy was quiet, cautious and generally conciliatory, even when championing the cause of Islam and the Arabs.

In Iraq – the third major oil-state in the Middle East – the Baathists recovered power in 1968, through a military coup after five years in the wilderness. In time they succeeded in gaining a firm grip on the country, largely due to the efforts of the civilian vice-president of the Revolutionary Command Council, Saddam Hussein, a natural leader of ruthless determination who established control over the internal security services and the military wing of the Baath to emerge as the strongman of the regime. President Bakr had little power. In June 1972 Saddam Hussein took the bold step of nationalizing the Iraq Petroleum Company. Times had changed in the twenty years since Iran's attempt to nationalize and the ten years since Kassem had expropriated most of the company's concession area. IPC's parent companies had been losing heavily through their cut-back in Iraq's production. After vigorously protesting, they accepted the act of nationalization in return for fair compensation.

The breaking of the twelve-year impasse in its oil industry combined with the quadrupling of prices in 1973–4 transformed Iraq's economic outlook. Revenues rose from $584 million in 1972 to $7.5 billion in 1974. The prospect of realizing the country's huge natural potential, which had been hampered for so long by political instability, seemed more easily attainable. However, Iraq's perennial problem with its largest Kurdish minority, which had threatened its stability since its foundation as a nation-state, remained. In 1970 Saddam Hussein hoped that this problem had been laid to rest when he reached an agreement with the veteran Kurdish leader Mullah Mustafa al-Barzani and his followers, providing for the appointment of a Kurdish vice-president in the central government and the creation of a Kurdish Autonomous Region in the north-east where the Kurdish language would have equal status with Arabic. But although relations improved for a time, they deteriorated again during the four-year proposed transitional period, and in March 1974 Barzani rejected Baghdad's offer of autonomy as hypocritical and inadequate and rose once again in rebellion. The war between Iraqi forces and Kurdish irregulars was renewed with customary ferocity.

The Kurds conducted their war with support from Iran and from sanctuary inside Iranian territory. Relations between the shah's government and the Iraqi Baath, with territorial disputes and mutual charges of subversion, had been bad for some years and at times on the brink of war. Saddam Hussein decided on drastic action. In March 1975 he accepted public reconciliation with the shah at an Algiers summit meeting of OPEC states. According to the terms of the ensuing agreement, the shah cut off his aid and closed his borders to the Iraqi Kurds. The Kurdish revolt collapsed and Barzani went into exile. However, in return, the Iraqis had to concede that the Iran–Iraq frontier on the Shatt al-Arab waterway – the joint outlet of the Tigris and Euphrates rivers to the Gulf – should pass along the *thalweg* or median line rather than the eastern shore, as had been agreed in 1937 when Iraq had been diplomatically supported by Britain. The resentment felt by the Iraqi Baathists over this concession to its larger neighbour at a time of weakness rankled deeply and would return to the surface in a few years.

The end of the Kurdish rebellion was only temporary, but with the greater feeling of security and vastly increased revenues Iraq was able to play a more prominent role on the Arab stage, where it had been marginalized for some years. Saddam Hussein, who succeeded as president in August 1979, used harsh and dictatorial methods but he showed considerable qualities of leadership. In accordance with his pan-Arab ideology, he invited tens of thousands of Egyptians to settle in Iraq and assist in the country's accelerating development. He also went out of his way to conciliate Iraqi Shiite Muslims who, although numerically superior, had always been dominated both politically and socially by the Sunnis. The sense of Iraqi nationhood received a powerful boost among its Arab population. The new, more dynamic Iraq, with its radical ideology, began to cause some alarm among its more conservative neighbours in the Arabian peninsula.

The intensification of the rivalries between the oil-producing states of the Middle East did not alter the fact that collectively they had gained immensely in world importance as a consequence of the sudden transformation of the international oil industry. In the first place they had formed the vanguard among Third World countries in fulfilling the 1966 UN General Assembly resolution which called for all states to acquire permanent sovereignty over their natural resources. Iraq and Algeria were the first to succeed in nationalizing their oil industries. The more conservative states, such as Saudi Arabia and Kuwait, preferred the course of acquiring increased state participation in the companies operating in their territory. The result was the same: within the decade from the mid-1960s, the role of the international oil companies had been reduced to one of drilling for oil, producing it and marketing it on contract to the owner states.

Within the Arab world, the shift in weight and influence from the traditional political power centres of Cairo and Damascus eastwards to the Arabian peninsula, which was already perceptible in the 1960s, now became fully apparent. Not only manual workers but also those with high skills and professionals from the Levant states and Egypt looked to the eldorado of the Arab Gulf countries as a means of transforming their living-standards.

However, it was their enhanced role in the world economy which gave the oil-producing states their new international status. The decisions of OPEC – in which the Middle East countries were overwhelmingly dominant – were headline material; the investment of the 'petro-dollars' of its members' huge and growing surpluses affected not only international currency markets but the business climate in many of the advanced industrial countries.

There was a reverse side to all this. In the first place the oil states – invariably personified in the Western media as 'the Arabs' – became the target of widespread hostility and resentment. The wealthier industrialized countries blamed them for the global inflation of the 1970s; Third World states without oil of their own saw their development plans shattered by the huge increase in the price of imported fuel. Where the Arab oil states were able to use their increased influence to secure some improved international appreciation of the Arab position on Palestine, those hostile to their cause attributed this to 'oil blackmail'. Israel understandably did everything to encourage this view.

The OPEC states soon discovered the limitations to their power. At the time of the 1973 war the Arab states declared that they would continue their embargo of Western countries supporting Israel until Israel had withdrawn from all occupied Arab lands. But the real fear that the United States and its allies, faced with disaster to their industrialized economies, might invade and occupy their oilfields forced the Arabs to lift the embargo in March 1974. As this fear receded, it became apparent that the quadrupling of prices was leading to a reduction in the rate of consumption and that this, combined with the increase in output, would soon result in a world oil surplus. The industrialized countries, having been startled into awareness of the dangers of dependence on cheap oil, began to seek to conserve their own resources and to exploit alternative sources of energy such as coal, nuclear power or oil-bearing shale deposits. The threat of a collapse in oil prices showed that OPEC was far from being a monolithic bloc – there was a huge difference in outlook between those countries such as Iran or Algeria whose needs exceeded their revenues and those such as Kuwait, Libya or Abu Dhabi, with small populations, which could afford to cut back production in order to maintain prices. This placed additional responsibility on Saudi Arabia as the OPEC 'swing' producer, responsible for one-third of OPEC's output and, with its immense spare capacity, capable of doubling or halving its production in order to reduce or raise prices on the international market.

As a sharp and sometimes acrimonious debate continued within OPEC, it seemed at times that the organization might break up, and its demise was regularly foretold by some international economists. But this did not happen. When disaster threatened, the necessary minimum agreement on the sharing of output was reached. Much of the credit for this was due to Saudi Arabia's willingness to use its power to stabilize the market. OPEC even survived a new and potentially disastrous surge in oil prices in 1979–81 caused by a panic among consumers on the outbreak of the Iraq–Iran war. The artificial boom, which took prices as high as $34 a barrel, was followed by a prolonged glut in the 1980s, during which OPEC with difficulty maintained prices at around $18 a barrel.

OPEC's share of world oil exports fell from its height of 90 per cent when the organization was founded to about 40 per cent as production from non-OPEC sources such as the North Sea, Alaska and Mexico was stepped up. Faced with increasing budget deficits, Saudi Arabia and Kuwait had to begin drawing on their foreign reserves. The enormous material losses caused by the Gulf War meant that Iran and Iraq could no longer be regarded as among the more affluent of Third World countries. However, the underlying fact remained that more than 60 per cent of all the proved reserves of crude oil in the world were in the territory of the states bordering on the Persian/Arabian Gulf, easily accessible and cheap to produce. Hence the relative decline of these countries' importance in the world economy from its high point in the 1970s was likely to be temporary. The creator of the universe gave Arabs and Persians an instrument of power which was discovered and realized in the twentieth century and will no doubt continue to be wielded in the twenty-first.

Egyptian Initiatives

In 1970 the death of Nasser, who had dominated Egypt's political life for sixteen years, left a vacuum. However, when, in declining health, Nasser had left Egypt for an Arab summit meeting in Morocco in 1969, he had appointed Anwar Sadat as his sole vice-president to manage the country's affairs in his absence. Sadat was the same age as Nasser and a former fellow-officer and conspirator (although a civilian at the time of the 1952 revolution); he came from a similar moderately prosperous village background. Although Sadat had been a member of the original Revolutionary Command Council, Nasser never appointed him to ministerial office but he made him the speaker of parliament after 1956 and occasionally used him on important diplomatic missions. The public did not regard him as a political heavyweight; he was the butt of many of the famous Cairene political jokes. However, as the sole vice-president, his election as president was a foregone conclusion under Egypt's constitution.

Initially Sadat promised only to follow in Nasser's footsteps, but a change of emphasis towards more 'Egypt first' policies soon emerged. Relations with Turkey, Iran and some European states which had long been hostile were repaired and improved. There was a perceptible relaxation in the atmosphere of public life.

In April 1971 Sadat made more decisive moves to stamp his mark on the regime. He dismissed his vice-president, Ali Sabry, formerly one of Nasser's closest aides, who had challenged his policies in the Arab Socialist Union, and when, two weeks later, seven ministers and officials resigned *en bloc* he had them arrested and charged with attempting a coup. They had been hoping to maintain a collective leadership with Sadat as little more than a figurehead, but Sadat was popular with the general public, who wanted firm leadership, and he had the support of the army.

Sadat was announcing that the Sadat era had begun. In his speeches he increasingly denounced the errors of the Nasser period. He promised that the police-state apparatus would be destroyed, that the rule of law would be restored and vigorously applied, and that genuinely free parliamentary elections would be held. He called this his Corrective Movement.

But although these moves enhanced his popularity, he was threatened by the lack of any progress in the Arab–Israeli dispute. The US government showed no willingness to follow up the Rogers Plan of 1970 by enforcing an Israeli withdrawal from Sinai. Sadat's offer in February 1971 to reopen the Suez Canal in return for an Israeli withdrawal to the Mitla and Geddi passes in central Sinai received no response. On the other hand, the Soviet Union rejected Egypt's repeated appeals to supply the types of arms that made the crossing of the Canal a feasible alternative. The two superpowers were becoming increasingly interested in their own *détente*. President Nixon and his national security adviser, Henry Kissinger, were not unhappy that a closed Canal should hamper communist supplies to

North Vietnam. On the other hand, Secretary-General Brezhnev did not want to risk another Middle East war on the very doubtful assumption that it would mean Egypt's recovery of the Canal and of Sinai. Israel was naturally content with the *status quo*.

At home Sadat had to face an increasingly restive people. Left-wing students demonstrated against the impasse. The morale of the army, paralysed on the Canal, sank lower. Sadat's repeated promises that action would shortly be taken to recover lost territory aroused increased scepticism.

In July 1972 President Sadat made what seemed like a desperate throw to restore his popularity when he ordered the withdrawal of all the 15,000 Soviet military advisers and service personnel from Egypt. The move was popular because the Soviet presence was widely disliked, especially by the army, but at that stage Egypt had no real alternative to Soviet aid. The West's relations with Egypt were improving but not to the extent of providing arms. Popular impatience exploded in fiercer rioting in January 1973, raising doubts as to whether the Sadat regime could survive.

In fact by this time Sadat had already decided that he had no alternative but to launch against Israel a war of limited objectives which would oblige the West and the Soviet Union to reassess the situation. The risks were enormous, but inaction was no longer possible and he was helped by the fact that Israel and the superpowers contemptuously assumed that he could not possibly succeed.

In preparing the ground, his objective was to secure Syria as his military ally and Saudi Arabia as his diplomatic and financial ally. Relations with the Saudi kingdom had been transformed for the better since Nasser's death, but Syria presented greater difficulty. Its leader, Hafez Assad, was twelve years younger than Sadat and came from Syria's Alawite minority, the sub-Shia sect of Islam which had traditionally formed the Syrian underclass but was disproportionately represented in the armed forces. Assad had risen rapidly in the ranks of both the air force and the Baath Party, in which he belonged to the radical wing in opposition to the more moderate elements such as the veteran Baathist leader Salah Bitar who favoured conciliation of the Syrian middle class. When the radicals or neo-Baathists ousted their opponents in a coup in 1966, Hafez Assad became defence minister. Salah Bitar and Michel Aflaq, the original founders of the Baath, went into exile.

The new regime survived the Palestine catastrophe of 1967 with difficulty. But the experience served to broaden Assad's horizons, and he began to show his masterly aptitude as a political strategist. Seeing that the somewhat faceless men of the regime who belonged to the civilian wing of the Baath were leading the country to disaster by stridently rejecting all political solutions to the Arab–Israeli conflict without being capable of any military initiative, he moved in 1970 to impose the authority of the military wing, secure in the support of the Syrian armed forces. He became prime minister, and in 1971 he took over the presidency with a revised constitution which gave him supreme executive power. Despite the drawback of being an Alawite in predominantly Sunni Syria, he succeeded in creating a highly personified rule which was not under serious challenge. Briefly he became Anwar Sadat's ally, but he would soon become his most formidable opponent. The two men mistrusted each other, and there was a fundamental difference in their war aims. Assad hoped to drive Israel out of Syrian territory and to inflict a sharp military defeat on the enemy. Sadat wanted victory for the essential purpose of obliging the West – especially the United States – to revise its view of the Middle East conflict; he hoped that Washington would take Egypt as seriously as it took Israel.

The Syrians and Egyptians co-ordinated their plans during the summer of 1973 and launched their attack simultaneously on the night of 6 October, the Jewish feast of Yom Kippur. Their initial success was stunning. Within twenty-four hours the Egyptians had put 90,000 men and 850 tanks across the Suez Canal, seized Israel's fortified Bar–Lev line and established bridgeheads along the Canal. Israel lost some 300 tanks. At the same time, three Syrian divisions and an armoured brigade broke through Israel's defences in the Golan Heights and were poised to descend on to the plains of Galilee.

The Arabs' strongest weapon was the element of total surprise, which was helped by Israel's complacency. In the Egyptian forces improved training and officer–men relationships and the high quality of logistical planning helped to maintain morale. Israel's qualitative advantage in air power and armour over Egypt was partially neutralized by the Soviet-supplied missile defence system and by anti-tank 'suitcase missiles' capable of being held by a single infantryman.

Egypt and Syria had deliberately excluded Jordan from joining the offensive because, lacking Soviet missile air defences, Jordan would have been unable to prevent a potentially disastrous Israeli thrust through its territory into southern Syria. But Jordan did send two armoured brigades to Syria after the war began. Iraq contributed three divisions and three fighter squadrons, which suffered heavy casualties on the northern front, while 1,800 Moroccan troops were involved in bitter fighting around Mount Hermon on the first day. The main contribution of the Arab oil-producing states, led by Saudi Arabia, was the use of the oil weapon in declaring an immediate cut in production and a boycott of countries supporting Israel. However, this could not affect the military outcome.

Israel's military recovery was swift, helped by an immediate and massive airlift of the most sophisticated arms from the United States. Israel struck first at Syria, which directly threatened its territory, and by 12 October had pushed the Syrian forces back to their main defensive lines until the front was stabilized some thirty miles from Damascus. (It is possible that Israel feared Soviet intervention if it tried to advance on the Syrian capital.) It was now able to turn its full weight against the Egyptian forces in Sinai, where its initial counter-attacks had been thrown back with further heavy losses. Shortly after the American aid to Israel, the Soviets began an airlift of arms to Egypt. However, on the night of 15 October an Israeli force led by General Ariel Sharon succeeded in crossing to the West Bank of the Canal in a gap between the Egyptian armies and establishing a bridgehead. The Egyptian high command, reluctant for reasons of prestige to withdraw forces from Sinai to deal with the threat, reacted too slowly. The Israelis broke out of their bridgehead and came within fifty miles of Cairo. Egypt's Third Army was surrounded and cut off in Sinai.

The United States and the Soviet Union jointly sponsored a Security Council resolution calling for an immediate cease-fire, the implementation of UN Resolution 242 of 1967 and negotiations for a peace settlement 'under appropriate auspices'. This became UN Resolution 338 on 22 October 1973. Egypt and Israel accepted, as did Syria after twenty-four hours' delay. The cease-fire was due to come into force on 22 October, but it immediately broke down. At this point the superpowers came as close as ever before to a direct clash over the Middle East. The Soviets threatened to respond unilaterally to an Egyptian request for US and Soviet troops to be sent to the Middle East to enforce the cease-fire, and the US responded by placing its forces on Defence Condition Three in the early hours of 25 October. The Soviet Union backed down and agreed instead to the formation of a UN Emergency Force in the Middle East from which the troops of the permanent members of the Security Council would be excluded.

The consequences of this fourth Arab–Israeli war (or fifth if the 1968–70 war of attrition along the Suez Canal is included) were substantial and far-reaching, but they were not all immediately apparent and took time to have their full effect.

Israel had snatched a stunning military victory from initial defeat, but the cost was heavy and the psychological effects were deep. Losses in tanks and planes were much heavier than in previous wars; 2,521 Israelis were killed and 7,056 were wounded – about half of them permanently maimed. Arab losses were greater but much less as a proportion of the population, and the performance of the Arab armies had been sufficient to destroy the myth of Israeli military invincibility. The Israeli public, led by the press, launched a form of witch-hunt to apportion blame, focusing on the Labour coalition cabinet of Mrs Golda Meir and especially the defence minister, Moshe Dayan, who was known to have lost his nerve on the initial surprise Arab assault. The Israeli Labour Party had effectively governed the country since the foundation of the state, with the support of the more affluent and better educated Ashkenazi Jews of European origin, but it now began a slow but inexorable political decline. The gainer was the right-wing ultra-nationalist Likud Party, led by Menachem Begin. This had previously been regarded as unelectable, but it now won widespread support from the mass of Sephardic or oriental Jews, who resented the political and social dominance of the Labour establishment. In elections in March 1977 the normal Labour vote of about 40 per cent sank below 25 per cent, while the Likud won 33.4 per cent. Begin became prime minister, and the prospects darkened for any settlement of the Arab–Israeli dispute.

The near defeat in 1973 reinforced Israel's determination to ensure its military superiority over the combined forces of the Arabs and to use this as the main instrument of its diplomacy. With massive US aid and support, Israel's forces by the end of 1974 were proportionately larger than in October 1973 and qualitatively much improved.

In contrast Egypt's near-victory in Sinai had a harmful effect on President Sadat's diplomacy. Whether or not he totally believed it, he continued to claim that it had indeed been a glorious triumph, and this fiction weakened his hand in subsequent negotiations. On the other hand, he had achieved his most immediate aim of breaking the Middle East impasse and causing a reassessment of US policy in the region. The basis of the Egyptian president's policy was his declared view that the United States always holds 99 per cent of the cards in the Middle East. Immediately following the war he renewed diplomatic ties with Washington after a break of seven years and established a close working relationship with Dr Henry Kissinger (who had been confirmed as secretary of state just two weeks before the outbreak of the war). Through Kissinger's tireless mediation, Sadat secured two military disengagement agreements with Israel – Sinai 1 in January 1974, under which Israeli troops withdrew from the east bank of the Suez Canal and light Egyptian forces occupied a six-mile strip along the shore, and Sinai 2 in September 1975, which took the Israeli forces behind the key Mitla and Geddi passes in Sinai. Early-warning stations manned by US civilians were set up on the passes. The disengagement enabled Egypt to clear and reopen the Canal by June 1975, to start work on the rebuilding and repopulation of the Canal cities and to recover its oilfields in Sinai.

The obverse side to these achievements was that they finally shattered the wartime alliance with Syria. President Assad's mistrust of Sadat turned to bitter contempt as he believed that the Egyptian was ready to opt out of the Arab front against Israel in order to embrace the United States and concur with its wishes. He regarded Egypt's acceptance of US manning of the early-warning stations in Sinai as proof of this. Assad was prepared to end Syria's long diplomatic breach with the United States and to respond to Dr Kissinger's diplomacy as the secretary of state shuttled relentlessly between Middle East capitals, but the Syrian was much more wary than the outgoing and uncomplicated Sadat.

Assad too accepted a disengagement agreement with Israel, engineered by Kissinger in May 1974, under which Israelis withdrew from a small band of territory in the Golan, including its capital, Quneitra, which they first destroyed. But he hoped and believed that it was the United States' intention to proceed to an overall Arab–Israeli settlement based on UN Security Council Resolutions 242 and 338 through the reconvening of the Geneva Middle East peace conference under UN auspices. Later he came to believe that, through his lack of experience in international diplomacy, he had allowed himself to be deceived by Dr Kissinger, who had no intention of trying to persuade Israel to withdraw to its 1967 borders or to agree to Palestinian aspirations. The secretary of state's overriding aim was to exclude the Soviet Union from the Middle East.

President Sadat had no reluctance about excluding the Soviet Union from the Middle East. While his relations with Moscow, which halted all military supplies to Egypt early in 1973, deteriorated to breaking-point, he turned increasingly to the United States and the West. The reversal of alliances corresponded to his deepest political instincts and was reflected in many aspects of his domestic policy. The political opening to the West was matched by an economic and financial open-door policy (*infitah* in Arabic) to encourage non-communist investment in Egypt through tax holidays, freedom to repatriate profits and guarantees against nationalization. Liberalization of the economy brought some results, but the *infitah* policy was often mishandled and critics complained that it failed to treat the real needs of the people. A new-rich class and the old-rich who had recovered their property flaunted their wealth. As foreign banks and businesses opened branches in Cairo, the price of property and services rose steeply. The country's huge indebtedness received some relief from the Arab Gulf states, which were not averse to Egypt's Westward leanings.

Sadat had partially fulfilled his promises to relax the political repression of the Nasser era and to restore the rule of law, but government remained authoritarian. Although he allowed political parties to operate again, the electoral system ensured that the government party dominated parliament totally and the opposition was marginalized. A little criticism was tolerated, but an overwhelmingly pro-government press was ensured. When severe rioting broke out in all major Egyptian cities in January 1977 in protest against sharp price rises for essentials, President Sadat blamed the disturbances exclusively on the left. The rioters had changed Nasser's name, but he declared that Nasser and Nasserism had been dead since 1967. From then on he was openly critical of all aspects of the Nasser era except for the immediate achievements of the revolution in which he had participated. At the same time he gave quiet but effective support and encouragement to the Islamic militant trend as the best barrier against Nasserism and the left. One consequence of the surge in Islamic feeling was that relations between Egyptian Muslims and the Christian Coptic minority deteriorated to an extent that had not occurred in Nasser's time.

The need for a peace settlement with Israel in order to relieve Egypt's disastrous economic difficulties seemed even more acute. The election of Jimmy Carter to the US presidency in 1976 raised the hopes of all the Arab states, as Carter and his secretary of state, Cyrus Vance, showed that they were prepared to launch a serious new initiative through the reconvening of the Geneva peace conference. President Carter spoke openly of the need for Israel to withdraw from occupied Arab lands and became the first US president to refer to the need for a Palestinian 'homeland'. He met all the principal Arab leaders (including President Assad) and convinced them of his sincerity. However, hopes of resuming the Geneva conference always came up against the same obstacle: the refusal of the Israelis, which still had US backing, to have dealings with the Palestine Liberation Organization, which the Arab states had committed themselves to recognizing as the sole legitimate representative of the Palestinian people. The election of a Likud government headed by Menachem Begin in March 1977 further dimmed the prospects of any progress towards peace. President Carter continued to persevere and some hopes were raised on 1 October when a joint US–Soviet statement on the Middle East outlined the principles and objectives for a full Arab–Israeli peace settlement and a common approach to Geneva. This was the first superpower accord on the Middle East of its kind, and the first occasion on which the US officially subscribed to the term 'the legitimate rights of the Palestinians'.

The superpower agreement seemed like a milestone; but it was not to be. President Carter, taken aback by the harshness of the reaction of Israel and its Zionist supporters in the US, emphasized that all US moves would be co-ordinated with Israel – the United States still felt committed to Dr Kissinger's undertaking to Israel that it would never expect it to deal with the PLO.

Meanwhile, President Sadat had been planning his own dramatic initiative without the knowledge of his foreign minister and most of his advisers. Having sounded out the Israeli government's reaction through mediators in Romania and Morocco, on 9 November 1977 he announced to an astonished Egyptian parliament that he would go to Jerusalem to address the Israelis directly in the Knesset. Mr Begin warmly responded to this proposal and the visit was fixed for 19 November.

Sadat was impatient, and the high theatre of his action appealed to him. He was also happy to take a road to peace which excluded the Soviet Union he detested. But while most of the rest of the world was delighted and admiring, the Arab states were generally dismayed. Some were simply shocked at the gesture of speaking directly to the enemy in of all places the Holy City of Jerusalem, but all sensed that Egypt, despite Sadat's vigorous denials, was starting on the road towards a separate peace with Israel. That was the accusation from an angry President Assad when Sadat vainly tried to reassure him.

Sadat's speech to the Knesset caught the imagination of millions around the world who watched the spectacle on television. He spoke with eloquence and dignity, invoking the spirit of tolerance in Islam and the equality of Jews, Muslims and Christians in the sight of God. But he also spoke of Palestinian rights and his rejection of Israel's annexation of Jerusalem. The occasion revealed the immense gulf between him and the Israeli leaders. In his polite but intransigent reply, Begin said that the Jews were back in their God-given land of Israel by right and there was no question of it being divided. He was not specific about territory but left the clear impression that Judaea and Samaria (i.e. the West Bank) were part of Israel and that the 'Arabs of the Land of Israel' (i.e. the Palestinians) at best were tolerated guests.

Peace negotiations between Egypt and Israel began almost immediately. The United States had not been privy to Sadat's initiative, but President Carter now committed his country to 'full partnership' in the peace process. His attempts to persuade other Arab states to revise their attitude were in vain. Libya, Algeria, Syria, the PLO, South Yemen and the Yemen Arab Republic formed a 'Front of Steadfastness' to oppose Sadat. (Iraq shared their views but failed to join because of its regime's antagonism towards Syria.) Saudi Arabia and Jordan were apprehensive but prepared to await events.

Sadat repeatedly affirmed that he had no intention of abandoning the Palestinian cause, despite PLO ingratitude, but his assertions carried declining conviction. He threatened to break off the negotiations with the United States and Israel, but he could not afford them to fail, as the Israelis well knew. A proud and inordinately vain man, he was infuriated by Arab criticisms. He broke off relations with the Front of Steadfastness states and closed down the PLO offices in Cairo. He had promised his poverty-stricken people that there would be no war and had hugely raised their expectations. Moreover, he had aroused a spirit of Egyptian nationalism based on a feeling that Egypt had made the greatest sacrifices in blood and treasure on behalf of the Arabs, who were now showing their ingratitude.

In September 1978 President Carter succeeded in bringing Sadat and Begin together at his Camp David retreat where, after twelve days of negotiations, two agreements were signed: 'a framework for peace in the Middle East', which was intended to deal with the Palestinian question, and 'a framework for peace between Israel and Egypt'.

The second of these was fairly straightforward – providing for the restoration of Egyptian sovereignty over its territory (except for the partial demilitarization of Sinai) and the normalization of relations between the two countries. The former was more complex, providing for a transitional period in the occupied territories of a maximum of five years during which a local 'self-governing authority' would be established to provide 'full autonomy' for the inhabitants. The 'final status' of the occupied territories would be decided before the end of the transitional period. There were loopholes and ambiguities. It was unclear who would represent the Palestinians in the negotiations; Jordan was expected to take part, but Jordan had not accepted and was refusing to speak on the Palestinians' behalf. Nothing was said about the vexed question of the future of Jewish settlements in the occupied territories. Above all there was nothing to link the two agreements on peace between Israel and Egypt and a solution of the Palestine problem. On this crucial point Sadat gave way on the last day of the negotiations when he was threatening to leave. He said it was a response to the urgent pleading of President Carter.

Egypt was now set on the inevitable course towards a separate peace with Israel which President Assad and others had predicted. No serious obstacles to this remained. The most difficult obstacle was the presence on Egyptian territory of Jewish settlements which had been established since 1967, but Israel saw the neutralizing of Egypt – the biggest Arab military power – as a far greater prize. Ironically, it was some politicians of the more moderate Israeli

Labour Party who were anxious about giving up a strategic hold on Sinai. For Mr Begin, what mattered most was that Israel could consolidate its hold on 'Judaea and Samaria'. He never concealed his belief that Israeli sovereignty extended over them, even if for tactical reasons he refrained from declaring this officially. (Israel did, however, on 30 July 1979 declare the whole of Jerusalem, including the Arab eastern part, to be part of the united and eternal capital of Israel. As a result the slim chance that the Palestine part of the Camp David agreements might achieve anything disappeared.)

The Treaty of Washington was signed on 26 March 1979, bringing to an end thirty-one years of the state of war between Israel and Egypt. Ambassadors were exchanged in 1980, and Israel finally evacuated Sinai on schedule in March 1982. The borders were open, but relations were hardly those normal for neighbouring states. Trade and economic exchange remained minimal and, although Israeli tourists began to come to Egypt, hardly any Egyptians went to Israel. Three decades of hot and cold wars were replaced by a cold peace. Yet the treaty endured, because it was greatly in Israel's interest and cancellation was scarcely an option for Egypt. Israel made clear it would regard cancellation as a *casus belli*, and Egypt, having turned to the West and renounced its friendship with the Soviet Union, was heavily dependent on the United States, which was Israel's ally.

Egypt was not only tied to the United States: it faced isolation from nearly all the Arab states. At a Baghdad summit meeting in November 1978, following the Camp David accords, they decided to move the headquarters of the Arab League from Cairo to Tunis. They agreed to impose sanctions on Egypt if the accords led to a peace treaty, which Saudi Arabia, Jordan and the moderate states still hoped would not happen. After the signing of the Treaty of Washington in March 1979, they closed their embassies and broke off trade and diplomatic relations with Egypt. The Arab oil states cut off the aid and investment which was crucial to Egypt. A Tunisian lawyer, Chedli Klibi, was elected secretary-general of the League – the first non-Egyptian to hold that post in the twenty-four years of the organization's existence.

For a whole decade Egypt stood outside the mainstream of Arab politics – no longer the centre of gravity of the Arab world. But its isolation could never be complete. Most of the hundreds of thousands of Egyptians working in the Arab oil states remained. Cairo was still the greatest Arab city, and a major centre of Arab cultural life. Fewer Arabs visited Egypt, but a range of private contacts continued. But the fact remained that the political decisions made in Cairo were no longer of major importance in the affairs of the Middle East.

For their part the Egyptian people had mixed feelings about the trend of events. While there was relief that there was to be 'no more war', as Sadat had promised, there was disappointment that peace had brought fewer benefits than had been hoped, except to the small class of beneficiaries of the *infitah*. Although US aid to Egypt now came close to matching that to Israel, it made much less difference to Egypt's larger population. But the doubts went deeper than this.

Sadat had touched a chord of Egyptian nationalism and resentment against the other Arabs. Some of the country's leading intellectuals, who had once been supporters of the Nasser Revolution and its pan-Arabism, rationalized these feelings by talking of an Egyptian identity and destiny which were separate from those of the other Arabs. Yet Egyptians could not easily abandon their feeling that Egypt was naturally placed for Arab leadership and for a major role in the wider Islamic world. Sadat's declarations that the Arabs must first beg for Egypt's forgiveness if Egypt was to help them were taken seriously only by a small group of sycophants. There were growing doubts about the president's eagerness for Egypt to replace Israel as the United States' principal surrogate in the Middle East.

As Sadat's natural vanity was fed by the adulation of the West's media, he became increasingly intolerant of criticism at home. His earlier reputation for liberalism was destroyed by new repressive laws to restrict political life and muzzle freedom of expression. Islamic activists, whom he had originally encouraged as a bulwark against the left, now turned outspokenly against him because of his peace with the Zionist enemy and his contemptuous hostility towards the Islamic Revolution in Iran. In September 1981, imagining a concerted move to overthrow him, Sadat ordered the arrest of 1,500 personalities covering the whole political spectrum and including Muslim divines and Coptic bishops. One month later, during a Cairo military parade, he was assassinated by a small group of Islamic extremists within the army. The great majority of Egyptians did not approve of the murder, and there was no general uprising of the Muslim population as the assassins had hoped, but neither did the Egyptian public grieve. The crowds in the Cairo streets were unusually silent.

The succession of Vice-President Husni Mubarak, who was slightly wounded in the attack, proceeded smoothly. A former head of the air force, Mubarak was regarded as honest and straightforward, if uninspiring. He lacked the very different kinds of political charisma of his two predecessors, but he showed both wisdom and common sense. He released Sadat's political prisoners and established a dialogue with the opposition. There was no question of the presidency abandoning its authoritarian power, but he successfully calmed the domestic political scene. At the same time he halted the media attacks on Egypt's fellow-Arabs and began his country's rehabilitation in the Arab world. The process was gradual, and restrained by the necessity of maintaining the peace treaty with Israel and the dependent relationship with the United States, but it was helped by the inescapable fact that Egypt's isolation had drastically reduced the Arabs' political strength in the world. With the notable exception of Syria, the Arab regimes had good reason to want Egypt back in the Arab fold.

Israel/Palestine and the Lebanese Victim

Israel's devastating victory in the June 1967 war and the catastrophe suffered by the Arab armies provoked the rise of the Palestinian guerrilla organizations as an independent force in the Arab world. However, their significance was political rather than military. Israel was not seriously concerned by guerrilla activity on its new borders – casualties had been considerably heavier on the Suez Canal front during the 1969–70 war of attrition. The Israeli defence minister, Moshe Dayan, exercised virtually complete control over the occupied territories of the West Bank and Gaza, and he adopted a policy of consolidating Israel's economic and political hold over them while awaiting a time when the Arabs would be ready to make peace on Israel's terms. Israel wanted direct negotiations leading to peace treaties with the neighbouring Arab states, and it did not consider it had any prior obligation under UN Security Council Resolution 242 to withdraw from all the occupied territories. In fact it envisaged only a partial withdrawal and continued military control of the occupied territories even in the event of peace. The permanence of the occupation was underlined by the launching of a colonization drive in 1968 with a series of military settlements which were established along the Jordan Valley. Most of these were later handed over to civilian settlers. There was no question of negotiating with leading Palestinians for the establishment of an autonomous Palestinian state on the West Bank, although this idea was entertained by some prominent Israelis outside the government.

General Dayan's method in the occupied territories was to deal firmly with opposition and unrest while making the occupation as inconspicuous as possible. An 'open-bridges' policy which allowed Arabs of the occupied territories to travel to Jordan and other Arab states was maintained.

For their part the Palestinian guerrilla organizations, grouped together in the reconstructed Palestine Liberation Organization, did not at this stage foresee the establishment of a small Palestinian state alongside Israel any more than the Israelis. The Palestinian National Covenant, which was adopted in 1968 by the Palestine National Council (the Palestinian quasi-parliament in exile) looked forward to the total Arab liberation of Palestine and the disappearance of the state of Israel. Palestine would be for the Palestinians, who were defined (Article 5) as 'the Arab citizens who were living permanently in Palestine until 1947' and 'whoever is born to a Palestinian Arab father after this date'. Jews who were living permanently in Palestine 'until the beginning of the Zionist invasion' would also be considered Palestinians (Article 6), but by implication this excluded the majority of Israeli citizens.

Despite their failure to cause Israel any serious military problem, the Palestinian guerrilla organizations enjoyed high prestige. Their morale reached a climax with the battle of Kerameh in the Jordan valley in March 1968, when the Jordanian army and Palestinian commandos co-operated in a major engagement against an Israeli reprisal raiding force which inflicted heavier losses on Israel than on previous occasions. But the increasingly independent activities of the Palestinian organizations, which brought heavy Israeli reprisals against Jordanian territory, threatened Jordan's stability. The Jordanian civilian and military authorities were divided between those who wished to accommodate the commandos and those who wanted to restrict and control their activities. Both King Hussein and the PLO chairman Yasir Arafat favoured compromise, but the king had to contend with increasing anti-Palestinian resentment in his army, especially among ultra-loyalist elements of beduin origin, while

Arafat was unable to control and discipline the smaller extremist groups in the PLO. Under pressure, the king agreed to the formation of a provisional military government.

The spark of civil war was lit in September 1970 when the left-wing Popular Front for the Liberation of Palestine hijacked three Western airliners to a deserted airstrip in east Jordan. From 17 September fighting was general between army units and guerrillas until on 25 September a cease-fire was arranged by an inter-Arab mission representing Arab heads of state who had hastily met in Cairo at President Nasser's invitation (shortly before his death). King Hussein and Arafat reached a fourteen-point truce agreement providing for a return to civilian rule. Although the guerrillas still held some strongholds in north Jordan and certain quarters of Amman, they had been fatally weakened by the fighting. The king made prime minister one of his closest advisers, Wasfi Tel, who adopted an uncompromising attitude towards the guerrillas.

Gradually the full weight of the Jordanian army was used to expel the guerrillas from the country, and by July 1971 their last military bases in Jordan had been eliminated. Other Arab states expressed outrage but could do little to help the guerrillas, and Jordan, although isolated, stood firm. The frustration and despair of the Palestinians gave rise to the self-styled 'Black September' movement, a shadowy and undisciplined group bent on revenge. In September 1971 Wasfi Tel was assassinated in Cairo. Black September was responsible for a series of incidents – mainly outside Israel – involving hijacking, bombing and attempts to take hostages. The most sensational, during the Olympic Games in Munich in September 1972, led to the death of nine Israeli athletes who had been taken hostage by Black September terrorists. The world reacted with horror, but the Palestinians, with nothing left to lose, felt that their cause was at least attracting public attention.

The expulsion of the Palestinian guerrillas from Jordan caused the PLO to concentrate its activities in the one remaining Arab country where they could enjoy some freedom of action – Lebanon. While many Lebanese – especially the Muslims – had some sympathy for the Palestinians' struggle, the majority of Lebanese Christians were hostile and the Maronite political leaders demanded that the guerrillas be excluded from Lebanese territory. But the Lebanese state, built on a delicate political compromise, was weak and unable to defend its interests. All Lebanese were sharply aware of their country's defencelessness in the face of Israeli reprisals against Palestinian guerrilla activities.

For a time the clashes between the guerrillas, the Lebanese army and armed civilian groups of various loyalties were prevented from deteriorating into a general conflict through a series of patched-up compromise agreements achieved through Arab mediation. But such mediation became increasingly difficult after 1971, when the PLO transferred its headquarters from Jordan to Lebanon, where it had the last opportunity for building up a 'state within a state'.

The 1973 Arab–Israeli war and its aftermath brought some benefits to the case of the Palestinians on the international level. The feeling that Israel was no longer invincible, the improved performance of the Arab armies and the great increase in wealth and influence of the Arab oil states were reflected in a new awareness of the Palestinian struggle for self-determination. West European states inclined more strongly towards the Arabs, while Cuba and twenty-seven African states, several of which had been friends of Israel, broke off diplomatic relations with Israel by the end of 1973. In September 1974 the UN General Assembly for the first time agreed to include 'the Palestine question' as a separate item on its agenda and then invited the PLO to take part in the debate, and on 13 November Yasir Arafat, accorded the honours of a head of state, addressed the UN General Assembly. 'I have come bearing an olive branch and a freedom fighter's gun. Do not let the olive branch fall from my hands,' he said. The PLO now had quasi-official status in various international organizations.

After the UN's action the Arab states felt they could do no less in recognizing the PLO. At their summit meeting in Rabat in October 1974, King Feisal of Saudi Arabia took the lead in persuading a reluctant King Hussein to accept a resolution endorsing the right of the Palestinian people to establish an international authority under the direction of the PLO 'in its capacity as the sole legitimate representative of the Palestinian people'. Subsequent attempts to dispute this title by proposing an alternative Palestinian leadership consistently failed.

Yet there was a weakness at the heart of the PLO's position, as Arafat could not fail to be aware. The 1973 war had helped its cause, but the Palestinians had played no part in the decision to go to war and had fought only minor actions on the Lebanese border. World recognition of the justice of Palestinian claims depended heavily on Arab diplomacy, and the key Arab states (notably Egypt) wanted peace. The prospect of recovering Palestine for the Arabs was as remote as ever.

This paradox was reflected within the Palestine Liberation Organization. Some of the Palestinian leaders, including Yasir Arafat, had reached the conclusion that Palestinian aims should be scaled down to the creation of a Palestinian 'mini-state' in the West Bank and Gaza and that the PLO should seek a settlement in co-operation with Egypt through a UN-sponsored conference at which they would be represented. This was bitterly opposed by others – the rejectionists – who refused to abandon, even temporarily and tactically, the goal of making the whole of Palestine a 'democratic, non-sectarian state'. Arafat and his colleagues did not admit that they had abandoned that aim, which was the theme of his speech to the UN General Assembly, but, as he said later, it was a dream and 'Is it a crime to dream?' The reality was that the Palestinian mini-state was now the objective, and the formula that was successfully adopted was to have the Palestine National Council pass a resolution calling for the establishment of a 'national authority' on any Palestinian territory that might be liberated.

However, as Israel, with the support of the United States, stood by its refusal to grant any recognition to the PLO, the chances of recovering even a small portion of territory to set up a PLO state seemed remote. The PLO concentrated on building up its shadow state in Lebanon. Here the situation was rapidly deteriorating and the Palestinian presence was far from being the only reason. The Shiite Muslims who were the majority of the population in southern Lebanon and had traditionally been the country's social and political underclass had found a charismatic new leader in Imam Moussa al-Sadr, a cleric of Iranian origin, who organized a Movement of the Disinherited with its own armed militia – Amal ('hope'). The deprived southerners suffered most from Israel's reprisal raids against the Palestinian guerrillas, and some fled their homes to the relative safety of the suburbs of south Beirut. The social and economic disparities in Lebanon, always dangerously strong, were being increased by the effects of the great Middle East oil boom, which brought added prosperity to the country's affluent business classes. Meanwhile the plethora of armed militias representing Lebanon's many sects and political trends acted with increasing independence in open defiance of the inadequate Lebanese armed forces.

In 1975 the unrest developed into full-scale civil war. At first it was mainly a conflict between the right-wing Christian militia and an alliance of leftists under the leadership of the Druze politician Kemal Jumblatt. The conflict was fuelled from outside by the supply of arms and money from various quarters, including Israel, some Arab states and very probably the CIA. The Palestinian leaders initially tried to keep out of the civil war but were dragged in remorselessly, until by January 1976 they were fully engaged on the side of the leftists. After initial successes, the leftist–Palestinian alliance gained control of some 80 per cent of the country, but at this point Syria began to intervene in force, fearing that Lebanon would be partitioned into a tiny Christian state, which would be in alliance with Israel, and a remainder in the hands of Lebanese Muslims and Palestinians, outside Syria's control. President Assad, like any Syrian leader, regarded Lebanon as a vital Syrian interest. He also saw the Palestinian cause as the responsibility of all the Arabs – and especially of Syria, as the leading front-line state with Israel. He did not believe the PLO should act independently, and his personal relations with Arafat were characterized by deep mutual distrust.

Syria's intervention led to a bizarre alliance with the right-wing Lebanese Christians which, although short-lived, was sufficient to turn the tide against the leftist–Palestinian coalition. The Arab states reluctantly endorsed the presence of Syrian troops in Lebanon as the main body of an Arab peace-keeping force. The civil war died down, leaving some fifty thousand dead and many more injured, while about one million Lebanese were driven from their homes. As in all such wars, atrocious acts of massacre, kidnapping and murder were committed by both sides.

With their usual vigour the Lebanese set about restoring their economy. Trade and banking revived; the Lebanese currency remained strong and it seemed that Lebanon could not easily lose its commercial pre-eminence in the region. But it was soon apparent that the civil war had subsided rather than ended. The fears and hatreds which had been intensified by the war remained, and the Syrian forces were incapable of disarming the sectarian militias and pacifying the whole country. The Lebanese Christians, who had welcomed them in 1976, soon came to detest the presence of Syrian troops and demand their withdrawal. But Syrian domination was opposed by some in the opposite camp, too. In March 1977 the Druze leader Kemal Jumblatt was assassinated, almost certainly by Syrian military intelligence. Moreover, the continuing presence of the Palestinian quasi-state in Lebanon meant that Israel always found cause to intervene. The alliance between Israel and various branches of the Christian militia, which had begun during the civil war, continued to develop.

Since Israel's earliest days, its leaders had seen the advantages of promoting Christian separatism in Lebanon and the creation of a Maronite-dominated Christian state which would be in alliance with Israel. In southern Lebanon the Israelis had an opportunity to make a start by helping to establish a friendly border enclave controlled by a Lebanese Christian officer who had their full support. By Israeli–Syrian mutual agreement, mediated through the Americans, Syrian forces kept a substantial distance from the Israeli frontier. Lebanese southerners now crossed the 'open border' into Israel for refuge or medical treatment. The great majority were Shiites, and some of them, embittered by their suffering and antagonized by the frequently domineering and insensitive attitude of the PLO fighters towards them, joined the Christian militia.

The situation became more dangerous with the advent to power in Israel in May 1977 of a right-wing government headed by Menachem Begin. The virtual certainty that Israel need no longer be concerned about war with Egypt after President Sadat's visit to Jerusalem in November meant that Israel was free to concentrate on its northern front. In March 1978 it launched its first full-scale invasion of south Lebanon, with the aim of destroying the Palestinian guerrilla bases. The Palestinians melted away northwards and it was mainly the Lebanese who suffered. On this occasion, firm UN Security Council action, backed by President Carter, secured an Israeli withdrawal by June and the installation of a UN International Force in Lebanon (UNIFIL). But Israel continued to maintain and support the friendly border enclave over which UNIFIL had no control.

The years 1979–81 were a period of uneasy stagnation in the Arab–Israeli conflict. It became fully apparent that the conclusion of a separate peace between Egypt and Israel was not going to lead to any comprehensive settlement; in fact it made this more difficult in that Israel, faced with an Arab front in disarray from which the strongest member was excluded, was even more determined not to yield to the demands of Palestinian nationalism. In June 1980 the members of the European Community issued what was called the Venice Declaration, in which they said that the PLO should be 'associated' with any Middle East peace negotiations. But Israel could afford to ignore such suggestions as long as the Europeans still accepted President Sadat's view that the United States held 99 per cent of the cards in the Middle East.

In July 1986 the Israelis formally annexed east Jerusalem and declared the united city their permanent capital. In August 1981 the Saudi Arabians put forward their own plan, to be guaranteed by the UN, providing for Israel's withdrawal from the Arab territories occupied in 1967 and the creation of a Palestinian state in the West Bank and Gaza with east Jerusalem as its capital. All states in the region, including Israel by implication, should be able to live in peace. But Saudi Arabian influence, although strong, was not enough to secure Arab endorsement. A new disturbing factor had emerged in the outbreak, in 1980, of full-scale war between Iran and Iraq. This diverted attention in the Middle East and the rest of the world away from the Arab–Israeli conflict and caused further division among the Arab states.

During this period, Lebanon hardly enjoyed peace. Violence between sects and within sects, with their inevitable reprisals, and massive Israeli retaliation for Palestinian guerrilla attacks resulted in many thousands of dead and injured. Some partial respite was achieved when, in September 1981, the PLO arranged an unofficial cease-fire with Israel through US mediation. But Israel had not abandoned its aim of finally destroying the Palestinian quasi-state in Lebanon. An assassination attempt on the Israeli ambassador in London by young Palestinian extremists provided Israel with a pretext: on the following day – 6 June 1982 – it launched another full-scale invasion of Lebanon but this time it did not halt at the River Litani, some twenty miles from the border, but went on to besiege Beirut for two months. Thousands died and tens of thousands were made homeless in the capital and the cities and villages of the south.

The Arab states were appalled, but frustrated and humiliated because of their inability to influence events. Many Lebanese

Christians greeted the Israeli invaders as friends and deliverers, while even some Muslims showed that they had come to detest the Palestinian presence in their country. Syrian forces put up some resistance but, after Israel destroyed their missile sites without losing any planes, Syria agreed to a cease-fire. The Israelis secured a stranglehold on the PLO headquarters in Beirut but the Palestinians, supported by some Lebanese allies, were able to demonstrate that what would have been Israel's first occupation of an Arab capital would be extremely costly. Faced with tremendous odds, Palestinian fighters put up a fair resistance although they lacked an effective strategy.

The Arab gains from this – which might be called the sixth Arab–Israeli war – were negative but important. The heavy civilian casualties among Lebanese and Palestinians, the huge destruction of property and the callous saturation bombardment of Beirut all helped to swing world opinion against Israel, and began to divide public opinion inside Israel itself.

President Reagan, responding to desperate appeals from King Fahd of Saudi Arabia, began to show public disapproval of Israel's actions and to exert pressure for restraint. Through US mediation an agreement was reached whereby Israel would stay outside Muslim west Beirut and Yasir Arafat and 13,000 Palestinian fighters would be evacuated under US military supervision. The evacuation began on 22 August. On the following day Bashir Gemayel, the young leader of the combined Christian militias, was elected president under the shadow of Israeli guns. But on 14 September, before he could take office, he was assassinated – almost certainly by Syrian agents – and Israeli troops, against vigorous but vain US protests, entered west Beirut 'to maintain order'. Two days later atrocious massacres of Palestinian civilians by Lebanese rightist militiamen took place in the Sabra and Shatila refugee camps – in areas now under Israeli military control and without any Israeli attempt to foresee or prevent them. The event provoked huge protests by the peace movement in Israel. The frustrated Arabs could only denounce the USA for breaking its promise that Palestinian civilians would be protected after the fighters had been withdrawn.

Nevertheless, there seemed for a time to be a chance of a new understanding between the United States and the Arabs. On 1 September 1982 President Reagan announced comprehensive proposals for a Middle East settlement which for the first time showed equal concern for Arab and Israeli interests. Although he ruled out the creation of a Palestinian state, he said that permanent Israeli control over the occupied territories was unacceptable and proposed instead the establishment of an autonomous Palestinian entity linked with Jordan. While Mr Begin angrily rejected the Reagan plan, the response of the Arab states was more conciliatory. At a summit meeting in Fez, they put forward their own plan – which was in fact identical with the Saudi proposals of the previous year. Although it differed from the Reagan plan in important respects – notably in demanding the creation of an independent state – the US and the Arab proposals were not too far apart for their reconciliation to be inconceivable. On the other hand, US–Israeli relations were distinctly cool.

However, this was only one of many false dawns in United States relations with the Arabs. It was not only that the US government in reality still supported Israel in its rejection of Palestinian self-determination; the more immediate problem was that US strategy in the Middle East ignored the role of Syria and, by extension, that of Syria's ally, the Soviet Union, which had more than replaced the Syrian weapons lost in the fighting with Israel. The Kissinger Doctrine of excluding the Soviet Union as far as possible from Middle East diplomacy still held.

In September 1982, US marines returned to Lebanon to form part of an international peace-keeping force with similar Italian and French and much smaller British contingents. United States declared policy was to secure the evacuation of all foreign troops – Israelis, Syrians and the remaining Palestinians – to enable the new Lebanese president, Amin Gemayel, to establish the authority of the Lebanese state throughout its territory. Vigorous US mediation between Lebanese and Israeli negotiators finally produced, on 17 May 1983, an agreement between Israel and Lebanon which fell short of a peace treaty but which was clearly intended to establish normal relations between the two countries in every respect. But President Assad, who was outraged at this attempt to remove Lebanon from Syria's influence and link it with Israel, had the means of aborting the agreement. Neither the United States nor Israel was able to force him to withdraw his troops, and the Lebanese state was far too weak. In November, suicide-bombers blew up the US marine headquarters and that of the French contingent, leaving more than three hundred dead. Although the United States attributed the direct responsibility to extremist Shiite militia, it considered that Syria must have approved and backed the action. The United States identified Syria, with its Soviet backers, as the obstacle not only to a settlement of the Lebanese problem but also to peace in the whole area. Its response was to move closer to Israel – with Israel's actions in invading Lebanon forgotten and forgiven – by adopting a common strategy towards an Arab–Israeli settlement and greatly increasing military and economic aid.

The United States was forced to accept that its strategy for Lebanon had failed. The American public would not have accepted any deeper involvement of US troops in the hopeless cause of pacifying Lebanon. In February 1984 the US marines were withdrawn from Beirut, and the other European contingents soon followed.

Israel also found that the objectives of its invasion of Lebanon were far from achieved. The PLO structure in Lebanon had been destroyed and its fighters scattered, but Arafat and the PLO survived and eventually made their headquarters in Tunis. Israel's dream of having a friendly neighbour to the north, dominated by Christian Maronites, had rapidly faded. The Israeli forces were quite unable to control the multi-factional civil war that was raging and turning Lebanon into a partitioned country with shifting internal borders. In southern Lebanon the mainly Shiite population, who had not initially resisted the Israeli invasion because of their sufferings caused by the Palestinian presence, turned bitterly against the Israelis, who too often behaved as conquerors. The Israeli forces faced increasing attacks from Lebanese fighters, who now included members of Hizbollah ('the party of God') – Shiite extremists supported by revolutionary Iran. As Israeli casualties mounted, Israel's intervention in Lebanon became increasingly unpopular at home.

In September 1984 the Israeli Labour leader Shimon Peres became prime minister of a Labour/Likud coalition after a tied election.

The Labour Party had not been responsible for the invasion of Lebanon, although it had not effectively opposed it. By June 1985 Peres was able to secure the withdrawal of Israeli forces from Lebanon. However, Israel kept military advisers with the South Lebanon army, composed mainly of Christians in a ten-mile buffer zone along the border, and to this extent could still interfere in Lebanon's internal affairs. But it had abandoned its opportunity to influence directly the character of Lebanon's regime.

It seemed to many that, although Arafat and his PLO colleagues had survived the siege of Beirut, their organization's effectiveness was ended. Moreover a worse blow was to come in April 1983 when a rebel movement within the PLO, supported by Syria, declared Arafat's leadership to be corrupt and denounced what was seen as his intention to abandon the armed struggle in favour of diplomacy in collaboration with Jordan. Expelled from Syria by President Assad, Arafat made his headquarters in Tripoli in north Lebanon, where he faced attacks by the rebels backed by Syrian and Libyan troops. After lengthy negotiations, Arafat and 4,000 loyalists were evacuated by Greek ships flying the UN flag.

This was surely the end. The PLO's fighters were scattered to the farthest corners of the Arab world, and its headquarters was 2,000 miles away from Palestine in Tunis, at the opposite end of the Mediterranean. But in fact these disasters caused most of the four million Palestinians, whether in the diaspora or in Palestine, to cling more tightly to Arafat and the PLO as the only effective symbols of national identity. To the outside world the pudgy and half-shaven figure of Arafat seemed to lack appeal, but to his own people he had powerful charisma and magnetism, especially when speaking in his Arabic tongue rather than coping with Western interviewers. There was still no real alternative to him as 'Mr Palestine', as Israel acknowledged by attempting to destroy him and his headquarters in an air raid on Tunis in October 1985. He was also a subtle politician. He infuriated Western well-wishers by refusing to state clearly what they knew to be true – that he was ready to recognize Israel and abandon the armed struggle in return for an independent Palestinian state – and he opened himself to the charge of changing his words to suit his audience, but he knew that he had first to convince the great majority of Palestinians or their movement would shatter and dissolve. It was to prevent internal differences from emerging that he consistently refused, despite the urging of outside sympathizers, to form a provisional government-in-exile whose policy decisions would have had to be binding on all its members.

The PLO survived as an organization, and Arafat pursued a diplomatic offensive as he shuttled between the many capitals of the world that were ready to receive him, but Western governments remained wary and the United States continued to back Israel's refusal to have any dealings with the PLO. Both countries still hoped that the Palestine problem could be solved through an agreement with Jordan which would leave the Palestinians in the occupied territories under some form of Jordanian–Israeli condominium. In February 1985 the stalemate appeared to be broken down when King Hussein and Arafat agreed on a joint Palestinian–Jordanian peace initiative, based on the exchange of territory for peace. But a year later the initiative collapsed, for reasons which had become familiar: the Jordanian monarch felt that Arafat had reneged on his undertaking to declare his willingness to recognize Israel, while Arafat refused to give up this last Palestinian card of negotiation or even to negotiate without at least securing United States recognition of the Palestinian right to self-determination and hence the right to establish an independent state.

The impasse was broken by a development which none of the parties to the Arab–Israeli conflict – including the PLO – had foreseen. In December 1987 the Palestinians in the occupied territories began an uprising against the Israeli occupiers. The uprising or *intifada* – an Arabic word which was to become as much part of the international vocabulary as the Russian *glasnost* – was unexpected because, although there had been days or even weeks of sporadic unrest, the Israeli occupiers had faced a relatively easy task for two decades. Guerrilla attacks had never been a serious military problem; internal resistance had not been prolonged or organized. When a hostile political leadership had looked like emerging, its members were imprisoned or deported. In December 1987, however, a minor incident in Gaza sparked off a resistance movement which, although unplanned and at first unorganized, refused to die down. The half of the population who had not yet reached twenty years of age had known only foreign occupation. As the occupiers seized more land and water and planted new Jewish settlements on their territory they saw a future that could only become darker. Some 200,000 crossed each day into Israel to work, but it was generally to perform menial and unskilled tasks – the Palestinian economy was entirely colonial in kind. The despair of the people of the occupied territories was increased by the fact that the Arab states appeared to have lost interest in them. For the first time ever at a meeting of Arab heads of state, in Amman in August 1987, the Palestine problem had been displaced from the head of the agenda by a different question – the Iraq–Iran war.

The *intifada* took the form of demonstrations, tyre-burning, the illegal raising of the Palestinian flag and strikes. Its characteristic feature was the hurling of stones at Israeli soldiers by Arab adolescents and even children. A significant innovation was that an anonymous National Unified Command of the Uprising emerged which, through pamphlets and a secret radio station on Syrian territory, gave some effective organization to the demonstrations and strikes.

The Israeli authorities, surprised by the intensity and persistence of the uprising, responded with mass arrests and deportations, curfews, beatings and the various forms of plastic bullet, which were often lethal or caused grievous wounds. In the first two years there was an average of about one Palestinian death each day.

After two years some 50,000 Palestinians had been arrested, 7,000 wounded and more than 500 killed. About half of those arrested were under the age of eighteen. The rebels rarely resorted to arms – their uprising was called the 'Stone Revolution' – but as its second year progressed it became increasingly bitter as the Palestinians began killing anyone suspected of collaborating with the Israeli secret police, and Islamic fundamentalists opposed to any political compromise came to the fore.

For Israel, the effort to suppress the *intifada* was costly and damaging – both to the morale of its troops, mostly untrained in putting down civil resistance, and to Israel's international reputation. There was no question that it was capable of opposing the insurrection militarily and economically – it was the political dimension that was important. Despite defiant assurances by Israeli political leaders that the rebellion would be ended, it became an accepted international truism – shared by the United States government and much of the Israeli public – that any purely military solution would be ineffective. Israel was faced with the prospect of a *de facto* Palestinian state being created west of the River Jordan.

The success of the uprising merely in staying alive gave a wholly fresh impetus to the PLO. Although it had neither timed nor organized the internal rebellion, and the amount of support and direction it could provide from outside was very limited, the Arabs under occupation left no doubt that they regarded the PLO as their representative and Arafat as their leader. Everywhere they displayed his picture as the symbol of their defiance. Paradoxically, this demonstration of the spirit of Palestinian nationalism enable the PLO leadership to adopt a more overtly moderate position which emphasized the common interest of Palestinians and Israelis in peace and security. At the same time it persuaded King Hussein of Jordan to destroy once and for all the credibility of the 'Jordanian option' – that is, the belief still entertained by many Israelis and some Western governments that Palestinian nationalism could remain under joint Jordanian and Israeli hegemony. In July 1988 the Jordanian monarch announced that he was finally abandoning all Jordan's responsibilities for the West Bank. From there it was only one step for the PLO to declare, through its quasi-parliament meeting in Algiers in November, the establishment of an independent Palestinian state with Arafat as its president. But simultaneously the Palestine National Council for the first time unambiguously declared its acceptance of UN Security Council Resolution 242 of 1967 – the step which the United States had long been demanding as a demonstration that the PLO was willing to recognize Israel. It also declared that it was renouncing all forms of terrorism.

Arafat spelled this out more clearly in other world capitals. He was advocating a 'two-state solution' – that is, a small independent Palestinian state living alongside Israel. This had been his objective for years, but he had never felt confident enough to declare it unambiguously for fear that abandoning the dream of liberating all Palestine from Zionism would divide his people against each other.

Israel's leaders denounced the PLO's new stand as false and treacherous. The threat to their position was underlined when for the first time the United States declared that it was prepared to begin a dialogue with the PLO through its ambassador in Tunis.

However, Palestinian hopes of rapid rewards for their new concessions were not realized. In March 1990 Yitzhak Shamir, the Israeli premier from 1988 to 1990, dismissed his Labour partners in his coalition and eventually succeeded in forming a right-wing Likud government. Although the United States showed increasing impatience with Shamir's stubborn rejection of any plausible formula for Palestinian autonomy it was still unprepared to exert concentrated pressure on its Israeli ally to change its attitude. An increasingly disillusioned Arafat, faced with a growing Islamic fundamentalist element in the *intifada* that rejected any two-state solution in favour of the old slogans of total liberation, began to look towards President Saddam of Iraq who was posing as the champion of the Palestinians and threatening Israel with its missiles. After a botched terror raid on an Israeli beach by a PLO splinter group, almost certainly promoted by Iraq, the United States broke off its listless dialogue with the PLO.

Consequently, Arafat showed some evident sympathy with Saddam's invasion of Kuwait in August 1990, though formally advising an Iraqi withdrawal, while ordinary Palestinians in Jordan and the occupied territories cheered Saddam as a hero. Powerful anti-Palestinian feelings were aroused among the Gulf Arabs, and Western governments declared that the PLO had marginalized itself in the Gulf conflict. But this was premature and unrealistic. The *intifada* had superficially subsided in the first half of 1990, partly through exhaustion and partly through a more restrained Israeli policy of repression, but in October a renewal of violence enhanced extremism on both sides and further envenomed relations between Arabs and Jews. In these circumstances there was no way that either the United States or Israel could promote an alternative Palestinian leadership to the PLO.

Forty years after the triumph of Zionism in the creation of a Jewish state, a new stage had been reached in the Palestine problem that this had created. This emphatically did not mean that the problem had been solved, or even that it was nearer a solution – a 'solution' that would be satisfactory to all the parties concerned is in any case inconceivable. The original concept of the partition of Palestine into an Arab and a Jewish state – approved by the United Nations in 1947 with so little concern for its consequences, and so bitterly rejected by the Arabs of Palestine at the time – had come to be accepted by a new generation of Palestinians and much of the rest of the world. But it was no longer accepted by Zionist Jews, except for a small, albeit growing, minority. Some, represented by Israel's prime minister Yitzhak Shamir, saw the West Bank (or Judaea and Samaria) and Gaza as part of the Land of Israel and could not contemplate abandoning it to an Arab sovereignty. Others, represented by the Labour leader Shimon Peres, although ready to give up some land for peace, still could not face the prospect of an independent neighbouring state which would surely be governed by the PLO under President Arafat. In this rejection of an independent Arab Palestine, Israel had the support of the world's most powerful state, and experience had shown on multiple occasions that the United States government, however much it disapproved of certain Israeli acts or attitudes, would exert pressure to change them only on the rarest occasions and never for long. It remained a cardinal principle of the US–Israeli alliance that the United States would sustain Israel's military machine and economy to ensure that Israel remained the most powerful state in the Middle East.

Syria's crucial role in trying to restore peace and unity to the Lebanese state was grudgingly acknowledged by most of the world after the withdrawal of Western and Israeli troops in 1984 and 1985. But if Syria was dominant in Lebanon, it was far from all-powerful. Even President Assad's supreme abilities as a political tactician could not resolve the multifarious conflicts of Lebanon. It proved impossible to secure the essential minimum of an agreement among the factions to reunite the country. While Syria had some friends among the Maronites, these were outnumbered by its bitter enemies who controlled the strongest militia, the Lebanese Forces. Even Syria's allies in Lebanon – the Druze, the Shiite Amal militia and the extremist Hizbollahis – were far from obedient and sometimes fought each other. An additional factor was that some of the Palestinian fighters, now fiercely anti-Syrian, had returned to Beirut and the south and had become engaged in fighting with the Amal militia who besieged the Palestinian refugee camps. By sending their forces into Muslim west Beirut, the Syrians were able to reduce the fighting between the militias, but Christian east Beirut and the Shiite southern suburbs remained outside their control.

When President Amin Gemayel's six-year term of office ended in September 1988, the anti-Syrian Maronites prevented the parliamentary deputies from electing a successor who would have been acceptable to Syria. After the failure of every alternative, Gemayel's last act as president was to appoint General Michel Aoun, the Maronite commander of the armed forces, as prime minister. Since Muslims refused to serve in his cabinet and the previous Sunni prime minister declared himself still in office, Lebanon had two half-governments and no head of state. It seemed as if the little republic of Lebanon was doomed to final destruction after less than seventy years of existence. The Lebanese economy, which had survived the first decade of civil war with amazing resilience, was on the point of collapse.

However, the peculiar circumstances of Lebanon, with its shifting balance of internal forces and external pressures, do not favour final solutions or dissolutions. The Arab states, backed by all the outside powers concerned with the region, made unsparing efforts to hold Lebanon together. This required an accommodation between Syria and its Lebanese Christian opponents which was difficult to achieve. General Aoun, who suffered from minor Napoleonic delusions, was uncompromisingly defiant. He was buoyed up by a vague and unwarranted belief that the Western powers would come to the aid of the Christian Lebanese, although he also received real help in money and arms from Syria's arch-enemy Iraq. He was unable to fulfil his boast of driving the Syrians out of Lebanon, but equally the Syrians and their allies lacked the power and will to overrun the Christian fortress enclave. In the summer of 1989 the two sides poured shells on to each other, causing atrocious suffering mainly to civilians.

Against most expectations, Arab mediators secured a cease-fire in September 1989 and persuaded the surviving and elderly deputies of the Lebanese parliament to meet in Taif, Saudi Arabia's summer capital, where they hammered out an agreement on a new political structure for Lebanon, through which the Maronites, who had been politically dominant since the French creation of Greater Lebanon, would relinquish some of their powers. Since it was a compromise, many were dissatisfied. The Christians had not secured Syria's immediate departure and the Shiites, now more numerous than Lebanese Sunnis, felt that they should have a more influential role. But the agreement made it possible for the deputies to meet in Syrian-controlled north Lebanon to elect on 5 November 1989 a new president – Rene Muawwad. General Aoun defiantly declared the election illegal and claimed that he was still Lebanon's constitutional leader.

Two weeks later Muawwad was assassinated by a car bomb in west Beirut. Under Syrian protection the deputies then elected yet another Christian president Elias Hrawi whom the rebel general found equally unacceptable. Although Hrawi was recognized by the Arab states and the rest of the world Aoun maintained his defiance. But his authority over Christian Lebanon was challenged by the Christian militia group in the Lebanese Forces. A bloody conflict ensued, causing atrocious suffering to the people of east Beirut and leaving General Aoun in control of only one third of the Christian enclave. The *de facto* partition could not be permanent and the issue of a death certificate for the Lebanese Republic was still postponed.

Aoun's nemesis was not long delayed. In October 1990, as world attention was diverted towards the Gulf and the containment of Iraq (which had supported Aoun in his hostility towards Damascus) the Syrians were able to overrun the general's fortress enclave in alliance with Lebanese forces loyal to President Hrawi and bring about his surrender. The Syrians now dominated all of central Lebanon but their first aim was to extend the Lebanese government's authority throughout the one hundred square miles of greater Beirut, ensure the withdrawal of the rival militias and reopen communications. If the Lebanese heartland could be secured, even under Syrian hegemony, the Lebanese Republic still had a chance of survival.

Islamic Reassertion, Revolution and War

With the decline and defeat and dismemberment in 1918 of the Ottoman Empire – the last Muslim great power in global terms – the world of Islam was on the defensive. In the nineteenth and early twentieth century the Arabs came under some form of Western colonial domination. The Muslims of central Asia were absorbed into the Russian Empire, the Muslim former rulers of India became part of the British Raj, and the Persian/Iranian Empire suffered a joint Russian–British hegemony. It was only in Turkey, the former heartland of the Ottoman Empire, that a nation-state which was strong enough to remain independent of the European colonial powers was forged, by the political and military genius of Kemal Atatürk. But his cause was secular Turkish nationalism and not Islam.

The Arab and Iranian response to European domination differed from Turkey's in that it was neither purely secular nationalism nor an Islamic counter-offensive but a combination of both. The Islamic cultural element was supremely important. As Frantz Fanon, the Martiniquais intellectual who joined the Algerian revolution against France, pointed out in his classic work *The Wretched of the Earth*: whereas European colonizers thought of black Africans in essentially racial terms, their attitude towards the Arab world was different. Here they were confronted by a specific and unified, if not homogeneous, culture which was derived from its Arab/Islamic tradition. Beyond doubt it was the indestructibility of this culture which prevented France from not only colonizing Algeria but also turning it into a permanent European dependency as at one time seemed perfectly feasible.

However, to say that Arab resistance to European domination drew its inspiration from Islam and its heritage does not mean that in this respect it was pure and uncompromising. The great nineteenth-century and early twentieth-century Muslim reformers such as Al-Afghani, Abduh and Rida reached the conclusion that the world of Islam began to decline when the Turks took over its leadership from the Arabs. Although this was not their intention, their ideas provided the intellectual basis for Arab nationalism. The Arabs of the Middle East formed an alliance with the European colonizers to overthrow Ottoman Turkish rule, but when this succeeded they were left with weak Arab nation-states under European domination. The pan-Arab nationalist movement which developed in the 1920s and 1930s was given a powerful fresh impetus by the loss of Arab Palestine in the 1940s and reached its peak in the 1950s under Gamal Abdul Nasser of Egypt, who aimed to overcome this weakness and throw off European hegemony. But although Arab nationalism was not purely secular, neither was it wholly Islamic. Unlike the nationalism of Atatürk, it could not be entirely secular for the obvious reason that for any Arab – even a non-Muslim – to cut himself off from his heritage of Islamic civilization would be to deny his own identity. But equally the pan-Arab movement could not be purely Islamic in its ideology, in the sense of regarding Islam as the sole path to the true self-determination of the Arab peoples. This was not only because some of the leading exponents of pan-Arabism, such as the Baath ideologist Michel Aflaq, were Christians: its Muslim leaders were also strongly influenced by European and American concepts of secular nationalism. Many had been educated at Western institutions or trained by European officers. However grudgingly, to some extent they accepted Atatürk's belief that it was reactionary Islam which had allowed the West (and the Zionists) to defeat and dominate the peoples of the Middle East – Turks, Persians and Arabs.

Among the Arabs who most fiercely resisted Western domination there were indeed some who saw nothing of value outside Islam. These were Muslim nationalists rather than Arab nationalists; today they are called fundamentalists. They had, and have, a utopian view that if Muslims were to set up an Islamic order in which the holy *sharia* would be the only authority, all the internal problems of government and society and the external problems of un-Islamic domination and influence would be solved. While their dedication and readiness for martyrdom made them formidable, they remained a minority in the Arab struggle for full independence from the West. Their refusal to compromise and their willingness to use violence against anyone who did not wholly share their views alienated potential allies. Whenever there seemed a chance that they might gain power, they deeply alarmed the majority. Their first organized movement in the modern Arab world – the Muslim Brotherhood, in Egypt – believed that it was on the point of overthrowing a corrupt monarchy but was then, as we have seen, swept aside by the Nasser Revolution.

A seeming exception to the rule that militant Islamic fundamentalists are unlikely to be successful in winning control of an Arab state in the twentieth century occurred in Arabia. Here the puritanical Wahhabi reformers, allied to the House of Saud, had in the eighteenth century been the first Arab movement to challenge the authority of the Ottoman sultan/caliph and to denounce the religious backsliding of their fellow-Muslims. Defeated in the early nineteenth century by the secular power of Muhammad Ali, the Ottoman governor of Egypt, they finally triumphed in the 1920s through the political and military genius of Ibn Saud. Here at last the uncompromising forces of Islam were in power. But King Ibn Saud knew his limitations. Although he enjoyed prestige as the custodian of the holy places of Islam, his new kingdom was remote, desperately poor and militarily weak. It was in no position to spread its puritan revolutionary movement northwards to the great centres of Arab population – Cairo, Damascus and Baghdad. Moreover – and most important – the grinding poverty of the people of Saudi Arabia caused Ibn Saud and his sons who succeeded him to ally themselves with the West – especially the supremely secular United States – to relieve the country's economic backwardness. Ironically, the puritanical Saudis subsequently proved to be endowed with unimaginable natural wealth, but, although the Saudi kingdom then acquired prestige and influence in the councils of the world, it needed non-Muslims even more – for the development and protection of its newly discovered resources. The alliance with the West deepened with the added spur of the Saudi fear and detestation of communism.

So it was that, although the Saudis were amazingly successful in preserving their identity through the retention of their system of government and laws and their conservative social mores, their inter-relationship with and dependence on the West was also undeniable. Saudi Arabia might take the lead in creating international bodies and organizations to increase the links between the Muslim states, and it lavishly endowed Islamic missions and mosques throughout the world – all of which powerfully assisted the reassertion of Islam in modern times – but the militant Islamic fundamentalists were not satisfied. They wanted to exclude the West from the world of Islam. In 1979 the House of Saud was made brutally aware of their existence even inside the kingdom when a group of young fanatics, denouncing the corruption of their rulers, seized and held for a time the Great Mosque at Mecca – the holiest shrine of Islam.

After the Arab catastrophe in 1967, volatile world opinion seized on the possibility of an Islamic fundamentalist revolution sweeping through the Arab countries. In the heyday of pan-Arab nationalism in the 1950s and 1960s, the importance of Islam as a political force was grossly underestimated by the majority of Western journalists and academics – and, indeed, by much of the Arab intelligentsia. A common view was that the Arabs were determined to catch up with the West's material and technical progress, and for this Islam had nothing to contribute. After 1967 there was a sudden reversal of this opinion. Secular Arab nationalism had been proved a failure and was dead; the masses would reject Western progress and turn to fun-damentalist Islam as their only hope.

Both views were misleading. Islam had never ceased to be a supremely powerful underlying force; it was only reasserting itself more openly in the wake of the Arab defeat. On the other hand, nationalism was far from dead, even if it had to modify its form. All the regimes of the Arab states – even in Saudi Arabia – still subscribed to the notion that the Arabs form a single nation which should be more closely united. There was no question of breaking up the League of Arab States. At the same time, it was apparent that there had been a strengthening of territorial nationalism – the local patri-otism that had grown up around the flag and capital of the individual Arab states (however artificial their creation by the West may have been) and that supported their particular interests. There was no likelihood that an Islamic revolution would be able to sweep all this away.

The Islamic revolution which did occur took place not in the predominantly Sunni Muslim lands but in Shiite Iran. All but a very few of the closest observers were taken by surprise.

Since the overthrow of Mossadegh in 1953, Iran had come to be seen as an example of the progress and development which were widely held in the West to be synonymous with westernization. In the 1950s, elections to the Majlis were carefully controlled to ensure that acceptable candidates were elected. The National Front ceased to function as an organized political force and the communist Tudeh Party was proscribed. Power was increasingly concentrated in the hands of the shah. However, the task of the shah's loyalist governments was not easy. Their hope was that economic growth would dampen opposition to the control of political life but, although oil revenues expanded, the large-scale projects to develop the infrastructure took time to mature and there was widespread corruption and inefficiency. Anti-Western nationalist feelings, inflamed during the Mossadegh crisis, were by no means extinguished. They gained strength from the regime's close identification with the Western camp, symbolized by Iran's adherence to the anti-Soviet Baghdad Pact in 1955.

In 1961 the unrest obliged the shah to appoint as prime minister Ali Amini, a wealthy aristocrat with a reputation as a liberal reformer. He tackled government extravagance and corruption and relaxed controls on the National Front and left-wing opposition. He brought into the cabinet as minister of agriculture Hassan Arsanjani, a radical politician committed to land reform and the break-up of the large estates consisting of scores of villages. Amini persuaded the shah to allow him to dissolve the Majlis and rule by decree to push through his reforms. But his reformist experiment was short-lived. He aroused opposition on all sides – from the land-owners and the army as well as the politicians who demanded the restoration of the Majlis. Within a year he had been forced to resign and the shah reasserted his authority.

The shah nevertheless pursued and even intensified some of the reform measures – notably land reform, which was extended to the Islamic *waqf* properties (whose revenues were used for the upkeep of mosques or charitable works), while the large land-owners were limited to the holding of one village. Female suffrage was introduced, and women's rights were legally extended. A Literacy Corps was founded to enable high-school students to teach in village schools as an alternative to military service. In this way the shah's government retained the initiative. The National Front declared that it favoured the reforms but said that they were 'unconstitutional', while the mullahs, whose most effective spokesman was Ayatollah Khomeini of Qum, denounced them as 'un-Islamic' as well as unconstitutional. In 1963 the National Front was disbanded by the government and then disintegrated. Khomeini and other religious leaders were arrested, and a year later Khomeini was sent into exile and took up residence in the Shiite region of southern Iraq. The religious opposition resorted increasingly to underground activity and violence, but this was ineffective and the government was able to denounce both the nationalists and mullahs as reactionary opponents of reform.

For more than a decade the shah could rule without serious opposition pressure. He reconvened the Majlis and allowed it to function with officially sponsored political parties and an opposition which consistently voted for government bills. Outside parliament the ubiquitous SAVAK secret police relentlessly suppressed dissent.

The shah showed increasing self-confidence and a vaulting ambition to make his country the indisputably dominant regional power. The West was always ready to provide him with the most sophisticated modern weapons. Although remaining in the Western camp, however, he improved relations with the Soviet-bloc countries and signed with them a series of large-scale industrial agreements. He secured greatly improved terms from the oil companies, which amounted to the National Iranian Oil Company taking over control of operations. In 1967 he amended the constitution so that the queen would automatically become regent in the event of his death before the crown prince reached his majority, and in the twenty-sixth year of his reign he and the queen were crowned in a wholly un-Islamic ceremony. In 1971 he celebrated the two-thousand-five-hundredth anniversary of the Persian monarchy with colossal extravagance at the ancient capital of Persepolis.

The huge increase in Iran's oil revenues in 1973–4 drove the shah's ambitions to the border of megalomania. He began to proclaim that his country would be among the six most advanced industrial countries of the world by the end of the century. In fact – in spite of the real industrial progress, the extension of education and literacy, and the growth of the professional and business class – many of the standards of Iranian society remained those of the Third World. With hindsight it is possible to discern that the sudden vast increase in government revenues was the nemesis of the regime. The huge growth in spending which followed placed intolerable strains on the country's social and economic fabric. When overspending led to retrenchment and recession combined with continuing inflation, even the members of the new middle class who had benefited most from the shah's policies became disaffected, while the mass of the population tended to see the hasty westernization and un-Islamic modernization of the country as the source of all evil.

The shah, in common with most Western observers (including ambassadors), still underrated the opposition. He saw only an opportunistic alliance between the extreme left and the mullahs, and referred contemptuously to 'Islamic Marxists'. In fact it was the mullahs who were best able to articulate the discontent of the majority.

As the tide of unrest gathered momentum, it became apparent that popular opposition was massive and deep-seated. The huge coalition of discontent found its voice in Ayatollah Khomeini. After being ousted from his Iraqi exile by an embarrassed Iraqi government (which wanted stable relations with Iran), he took refuge in Paris, from where he issued uncompromising demands for the shah's abdication. As strikes and demonstrations spread, the shah attempted a series of measures, mixing concessions with firmness, in an effort to secure his power. But these were ineffective. The armed forces remained apparently loyal, but the shah had finally lost the will and determination to hold on to power through the massive repression which would have been necessary – his arrogant demeanour had always concealed a certain lack of decision. He was also suffering from the cancer which was to kill him two years later. Without the will to retain his throne, neither his loyal followers nor his US allies could help him. On 16 January 1979 he left Iran with his queen, ostensibly on holiday but never to return. His departure from Tehran was cheered by two million supporters of Ayatollah Khomeini. Twenty-five centuries of the Persian monarchy had ended.

Two weeks later the frail 76-year-old ayatollah showed that he could inspire millions of his people to frenzied enthusiasm when he returned in triumph to declare that, with his Islamic Revolution, a truly Islamic republic would be established.

This momentous event was soon to be compared in importance with the French Revolution of 1789 and the Bolshevik Revolution of 1917. For the comparison to be sustained it was necessary for the Iranian Revolution's influence to spread far beyond Iran's borders, and especially to the Muslim peoples of the Middle East. Khomeini and his clerical associates left no doubt that this was their intention. They proclaimed that all the regimes of Muslim countries in the region were corrupt, unworthy and un-Islamic and therefore deserved to be overthrown. They also denounced these regimes' association with the West. Khomeini declared that a true Muslim country should have no truck with either East or West, but his special hatred was directed towards the United States – 'the Great Satan', the former ally of the shah. Anti-American rage swept Iran and, when President Carter allowed the shah to travel from his retreat in the Bahamas to the United States for medical treatment, a crowd of militants stormed the US embassy in Tehran, seizing some fifty US hostages and all the embassy documents. This outrage against all the norms of diplomacy, which even the most radical and revolutionary regimes usually accepted, provoked the United States, with the support of its allies to declare Iran an international outlaw. Khomeini was not displeased. His uncompromising defiance of the West provoked admiration among all the Muslim masses to whom he wished to appeal. This was reinforced by his adoption of the cause of Palestine. He reversed the shah's *de facto* alliance with Israel and invited Arafat to Tehran, where he was greeted as a hero.

At home, Ayatollah Khomeini set about consolidating clerical rule under his leadership. His authoritarianism provoked the opposition of the secular nationalist and left-wing elements who had supported his revolution, but they were no match for the hold he had gained over the Iranian people. In fact the most serious opposition to his rule came from more senior Islamic clerics who challenged his religious authority. But even this he was able to contain. He had political genius, which they lacked. He based his rule on the doctrine of *velayat-e faqih* – that is, 'government of the Islamic jurist' – which he had expounded in lectures in exile. This holds that the true Islamic state must be based on the Koran and be modelled after the Prophet's Islamic community in the seventh century, and that it should be administered by the clerical class as the Prophet's heirs. As the self-appointed governing Islamic jurist, Khomeini was able to hold supreme power above that of the president, prime minister and elected parliament, which were all provided for in the new Islamic constitution. Under his authority, mass trials of the shah's former supporters were organized, leading to many executions. The educational system was purged of non-Islamic influences. Squads of young Muslim militiamen enforced a strict Islamic code of conduct. Educated Iranian women, who had reached an advanced stage of emancipation before the revolution, had their role in public life sharply reduced and all had to envelop their heads and bodies in Islamic dress in public.

The success of the Khomeini Revolution and its declared desire to export itself caused serious alarm among Iran's Arab neighbours, but nowhere more than in Iraq. With its secular pan-Arabist ideology and its large Shiite population with little share in political power, Iraq was a vulnerable target. Tehran Arabic broadcasts poured hatred and contempt on the Iraq regime and called on the Iraqi people to overthrow it.

Iraq's president, Saddam Hussein, decided to act first. Although Iran has immense resources and three times Iraq's population, he believed that the Khomeini Revolution could be overthrown by a swift blow. The Iranian regular armed forces were demoralized. Iran's large minorities – the Kurds in the north-west, the Turkomans of the Caspian plain and the Arabs of Khuzestan in the south-west – saw their religious and cultural identities threatened by the Shiite fundamentalist policies of the Revolution and were demanding autonomy and threatening revolt. The economy, facing a Western boycott, was in dire condition. Almost certainly, exiled royalist Iranian officers helped to convince President Saddam that it was time to move. On 17 September 1980 Iraq, alleging various minor acts of Iranian aggression, denounced the 1975 agreement with the former shah and invaded Iran.

The eight-year war which ensued was on an epic scale, with colossal casualties, massive material destruction and mutual rocket attacks on Baghdad and Tehran in 'the war of the cities'. Iraq initially advanced deep into Iranian territory, but its invasion soon proved the danger of attacking a revolution. Iranian morale was higher than expected, and the Arab Iranians of the south-west did not rise to support the invaders. Within a year Iraq had been forced back, and by May 1982 Iran had recaptured nearly all its territory. All Iraq's outlets to the sea were cut off. A prolonged stalemate ensued, interspersed by large-scale offensives which, as in the First World War, left many dead but the battle lines scarcely changed. Iraq, which could obtain arms from both East and West, had the advantage in weapons – especially tanks and artillery. Iran, lacking fresh supplies of its American weapons, was forced to turn to sources such as North Korea or the international black market in arms. It used its numerical superiority to launch human-wave assaults which often involved thousands of teenage youths imbued with the characteristically Shiite readiness for martyrdom.

For some time the Gulf War directly involved only Iraq and Iran. Initial world alarm caused a further steep rise in oil prices, but the reaction of the world outside the Middle East could be summed up in a possibly apocryphal comment ascribed to Dr Henry Kissinger: that the best result would be for both sides to lose the war. The war was prolonged because, while Iraq was prepared to settle for a return to the old frontiers, Iran demanded nothing less than the downfall of Saddam Hussein.

The six Arab Gulf states – Saudi Arabia, Kuwait, Qatar, Bahrain, the United Arab Emirates, and Oman – supported Iraq with varying degrees of enthusiasm and openness, and as the war progressed they helped to sustain Iraq with money and supplies. They were appalled at the prospect of an outright Iranian victory. The threatening situation, aggravated by the Soviet invasion of Afghanistan in 1979, acted as a catalyst for them to join together in self-defence in May 1981 to establish the Gulf Co-operation Council. This looked forward to a staged process of political and economic fusion, somewhat along the lines of the European Community.

Among the other Arab states, Jordan and Egypt declared their support for Iraq in the war even more openly. Jordan's Aqaba port became the principal route for Iraqi imports of war materials; Egypt supplied arms and ammunition. But President Assad of Syria declared himself Iran's ally in the war and closed Iraq's oil pipeline across Syrian territory. Although this bizarre friendship between a professed Arab nationalist and an Iranian Shiite fundamentalist might have had something to do with the fact that Assad came from Syria's sub-Shia Alawite minority, from his view it was primarily a strategic alliance against the detested rival Baathist regime in Iraq. Syria benefited from the supply of a regular quota of free Iranian oil and from the pro-Iranian sympathies among the Shiites of Lebanon. President Assad rejected all the repeated attempts by other Arab states to persuade him to change sides. The ideological cynicism of the Syrian–Iranian alliance was underlined when, in February 1982, the Syrian army ruthlessly repressed an armed rising in the city of Hama by the Muslim Brotherhood, whose aims were closely similar to those of Iran's Islamic Revolution.

While the fears of the Revolution among most Arab regimes were real enough, the danger that it could reach out to topple them receded as the war progressed – even when Iran appeared to have the advantage. Khomeini emphatically wished to appeal to all Muslims, not only to the Shiite minority, and he scorned any concept of nationalism within the Islamic *umma*. But he could not prevent the war from widening the ancient Persian–Arab rivalry or the Sunni–Shiite division. In the Arab Gulf states, any initial popular enthusiasm for the Islamic Revolution was soon confined to the Shiite minorities. This caused their Sunni rulers serious concern, but increased their determination to stand firm, and the bloodthirsty repression of all opposition in Iran also helped to antagonize their Sunni subjects. In Iraq, with its Shiite majority, territorial nationalism showed itself to be the stronger force. Just as the Arab-speaking Iranians had refused to side with Iraq, the great majority of Iraq Shiite Arabs remained loyal and showed no eagerness to be occupied and ruled by the Islamic Republic. It was Iraq's Sunni Kurds who gave the regime serious trouble.

In countries more remote from the Gulf War – in Egypt, Sudan and the Maghreb states – the Khomeini Revolution's defiance of both West and East retained it some prestige among Muslim militants who had no love for the Iraqi regime. But the Ayatollah's influence was symbolic. There was no question of accepting his political leadership – the Muslim Brothers of Egypt and Sudan had begun their own struggle long before the Iranian Revolution.

The murderous stalemate in the Gulf war continued from 1982 to 1987. 'The war of the cities', with rockets and shelling, was pursued sporadically at heavy cost. The Iranians alternated human-wave assaults with attacks on a smaller scale at varied points along the frontier to wear down Iraqi morale, but this was higher now that Iraqi troops were defending their own territory. In 1986 the Iranians captured Iraq's Faw peninsula on the Gulf coast but failed at heavy cost in an attempt to seize Basra. The focus of the war moved to the waters of the Gulf, where Iraq's air superiority could be used against Iran's vital oil exports but Iran's naval superiority enabled it to blockade Iraqi supplies. The danger that the tanker war might intensify and spread at last attracted the serious attention of the superpowers. In 1987 the United States offered to reflag Kuwaiti tankers to provide protection (following a similar offer by the Soviet Union), and by mid-year the USA was in full-scale naval confrontation with Iran. On 20 July the UN Security Council unanimously passed Resolution 598 calling for an immediate end to all hostilities. Iraq accepted this but Iran refused, on the grounds that at the very least President Saddam's responsibility for the war should be internationally accepted.

In 1988 the war took a new and final turn. Between May and June the Iraqis recaptured Faw and drove the Iranians out of other key areas on the frontier. With the numbers of willing Iranian martyrs declining and economic collapse looming, the closest supporters of the infirm octogenarian Khomeini persuaded him that there was no alternative to accepting the UN cease-fire. He told his people that taking the decision 'was more deadly than taking poison'.

The cease-fire held, with the help of the UN observers, but it was still only an armed truce. UN-sponsored peace talks failed to achieve a peace agreement to settle the outstanding border disputes, or even an exchange of prisoners. The two regimes remained deadly enemies, although they had to accept that renewed war was impossible for some years. They began to rearm even as they set about reconstructing their ruined economies.

A triumphant President Hussein declared that Iraq had won the war – which in a sense it had, even if he had not achieved his original war aims of overthrowing the Islamic Republic. He had won by not losing, just as Khomeini had lost by not winning.

On 4 June 1989 Khomeini's long-expected death finally occurred. The succession passed smoothly in spite of an underlying struggle for power between those, including Khomeini's son Ahmed, who wished to pursue his uncompromising hostility towards the West and those who sought to normalize Iran's relations with the world as an essential means of restoring the economy, while insisting that the Ayatollah's legacy would remain unchanged.

It was the pragmatists who won. The Assembly of Experts swiftly appointed the mild-mannered former president Khomanei as the new spiritual leader. Two months later the speaker of the Majlis, Ali Akbar Rafsanjani, a man of high political skill, succeeded in having himself elected president with greatly increased powers and promptly ousted the leaders of the hardline faction from the cabinet.

For the millions of Iranians who mourned Khomeini's death there was no one who could replace the man whom many of them had come to regard as God's embodiment on earth, even if anyone had wished to try. In the decade since the Revolution, hundreds of thousands had died and the economy had been ruined in a war which had ended in failure. Dissidence had been harshly repressed, and a large proportion of the skilled and educated had fled into exile. Yet the scowling figure of Khomeini, so deeply unattractive to most of the rest of the world, still represented to his intensely proud people a spirit of unyielding defiance after centuries of humiliation by stronger powers.

The question was, how much of Khomeini's legacy would survive? While clerical rule had been institutionalized and seemed likely to last for a time, Rafsanjani, with modest religious credentials, was essentially a secular figure. But he was not all-powerful – his hardline opponents had been bypassed but not subdued. He had to move cautiously towards calming and moderating the Islamic Republic's policies towards the rest of the world, in order to reconstruct the economy and encourage the urgently needed exiles to return.

Only one thing seemed certain: Iran's Islamic Revolution would not permanently change the face of the Middle East. This had proved beyond Khomeini's power, and it was certainly impossible for his successors. As the representative of militant Shiite Islam, Iran could count on the open allegiance of many Lebanese Shiites and the covert sympathy of Shiite minorities in the Arab Gulf states, but little more. With its fifty-five million people, and occupying a strategic position, it was still a major power in Middle Eastern terms and all states with interests in the region were therefore anxious to have dealings with Tehran. But its power to influence events outside its borders was no greater than in the time of the shah.

Iraq's World Challenge

The ambitions of President Saddam Hussein of Iraq, who had been the effective ruler of his country since 1968, were not exhausted by his eight-year struggle with his larger neighbour. Despite mountainous debts and an economy in desperate need of reconstruction he still maintained a huge military machine with nearly one million men under arms, and he poured vast sums into developing advanced weapons. During the summer of 1990 he threatened Kuwait because of its reluctance to allow Iraq secure access to the Gulf through its territory and its responsibility for the fall in the price of oil by producing in excess of its OPEC quota – a fall which he claimed was losing Iraq one billion dollars a month in revenues. In late July he massed troops on Kuwait's border. But despite this and the failure of Saudi Arabia's efforts to mediate there were few – except the Iranians – who expected his next move which on 2 August was to invade and occupy the whole of Kuwait on the spurious assertion that there had been a pro-Iraqi uprising against Kuwait's Amir. The Amir and his ministers fled to Saudi Arabia where they set up a government-in-exile. A week later Saddam announced the annexation of Kuwait as Iraq's nineteenth province. He declared that the child had been restored to its mother, regardless of the fact that the Kuwaiti emirate had been born some two centuries before its supposed parent – the Iraqi state.

If Saddam had successfully taken the world by surprise, he had also miscalculated the extent of its opposition. The UN Security Council unanimously imposed mandatory sanctions against Iraq that, following a series of resolutions, became almost totally effective in blocking Iraq's foreign trade and freezing its foreign assets. The first major crisis of the post-Cold War era offered the extraordinary spectacle of a country of eighteen million people defying the two superpowers and most of the world. As Iraqi troops advanced to the Saudi Arabian border there arose the alarming prospect that Saddam would seize the Saudi oilfields which, in conjunction with those of Iraq and Kuwait, would make him master of more than half the world's oil reserves. The United States, which had regarded an Iraqi victory in the Gulf war as preferable to the triumph of Ayatollah Khomeini, now denounced Saddam Hussein as an international outlaw. President Bush immediately responded to King Fahd of

Saudi Arabia's urgent invitation to send troops to defend the kingdom. Even after the initial threat had receded with the arrival of airborne forces, there was a continued build-up of naval, land and air forces totalling some six hundred thousand personnel, and carrying the most advanced weapons. The great majority were American but Britain and France sent substantial contingents and no less than fifty-four countries contributed either military forces or financial support. Of the greatest political importance to the United States was the addition, apart from the troops of Saudi Arabia and other Gulf states, of Arab forces from Egypt, Syria and Morocco, and others from Muslim Pakistan and Bangladesh. It was vital to demonstrate that this was not one more Western crusade against the Arabs and Islam.

In fact opinion among the Arabs was divided and confused on the issue. While the governments of the Arab League declared with varying emphasis that Iraq should withdraw from Kuwait, there were those, such as Jordan, Sudan, Libya and Algeria as well as the PLO, that showed some degree of sympathy with the Iraqi position. These governments gave priority to announcing the danger to the Arabs and Islam presented by the huge influx of infidel Western armies. King Hussein of Jordan and Yasir Arafat tried urgently to negotiate an 'Arab solution' to the crisis.

All Arab leaders had to take some account of public opinion, which often tended towards a simplistic view of Saddam Hussein as a twentieth-century Saladin who would defy the West and unite the Arabs. The great majority of Arabs who are poor felt little sympathy for the Gulf Arabs with their vast recently inherited wealth. Demonstrators in Jordan and the Israeli-occupied territories cheered Saddam as a hero while even some Islamic militants who had known him as a ruthless secular dictator felt some response to his appeal for *jihad* or Islamic holy war against the Western invaders.

President Saddam acted with some guile but also made gross miscalculations, which were partly due to his ignorance of the world and partly to his insulation from the advice and criticism of his colleagues, whom he had so intimidated. He shrewdly linked the Gulf crisis with the Palestinian cause by contrasting the West's instant reaction to his seizure of Kuwait with its failure to end Israel's occupation of Arab lands. He made some headway with his appeal to popular Arab and Islamic sentiment although he would never overcome the suspicion and hatred of those who had direct experience of his ruthlessness, such as the hundreds of thousands of Egyptian *fellahin* who were forced to leave their livelihood in Iraq. Two weeks after the invasion he took the risk of offering peace to Iran and formally abandoning all the aims for which he had gone to war, in order to ensure Iran's neutrality. This enabled him to with-draw vital troops from the Iranian border and reinforce his Kuwait defences. The Iraqi people seemed to accept the necessity for this drastic action.

Saddam's efforts to win over opinion outside the Middle East was grossly misconceived. Outrage was caused by his detention of hun-dreds of foreigners as hostages, mostly Westerners caught in Kuwait or Iraq; some were used as human shields by being confined close to potential military targets. Bad feeling was not assuaged by the release of selected groups of women, children, the sick and aged in a charade of humanitarian gestures. As news trickled out of the Iraqi troops' pillage of Kuwait and atrocities committed against the remaining third of the Kuwaiti population that had not fled, there were calls in the West for Saddam to be tried as a war criminal and for Iraq to pay war reparations.

In spite of the overwhelming array of force deployed against Iraq, the United States and its allies were faced with an acute dilemma. Their prime objective was clear: to force Iraq to withdraw from Kuwait to enable the legitimate government to be restored. But from the outset it was clear that other decisions would be necessary. There was a question whether, even in the event of an Iraqi withdrawal, it would be reasonable to leave Saddam with his formidable military machine intact (including chemical weapons) and with the continuing capacity to threaten the Middle East with his power. It also had to be considered whether the destruction of this power would not drastically unbalance the region. A more immediate decision had to be made as to how long it would be possible to wait to see if the sanctions decreed by the UN would be enough to weaken Iraq and force its withdrawal, before using military force. There was a danger that, as the weeks stretched into months, the motley coalition of the inter-national force opposing Iraq would break apart – especially if Iraq were to offer a compromise such as a partial withdrawal from Kuwait or propose that the Palestine problem should be solved simultaneously with that of the Gulf. But the unity of the international force might be even more strained if a lightning strike to destroy Iraq's air force and cut off its forces that were dug in behind formidable defences should fail in its objective and lead to a prolonged and costly campaign.

The anti-Iraq coalition hoped that awareness among the Iraqi people of the potential disaster facing their isolated country would lead to Saddam Hussein's overthrow. But the state of morale among Iraqi military and civilians and the relative proportions of fear and admiration in their attitudes towards their leader were hard to gauge; intelligence reports were remarkably conflicting. The desirable outcome was akin to that of a hundred and fifty years earlier when the powers of Europe combined to cut down to size another aspiring great power of the Middle East – Muhammad Ali's Egypt. But the repetition of history is always improbable – especially when it is deliberately intended.

13. Prospects for the Twenty-first Century

As the end of the second millennium of the Christian era approaches, there can be no doubt that the Middle East will remain one of the nerve-centres of the world. It may no longer be the source of great new civilizations – although we cannot be sure of this – or in the forefront of cultural and material progress as it was for much of the past five thousand years of its history. But neither will it be the relative backwater that it became after Europe had learned to bypass the Middle East by circumnavigating Africa *en route* to the treasures of India and the Far East. The peoples of the Middle East – mostly Arabs under Turkish rulers or Persians, both inheritors of proud and glorious civilizations – found that they had become second-class citizens of mankind. The situation worsened when the Middle East was once again invaded – this time by secular crusaders from the West, with Napoleon Bonaparte as their forerunner. Much of the Middle East became a quasi-imperial possession of Europe.

However, the Middle East was emphatically no longer a backwater. The reasons were initially strategic and commercial: as Bonaparte had understood so well, Egypt and the Levant were the keys to Africa and Asia, and the importance of this was increased as the Middle East once again became the principal route from Europe to India and China and as the European powers scrambled for colonies in Africa. A new dimension to the Middle East's importance was added by the discovery of oil in Iran at the end of the nineteenth century, and this importance steadily grew as it was gradually discovered that the region surrounding the Persian/Arabian Gulf was far the richest source of oil in the world. Domination of the Middle East was of crucial importance to the belligerents in the two World Wars and to the two superpowers in the Cold War which followed.

In the reawakening of Europe's interest in the Middle East which began two centuries ago, the fact that the region was the cradle of the world's three great monotheistic faiths was not a major factor – as of course it had been in the medieval crusades. That was a source of romantic, historical interest, stimulating the growth of the small clan of European orientalists, but there was no question of driving Islam out of the land that is holy to the three religions. Instead Muslims – no longer a challenge in terms of material power – were patronized by the West, while the Jews – a tiny minority in the Middle East – were virtually ignored. All this changed, firstly with the emergence of political Zionism in the twentieth century, culminating in the establishment of a Jewish state in Palestine after nearly two thousand years, and secondly with the growing awareness of Islam as a newly assertive political force and the fastest growing missionary religion. All these factors making the Middle East a focus of world interest will remain, although their consequences will vary. The region has seen extraordinary change and development during this century, and these are likely to continue. Further wars and upheavals in the region are more than probable, although they may not be of the same significance or scale as the Iranian Revolution of 1979 or the Iraq–Iran war of 1980–8.

Unless there are some gigantic new oil discoveries outside the Middle East – which is possible but unlikely – the region will remain the most important single source of energy for the world during the twenty-first century. There is disagreement among oil economists as to when the Middle Eastern oil-producing countries will recover their dominant position in world oil markets and oil prices and revenues will recover from the depression of the 1980s. Some believe it will happen by 1995, and others that it will not be until after 2000; but few doubt that it will happen. The timetable depends upon the effectiveness of OPEC, in which the Middle East producers are the dominant core.

Before the 1973 Middle East war, world oil consumption had been rising steadily by 7 to 8 per cent a year. After the quadrupling of oil prices in 1973–4 the rate of consumption increase began to fall sharply. After the Iraq–Iran war sparked off a second round of price increases (from $13 a barrel to a peak of $36), world consumption actually fell by over 10 per cent between 1979 and 1983. The advanced industrialized countries not only were passing through a recession but also were finding ways of conserving oil and switching to other sources of energy. However, this did not apply to the communist countries or to the developing countries of Asia, Latin America and Africa, which actually increased their consumption even after oil prices had risen. The pattern of world consumption was changing to an extent that had not wholly been foreseen. In the absence of a worldwide economic slump, at the start of the 1990s the trend seems set for a resumed steady increase in the world demand for oil, but this time led by the countries in the earlier stages of industrialization. The potential needs of China and India are clearly enormous.

The extent to which the OPEC countries will be able to influence events depends on their ability to co-operate and to learn lessons from the past. A huge increase in oil prices in the 1990s could have the same effect on the developing world as it did on the advanced industrialized countries in the 1980s. Within OPEC there is a clear division of interest: the countries with small reserves, such as Algeria, want to keep prices as high as possible in order to maximize their incomes, while those with huge reserves, such as Kuwait or Saudi Arabia, look more to preserving their share in the world energy market. But the underlying reality is inexorable: it is the holders of big reserves which have the power to influence events in the long term, and they are in the Middle East. At any conceivable rate at which they produce and export their oil, these reserves will last for a century.

Despite the relative, and almost certainly temporary, decline in interest in oil as a source of energy by the industrialized countries in the 1970s and 1980s, the Middle East remained vital to their economies. Western Europe obtained 70 per cent of its oil needs from the Middle East, Japan more than 60 per cent while for the United States the proportion had reached 50 per cent and was rising. Any threat to these supplies was a major concern for the industrialized democracies, of which the USA still regarded itself as the leader, and this was clearly demonstrated during the later stages of the Iraq–Iran war. Yet the containment and ending of this war, which were greatly assisted by a measure of US–Soviet understanding, also demonstrated something else: that the superpower Cold War was fading away in the Middle East. This struggle for hegemony in the region had lasted about forty years – or a similar period to the Anglo–French interregnum which preceded it.

The outlook in the new era must still be the subject of speculation. It would also be wrong to exaggerate the suddenness of the change. There have been periods of US–Soviet *détente* in the Middle East before – as during the Nixon–Brezhnev era preceding the 1973 Arab–Israeli war. The inescapable fact remains that the Soviet Union desires to play an active role in the Middle East (and still resents Dr Kissinger's efforts to exclude it), but in the Gorbachev era it seeks to do this through combined action with the USA and other outside powers rather than through confrontation. While, from the days of Stalin, the Soviet Union has always accepted Israel's existence and opposed any attempt by either side to resolve the Arab–Israeli dispute by military force, President Gorbachev has given much greater strength and clarity to these policies. He has moved towards the normalization of Soviet relations with Israel, which were broken off during the 1967 war, and he has thrown the Soviet Union's weight behind the mainstream of the PLO, led by Arafat, which seeks an independent Palestinian state in return for Palestinian recognition of Israel. At the same time, while continuing to support and rearm Syria, the Soviet Union has made it clear that the relationship with Syria is changing in the new era of Soviet regional diplomacy – which sees negotiation as the only way to peace and security – and that it regards Syria's declared aim of securing 'strategic parity' with Israel as futile.

Although, as we have said, the Soviet Union of President Gorbachev is anxious to participate in the search for a lasting peace between Arabs and Jews, the Middle East is no longer among the principal policy concerns of the Soviet government, as it was in the 1950s and 1960s – the future of its own disintegrating empire will absorb the attention of any Soviet leadership. But while this more relaxed Soviet attitude is generally welcome to all the states in the region which have feared Soviet ambitions in the past, the reaction of Israel in particular is ambiguous. This is because it fears a similar withdrawal of interest by the United States.

Israel had reasons to welcome a thaw in its relations with the Soviet Union – especially since it means a relaxation in the restrictions on emigration by Soviet Jews. Ironically, Jews have been encouraged to leave the Soviet Union by the revival of open Russian anti-Semitism in the time of *glasnost*. Even more ironically, Soviet Jews began emigrating to Israel rather than to the United States, which they had shown was their preferred destination, because in 1989 the United States began to impose restrictions on their entry since it no longer regarded them as refugees. Any increase in its Jewish population is welcome to Israel, because of its fears that the demographic balance within Israel and the occupied territories (that is, the Land of Israel in the eyes of Mr Shamir and his Likud Party) might swing in favour of the Arabs. Nevertheless this benefit to Israel is more than balanced by the fear that its ally, sponsor and financial supporter, the United States, might reduce its support and adopt a policy of seeking to impose a Middle East peace settlement in co-operation with the Soviet Union and other permanent members of the Security Council. That could only mean United States support for an independent Palestinian state in the occupied territories.

The United States alliance with Israel rests on two elements which overlap but do not entirely coincide. One of these is the United States' view of Israel as the only state in the Middle East which has Western-style democratic institutions but is also a strong military power capable of defending US and Western interests in the region. The other element is the Zionist factor: the extraordinarily powerful and pervasive influence of American Zionist Jews on the US political system. A decline in the first of these factors is inevitable as the Cold War subsides and the United States ceases to regard the Soviet Union as a serious threat in the Middle East. But there are other reasons for a decline. Israel's colonial-style efforts to suppress the Palestinian *intifada*, which have been given wide publicity in the American media, have damaged its credentials as a democracy. In 1989, further damage was done by revelations of the extent of Israel's relations with South Africa, especially in the field of arms development, including nuclear weapons. South Africa is an emotive issue among many US politicians and large sections of the US public. Finally, Israel's reputation has also been tarnished by reports of close Israeli connections – not necessarily at the highest level – with elements in Latin America which are the subject of the highest US disapproval, such as the Colombian drug-barons and former president Noriega of Panama.

All these doubts about the virtue and necessity of the US–Israeli political and military alliance have affected the other pillar which supports the alliance – the almost unquestioning loyalty to the Israeli state among the American Jewish community. While proclaiming that this loyalty remains undiminished, the majority of the representatives of American Jewish organizations began openly to cast doubts on the wisdom of the Israeli government's policies and notably of prime minister Yitzhak Shamir's refusal to consider exchanging land for peace. It could be said American Jews no longer consider it feasible that US power can or will indefinitely sustain Israel as a fortress state in control of the whole of the former land of Palestine.

At the start of the 1990s the United States president George Bush and his secretary of state James Baker, taking a markedly less sentimental view of US–Israeli ties than any of their predecessors, appeared to be transforming the relationship. In Israel there were two distinct views of this matter. One was that the change was superficial – that the clouds would pass and US support for Israel would remain undiminished. Many Arabs agreed with this view, on the basis of recent historical experience which showed that rifts between the United States and Israel were always brief and unimportant. These Arabs included a substantial proportion of Palestinian political leaders, some of whom had always been sceptical about the US–Palestinian 'dialogue' while others had come round to the view that it had been intended only to weaken and divide them.

However, there was a differing view in Israel, represented broadly by the Israeli Labour Party and all political groupings to its left, which was that Israel's policies had to change substantially if the US–Israeli relationship were to be preserved. It assumed that the Palestinian uprising could not be ended by repression alone, except at too great a cost, and that there had to be concessions to Palestinian nationalism.

On one point all but a small minority of mystical fanatics in Israel are agreed: the Jewish Zionist state of Israel as it now exists cannot survive in the heart of the Middle East in its present form without the support of the United States. This is not because all other outside powers – the Soviet Union, the Europeans and Japan – are hostile, and it is still less that they want Israel to disappear. It is because Israel has come to see its own survival as depending on its extraordinarily powerful but expensive military machine. Since the Israeli economy, while highly developed, is hugely in deficit, the machine can be maintained only with outside help. In Israel's earlier years this help came from many sources, but in the 1990s it can come on the scale that is required only from the United States. All history shows that no small state, however strong and resolute, can rely on such external support from a world power.

At the end of the twentieth century, Israel therefore faces a huge and cruel dilemma, which has been best expressed by a former head of Israeli military intelligence, Yehoshafat Harkabi, who on his own admission has been converted from a hawk into a 'pragmatic dove'. In his book *Israel's Fateful Decisions* (London, 1988) he sees his country as standing at a crossroads, with one path leading to national suicide. By this he means the attempt to destroy Palestinian nationalism by force and to annex the occupied territories. This would destroy Israel's democracy and forfeit the international sympathy on which the Zionist state has depended since its foundation. There are obvious differences between Israel and the white South African regime, as well as similarities, but in the matter of survival in the face of growing world-wide hostility the analogy is clear. Israel could wither away like one of the crusader states – a comparison of which Arabs are understandably fond.

Harkabi says, 'The choice facing Israel is not between good and bad, but between bad and worse.' The bad alternative to national suicide is acceptance of the 'two-state' solution – a small state of Palestine alongside Israel. This only underlines the extent of the dilemma. Israel's opponents of a Palestinian state – who are still a large majority, although probably declining – can justifiably argue that, if a Palestinian state is granted the 'right to exist' in a small part of Palestine, there is no moral or legal justification for denying the right in the rest of Palestine. If Palestinians can win control over Nablus, Hebron and Gaza, why should they abandon for ever their claims to Nazareth and Haifa – or indeed Jerusalem? This is the gnawing doubt which sustains Israel's intransigence. Yet, as Harkabi argues, the risk of accepting the existence of a Palestinian state must be taken or the Israeli state will destroy itself.

Theodor Herzl, the founder of political Zionism, saw the future Jewish state as a bridgehead of the advanced and enlightened West in the backward and obscurantist East. It would bring the elements of progress to the peoples of the surrounding region. However, the early Zionist pioneers were more concerned with 'redeeming the land' on their own, with Jewish labour and capital. They wished to remain separate and different – speaking the classical Hebrew language. Although the men who realized the revived Zionist dream, such as Chaim Weizmann, argued like Herzl that a Jewish state in Palestine would bring great benefits to the region, their primary concern was with the development of the state itself. It should have high cultural and living standards, to attract all the Jews of the world to their new

homeland. David Ben Gurion, the state of Israel's first prime minister, believed that, while Israel should be powerful and dominant in
the region, it must not adopt the ways of the Middle East or become
part of it. Israel should never become just another Levantine state.
Even today, when the great majority of Israeli Jews have either been
born in the Middle East or originate from Arab countries, Israel
regards itself and likes to be regarded as an outpost of the West in a
more backward and undeveloped region of the orient. This on the
whole is still a view that the West accepts.

In a real sense the Arabs also accept it. From Israel's beginnings
they regarded it as a cancerous growth implanted in their body by the
West, and that view has not changed – even if they now accept that
they can live with it, provided its growth can be contained by modern
methods of treatment. But the fact that a militarily and economically
powerful state of four million Jews has enforced its acceptance in the
heart of the Islamic world, surrounded by 120 million Arabs, is a
source of deep humiliation to the Arab nation. Whatever they may
say, the Arabs know that the support Israel has received from the
West provides only part of the explanation for its survival.

In surveying all the developing countries of the Third World, the
Arabs are conscious of the fact that, while they have made greater
progress than many of the countries in Africa and Latin America
since achieving independence from the Western colonial powers, they
are a long way behind the more advanced countries in Asia –
especially those of the Pacific rim. Japan – the first oriental nation to
defeat a Christian European power in modern times, in its 1904–5
war with Russia – has long been an inspiration to Arabs. The
Egyptian nationalist leader Mustafa Kamel published a book about it
– *The Rising Sun* – in 1904. More recently the Arabs in the oil-
producing states have regarded the Japanese as an example of a
people who have triumphantly matched and even surpassed the
economic performance of the Western industrialized countries without losing their own identity. But Japan's achievements are a distant
goal for the Arabs. In terms of eliminating illiteracy, developing a
skilled and educated labour-force, increasing food production for an
exploding population and fostering diversified industries, progress in
the Arab world as a whole has been patchy and disappointing.
Admittedly, progress has been spectacular in some areas, but this is
largely the consequence of the discovery of vast natural wealth in

those parts of the Arab world which were most underpopulated and economically backward. Collectively the Arab peoples form a bloc which carries less weight in the world than might be expected in view of their resources and the strategic position they hold.

There are two kinds of response to the shame and humiliation which the Arabs find in this situation. The first is simplistic or Utopian and is shared by Islamic militants or fundamentalists and pan-Arabists. The Islamic militants believe that the introduction of what they would regard as a true Islamic order in the Arab states would solve all their social, economic and political problems. They are not very interested in matching the West, which they regard as hopelessly decadent, although they believe that the Arabs, as part of the wider Islamic *umma*, should be strong enough to prevent Western military and economic domination. But they see no reason why this should not be achieved under Islamic laws.

The pan-Arabist response is similarly simplistic, in that it holds that the humiliating weakness of the Arabs is due to the artificial division of the Arab nation – first by the colonial powers and then by Israel. (This is not incompatible with the common Western view that hatred of Israel is the only thing which unites the Arabs – a shared enmity is an unsatisfactory cement). But the pan-Arab creed in its simple Utopian form is now in abeyance. Even Colonel Qaddafy of Libya, its last disciple among Arab leaders, has come to accept that smaller regional groupings – such as the Union of Maghreb States, established in 1989 – are the best way forward. A more gradualist and pragmatic approach is favoured. While the Arab bloc would clearly be stronger if there were no bitter rivalry among its members, as there is between Iraq and Syria, no Arab now expects the bloc to merge into a United Arab States under one government, even with a federal constitution. The most that can be expected is what is known in the bureaucracy of the League of Arab States as 'Arab joint action' to meet specific problems. The way in which this could be effective was demonstrated by the way in which the Lebanese factions were brought together through the League in the Taif accords of September 1989.

The second type of reaction to the immaturity and inadequacy of Arab political life is neither simplistic nor Utopian. While it accepts that there is no easy or uniform solution, it believes that the problem itself can be stated in simple terms: that in the 1990s the Arabs are still awaiting both *glasnost* and *perestroika*. Among Arab thinkers who are not of the Utopian persuasion there has developed a remarkable consensus that what the Arab world urgently needs is more democracy, wider political participation and much greater respect for human rights. While the situation is not equally unsatisfactory in all the Arab states, the fact remains that the large and growing educated middle classes have almost no influence on the major policy decisions of their governments or the way in which these decisions are reached. The consequences are striking. One is that a high proportion of the Arab educated élite has chosen to work abroad in a more liberal atmosphere. Another is the remarkable growth in the 1980s of a relatively free Arab press in London and Paris, in contrast to the paralysing tedium of the government-controlled media in the Arab states, which resemble those of pre-*glasnost* eastern Europe. The situation is markedly worse than in the quasi-colonial period of the mandates.

It is a civil society which is still generally lacking in the Arab world. In the expression of one leading Arab intellectual, the Moroccan Abdallah Larawi, the Arab states have legality but not legitimacy in the eyes of their people. The regimes of the nation-states which emerged from the Ottoman Empire are helped to remain in power by the instruments of repression in their hands, of which their control of the media is not the least important. This gives them stability – and most of these regimes have been remarkably enduring for the past two decades – but it is a stability which ultimately means stagnation. There is no democratic tradition to which to appeal, and those who would normally participate in political life have to choose between exile and working within the system. Lawyers have to work without the rule of law, journalists without freedom of the press, and businessmen in an economy which may be called 'socialist' or 'capitalist' but in either case is controlled by the state.

But the picture is not all dark at the end of the twentieth century. Egypt has developed and maintained elements of a civil society and separation of powers within the state in spite of its long tradition of authoritarianism – from the Pharaohs, through Muhammad Ali and Cromer, to Nasser and Sadat. The Arab Maghreb states, largely insulated from the insidious effects of the Arab–Israeli conflict, show a clear trend towards more pluralist political systems. In the Arab Gulf states, where sudden wealth placed enormous additional power in the hands of the ruling families, and therefore of the state, a growing and flourishing private business and industrial sector – deliberately fostered by the same rulers – is gradually but inevitably taking power from the centre. Kuwait twice instituted representative government through an elected parliament and twice closed it down when it became too obstreperous, but the ruling Sabah family showed its determination to maintain the experiment in some form and in exile promised further democracy once it was restored. In a different context, King Hussein of Jordan, partly influenced by events in eastern Europe, relaxed his kingdom's semi-military form of government by holding free parliamentary elections in October 1989 in a clear attempt to legitimize his rule in the face of growing criticism. In contrast, however, there is little sign of Arab *glasnost* in the key countries of Syria and Iraq, where, in spite of some cosmetic moves to liberalize the political and economic systems, power remains in the hands of the head of state and the ruling Baath Party. In Iraq, following the humiliation of Iran in the Gulf War, the cult of personality of the triumphant President Saddam reached Orwellian proportions.

The possibility remains that in any of these states the evolution towards a more liberal, pluralist and democratic society with wider public participation in the political process will be swept aside by the tide of militant Islamic fundamentalism. The threat should not be underestimated. Whether the Islamists can act openly, as in Egypt and Jordan and the chaos of Lebanon, or whether they have to work underground, as in Syria and Iraq, they demonstrate that they have the active support of a substantial minority of the population and the passive sympathy of many more. Where they are tolerated, they have learned to work within rather than against the political system – they usually show greater regard for the immediate needs of ordinary people than does the official bureaucracy. Yet the absolutist and intolerant nature of their ideology and their refusal to address the real problems of government of a modern state make it unlikely that they can achieve and hold the unlimited power they seek except through violent revolution. In this respect the forces opposing them are still stronger. Most Arabs would like to live in a more tolerant and open society. They want their children to be better and more widely educated in a system which is not dominated by religious bigots. They would prefer to live under

efficient modern governments capable of responding to contemporary needs which are increasingly of a global nature.

The popularity of the Islamic Revolution in Iran might seem to
contradict these assertions. But in the first place this Revolution was
Shiite and Iranian rather than Sunni and Arab. Nothing has done
more to discredit the very concept of Islamic Revolution among the
Arabs than the bloodthirsty intolerance of the Iranian Revolution and
its followers such as the Hizbollahis who seek to establish an Islamic
Republic of Lebanon. Secondly, since the death of Ayatollah Khomeini, Iran's rulers have quietly but convincingly demonstrated their
understanding that most of the intolerant ideology must be abandoned
if Iran is to flourish in the modern world.

Iraq's seizure of Kuwait in August 1990 and the ensuing world
crisis was a seismic event. It was certain there would be widespread
consequences but their scale and nature were hard to predict. Those
who had previously detected clear trends in Middle Eastern society
such as towards Islamic fundamentalism, xenophobic nationalism or
liberal democracy were forced to re-examine their assumptions. The
Arabs of the Middle East were placed in a state of moral and
emotional confusion which can only be compared with that of 1915–
16 when they had to choose between loyalty to the Ottoman Empire,
the only Muslim power in the world, and the opportunity for creating
an independent Arab nation through an alliance with the British and
French imperialists.

Saddam Hussein appealed to their potent feelings of outrage against
their long humiliation at the hands of the West. He merged the
secular ideology of pan-Arabism with Islam and unashamedly called
for a *jihad* against the conservatively religious Saudi Arabians who
had allied themselves with the West against him. In this he successfully demonstrated that Arab nationalism and Islam could never be
mutually exclusive, as had sometimes been claimed. His appeal
enjoyed some success. Many Arab intellectuals who had previously
been concerned with the questions of human rights and the need for
a more liberal Arab society, felt that Saddam, however unattractive
the character of his regime, offered through his defiance of the West
the hope of a new order in the Middle East in which the 'artificial'
frontiers imposed on the Arabia world could be redrawn and the
natural resources of what was formerly Arabia be more equitably
distributed. Such intellectuals ignored the fact that Eastern Europe,

Japan and most of the Third World, along with the West, regarded Saddam as a deadly and unpredictable danger to the post-Cold War new world order and not as a leader with legitimate patriotic aspirations. Their protest found expression in a revived United Nations.

An immediate consequence of the crisis was disruption to the gradualist approach to Arab unity. The League of Arab States was shattered and virtually ceased to function; the League's Tunisian secretary-general resigned although the majority of members had their way in returning the headquarters from Tunis to Cairo in November 1990. The Arab nation-states were more divided than at any time in their seventy-year history.

These events could not be extrapolated into the future. It was far from certain that Saddam Hussein would remain an inspirational figure in Arab history. He was neither an Iraqi Nasser nor an Arab Bismarck and still less a new Saladin as some Arabs vainly hoped. (Mussolini was a more likely antecedent.) But he undoubtedly shook the established order in the Arab East – especially in the Arabian Peninsula. The threat he presented caused all Arab regimes to concern themselves with ensuring greater popular consent for their rule and there was an ironic possibility that the reaction to his aggressive ambitions might be a move towards greater freedom in Arab political life. But the belief that Saddam Hussein would lead the Arabs towards a revolutionary new order which would transcend all the humiliations of the past was as futile as any other Utopia.

The third main group of peoples inhabiting the Middle East – and its former imperial rulers – the Turks – have provided a different model in the twentieth century. Unlike the Arabs, they have the advantage that their homeland occupies a single cohesive territory; they have no feeling that they have been artificially divided.

The peaceful transfer of power by the Kemalist semi-dictatorship to the opposition Democratic Party in 1950 was a remarkable achievement, but Turkey's parliamentary democracy was still fragile. The new prime minister, Adnan Menderes, had initial success in denationalizing state industries and liberalizing the economy. He won support from the countryside by increasing food prices and making concessions to religious feeling. But government overspending and consequent inflation provoked increasing opposition among the urban middle class, the bureaucracy and army officers, who considered that Menderes was wooing the peasantry at the expense of the westernized elements of the population. Intolerant of any criticism, Menderes introduced his own highly authoritarian legislation. In May 1960 the army seized power from him. (He was later tried and hanged.)

Turkish democracy was not obliterated. In 1961 the army honoured its pledge to hand back power to an elected parliament under a revised constitution. The Democratic Party, renamed the Justice Party, was allowed to resume activity. However, various threats to the parliamentary system remained as the Justice Party and the Republican People's Party, failing to secure adequate majorities in elections, sought to govern through unstable coalitions with smaller parties. The introduction of martial law in most of Turkey's provinces failed to quell increasing violence from trade unionists and between left-wing and right-wing students and sectarian strife with the Shiite minority and with Kurds in eastern Turkey. In a bloodless coup in September 1980, the armed forces again intervened and dissolved the political parties. But once more the army refused to contemplate a military dictatorship. A Constituent Assembly again revised the constitution. In 1983 power was restored once more to an elected parliament and restrictions on civil liberties could gradually be eased, although many aspects of Turkey's human-rights record continued to provoke criticisms among the Western democracies to which Turkey's rulers felt their country belonged.

The conservative rural population never wholeheartedly accepted Kemalist secularism, and Turkey was not immune to the growth of Islamic militancy in the 1980s. Yet the chances that parliamentary democracy will be permanently overthrown remain small. The armed forces have twice demonstrated their readiness to intervene to preserve rather than destroy it.

Two forces have combined to turn Turkey Westwards: one is the feeling that its Arab co-religionists abandoned Turkey when they allied with its enemies in the First World War; the other is the Kemalist reforms which drew strength from this sentiment.

In 1952 Turkey demonstrated its adherence to the Western camp in the Cold War when it became a full member of NATO, although the transfer to the Soviet Union of its long-standing fears of Russian expansion played a part in the decision. The Westwards trend of Turkish interests was little affected by Turkey's membership of the short-lived Baghdad Pact in the 1950s. In 1963 Turkey signed a treaty of association with the European Economic Community, causing the President of the European Commission to remark, 'Turkey is part of Europe,' and in 1980 Turkey made its first application for full membership of the Community. Problems with Greece over Cyprus and other matters remained as obstacles to Turkey's European destiny but they also underlined the reality that Turkey's foreign policy interests lay in Europe rather than the Middle East.

Paradoxically, however, Turkey's application to become the thirteenth member of the European Community, on which a decision has been repeatedly postponed, is the one factor which might cause a serious crisis of identity. It raises the question of whether what remains a Muslim nation, however secularized its public life, can become irrevocably part of a Europe in which it would be a lone minority. Doubts must remain as to whether the heritage of centuries of struggle for dominance between Islam and Christian Europe can be set aside in this manner.

The sweeping changes in eastern Europe and the nationalist turmoil within the Soviet Union will influence the Middle East, although their precise consequences cannot be calculated. If the Soviet Union were to break up, the links between the Muslim republics of central Asia would obviously be strengthened. It has been suggested by a historian of the Armenians that if Georgia and Armenia were to break away from Moscow's rule their most likely alliance would be with Iran.

If the Cold War fades into the past and the United States withdraws from Europe, it would hardly maintain its superpower role in the Middle East. The role of Europe in the region would again become more important, although hardly in its previous quasi-colonial form – a transmediterranean dialogue between equals is certainly what the Arabs would prefer. But however events inside the region and beyond its borders unfold, the Middle East will not be ignored.

Notes on Further Reading

The focus of this history is on the past two centuries since Bonaparte began the second invasion of the world of Islam by the West – the secular crusades. The background of the previous eleven centuries since the coming of Islam which led to the arabization and islamicization of most of the Middle East is covered by the *Cambridge History of Islam* (2 vols, Cambridge, 1971), but a new synthesis of much of this material which can be highly recommended is I. M. Lapidus's *A History of Islamic Societies* (Cambridge, 1988). The collection of essays edited by J. Schacht and C. E. Bosworth, *The Legacy of Islam* (Oxford, 1974), covers all aspects of Islamic society and civilization. For an understanding of Shiite Islam which plays such an important role in the modern Middle East, M. Moojan's *An Introduction to Shi'i Islam* provides a comprehensive account. A. H. Hourani's *Minorities in the Arab World* (London, 1979) is still the only survey of the religious and national minorities remaining in the Arab countries. The Christians are specifically dealt with in R. B. Betts's *Christians in the Arab East: a political study* (London, 1979).

B. Lewis's *The Arabs in History* (4th edn, London, 1968) is brief but still unequalled in its account of the Arabs at the apogee of their power. A more detailed history of the Arab expansion and empire appears in J. B. Glubb's *The Great Arab Conquests* (London, 1963), *The Empire of the Arabs* (London, 1963) and *The Last Centuries, from the Muslim Empires to the Renaissance of Europe 1145–1453* (London, 1967).

For the first Western invasion of the Middle East, see Steven Runciman's monumental *A History of the Crusades* (3 vols, Harmondsworth, 1978), although in some respects this has been overtaken by more recent research. A. Maalouf's *The Crusades Through Arab Eyes* (London, 1984) is a personal favourite.

My own *The Arabs* (2nd edn, Harmondsworth, 1985) was an attempt to bring the story of the Arab peoples up to the present day but A. H. Hourani's account of the same subject expected in January 1991 is likely to become indispensable. J. Berque's *The Arabs: their History and Future* (London, 1964) provides the perspective of an outstanding French historian of the Arabs and Islam.

The work of another French scholar, M. Rodinson, *Islam and Capitalism* (London, 1966) helps to enlighten the subject of Chapter 2, 'Islam on the Defensive'. Lord Kinross's *The Ottoman Centuries, the rise and fall of the Turkish Empire* (London, 1977) is a highly readable but reliable account of the last Muslim world power and B. Lewis's *The Emergence of Modern*

Turkey (2nd edn, London, 1968) remains the best history of the transformation of its heartland into the Turkish Republic. A. Lutfi al-Sayyid Marsot's *Egypt in the reign of Muhammad Ali* (Cambridge, 1984) is an outstanding study by an Egyptian historian of the Muslim power which came close to replacing the Ottoman Empire.

Modern Egypt by E. Baring, First Earl of Cromer, (2 vols, London, 1908) is still essential not only for its account of the British occupation but also as a classic exposition of the British imperial view of the Middle East. It may be balanced by a French view in J. Berque's *Egypt, Imperialism and Revolution* (London, 1972), by an Egyptian one in A. Lutfi al-Sayyid Marsot's *Egypt and Cromer: a study in Anglo-Egyptian relations* (London, 1968) and possibly by P. Mansfield's *The British in Egypt* (London, 1971).

For the development of Arab nationalism and relations between Arabs and Turks, *Arab Nationalism, an Anthology*, edited by S. Haim, remains invaluable as much for the editor's introduction as for the rare anthology of Arab writing on the subject. E. Dawn's *From Ottomanism to Arabism, essays on the origin of Arab nationalism* (Chicago, 1973) also makes a useful contribution to the subject. *The Arab Awakening: the Story of the Arab National Movement* (Beirut, 1962) by the Palestinian George Antonius is still unique in the way it shaped the thinking of a generation, but it should be balanced by the differing perspective of Z. Zeine's *Arab–Turkish Relations and the Emergence of Arab Nationalism* (Beirut, 1958).

On the subject of modernization and the impact of the West on the Middle East, A. H. Hourani's *Arabic Thought in the Liberal Age 1798–1939* (2nd edn, London, 1983) and his two collections of essays *Europe and the Middle East* (London, 1980) and *The Emergence of the Modern Middle East* (London, 1981) are exceptionally rewarding. *Beginnings of Modernization in the Middle East: the Nineteenth Century* edited by W. R. Polk and R. L. Chambers (Chicago, 1968) also contains useful material. R. Owen's *The Middle East in the World Economy 1800–1914* is a splendidly lucid and comprehensive study of its subject. A unique work of reference is J. C. Hurewitz's *The Middle East and North Africa in World Politics, a documentary record: Volume 1 European Expansion 1535–1914* (2nd edn, New Haven, 1975); *Volume 2 British–French Supremacy 1914–1945* (2nd edn, New Haven, 1979).

Sir P. M. Sykes's *History of Persia* (3rd edn, 2 vols, London, 1930) still holds its own for the period before Reza Shah. E. Monroe's *Britain's Moment in the Middle East 1914–71* (new and revised edn, London, 1981) is unlikely to be surpassed as an account of its subject and P. S. Khoury's *Syria and the French Mandate: the politics of Arab nationalism 1920–45* is a penetrating study of the French role in the Anglo-French interregnum in the eastern Arab World. J. Wilson's *The Authorized Biography of T. E. Lawrence* (London, 1987) is so exhaustive that it covers most aspects of this period of modern Arab history.

For Turkey since the demise of the Ottoman Empire there is Lord Kinross's *Atatürk: the rebirth of a nation* (5th edn, London, 1971) and for the post-Atatürk period of troubled Turkish democracy G. Lewis's *Modern Turkey* (4th edn, London, 1974) and W. R. Hale's *The Political and Economic Development of Turkey* (London, 1981). Iran in the modern period before the Islamic Revolution is well covered in P. Avery's *Modern Iran* (London, 1965) and N. Keddie's *Iran: religion, politics and society* (London, 1980). J. A. Bill and N. R. Louis's *Musaddiq, Iranian nationalism and oil* (London, 1988) is a useful account of this crucial episode in modern Middle East history.

There are several books on the Arab states since the end of the Ottoman Empire and their eventual achievement of full independence from the European powers:

1. Egypt

P. J. Vatikiotis's *The Modern History of Egypt* (London, 1969) and T. Little's *Modern Egypt* (London, 1967) are to be recommended. More specifically on the Nasser era, Gamal Abdul Nasser's *Egypt's Liberation: the Philosophy of the Revolution* (Buffalo, 1959) still repays study as a seminal manifesto. A. Nutting's *Nasser* is an outstanding biography. P. Mansfield's *Nasser's Egypt* (2nd edn, London, 1969) was an attempt to outline his achievements during his lifetime. A. Sadat's *In Search of Identity: an autobiography* (London, 1978) reveals the profound difference in outlook of Nasser's successor. W. R. Louis and R. Owen's *Suez 1956: the crisis and its consequences* (Oxford, 1989) provides an essential assessment of this watershed in the modern history of the Middle East.

All the books by Mohammed Heikal, Egypt's leading journalist and Nasser's close friend, provide valuable insight but notably *The Road to Ramadan* (London, 1975) on Arab preparations for the 1973 war and *Autumn of Fury* (London, 1983) on the events leading to Sadat's assassination. D. Hopwood's *Egypt: Politics and Society 1945–1981* can be warmly recommended and A. McDermott's *Egypt from Nasser to Mubarak: a flawed revolution* (London, 1988) is a useful assessment of the whole post-revolutionary period.

2. Syria

N. A. Ziadeh's *Syria and Lebanon* (Troy, 1968) covers the French mandate and the earlier years of independence. Two outstanding books by Patrick Seale are essential reading not only for Syrian affairs but also for the post-war history of the Arab World: *The Struggle for Syria: a Study of Post-war Arab Politics, 1945–1958* (2nd edn, London, 1987) and *Asad: the Struggle for the Middle East* (London, 1988). T. Petran's *Syria* (London, 1972) is still rewarding and D. Hopwood's *Syria, 1948–1956 politics and society* is an excellent short survey of its subject. M. Ma'oz's *Asad: The Sphinx of Damascus* (London, 1988) provides a useful Israeli view.

3. Lebanon

First and foremost are the books by the Lebanese historian Kamal Salibi, notably The Modern History of Lebanon (London, 1977), *Crossroads to Civil War: Lebanon, 1958–1976* (Delmar, NY, 1976) and most recently *A House of Many Mansions: The History of Lebanon Reconsidered* (London, 1988). There are various books by close Western observers of the modern Lebanese tragedy of which H. Cobban's *The Making of Modern Lebanon* (London, 1985) and J. C. Randal's *Going All the Way: Christian warlords, Israeli adventures, and the war in Lebanon* (New York, 1983) are perhaps the best. Z. Schiff and E. Ya'ari's *Israel's Lebanon War* (New York, 1984) adds the Israeli dimension, but the impossibility of writing an up-to-date history of modern Lebanon is obvious.

4. Jordan

M. Wilson's King Abdullah, Britain and the Making of Jordan (Cambridge, 1987) deals with the mandate and the early years of independence, as does A. Dearden's *Jordan* (London, 1958). The autobiography by Hussein, King of Jordan, *Uneasy Lies the Head* (London, 1962), may be read in conjunction with an assessment after his thirty-five years on the throne in J. Lunt's *Hussein of Jordan* (London, 1989). P. Gubser's *Jordan: crossroads of Middle Eastern events* (London, 1979) places the kingdom in its modern context, although the latest events show that the Jordanian role is subject to continuous change.

5. Iraq

For the early modern period S. Longrigg's Iraq 1900 to 1950 (London, 1953) remains the best, and for more recent times P. Marr's *The Modern History of Iraq* (Boulder and London, 1985) and P. Sluglett and M. Farouk-Sluglett's *Iraq since 1958: from revolution to dictatorship* (London, 1987). H. Batatu's *The Old Social Classes and the Revolutionary Movements of Iraq: a study of Iraq's old landed and commercial classes, and its Communists, Ba'athists and Free Officers* (Princeton, 1978) is still unequalled as a study of contemporary Iraqi society.

6. Arabia and the Gulf

H. St J. B. Philby's Saudi Arabia (London, 1968) is a detailed account of the Saudi kingdom before it became wealthy. The two modern studies of the kingdom which appeared almost simultaneously – R. Lacey's *The Kingdom* (London, 1982) and D. Holden and R. Johns's *The House of Saud* (New York, 1981) together provide a highly comprehensive modern history. F. al-

Farsy's *Saudi Arabia, a case study in development* (revised 2nd edn, London, 1983) is a useful factual account by a senior Saudi official, and two recent American studies – W. Quandt's *Saudi Arabia in the Nineteen Eighties: foreign policy, security and oil* (Washington, 1981) and P. N. Woodward's *Oil and Labor in the Middle East: Saudi Arabia and the oil boom* (New York, 1988) – are both to be recommended. A. M. Abu-Hakima's *The Modern History of Kuwait 1750–1965* (London, 1983) is very reliable, as, for the more modern period, is H. V. F. Winstone and Z. Freeth's *Kuwait: Prospect and Reality* (London, 1979). N. Sakr's *The United Arab Emirates to the 1990s* (London, 1986) can be highly recommended, as can R. S. Zahlan's *The Making of the Modern Gulf States* (London, 1989). An entertaining but scholarly study of southern Arabia is provided by R. Bidwell's *The Two Yemens* (London, 1983), and a salutary radical view of the Arabian peninsula is contained in F. Halliday's *Arabia without Sultans* (Harmondsworth, 1974).

7. Israel/Palestine

The literature on the two subjects, whether treated jointly or separately, is large and growing rapidly as contemporary studies soon become out of date. W. Z. Laqueur's *A History of Zionism* (London, 1972) provides the essential background to Israel, and C. Sykes's *Crossroads to Israel* (London, 1965) remains the best account of the moves which led to the creation of the state of Israel, although an Israeli historian, Avi Shlaim, provides some startling new material in *Collusion Across the Jordan: King Abdullah, the Zionist movement, and the Partition of Palestine* (Oxford, 1988). M. Bar-Zohar's *The Armed Prophet: a Biography of Ben Gurion* (London, 1967) illuminates the creation and early years of the state, and N. Lucas's *The Modern History of Israel* (New York, 1977) is an excellent history of its first three decades. A. Perlmutter's *Military and Politics in Israel: Nation-building and Role Expansion* (London, 1969) remains highly relevant, as does Y. Peri's *Between Battles and Ballots: Israeli Military in Politics* (Cambridge, 1983). Golda Meir's autobiography *My Life* (London, 1975) illustrates old-style Zionist politics, while that of Ariel Sharon, *Warrior* (New York and London, 1989), may do the same for those of the future. There are several important critiques of official Israeli policies, among which S. Flapan's *Israel: myths and realities* (London, 1987) and Y. Harkabi's *Israel's Fateful Decisions* are outstanding. A well-researched account sympathetic to the Palestinian Arabs is D. Hirst's *The Gun and the Olive Branch: The Roots of Violence in the Middle East* (London, 1977), and A. Hart's *Arafat: Terrorist or Peacemaker?* (London, 1984) contains useful material even if it is not always rigorous in its assessment of sources. Andrew Gowers' and Tony Walker's *Behind the Myth: Yasser Arafat and the Palestinian Revolution* (London, 1990) is a major new contribution. There are a growing number of works by Palestinian writers, such as H. Cattan's *Palestine and International Law, the Legal Aspects of the Arab–Israeli Conflict* (2nd edn, London, 1976), E. W. Said's

The Question of Palestine (London, 1980) and M. Tarbush's *Reflections of a Palestinian* (Washington DC, 1986).

On relations between the Middle East and the superpowers M. Heikal's *The Sphinx and the Commissar* (London, 1978) is the illuminating and highly readable contribution of an insider, and E. Karsh's *The Soviet Union and Syria, the Asad Years* (London, 1988) is the useful objective work of an Israeli. The general history of US relations with the Middle East still awaits a new chronicler; meanwhile there are W. R. Polk's *The United States and the Arab World* (Cambridge, Mass., 1965) and personal memoirs such as J. Carter's *The Blood of Abraham, Inside the Middle East* (Boston and London, 1985) and passages in H. Kissinger's *White House Years* (New York and London, 1979) and *Years of Upheaval* (New York and London, 1982). G. Sick's *All Fall Down: America's fateful encounter with Iran* (London, 1985) goes far to explain the US débâcle in part of the Middle East.

For the role of oil in Middle East history, S. H. Longrigg's *Oil in the Middle East* (3rd edn, London, 1968) and G. W. Stocking's *Middle East Oil* (London, 1971) are both excellent on the period when the international oil companies were dominant, and A. Sampson's *The Seven Sisters* (London, 1975) sceptically examines the decline in their power and the rise of OPEC. That a general study of Middle East oil has been lacking since then is not surprising in view of the subject's complexity. OPEC's fortunes and prospects change swiftly and any history soon becomes outdated, but there is A. Skeet's *OPEC: 25 years of Prices and Politics* (Cambridge, 1988), and M. Arari's *OPEC: The Failing Giant* (Kentucky, 1988) is a recent pessimistic assessment. W. I. Sharif's *Oil and Development in the Arab Gulf States* (London, 1985) is an annotated bibliography of special value.

Islamic reassertion in the modern world and the Islamic Revolution in Iran are the subjects of numerous books of varied quality. Two which are likely to stand the test of time are E. Mortimer's *Faith and Power, the Politics of Islam* (London, 1982) and M. Ruthven's *Islam in the World* (Harmondsworth, 1984). On the Khomeini Revolution, S. Bakhash's *The Reign of the Ayatollahs: Iran and the Islamic Revolution* is outstanding, and R. Mottahedeh's *The Mantle of the Prophet: Religion and Politics in Iran* (London, 1986) is a brilliant analysis of the Revolution's antecedents. On the Gulf War, S. Chubin and C. Tripp's *Iran and Iraq at War* (London, 1988) is the best study to date.

Political futurology in the Middle East is perhaps best left to astrologers, but some attempts to analyse the present with an eye to the future are worthwhile. Two works by Lebanese writers are F. Ajami's *The Arab Predicament: Arab Political Thought and Practice Since 1967* (Cambridge, 1981) and G. Corm's *Fragmentation of the Middle East* (London, 1988). There are also two excellent collections of essays: H. Sharabi's *The Next Arab Decade: Alternative Futures* (Boulder and London, 1988) and the series in four volumes edited by Giacomo Lucini of the Istituto Affari Internazionali, Rome, under the general title *Nation, State and Integration in the Arab World* (London and New York, 1988). Y. Sayigh's *The Arab Economy 1930–1980: Past Performance and Future Prospects* (Oxford, 1982) is by one of the Arab World's leading economists.

For general reference, Europa Publications' *The Middle East and North Africa* (London, 1948–) is published annually. Two more reference works of high standard are *The Cambridge Encyclopaedia of the Middle East and North Africa* (Cambridge, 1988), executive editor Trevor Mostyn and advisory editor Albert Hourani, and the second revised edition of *The Middle East* in the 'Handbooks to the Modern World' series (New York and Oxford, 1987), edited by Michael Adams.

Index